REIMAGING BRITAIN

Five Hundred Years of Black
and Asian History

RON RAMDIN

Pluto Press
LONDON • STERLING, VIRGINIA

First published 1999 by Pluto Press
345 Archway Road, London N6 5AA
and 22883 Quicksilver Drive,
Sterling, VA 20166–2012, USA

British Library Cataloguing in Publication Data
A catalogue record for this book is available from the British Library

ISBN   0 7453 1600 X hbk

Library of Congress Cataloging in Publication Data
Ramdin, Ron.
    Reimaging Britain : five hundred years of Black and Asian
    history / Ron Ramdin.
        p.   cm.
    Includes bibliographical references (p.   ) and index.
    ISBN 0–7453–1600–X (hc.)
    1. Blacks—Great Britain—History. 2. Great Britain—Emigration
and immigration—History. 3. Great Britain—Race
relations—History. 4. East Indians—Great Britain—History. 5.
West Indians—Great Britain—History. 6. Immigrants—Great
Britain—History. 7. Africans—Great Britain—History. 8.
Asians—Great Britain—History. I. Title.
DA125.N4 R36 1999
305.8'00941'0904—dc21
                                                    99–34705
                                                    CIP

Designed, typeset from disk and produced for Pluto Press by
Chase Production Services, Chadlington, OX7 3LN
Printed in the European Union

THE LION BEATEN BY THE MAN

A picture was exhibited
in which the artist had depicted
a lion of immense stature
floored by a single man

Those who were viewing were drawing pride from this.

A lion when passing, stopped their chatter
'I can see', he said, 'that in fact
you are given the victory here;
But the artist has deceived you:
he had the freedom to invent.
More reasonably we should have the upper hand,
if my brothers knew how to paint.'

La Fontaine, *Fables*, Book III, No. X1

Quoted by Chateaubriand in *Adventures of the Last Abencerage*,
in which a Moor in Spain during the Christianisation
of the country laments, 'We don't know how to paint.'

'History, in other words, is not a calculating machine. It unfolds in the mind and the imagination, and it takes body in the multifarious responses of a people's culture, itself the infinitely subtle mediation of material realities, of underpinning economic fact, of gritty objectivities.'

Basil Davison, *Africa in Modern History*

FOR GEORGIA AND JOSHUA

CONTENTS

PREFACE

This book adopts an integrative approach to black and Asian history in Britain, which encompasses the period from Britain's early Empire aspirations to the 'Empire Within'. Its aim is to put Britain and its African- and Asian-descended settlers into historical perspective, a history of British domination which devalued the cultures and economic contribution of the peoples of Asia, Africa, the Caribbean, the Americas and the Middle East as 'inferior'.

Britain's imperial conquests were an astonishing, rapacious achievement. Vast regions of the world were colonised and – after initial private ventures – administered and controlled by government officials, who, over the centuries, behaved autocratically.

From the sixteenth to the twentieth centuries, the majority of black (African) and Asian people in Britain have been among the poorest, excluded from society and unreservedly exploited. Their labour value, the *raison d'être* of the black and Asian presence in Britain, has been (and remains) a reminder of the importance of the colonial and postcolonial contribution to the British economy.

Unlike my earlier book, *The Making of the Black Working Class in Britain*, which explored the industrial and related struggles of blacks and Asians, especially in the twentieth century, *Reimaging Britain* is a work of wider scope. Not only does it point to similarities and differences, but it indicates and makes connections between the various indigenous and migrant groups. Blacks and Asians in Britain are considered significantly in the context of the British Isles, with which these 'subject' peoples were closely bound for centuries.

While much of what constitutes black and Asian history in Britain focuses largely on the period from the sixteenth to the eighteenth centuries, *Reimaging Britain* broadens the scope and brings the history up to date in the late twentieth century. Moreover, the book takes a new approach to 'British' history, reconfiguring the images of Britain that arise from relations with its colonial and former colonial possessions – a perspective that contextually juxtaposes the Scots, Irish, Welsh and English (the British) with black and Asian peoples, whose histories, until recently, have more often than not been considered separately rather than seen as reflecting the interdependence of their histories. Blacks, Asians and whites in Britain have been influencing each other for centuries, and this legacy is reflected in the hybridised lifestyles of Britain's black and Asian British youth. British history should no longer be written from the point of view of English nostalgia. Rather, it needs to reflect multiculturalism, for this has been Britain's identity for centuries. It is my hope that this book will lead to a reappraisal of how we approach 'British' history in the future. In this sense, *Reimaging Britain* makes an important and timely contribution to British historiography.

The words 'black' and African are used interchangeably and, as a 'political colour', 'black' also refers to the various groups and their descendants from the former colonial and Commonwealth countries. 'Asians in Britain' refers to people originally from the Indian subcontinent, but also, more generally, people from the whole of Asia, including the Chinese. Indians from the Caribbean are identified as either East Indians or Indo-Caribbeans.

I would like to pay my respects to the memory of my dear old friend Louise Floyd, who had been anticipating publication of this book, but died suddenly in early 1999. My special thanks to Anne Beech, Rozina Visram whose own work is an invaluable source of reference, the staff of the India Office Library and Records, the Public Records Office and other sections of the British Library, the Policy Studies Institute and Anthony Rhys-Jones, Brian Rooney, Professor David Skilton, Melissa Slater, Michael Woods and Roger van Zwanenberg. Finally, I am most grateful, as always, to my son, Ronnie.

Ron Ramdin
The British Library,
London, 1999.

PROLOGUE

In recent years, as ethnic groups assert their presence and identity in Britain – and indeed elsewhere in the world – much attention has focused on Africa as the cradle of humanity. Since *Homo sapiens* emerged there and evolved to bring the first flowering of human civilisations to the Middle and Eastern regions of the world, pre-eminently the Mesopotamian and Egyptian river valleys, in Asia, Africa and Europe, some things have changed little, namely the division of societies into categories (classes), with the higher dominating the lower. This dichotomy, emphasised by war, served the interests of the higher – a feature that characterised 'most civilisations through most of history, and Europe's most of all'. Stretching back deep into the past, a language spoken throughout Europe, Persia and northern India was identified as deriving from an 'Aryan' or 'Indo-European' grouping. Geographically, Europe was formed as a 'continuum' with western Asia and northern India.

Europe underwent a series of epochal shifts, each one deeply marked by residual elements of its predecessor. Having acquired an indispensable body of knowledge from the Egyptians, the Greeks introduced 'democracy'. Subsequently, the Romans learned from the Greeks how to promote civilisation – as opposed to barbarism – during the expansion of their Empire into Africa. However, while parts of Europe were invaded by the tribal Huns and Mongols, the more menacing threat nearer its borders was the growing militancy of the Islamic world, led by the 'less civilised' Moors and Berbers, who had gained ascendancy in Spain and parts of Asia. While these devout believers continued to perceive Europe as 'Rome' or 'Byzantium', Western Europeans preferred their region to be known as 'Christendom' and their foes as pagans, thus disclosing their indifference and ignorance of the Muslims' faith, while generating a religious tension that would deepen with time.

In the Middle Ages, Christian Crusaders attacked and raided Jerusalem in an attempt to reclaim it from the Muslims. And when in 1453 Christian Constantinople was overrun by Muslims (and renamed Stamboul) the vigorous growth of Islamic militancy posed a new danger to Europe. However, the Muslims were constrained, to some extent, by a lack of inventiveness. Western Europe, on the other hand, was at last showing signs of buoyancy and optimism as it emerged from the Middle Ages.

The two Western European countries that had been most threatened by Islam, Spain and Portugal, initiated European expansion. Portuguese voyages of discovery circumnavigated Africa in 1486 and again in 1497, thus avoiding the 'Turkish barrier' between Europe and the Far East. This was a long hoped for breakthrough, not just because of the prospect of the vast wealth which the East promised, but also, importantly, as a way of countering Islam, the 'old enemy' of the Christian Iberians.[1] In 1492, Christopher Columbus, who had been seeking a sea route to the East, found the West Indies. As a result, by 1520 the Aztecs had been robbed of Mexico, and ten years later, the Incas no longer ruled Peru. Such European (especially Spanish) victories were profitable and generated further confidence and daring. European military victories also had a spiritual dimension, which was integral to Spain's imperial design: native American Indians who were conquered were subjugated to the edicts of Christendom; they became 'Christians of a sort'. Furthermore, they were taught Spanish, a crucial means of enablement for the Spanish Empire.

However, what the Spanish conquests in the Americas and the Portuguese conquests in Asia demonstrated was how thin the veneer of civilised behaviour was when customary restraints were removed. Indeed, the colonial encounter between Europe and the Caribbean would inform European writings and policies, which were shot through with constructions of European political dominance and superiority. The first meeting between Europe and America in 1492, recorded in Columbus's log book, had described kind and helpful strangers, but a change of perception soon followed vis-à-vis 'native' Indians, with cannibalism powerfully evoked in a number of European texts over a period of some 300 years. It was, as Peter Hulme has noted, an encounter that has dominated colonialist writing, an obsession which appeared from the seventeenth century in such texts as the John Smith and Pocahontas stories, in Shakespeare's *The Tempest*, and, some 200 years after Columbus's first landfall, the 'idea of a pristine' encounter recurred in Robinson Crusoe's highly symbolic rescue of the Carib Indian Friday. There was also the well-known tale of Yarico and Inkle, about the betrayal of an Indian woman by a European man, which coincided with the ultimate subjugation of the native Indians in the Caribbean in the late eighteenth century.[2]

However, this Caribbean contact was a mistake. Though Columbus and other European explorers were intent on finding India, Cathay and the riches of the East, more immediately, they settled for – and indeed increasingly declared their hegemonic and aggressive interest in – Africa, India and the rest of the as yet unexplored world. Thereafter, writing 'history' became a reflection of European colonial and postcolonial ambitions.

PART ONE

THE 'BLACKAMOORES'' PRESENCE
(1500–1900)

1 AFRICANS AND ASIANS IN THE BRITISH ISLES (1500–1833)

BRITAIN, AFRICA AND THE WEST INDIES

Difference has always been a feature of humankind. Indeed, difference was present and integral to human civilisation long before Britain became an expanding empire in the sixteenth century. Historically, and crucial to the making of this 'Empire', was the element of difference in the relationship between England, Scotland, Wales and Ireland, whose histories were intertwined. With the passage of time, differences in colour, race, religion and culture would become central to the images and imagery in the history of black and Asian people in Britain. Before the European colonial encounter in the fifteenth century, and contrary to the popular view that 'black' people first came to Britain after the Second World War, there was an African presence in Britain during the Roman occupation,[1] and some argue even before that. Asians too had early contacts with Britain – according to one source, it began some ten thousand years ago.[2] For more than a thousand years,[3] prior to the sixteenth century, many cultures vied for hegemony within the British Isles. In the aftermath of the Hundred Years War and the Wars of the Roses the different cultures were able to function more or less autonomously, but from about the mid-sixteenth century, which marked the beginning of the 'modern period', England was in the ascendant. Yet the façade of a united polity headed by a monarch could not disguise the diversity of distinctive cultures and religious identities. Even earlier, English expansionism had been evident in Ireland, where in the twelfth century Henry II proclaimed himself Lord, thus bringing Dublin and its hinterland under England's control[4] – a portent of things to come.

The East held a strong fascination for many Europeans. Indeed, trade in high-value commodities such as silks, spices and textiles, particularly between Britain and India, flourished, until the Turkish blockade of the overland passage to India in the fifteenth century encouraged the search for an alternative route. The impulse of trade preoccupied questing European nations. Consequently, the acquisition of knowledge of distant lands was highly prized, especially in printed form, following the introduction of the printing press to England in 1477.[5]

The belief that the British Empire was made possible by 'push' factors, including 'domestic economic pressures, ambitious and wise rulers, clever merchants, adventurous seamen and the zeal to carry Christianity abroad', was questioned by John Parker, who pointed out that such forces could not have had the desired impact had the English not developed a knowledge of foreign lands, the means of oceanic travel and a zeal for overseas expansion sufficient to attract large numbers of people to settle in these new territories.

The literate public was crucial at this time, for it was to them that the transmission of 'knowledge and enthusiasm' was aimed. Among this *literati* were authors, translators, patrons and publishers, whose importance equalled that of statesmen. It was they who had introduced the 'idea of empire' to the English and made available books on geography and travel. In this way a wider public was informed and the basis of an empire created.

The arrival of William Caxton and the establishment of his printing press at Westminster set the scene for a period of rapid development as the English looked further afield. As new lands were reached, the printing press disseminated the news and the extent to which ambitious Englishmen were able to open up distant lands can be measured by the influence of books which came off the English presses.

Travel books met a growing need as the English language developed and became the medium through which fifteenth-century travel narratives were expressed and acted upon. Gautier of Metz's *The Mirrour of the World* (1481), Ranulf Higden's *Polichronicon* (1482), Wynkyn de Worde's *Proprietatibus Rerum* (1495) and *Informacon For Pylgrymes Unto the Holy Lande* (1498), Sir John Mandeville's *Travels*, Richard

Arnold's *Chronicle* (1503), Sebastian Brant's *Ship of Fools* (1509), the *Book of Robert Thorne*, Roger Barlow's *A Brief Summe of Geographie*, Richard Eden's *Of the Newe Found Landes*, Richard Hakluyt's *Principall Navigations and Voyages Touching the Discoverie of America* and the publication of part of Sebastian Muster's *Cosmographia* entitled *Treatise of the Newe India and Decades of the Newe World* (1555) are just a few of the many that were published in this period.

The main attraction of this literature was commerce and religious pilgrimage; and while England became more independent commercially and doctrinally in the fifteenth and sixteenth centuries, there was a parallel development in the English language. Early Modern English was crucial in advancing literature and education in the fifteenth century, and this reflected an emergent English nationalism, as expressed in 'ballad literature' after the Battle of Agincourt and again in the defence of Calais. Nevertheless, compared with the Continent, England lagged behind. The Dutch, for example, printed an estimated 2,000 books prior to 1500, while England produced a mere 360. Nevertheless, the English book trade was firmly established during the first three decades of the sixteenth century, the sales of books reflecting intellectual life in England.

By 1620 England had put in place the 'cornerstones of empire' and few in England doubted the potential of these enterprises. The benefits to ordinary Englishmen were loudly proclaimed and emigration to North America was seen as essential to realising its economic potential. However, such benefits that accrued to Britons were not without their consequences, for inevitably this meant a movement and a commingling of different peoples abroad and at home. In fact, much earlier, almost 500 years after the departure of the Romans from Britain in the fourth century, there was, according to the *Notitia Dignitatum* and *Hadrian's Wall*,[6] evidence of an African presence in Ireland. Again, after a long interval, the presence of black people in the British Isles was recorded, this time in Scotland in the sixteenth century, where they were associated with the court of James IV. Many of these people were skilled musicians and dancers, dark performers dressed in black and white costumes, as if to stress a point of social reference and distance, as well as the deference expected of them. Amongst the majority white population they were strikingly conspicuous. It comes as no surprise, therefore, that one black woman should have been immortalised by the Scottish poet William Dunbar in his poem 'Ane Blak Moire', which has been read variously by critics as a good-natured jest, a joke in poor taste and a 'deeply offensive smear'. Dunbar's imagery underscores his lyrical lines which refer to 'My ladye with the mekle lippis', a black woman with 'thick lips' and a 'short cat-like nose'. The poet exclaims how 'like a monkey' she is,[7] thus revealing contemporary white attitudes towards black people.

Such attitudes were derived from the image of black Roman soldiers as buffoons and jesters, whose colour typecast them as devils in later drama, folklore and witchcraft. The mirth that black entertainers provoked released white people from their fear, but did little down the centuries to correct the distorted image of black people amongst the white population in Britain.[8]

Until recently very little was known about Asians in England and much less about them in Scotland. As one writer noted, in 1505, 'certain foreigners' were at the court of James IV of Scotland, who received them well, presented them with gifts and gave one, described as an 'Earl of little Egypt', a letter of recommendation. During the reign of James V, the Privy Council of the Kingdom of Scotland issued a writ in the name of the king, recognising the Gypsy kingdom of 'Little Egypt'. But the identification of gypsies with Egypt, Bashir Maan tells us, is fallacious. He believes these people had come from India, and were members of a tribal people known as Doms, who lived in northern India. They reached England at the beginning of the sixteenth century, and in 1505 entered the Scottish court.[9] Between the sixteenth and seventeenth centuries this first recorded group of Indian migrants was assimilated into Scottish society, without identifiable trace, the precursors of today's 'new Scots'.

Scotland was not alone in its response to black and Asian people. In England, Henry VII hired a black trumpeter and from this time, if not before, black people were employed at court as servants and as pageant performers, jesters and musicians.

There was a growing curiosity about the lands from which these people came, but little was known about Africa except through Pliny, Herodotus and other classical writers. By the second half of the sixteenth century, however, European literature on Africa had grown and 'dramatists were not slow to realize the value of the "new" continent as a source of spectacle, plot, character and imagery'.[10]

What images did the people of the British Isles have of themselves, though? We know that in the sixteenth and seventeenth centuries they had to contend with their own crisis, their own images of themselves. How was this 'crisis' viewed and interpreted in the nation's art?

IMAGES OF 'BRITAIN' AS A NATION

John Ruskin wrote that 'great' nations write their autobiographies in three manuscripts: the book of deeds, the book of words and the book of their art, the only 'quite trustworthy' one being the last. However, if British art approximates an 'autobiography' of the nation, then it is likely to be 'less than entirely trustworthy', as Andrew Graham-Dixon argues, in his *A History of British Art*, for it is the work of a 'divided personality ... a composite of self-invention, self-deception, willed amnesia and involuntary forgetting'. Nevertheless, it is 'revealingly unreliable'. English art is a flawed tapestry, damaged by 'radical, muscular acts of censorship and abolition', a history marked by the violent erasure of English painting and sculpture. This aspect of native history is less well known than it should be, for while we are taught in school that the English Reformation started in 1534, following Henry VIII's unsuccessful petition to the Pope to have his marriage annulled, that the monasteries were dissolved in 1536 and that the Church of England was established, what remains relatively obscure is the extent of destruction that followed.

Radicalism entered the Church as Protestants took entrenched positions against the 'rituals and imagery' of Roman Catholicism, committing acts of desecration in places of Chris-

tian worship, and stripping cathedrals and churches in England,
Wales and Scotland of their treasures. The serenity that is
evoked by today's British churches as symbols of peace and
continuity is misleading. Continuity there has been, but much
has changed; significantly, churches and cathedrals must be
viewed as 'battlefields', where once the 'most vigorous war for
the soul of the culture' was fought.

Another watershed in English history was the revolution of
1688 and the untroubled accession of William of Orange and
Mary, which promoted Protestantism and progress. Religious
tolerance empowered Dissenters, who were finally free to build
their own churches. From the broader perspective of the British
Isles though, the 'Glorious Revolution' looks quite different,
and the English Empire, composed of a variety of cultures and
events in England, Scotland, Ireland, Wales and colonial
America, must be seen, like this 'Revolution', as giving 'meaning to particular pasts'.

The art produced by pre-Protestant, Roman Catholic
England speaks, in Graham-Dixon's words, of a once 'zealous,
convulsive, rowdy, colourful and superstitious people, possessed by consoling dreams of other brighter worlds and by
nightmares of death and damnation, living their painful and
devoted lives in a world of smoke and incense and music and
hot, hot colour'. The art they produced was uncomplicated
and direct. Indeed art served the function of being the
pre-eminent 'form of instruction' in a society in which few
were literate. Art was also an 'aid to prayer and to
meditation', a means through which images of heaven and
hell were envisaged. Eamon Duffy has written of the 'intimate
interweaving' of the now and the hereafter in Catholic
England. What was also characteristic of English art at this
time was an irrepressible inventiveness which broke the rules,
a 'vigorous, eccentricity at the heart of the national
imagination'. By the end of Charles I's reign, by contrast,
many English people were attracted to a 'certain kind of art', a
'new consensus' that was more aligned to facts than to
'extravagant, irrepressible fantasy'; an approach adopted by
Samuel Cooper in his portrait of Oliver Cromwell, who was
told to paint Cromwell with 'all these roughness, pimples,

warts and everything as you see me'. The English people had reached a point of national self-discovery and national self-definition, evoked in literary works such as John Milton's *Paradise Lost*, which is regarded as 'a huge affirmation of the death of irresponsible fantasy ... the one great epic in English verse ... the grandest manifestation of the Protestant values that were to underpin a new Britain'.

Christopher Wren's St Paul's Cathedral was also interpreted as a 'broader kind of allegory' which summed up national achievement and aspiration as the 'most turbulent' period of English history drew to a close. What Wren set in stone was not simply a clear rejection of the old faith, but also of 'old ways of seeing and dreaming too'. The change was profound. Now the British had no hesitation in looking outwards. And as their vision expanded, they were imbued with a sense of bravado, bordering on national arrogance, for when they renounced fantasy for reality, 'they did not only discover the real world. They began to take possession of it.'[11]

The acquisition of ever-greater quantities of land and gold was necessary in the making of an empire. Meanwhile, as the nation-states of Europe emerged and evolved, Europeans increasingly turned their attention abroad to strengthen their Old World economies through exploitation of the resources of foreign lands. As the Caribbean historian Eric Williams has noted, economic considerations gave added force to the political, scientific and religious 'urge to discover a new world', a process of discovery which was being slowly realised through contact with West Africa. Among those who had negotiated this African coastline was the explorer Columbus, whose ambition was the conquest of new territory and wealth for the Spanish Crown, which he achieved in a display of determination, daring and courage. By opening up the Americas, the course of European, Asian and African history was changed, and the gradual invention and reinvention of the 'Otherness' of colonised peoples from Africa and Asia and their exclusion from the Western canon evolved.

England soon joined Spain and Portugal in their scramble for actual and potential colonial possessions.

AFRICAN SLAVERY

In Britain, African and Asian people continued to work as servants and performers with little, if any, improvement in their daily lives. But this small African presence would soon become significant as trade and economic expansion and the demands of British capitalism required African labour, which became all-important in the production of tropical staples, the 'fruits of the Empire', including sugar, tobacco and cotton.

It has been argued that the slave trade generated the capital which financed the Industrial Revolution, and that 'mature' capitalism in turn destroyed the slave system. Others have hotly disputed this thesis. Professor Anstey, for example, in his *The Atlantic Slave Trade and British Abolition*, goes beyond the economic (essentially, Eric Williams's) argument to emphasise the religious and political aspects of the abolitionists' cause. What is indisputable is that as a consequence of the commerce and trade in slaves, cotton and sugar, an increasing number of black people began to appear in Britain. After the establishment of the East India Company Asian labour too became a crucial factor in the development of the British economy. The insatiable demand for material goods could only be realised through an abundance of good land and cheap labour. To this end, it was clear that the best option for the Caribbean colonies (and the Americas) was slavery, and so Europeans turned to the people of Africa. The origin of slavery then, was economic, not racial, the cheapness of labour rather than the colour of the labourer being the decisive factor.[12]

Transatlantic trade in African slaves, the so-called Middle Passage, was preceded by trade in European indentured servants. Earlier still, the indigenous Carib and Arawak Indians had been subjected to forced labour in the mines and plantations, a work regime which, in a relatively short time, decimated the population. They had mounted a strong resistance to the oppression of the colonial societies that now constituted that peculiar European creation, the West Indies. Though the high expectations of the Indians were not realised, they were defended by Bartholomè de Las Casas, a Spanish priest and former slave owner, who ironically not only embraced colonialism, but also accepted that African labourers were more robust and therefore better suited to this kind of work.

The introduction of sugar cane to the West Indies by Christopher Columbus on his second voyage soon led to an insatiable demand for cheap labour to facilitate sugar production. As the African slave population in the West Indies increased, it soon became clear that African captives were victims of a callous brand of cruelty, and unlike other forms of labour control (indentureship, for example), Africans were condemned to enslavement for life. Their loss of freedom and the rigours of slavery brought resistance and regular revolts, with notable rebellions before the middle of the sixteenth century. But the Africans' destinies were determined by the issuing of *Asientos* (contracts for the importation of slaves) in order to increase the slave population upon which the imperial economy had become dependent.

Thus, by the seventeenth and eighteenth centuries, European enterprise and African slavery were closely connected, helping not only the spectacular rise of British, French and Spanish seaports, but also the manufacturing centres.[13]

The growing British Empire was founded on the economic exploitation of the Caribbean, the Indian subcontinent and Africa. Though English traders' interests were still based largely on gold, pepper and ivory, it was John Hawkins's slaving adventures that captured the business imagination. With an eye on the West Indies, he decided to break the pattern of English trade and compete with the Spaniards for slave cargoes. In keeping with the times, he seemed to have recognised the potential profitability of such a long haul. In essence, the 'Triangular Trade', described as possibly the 'most lucrative commerce of all', involved the sale of cheap manufactured goods in Africa to purchase Africans, who were then transported and traded with planters in the West Indies and the Americas for foodstuffs, raw materials and minerals, which were, in turn, brought over to Britain for sale in the European market. Of the profits made from this three-sided trade, the largest did not come from the sale of slaves to planters, but from demand in Europe for slave-grown products, notably sugar, which accrued

great wealth to many British investors.[14] This was, as one
historian has argued, perhaps the 'earliest form' of the international exploitation of black labour, and with the plunder of India
– Bengal in particular – Britain was richly rewarded with two
'transfusions'[15] of wealth feeding into and coincident with the
Industrial Revolution – wealth made possible by forced African
and Asian labour at its command.

By the end of the eighteenth century, few things could be
regarded as more British than sweetened tea and the potato. So
too was the aroma of curling puffs and wisps of smoke from the
substance known as tobacco. These tropical commodities had
become essential to British social life, a part of day-to-day living
for the masses of the British people. Significantly, during the
140 years from 1660, the products that flooded into the British
market not only changed people's habits, but also utterly
transformed the far-flung regions of the world and their peoples,
a transformation which reflected European imperial aggression
in the post-Columbian years. European expansion and determination to possess the world engendered a reimaging and
remaking of the world, as the colonised regions and peoples
were made subservient to European interests.

Five hundred years ago, the world looked very different. What
are now vast urban conglomerates were once pastoral, rural
areas, and in the West Indies, what are regarded as indigenous
flora and fauna were, in fact, transported there from other parts
of the globe. Sugar, banana and breadfruit trees and certain
palms were not part of the natural landscape of the islands in
the fifteenth century. Nor were the people who today inhabit
these islands, including Africans, Europeans, Indians, Portuguese and Chinese, among others, who, more often than not,
went there against their will, or as an act of last resort.

British colonial expansion was a significant part of this story,
the context which, as Walvin argues, 'shapes, directs and
determines' the global relocation of peoples, plants, diseases and
some tropical commodities in the years after the fifteenth
century. Underpinning such movements were the demands of
Empire. So, through the process of colonial and commercial
expansion, Britain (and other European nations) was able to
convert a few crops into 'major instruments of profit, public

taste and global exploitation'. These commodities increasingly became the means of imperial and commercial progress, and such advancement, evident in the emergence of British power in the seventeenth and eighteenth centuries, was reflected in the relationship between commerce and colonial plantations. Britain's global power was assured and, in turn, underscored the relationship between British consumers and the tropical commodities.[16]

The ever-growing demand for exotic products created a new culture of consumption and an addiction to tobacco which, as a consequence, exacted an even greater propensity on the part of the slave masters to exploit their charges to the limits of human endurance, all for the sake of ever-higher profit margins.

According to Walter Rodney, over 15 million Africans were taken to New World destinations, and investors in the slave trade made 'fabulous' gains. Michael Craton has calculated an income (aggregate profits) of more than £150 million profits made by West Indian planters over the entire period of slavery – a rate that averaged £1 million a year throughout the eighteenth century. Taking the Triangular Trade as a whole, from 1640 to 1838, English people concerned with slavery could well have accumulated profits of £450 million, most of it in the eighteenth century.[17]

Wealthy West Indian planters, among the most conspicuous capitalists in the mercantilist era, usually lived in England, far from their plantations. Among the most prominent of these absentee landlords were the Beckfords of Gloucestershire, the Hibberts of Bedfordshire and the Long family of Suffolk and Bloomsbury. To these men of power and influence[18] the black presence in Britain was a reminder of the slaves/profits nexus, and the beneficiaries were not only the English and other Europeans. Some Africans also profited from the slave trade. Indeed, in the debate on slavery much has been written about the complicity of Africans in the slave trade and compensation for the descendants of the slaves. The former seems of lesser concern among descendants of the enslaved Africans than is the issue of compensation. Nevertheless, some writers and historians are determined to keep the question of African involvement in the slave trade on the agenda, because it is argued there is much still to be explored. Hugh Thomas engages in this exploration in *The Slave Trade*.[19]

THE BLACK COMMUNITY (1550–1800)

In 1555, some eight years before John Hawkins sold his first group of Africans into slavery, John Lok had returned from his second voyage along the African coast, bringing to England with him 'certaine black slaves'. This was the inauspicious beginning of a trading connection between the English Merchant Adventurers and the West African people, a commercial and religious enterprise that would, in the years to come, lead to an increased black African (and African-descended) presence in Britain. Meanwhile as the East India Company gained a foothold and then expanded its operations in India, more and more Indians joined the black British population.

By the end of the sixteenth century, the 'blackamoores'' presence had come to the attention of Elizabeth I. The growth in the numbers of black people in London was now targeted by Elizabeth, who informed the mayors of the principal cities that there were too many black people in her realm. In her view, the black presence in England had become a 'problem' and in January 1601, she issued a proclamation to deport 'Negroes and blackamoores'.[20] In spite of this, as the slave trade grew, in addition to direct importations from Africa, more and more black people entered Britain via slavery in the West Indies and North American colonies where, especially after the War of Independence, the black slaves who had fought on the British side were promised their freedom.

The enlarged black community in the eighteenth century, however, introduced a new social 'problem'. The ownership of human beings was increasingly viewed as a challenge to the common law and this was reflected in a number of slave cases in which contradictory judgments were reached. Slavery was upheld in England until 1772, when the case of the runaway slave Somerset was brought before Lord Chief Justice Mansfield, who ruled that a master could not forcibly take a slave abroad against the slave's wishes. The verdict aroused much interest not only within the black community but among the ranks of the British Anti-Slavery Movement, which had formed to campaign for the mitigation and phased abolition of slavery. Even this decision though was not enough to stop the taking of slaves by force from England, because the 1772 judgment did not provide adequate protective cover for 'free' black persons in England against unlawful enslavement. In effect, they remained vulnerable, having to wait another 62 years before, as Shyllon notes, they were emancipated, like their fellow-Africans on the plantations.[21]

'Free' black voices echoed a multiplicity of concerns within their community, especially on the intolerable conditions of slavery and the continuing plight of the black poor in Britain. It is significant that not all blacks were illiterate and among those who expressed themselves in writing were Briton Hamon, Ukawsaw Gronniosaw, Phyllis Wheatley, Julius Soubise, John Julius Naimbanna, Philip Quaque, Robert Wedderburn and John Jea, each with his or her won experience and images of the people and the country they had been brought to. Outstanding contributions came from three Africans: Ignatius Sancho, Ottobah Cugoano and Olaudah Equiano. Cugoano and Equiano wrote for publication, while Sancho was published posthumously and became one of the best known Africans in London.

Unusually, Sancho wrote in a range of literary forms, including poetry, plays and on the theory of music. His *Letters of the Late Ignatius Sancho, An African* was published in 1782 and he also appeared on the stage. The actor David Garrick and the novelist Laurence Sterne were among his friends and correspondents, and his portrait was painted by Gainsborough. Sancho was perhaps best known for the representations he made on behalf of his more unfortunate fellow blacks during a campaign in which he solicited the help of the novelist Laurence Sterne by drawing attention to the acute distress of London's Black Poor. But this 'black Englishman' had little sympathy for the oppressed white people in London. He had witnessed the Gordon Riots in 1780, but was, it seemed, entirely without sympathy for the rioters, among whom were English radicals such as the young engraver William Blake. Sancho estimated that at one point there were 'a hundred thousand poor, miserable ragged rabble, from twelve to sixty years of age', including black men and women. Of these rampaging demonstrators, Sancho could only offer these words: 'Thank heaven, it rains, may it increase, so as to send these deluded wretches safe to their homes, their families and wives.' As a postscript to his account, he declared: 'I am not sorry I was born in Afric.'[22]

In his *Thoughts and Sentiments* (1787)[23] Cugoano denounced the evil of slavery and pleaded for human dignity, kindness and mercy, not the transportation of the black people from England to Sierra Leone, a matter with which he and others were deeply concerned. For though poverty was no respecter of persons, it was a condition that was synonymous with being 'black', especially in London. Many of London's black population had become beggars by the mid-1780s, and one proposed remedy was an 'experiment' of resettlement overseas which was seen by many in authority as the final answer; a remedy that was promoted regardless of its cost.

More political than either Sancho or Cugoano was Olaudah Equiano, whose best-selling autobiography *The Interesting Narrative of the Life of Olaudah Equiano Or Gustavus Vassa, the African, Written By Himself* (1789), made him famous. Among the memorable events he recounted, he gives a detailed and moving account of how he and his sister were kidnapped in Africa and taken aboard a slave ship, of his years in slavery, and of his employment as a sailor.

These talented black men appealed to the liberal instincts of a few enlightened English men and women (including Granville Sharp, who championed many slave causes, James Ramsay, Thomas Clarkson, William Wilberforce and the poet William Wordsworth) who campaigned on behalf of enslaved Africans at a time when the pro-abolition campaign was beginning to receive support from radicals and the British working masses. By contrast, opposition came from another group of writers among whom were the historians Edward Long, Bryan Edwards and Thomas Carlyle and the novelist Anthony Trollope.[24]

In England popular movements emerged in response to oppression and the institution of colonial slavery, but the condition of the Black Poor[25] at home was still distressing.

THE SIERRA LEONE EXPERIMENT

When the American War of Independence began in 1775 the British found it necessary to enlist as much support as possible and to that end offered enslaved black men and women in the American colonies their freedom if they joined British Loyalists in the escalating conflict. After the British defeat, some black Loyalists fled to the West Indian islands, others to Canada and many arrived in Britain with little or no prospect of securing a livelihood. And so a 'new group' of black people came to be 'free' in the country to which they had given their ultimate support.[26]

However, the dream of freedom and a better life was not realised and many unemployed and destitute wandered the streets, drawing the attention of the indigenous white people, especially a group of powerful merchants, bankers and MPs, who formed the Committee for the Relief of the Black Poor. Through public appeals for funds, money was raised to feed black people in need. Clothing was also provided for over 200 people, and another 50 received hospital care. By 1786, some 700 black people were on the relief list. But the committee made it known that the largesse it doled out was not to be encouraged and soon announced alternative measures to deal with the growing ranks of the Black Poor. Thus resettlement in Africa of this section of the British population gradually evolved from an idea to a plan – the Plan of a Settlement to be made near Sierra Leone, on the 'Grain Coast' of Africa – published in 1786, which was advanced by Henry Smeathman, who had visited the Sierra Leone River and its environs between 1773 and 1774.

On his return to England, Smeathman wasted no time in presenting his plan to establish a settlement in Sierra Leone. On at least three occasions, between 21 March and 10 May 1786, the Committee discussed details of Smeathman's plan and decided, in the best interest of the government and the British people, to expel the Black Poor – an operation which Smeathman estimated would take at most eight weeks. Smeathman contacted George Rose, Secretary of the Treasury Board, before informing Granville Sharp, the philanthropist, of the deal he had struck with the government, which would accrue £12 for each black person he could deliver. He could hardly believe his luck. His plan, though coincident with the government's and the Committee's designs, would, in practice, be less easily effected than he had expected.

Prior to the House of Commons' approval of Smeathman's plan, on 5 July 1786 the good intentions of the Treasury were evident in its payment of £400 over a period of six weeks from the 17 April to 30 May, to aid the Black Poor. Not only did the House sanction the allocation of public funds for the repatriation of the Black Poor, it also paid for the maintenance of those who had been recruited as potential settlers and were awaiting transportation. In all, more than £4,000 was spent by Treasury officials on the proposed 'plan' for resettlement.[27]

This outlay proved to be an irreversible commitment. With Sierra Leone as the site of the new colony, the Committee wasted no time in informing the Black Poor, through handbills signed by the Chairman, Jonas Hanway, that they would be removed from Britain, as humanely as possible. The 'Grain Coast of Africa' (evocative of abundance) was now proclaimed as the most suitable place on the continent, where the 'necessaries of life' were at one's disposal. Indeed, through a combination of 'industry and moderate labour', much hope was generated in the prospective comforts that could be had, and all the more so, when the destination was contrasted with the alternative, Nova Scotia. Finally, in a seemingly philanthropic gesture, Smeathman accepted the Committee's appointment to accompany the deported Black Poor.

In May 1786, those who were 'desirous' of taking advantage of this opportunity to settle in Africa, were urged to contact Smeathman for further information at the 'Office of Free Africans', in Canon Street. Destitution prompted many to consider what seemed like a reasonable and attractive proposal. Whereas in 1785 Smeathman had declared before the House of Commons that the climate of Sierra Leone was so inhospitable that an estimated 100 convicts would die each month should a convict station be sited on the coast there, a year later, and with the prospect of real gain, he praised its soil and climate and, ever helpful, gave his assurance that agricultural crops would flourish in the area he had chosen – an offer and an opportunity 'so advantageous' that to miss it would be to forgo the best chance of improvement they would ever have.

Interestingly, the Black Poor were not all of one mind on this matter. Many did see some merit in the plan and turned to their trusted confidant, Granville Sharp, for reassurance and advice. The 'plan', in truth, reflected some thoughts that had been in Sharp's mind for some time,[28] and there was no conflict of interest between Sharp and Smeathman, although Smeathman's view of an Africa-based settlement was essentially 'economic and commercial', while Sharp's was 'rational and humanitarian'. Unlike the Committee, Sharp did not regard 'indigent blacks' as a 'nuisance'. As far as he was concerned, their colour was not a problem, but he was convinced that they should be returned to their African homeland. So, he did what he could, counselling (but not putting pressure on) those who came to him, advising that they should seize the opportunity of returning to their African homeland. Unlike the Committee, though, Sharp was, it seemed, concerned during the weeks leading up to repatriation with the thoughts and feelings of those black people involved in the process.

By 7 June 1786, Hanway was reporting that he had 'harangued' a number of blacks who, though accepting the government allowance, were 'reluctant' to go to the Grain Coast of Africa. He complained that they demanded safeguards that would ensure their 'Liberty' and told the Committee that at a meeting he had selected eight of the 'most intelligent' from among the blacks and people of colour, named as James Johnson, John William Ramsay, Aaron Brookes, John Lemon, John Cambridge, John Williams, William Green and Chas. Stoddard. A ninth man, a 'person of weight' in the black community, left without committing himself.

Hanway's actions did not allay the mounting fears. Of the 208 black people who had volunteered, 30 had decided not to accept the allowance of 6d a day pending their repatriation. They needed more time to consider the proposal. Why? Hanway's insensitive attitude was unfortunate and contributed to the dwindling numbers of volunteers, and the insistent desire, the achievable goal of forcing the Black Poor out of the country, biased everything that the Committee did. It was up to Hanway's headmen (or corporals) to persuade members of the black community to join the scheme.

In spite of their glowing accounts of the promised land, black people were not forthcoming. The Committee now exerted the maximum pressure by calling on the government and the London authorities to 'persuade' Poor Blacks to leave England. Consequently, there was a continuous hounding of them as vagrants.

There was a second consideration at work too: How was the Committee's objective to be achieved without conflicting with the rights of slave owners whose chattels might see repatriation as a means of escape to freedom? Such an eventuality had been considered: when the enlisted blacks for the Sierra Leone settlement congregated for their allowances each Saturday, they were screened not only by Hanway himself, but also by masters looking for their 'property'.

By the second half of 1786, the Committee had been well rewarded. Smeathman himself had died at the beginning of July, but by then more than 400 black people had been engaged as transportees. Smeathman's death opened up the possibility of another destination: the Bahamas. This, though, met strong opposition from the headmen, who petitioned the Committee and the Treasury. The plan anyway was now too far advanced and, almost as an epitaph to Smeathman, the diversion of another destination seemed to give added credence to the choice of Sierra Leone. Joseph Irwin now succeeded Smeathman as Government Agent charged with the responsibility of accompanying the repatriated Black Poor.

In the Committee's view, it was also necessary to appoint a Commissary, someone acquainted with the Sierra Leone coast 'to superintend and see justice done'.[29] With government approval, and at the Committee's suggestion, Olaudah Equiano was appointed Commissary to the Black Poor. At first, he declined the position; understandably, slave dealers posed special difficulties for him. His subsequent acceptance of the post did not override the reservations he had about the motivation and actions of those whom he was likely to confront. Nevertheless, news of his appointment was encouraging to the Black Poor, and more came forward.

By early October, 500 had enlisted and so two ships, the *Atlantic* and *Belisarius*, were commissioned to transport the settlers. By the end of the month, as many as 700 blacks had signed up. Nevertheless, many still remained on the streets and, as this was contrary to the purpose of the plan, in the days that followed more determined efforts were made to round them up. Over 300 decided to stay in England and it seemed that, with each passing day, more and more had doubts and fears; doubts about why they were being removed from England and fears for their security and safety in Sierra Leone, matters to which Ottobah Cugoano, the 'person of weight' in the black community, alluded at the time, in his *Thoughts and Sentiments on the Evil of Slavery:*

> For as it seemed prudent and obvious to many of them taking heed to that sacred enquiry, Doth a fountain send forth at the same place sweet water and bitter? They were afraid that their doom would be to drink of the bitter water. For can it be readily conceived that government would establish a free colony for them nearly on the spot, while it supports its forts and garrisons, to ensnare, merchandize, and to carry others into captivity and slavery.[30]

Cugoano, a devout Christian, was at a loss to understand why another 'Christian', Jonas Hanway, was haranguing his fellow-blacks. Cugoano was fortunate in having the powerful support not only of his friend Olaudah Equiano, but also the *Morning Herald* newspaper in mounting the strongest possible opposition to repatriation of the Black Poor, and believed that 'racial considerations' were the motive force.

With so many questions still unanswered, some of the black community leaders sought the advice of Lord George Gordon on the system of their governance in the intended place of settlement. Gordon saw insurmountable difficulties and advised them to give up the repatriation idea.

The unrelenting pressure on black people to leave England (as a 'British nation'[31] was being established) reached a climax late in 1786 when the aggrieved community felt the time had come to voice their discontent. But, a meeting called in December 1786 was banned and, as on the Caribbean slave plantations, the fear in Britain was that oppressed blacks congregating anywhere were dangerous and therefore had to be outlawed, because combinations – organisation of any kind among disparate, small groups – threatened the peace and security of those in control. In the case of the indigent Black Poor, perhaps, the Committee's real fear was the respected leadership of Equiano, who had now been officially endorsed as Commissary. To his credit, he did not hide his feelings and intentions in relation to the 'slave dealers', but this was no comfort to the Committee or the government. Both Equiano and the Committee were aware of the tension between them, and following the ban, Equiano leaked the news to the *Morning Herald*. On 29 December, the newspaper broke the story in an article that was extremely valuable to the Black Poor, who were all now at risk of being transported. More about this banned assembly was published in letter-form in the *Morning Herald* early in January 1787; and the next day, Joseph Irwin, the Government Agent, replied in the same newspaper. The main thrust of the letter issued by the representatives of the Black Poor was two-fold: that Irwin was exploiting his position for self-gain, and that those black people already on board the ships were being treated with iron discipline, not far short of that imposed on the enslaved Guinea men, awaiting shipment to the New World colonies.

To his credit, from the moment he began his job as Commissary, Equiano acted with diligence and a deep sense of responsibility. He quickly uncovered, as he suspected, Irwin's 'flagrant abuses', such as the non-existent stores that had already been paid for and the fact that members of the Black Poor were placed at the greatest disadvantage, their accommodation being the 'most wretched': many had no beds, while a greater number were without clothing and other essential items. Not only did Equiano feel aggrieved by the injustice done to his fellow countrymen, he also felt it was his duty, as Commissary, to inform the Navy Board of such wrong-doing. In taking this action, he was confident that he would get the support of Captain Thompson, commander of the *Nautilus*.

In the days that followed, Cugoano, Equiano and the *Morning Herald* persisted in their criticism of the Committee's settlement plan and its handling of the affair. Earlier fears and doubts had now become undisguised disenchantment, as many more black people avoided the ships. The *Morning Post*, and later, the *Public Advertiser*, took the Committee's and the government's side, using crude attempts at refinements of race and colour as their arguments became more hysterical.

Eventually, on 11 January 1787, the drama of the back-to-Africa experiment began as the *Atlantic* and *Belisarius* sailed from Gravesend bound for Sierra Leone. They stopped at Portsmouth where they were joined by the escort vessel, *Nautilus*, but before setting sail again, tragedy struck: 60 of the black deportees died of hypothermia and associated afflictions. Later, after a storm had damaged two of the ships while they lay at anchor in Plymouth, as Cugoano recorded, some of those on board, desperately unhappy with the prospect before them, leapt into the sea, no doubt in the full knowledge that should they survive the attempt to escape, they would be recaptured for the journey. Indeed, of the many blacks who headed for the shore, some were apprehended, while others disappeared, much to the annoyance of the Committee and the captain in command of the ships at port.

While the ships were still in Plymouth, much had transpired behind the scenes. Equiano may have had too much faith in Captain Thompson, who wrote to the Navy Board on 21 March 1787 that Equiano as Commissary was entirely 'turbulent and discontented', and used every means at his disposal to 'activate the minds of the blacks to discord'. Thompson also censured Irwin. Knowing of Equiano's commitment to his countrymen, Thompson said that if Equiano's 'spirit of sedition' was not dealt with, there was no doubt in his mind that it would prove 'fatal to the peace of the settlement'.[32] So, Equiano, the most outspoken and articulate black person of his time in Britain, was labelled a 'troublemaker'.[33]

In response, the Navy Board found that in all the work he had done as Commissary, Equiano had 'acted with great propriety' and 'had been very regular in his information'. Nevertheless, the judgement of the Lords of the Treasury was clear. They called for his dismissal, but decided that Irwin must be retained to discipline the Black Poor bound for Sierra Leone.

Predictably, Equiano was not pleased and discussed the matter with his friend Cugoano. As the foremost spokesman and black writer, Equiano again decided to write to the *Public Advertiser* early in April 1787, reiterating that Irwin 'never meant well' to the Black Poor. He also hoped that in time he would become 'very useful'. In this sense, his dismissal was fortuitous, for had he continued as Commissary, he might not have survived to become active in the anti-Slavery movement, which gained momentum following expulsion of the Black Poor.

At last, on 10 April 1787, the ships left England with 441 settlers.[34] But, although the repatriated Black Poor arrived safely at Sierra Leone on 9 May 1787, all was not well. In his report to the Navy Board, Captain Thompson complained that he could not 'subdue' the blacks; heavy rains, fevers and other physical complaints reaped a grim harvest as more settlers, including Irwin, died each day.[35] It was a sad realisation of a grand plan. The extent of the tragedy was revealed when Captain Thompson left Sierra Leone on 17 September 1787: of the 441 who had set sail from England, only 268 were still alive, thus justifying not only Equiano's distrust of Irwin, but also his fears for the welfare of his countrymen. Two years later, at the end of his book *The Interesting Narrative ...*, he referred to this episode in his eventful life:

> I wish to stand by my own integrity, and not to shelter myself under the impropriety of another; and I trust the behaviour of the Commissioners of the Navy to me entitled me to make this assertion; for after I had been dismissed, March 24, I drew up a memorial ... [which] was delivered into the hands of their Lordships, who were kind enough, in the space of some few months afterwards, without hearing, to order me £50 sterling – that is ... wages for the time ... I acted a faithful part in their service.[36]

The Sierra Leone settlement 'plan' did not, however, rid Britain of all its Black Poor. Beggars continued to live precariously, always liable to be imprisoned, flogged and/or taken overseas, often to the West Indies, which meant slavery. Some had begged for so long that they had become adept. One among them, Billy Waters, a one-legged fiddler, became a role model, being elected by his peers as King of the Beggars.[37] His music evoked a range of moods suggestive of the brevity and transience of life and the importance of living for the moment. He was a man who, in dire circumstances, displayed human creativity and gave hope and encouragement to others in the community.

Endless inventiveness kept the black population a vibrant and distinctive community, which rejoiced when the slave Somerset was freed and was saddened when members of their family, friends and colleagues were deported to Sierra Leone. It was also a varied community, incorporating the few like Jack Beef and Julius Soubise who were privileged and the less fortunate majority who lived 'below stairs'.

How were members of this community perceived in the eighteenth century? The images of black people in Britain at this time are revealing. Paintings, for example, depict their low status, while prints by William Hogarth and others portray them as equal participants in the subculture of life below stairs, in essence, a culture of 'violence and vulgarity'. Sexual relations between blacks and whites were illustrated as in William Humphrey's 'High Life Below Stairs'.[38] There was much camaraderie among them. Enjoined by the common bond of survival, black people combined with poor whites in demonstrations and riots, risking their lives for bread. Black people had indeed become an integral part of the lower classes in English society. What was recorded in visual images and in literature were interpretations of black people from a white, often privileged viewpoint. Historical evidence was therefore 'white' evidence of black people in English society.

By the last third of the eighteenth century, there were an estimated 10,000 black people[39] in Britain. Many had become so integrated in working-class life and the concerns of the wider society that they became, in some cases, passionate advocates of radical causes, struggles linked to, and reflective of, their fellow-Africans in the colonies, where plantocracy racism, so endemic in slavery, imposed a harsh regime to which the African slaves offered resistance, both as individuals and collectively. The frequency of serious uprisings has been well documented. Like the deprived people in Britain, the enslaved in the British colonies were no less insistent in their desire for freedom, as were oppressed people elsewhere in Britain's Indian Empire.

BRITISH INDIA

The route facilitating trade between Europe and India, conducted overland by way of Constantinople, was blocked by the Turks in the fifteenth century, a disruption that was eventually circumvented when Vasco Da Gama, flying the flag of Portugal, negotiated a new route, via the Cape of Good Hope, and landed at Calicut in 1498,[40] six years after Columbus's first landfall in the West Indies. Goa, off India's western coast, became a Portuguese stronghold, from where they launched their colonial exploits. The Dutch, British and French soon sought to emulate the Portuguese in order to gain a share of the Indian trade.

Almost one hundred years after Da Gama's arrival in India, the East India Company was inaugurated in London, and the following year, Elizabeth I conferred on the Company sole trading rights with India and the East Indies. Thwarted in its ambitions to participate in the spice trade which had been conducted earlier by Dutch traders, the East India Company could now survey the profitability of the nearby Indian subcontinent. Just over a decade later, encouraged by its success in winning the Mughal Emperor's approval, the Company had become the pre-eminent agency and institution of European power.

With a free hand, the Company had the latitude to plan its operations as it thought best, and soon enough found it expedient, for administrative purposes, to divide India into three main provinces, the Bengal, Madras and Bombay Presidencies, each functioning independently, but with ultimate responsibility for them resting with the Court of Directors in London. To monitor its activities competent administrators were required and, with the passage of time, a staff structure of English merchants, factors and writers was established in India, along with British legal, civic, religious and artistic institutions, together constituting communities which evolved as essentially British, separated from the Company's indigenous workers and from the rest of the Indian people.[41]

To protect these privileged white enclaves, the Company engaged armed British and Indian personnel. But with few English women among the Company's recruits, social mixing between Indians and the English took place until the latter part of the eighteenth century, when the Indian rulers were in disarray and the Mughal Empire was on the verge of decline. Indian disunity and competition from the French was enough to propel the Company to move swiftly to eliminate the threat their fellow-Europeans posed. After successfully dealing with this matter and exploiting the troubled relations between the Company and the ruler of Bengal, Robert Clive's soldiers forced the Indian overlord to surrender, a victory which established the Company's dominion over the Province, thus paving the way for Britain's Indian Empire. Now, the Company, recognised by the Mughal Emperor, was able to manage the affairs of Bengal, most importantly by becoming the tax collector; and with the Province under the Company's control, the 'nabobs' (expatriate Britons) could exploit every commercial avenue. In this process, the autonomy of the Provinces was abolished and, in 1773, responsibility for them was entrusted to the newly appointed Governor-General, Warren Hastings, an Orientalist, who, it was said, respected India's ancient civilisation and became a student of its religion, art, literature and languages.

Eleven years later, more changes to the Company's administration were introduced, one of which was Europeanisation. Indians were allowed to occupy only lower levels of the public service hierarchy, while the middle to higher reaches of the employment structure were the exclusive domain of Europeans who, with their Eurocentric attitudes, became socially more aloof. When Charles Cornwallis succeeded Hastings as Governor-General, he saw nothing in India or among Indians to convince him that they were civilised, and felt justified in imposing British standards upon India, to the further detriment of native Indians generally, and in particular, the landless, dispossessed peasants and the poor.[42]

In Britain, industrial workers also suffered the inhuman treatment of their employers who, in many cases, were members of the same class that drove slaves to the limits of planter profitability in the West Indies. Those who worked in the textile mills of northern England, for example, were equally victims of capital's inherent greed. This was the workforce which, Fryer claims, produced the textiles exported to Africa for the purchase of slaves. Among those who laboured in the Lancashire mills were children, whose parents were trapped in the cycle of poverty so characteristic of the poor city-dwellers of the time. Forced to seek refuge in the workhouses, some parents had no choice but to abandon their children, a loss which was, for the cotton factory owners, highly profitable. So, black cotton slaves in the United States had their white cotton counterparts in northern England. J.L. and Barbara Hammond have written perceptively and with sensitivity about this relationship: 'An age that thought of the African Negro, not as a person with a human life, but so much labour power to be used in the service of a master or a system, came naturally to think of the poor at home in the same way.'[43]

This was a system that could find an apologist in Parliament. There, a Mr Wortley said that while in the higher reaches of society it was true that cultivating the 'affections of children for their family was the source of every virtue', he could not concede that this was so among the 'lower orders' and therefore it was of 'benefit' to those who were taken away from their 'miserable and depressed' parents and insisted that it would be highly injurious to the public to stop the 'binding of so many apprentices to cotton manufacturers' because it would necessarily 'increase labour costs and raise prices'. The connection between the black slaves and the white poor in Britain though is incomplete without its Indian linkage, for the Imperial enterprise of profiteering in the West was increasingly being complemented in the East.

By the 1770s, Bengal had become a place of desolation, the combined effects of plunder and the subsequent famines which took the lives of some ten million people. This once thriving region, the granary of the East, was reduced to a near-desert, its fields left uncultivated.

At the time of the Indian Mutiny in 1857–8, the British Chancellor of the Exchequer would reflect that under the guise of being civilised, no government had existed which was 'more corrupt, more perfidious and rapacious' than the government of the East India Company in the years from 1765 to 1784. Not surprisingly, the Hindi word 'loot' became an integral part of the English vocabulary. In the years from 1757 to 1815, from the Battle of Plassey to the Battle of Waterloo, an estimated £500 million–£1,000 million from India flowed in[44] to lubricate the engines that drove Britain's Industrial Revolution. Coincident with the Battle of Plassey, and in the three succeeding decades, a number of crucial inventions and technological breakthroughs saw a dramatic rise in Britain's industrial output, including cotton manufacture, which reversed the trend of trade for products that had once been imported from India.

Like African servants in Britain, Asians were sought by wealthy families. As cheap labour, they were little more than slaves, their 'reliability' masking a desperate desire for liberty. The close attachment between servant and master, manifested in different forms of bondage was not unusual, for slavery, regardless of age or sex, was a well-known aspect of life at this time in British India. Although the ancient trade in African slaves along India's West Coast persisted until 1789, these Africans were expensive and the vast multitude of Indians (either as slaves or servants) sufficed.[45] Thus the eighteenth-century novelty of importing Indians as servants and ayahs became a custom that seemed appropriate in the age of Empire as many British employees of the East India Company became rich and powerful and were able to live in luxury with Indian servants attending to their every need. On their return to Britain, some of these nabobs and Army officers brought their Indian servants, many of whom were devoted and caring. Others fled from their masters' homes, with little concern for the consequences, thus joining the growing ranks of the non-white population engaged in the familiar and urgent struggle for survival.

BREAKING FREE (1780s–1820s)

Whether in Britain or abroad, whatever pressures were placed upon blacks and Asians, it would be misleading to assume that they were uniformly passive. Indeed the years from 1780 to the 1820s span an extraordinary period of struggle and change as black men and women took a stand.

Black people were united by common problems and interests; and with the diminution of their numbers in the nineteenth century, their poverty not only remained more or less the same, but was also accounted for in community activity on common causes that were shared in large part by the ranks of the British working classes.

At the beginning of the nineteenth century, the Anti-Slavery campaign was winning growing support from the churches and especially among the lower orders of the British working people. But, paradoxically, in spite of this sympathetic shift in British public opinion, black people were confronted with the naked prejudices of English society. It had become necessary for them to act, to be inventive. Accordingly, their struggles now merged into a larger movement, with the black slave increasingly being used as an argument against 'white slavery' in Britain. It should therefore not surprise us that between 1800 and 1850 black leaders were accepted as playing an essential part in the vanguard of the radical movement, a period during which three exceptional black men rose to take leading positions in the British working people's agitation. Two of these men, William Davidson and Robert Wedderburn, were revolutionary socialists, members of the most radical organisations of the time, and followers of Thomas Spence (Secretary of the London Correspondence Society and editor of radical newspapers) who was imprisoned for his radicalism.

Robert Wedderburn

Wedderburn was born in Jamaica in 1762, the son of Roseanna, a slave, and James Wedderburn, her Scottish owner, who granted his son his freedom at birth, a freedom which did not, however, spare him from being witness, at the age of eleven, to the distressing spectacle of his 70-year-old grandmother being flogged so severely that she would have died if a neighbour had not intervened. And to further scar his impressionable mind, Robert saw his pregnant mother receive repeated blows. These violent scenes would haunt him for the rest of his life.

Responding to the pull of his father's ancestry, after arriving in England at the age of 17, he found employment at sea before he became a tailor. There were few (if any) times when he was not aware of the great divide between rich and poor, especially in class-ridden England, where his social sense was honed to the point of taking action for his beliefs.

He felt powerfully drawn to outspoken men of conscience, to preachers at London's Seven Dials, especially the Wesleyans, and to radical activities. And so Wedderburn became the 'Reverend' Robert Wedderburn, a committed Unitarian preacher and writer. In his *Truth Self-Supported, Or A Refutation Of Certain Doctrinal Errors Generally Adopted In The Christian Church*, he expressed his unorthodox views. At the age of 52, he became involved with the Society of Spencean Philanthropists, having met Spence shortly before his death.

Gradually, he rose to prominence. A vigorous campaigner for English workers' rights, he displayed his unusual ability in literature by launching a periodical publication, *The Forlorn Hope*, in 1817, through which he hoped something approximating a free press would emerge. He was bold in debate, clashing occasionally with the most prominent Spencean leaders. His enthusiasm was recognised by young people, who approved of his teachings and applauded his ridicule of parts of the Scriptures. He was also proud of his African ancestry and very satisfied with the result of a debate on the slave's right to take his or her master's life. By championing the cause of the enslaved against their pious Christian masters (whether apparent or real), he posed a threat, and not surprisingly, he was prosecuted for 'sedition and blasphemy'.

After serving a prison sentence, Wedderburn found that his freedom was still proscribed by the presence of spies and informers: the struggle for survival had become more intense.

Then came the Peterloo Massacre in 1819, which bloodied the streets of Manchester; an occasion and a time when 'class war' was starkly evident and workers bore the brunt of unbridled violence.

Wedderburn worked desperately to counteract the policies and practices of the perpetrators of this evil, becoming more and more politically committed. His desire to bring political change was so great that at the age of 57 he began to prepare himself for what he believed would be the moment of confrontation, when the poor would rise up and overthrow their oppressors, the tyrannical government ministers and the Prince Regent. He had no doubts as to where he stood. Put simply, given his colonial background, he lived in hope of seeing a victorious revolution. His early life in Jamaica gave perspective to his struggle in England which, in turn, related to the enslaved on the plantations. He believed that both the black and white struggles were interconnected, for after all he was part white and part black.

In the 1820s, his Spenceanism was still strong and pursuing his passion for, and belief in the power of, the written word Wedderburn published *The Horrors of Slavery*, an autobiographical pamphlet in which he described the planters' hatred and oppression of black people. A decade later he was again imprisoned. He was then 68 but still felt spirited and capable enough to engage in violent confrontation, should it come.[46]

Not much is known about the rest of Wedderburn's activities or the date and circumstances of his death, but we are left in no doubt that his exemplary life was characterised by an undiminished desire for freedom and self-respect.

William Davidson

William Davidson was born in Jamaica in 1786. Like Wedderburn, his mother was a slave and his father a plantation owner. William came to England to be educated and to apply himself especially to the study of law. But like Wedderburn, he went to sea before taking a job as a cabinet-maker. This proved to be undemanding and soon he became an ardent reader and supporter of Thomas Paine's revolutionary ideas.

He was a lively, energetic man, full of life, who also enjoyed singing, the company of friends and the warmth of family life. However, it was his radical activities which, like his colour, made him conspicuous. He was targeted for special surveillance by an *agent provocateur*, George Edwards, who posed as a fellow-radical, at a time of rising political and class tension. Disappointing harvests and the effects of the Napoleonic blockade prompted riots and demonstrations against the government, bringing London to the brink of crisis, as once more it became, as Peter Ackroyd described it, a 'city of famine'.[47] In Spitalfields more than 45,000 hungry people sought entry to the workhouse. Starvation fuelled highly charged protests and the 'fear of insurrection' gripped the capital and the provinces. The violent Luddite actions of 1812 and 1813 reflected the general feeling of disenchantment among radicals, who railed against 'Old Corruption'. Their periodicals, *Pig's Meat*, *Black Dwarf* and *Axe Laid To the Root*, complemented their ale-house meetings, discussions and public demonstrations, responses to what they regarded as state oppression. Adding to their discontent, after 1814 unemployment rose, as did the number of beggars in London; and with a series of bad harvests and the introduction of the Corn Laws in 1815, there was a depression in trade.

Against this background of local revolt, Davidson could not remain politically neutral. He had become involved with a group of radicals (including Arthur Thistlewood, Richard Tidd, James Ings and John Brunt, who were implicated in the Cato Street Conspiracy) intent on overthrowing the government by murdering government ministers. Whereas Wedderburn exercised patience in his approach to the possibility of an uprising, Davidson could wait no longer. Direct action was the only course open to him. Accordingly, certain responsibilities were delegated to him, one of which was fund-raising for the purpose of acquiring weapons and guarding them.

In the wake of attempted insurrections in Sheffield, Barnsley, Huddersfield, Glasgow and Paisley, Thistlewood, Davidson and their fellow-radicals Ings, Brunt and Tidd, were put on trial for treason for their part in the Cato Street Conspiracy, which had resulted in the murder of a policeman. For his part, Davidson pleaded not guilty and when he suggested that his colour might lead to his conviction, one of the judges said: 'God forbid that the complexion of the accused should enter, for a single moment, into the consideration of the jury.' In his defence, Davidson informed the Court that although his house had been searched, nothing was found that could be used as evidence against him. However, these times were unpropitious for clemency and the five radicals were condemned to be publicly hanged, beheaded and quartered, early on the morning of 1 May 1820 in what turned out to be the 'grimmest' and most 'sickening' scenes at Newgate.[48]

So the dream of revolution harboured by these desperate men failed miserably. But like William Blake, who had been a radical in his early years, but later was content to be a visionary with no involvement on politics, Davidson also had a vision of freedom, which led him to die like a man and not like a slave.

Mary Prince

Another black person who was engaged in freeing herself from the stranglehold of her owner and master was Mary Prince, who fought against the male-dominated, class-oriented world of the nineteenth century.

She was born a slave in Bermuda on a farm owned by Charles Myners. Her mother was a house slave, and her father, a sawyer, carried the name Prince. In this violent household, Mary's owner flogged her frequently and his mistress displayed sadistic tendencies. She not only instructed Mary in her household duties, but also impressed upon her the difference between the 'smart of the rope, the cart-whip and the cow skin'.

Mary was subsequently sold into the service of Mr and Mrs Wood, and the change in ownership brought conditions that were no less hard. Years of work, washing clothes and standing in the water of salt ponds took their toll and Mary developed rheumatism. By the time she arrived in England with Mr Wood, her body was swollen 'dreadfully'. Her increasing disability was met with rising anger and impatience on the part of the Woods, who ordered her to leave their house, which she did, sustained by a determination to be free. After finding refuge with the

Moravian missionaries in Hatton Garden, she made her way to the Anti-Slavery office in Aldermanbury where her case was referred to George Stephen for investigation.

In spite of the Anti-Slavery Society's efforts, Mr Wood refused to let her return to her husband in the West Indies. After working for a while as a charwoman, relative good fortune befell Mary when she went into service with a Mr and Mrs Thomas Pringle, where she remained, until the publication of her life story, *The History of Mary Prince Related By Herself*. According to Pringle, the idea of writing her story was Mary's own and in it a unique view is presented of every facet of the life of a black woman in the service of her oppressors, first, as a slave, and then, seemingly more charitably, as a 'servant'. Indeed, black women were so taken for granted, so invisible, that they were often disgraced and, in Mary's words, thought of as 'no more than beasts'.[49] Her service in England was tangible evidence and a reminder of the depths of human debasement and the consistent degree of vindictiveness practised by her 'superiors'. Although her master had returned to the West Indies, he still refused to set Mary free for, in his interpretations of the relationship, legally she was his property for the rest of her days.

Little or nothing more is known of the life of Mary Prince and the unanswered questions remain: Did she eventually get her freedom and return to her husband in Antigua? Or did she spend the rest of her life in England? Whatever the answer, this patient and courageous woman, both as slave and 'servant', was the historical precedent of her countless sisters in the service of Britain.

In breaking free, these outstandingly brave individuals, Wedderburn, Davidson and Prince, were in the vanguard of millions of people (including a considerable number of whites) who felt deeply the wrongs of the brutality endemic in the kidnapping, ill-treatment and eventual enslavement of Africans. And so in the final decades of the eighteenth and the first third of the nineteenth centuries, as the tide of opinion in Britain and resistance on the plantations rose to new heights to counteract this crime against humanity, both the African slave trade and

African slavery were abolished, by Acts of the British Parliament. But although such abolitions had freed the slaves, the true cost of this freedom was about to be compounded by the employment of those who would replace them, almost immediately, through another form of bondage.

2 AFRO-ASIANS AFTER EMANCIPATION (1833–1900)

BRITAIN IN THE NINETEENTH CENTURY: AN HISTORICAL OUTLINE

> Assessment of the impact [of Empire] on Britain's sense of identity
> has to face the obvious problems that the British had and have many
> senses of identity and that empire, even as a system of rule, could be
> interpreted in different ways to fulfil differing aspirations to identity.
>
> Peter Marshall, *An Agenda for the History of Imperial Britain*,
> quoted in Linda Colley, *The Significance of the Frontier in British History*
> (1995)

Before moving on to the post-Emancipation story of Africans and Asians, let us first consider the context of developments in nineteenth-century Britain. Once again, the balance of cultures within the British Isles shifted radically in the nineteenth and twentieth centuries, and in England certain social, demographic and economic changes arising from industrialisation brought a new culture to the North, incorporating the subcultures of the Midlands, Merseyside, Manchester and its environs, the West Riding, Tyneside and Teesside. The divide between North and South demarcated the relative prosperity of the North and the lack of industrial enterprise in London.

Elsewhere in the British Isles change was relative. Ireland, which became a part of the United Kingdom in 1800, was the subject of much debate and government action, as a country that was on the 'periphery'. So too were Wales and Scotland, which resisted unwelcome intrusions. In the former, there were serious disturbances – the Merthyr Rising of 1831, the Chartist convergence on Newport in 1839 and the Rebecca Riots; while in Ireland, the Ribbonmen stood their ground. In Scotland,

Glasgow was the scene of unrest in the 1820s. If the government of the United Kingdom was dependent upon alliances formed between the Welsh, Irish and Scottish ascendancies and Parliament in London, by the 1850s there was some change when Irish Catholicism, Welsh Nonconformity and the Free Churches of Scotland combined with 'English dissent to bring pressure to bear upon the English establishment'.[1] This cooperation, founded upon opposition to the English ruling elite, gave rise to the Liberal Party. Thus political clout from the 'periphery' was exerted on the 'centre'. In less than a decade, resistance from more remote colonial possessions would come from the Indian Empire.

Moreover, with a better communications network incorporating road, rail and sea, Ireland, Wales and Scotland became more accessible and therefore more exposed to English political influences. Ireland was less of an issue in English national politics than it was in 1850, while Wales and Scotland were constituent parts of the class politics of the rest of the kingdom. With time, Ireland proved to be more susceptible to outside influences than Wales and Scotland, its Irish-born Gaelic speakers declining drastically in the latter part of the nineteenth century. However, although the southern English culture would come to dominate the British Isles, the years from 1860 to 1914 would see the rise and proliferation of ethnic consciousness within the region.

The last three decades of the nineteenth century marked a period of transition, of important change among the peoples of the United Kingdom generally, which in turn had 'a subtle bearing on their place in the world'.

While the celebrations marking Queen Victoria's Jubilee were an exhilarating spectacle, they masked more sober realities. The impression of unity within the realm was misleading for, by its nature, the United Kingdom was 'a multinational state' with divisions enough to assemble it 'in a number of ways'. For instance, the four nations, England, Ireland, Scotland and Wales, could become a Federation of 'sovereign states', with Ireland perhaps exercising the option of becoming a 'separate polity'. These were possibilities, but the majority of late Victorians favoured a United Kingdom within which diverse cultures, languages and regions could coexist.[2]

ENGLAND, SCOTLAND, IRELAND AND WALES

In 1870 England was the dominant region within the United Kingdom. In terms of population, England had outstripped the other areas and, within its borders, though there were marked differences between Yorkshire and, say, Cornwall, English identity was unquestioned. To this land, migrants were drawn from various parts of Europe, Scotland, Ireland and Wales. England's gravitational pull was further strengthened for it was in its capital, London, that the British government sat and where unrivalled cultural institutions of international significance were located. In all, England set certain standards for the other parts of the British Isles.

Ireland was quite different. Its national identity was divided into two distinct religious groups: Catholics (an estimated two-thirds) and Protestants (about one-third). The conquest and settlement of Ireland by the English was evident in terms of language and geography. The traditionalists, speakers of the Irish language, among the poorer folk, were to be found in the West and South, and resented English domination. The Protestants, predominantly in the North, wanted to remain part of the United Kingdom. Unlike the other parts of the United Kingdom, Irish politics were difficult to incorporate and, from the 1890s, the 'Irish Question' was no longer simply a question of land; Irish identity was the issue. But culture and politics could not be separated. While English-speaking northern Presbyterians with their Scots-Irish culture were pro-British, the promotion of Gaelic in the south helped maintain their national pride and mutual distrust.

Scotland, Ireland and Wales were grouped together as a 'Celtic fringe' to distinguish them further from England, which was 'Anglo-Saxon'. However, far from describing a homogeneous society, the term 'Celtic' masked diverse groups and regions. During the 1870s, the question of a Scottish nation was far from clear, for while Scotsmen regarded Scotland as an independent entity, most of them accepted the 1707 Union, which allowed the Scots to administer their own legal, ecclesiastical and education structures, through which Scottish identity could be expressed. In spite of the urgings of Gladstone (himself of Scottish descent) for Home Rule in these years, the idea remained only nascent.

Increasingly, Wales became more prominent and in terms of law, politics, statistics and administration, England and Wales were firmly entwined. The Liberals gained ascendancy after the 1868 elections and Gladstone found it politically expedient to establish good relations with the Principality.

Viewed as a whole, for all its internal divisions and tensions, the United Kingdom was focused in its efforts to expand its overseas territories.

As an Imperial ruler, before the end of the nineteenth century, Britain could boast that it had the largest Empire in world history. The colonies were regarded as gardens to be cultivated, tended by British gardeners for their own benefit. However, grabbing more land could not in itself change the hegemonic challenge of the United States of America and Russia. As it was, Empire fever led to the 'scramble for Africa'; and the exploration of the continent by Livingstone, among others, led to the transformation of Africa, a process which at first combined 'a confused mixture of idealism, scientific inquiry and desire for profit'. Whatever reservations the Conservatives may have had, the Imperial enterprise rolled on until the entire continent was overrun.

Once vast stretches of land had been acquired, government officials emphasised the supremacy of British rule, so much so that they could not imagine Africans becoming a self-governing people. This was best left to the British. Africa's commercial viability, however, was not in dispute for it was, as Joseph Chamberlain put it, an 'undeveloped estate'.[3]

INDIA

Before the 'scramble for Africa' India held a special place in the British Empire. Nevertheless, the memory of the 1857–8 Indian Uprising (or 'Mutiny' as the British called it) rankled and to avoid a recurrence of this kind, the British government took overall responsibility for the administration of India, which increasingly gained in importance, as far as British Imperial need was concerned, during the reign of Queen Victoria. Underpinning their conquest of India, the British arrogated to themselves an attitude approximating a divine mission. Like Africans, Indians were thought to be incapable of self-government. This was an important matter of principle for some Western Europeans, whose Orientalist discourses, devaluing Indian political and social institutions, have been challenged by such critiques as Ronald Inden's *Imagining India*.[4]

Culturally, Britain and India could not avoid influencing each other. The wisdom of the East found a ready audience among British intellectuals, who pondered India as the mystical Other as opposed to the Imperial West, the one defining and therefore giving value to the other. The Anglo-Indian connections, so masterly interwoven by Rudyard Kipling, reached a vast British readership, and through the long-standing presence of the British Indian Army, thousands of Britons came to admire and 'love' India, though paradoxically, such strong feelings as they had for certain aspects of the country were attenuated by the fact that the 'burden of rule' was very much upon the British.

Another aspect of the Imperial domain was the ever-growing settlements of the British in Australia (land of the Aborigines), New Zealand (land of the Maoris), Canada (land of the native Indians) and South Africa (land of the Zulus and other Africans). In the last half of the nineteenth century, an estimated 7,500,000 Britons went to these outposts of the Empire, although by the end of the century colonial ties had begun to loosen. But even as the United Kingdom struggled to maintain its Empire, it could not ignore its role as a European power, and as such, in the last years of the nineteenth century it faced threats from other major European powers. The Anglo-Boer War of 1899 afforded the government the opportunity to appraise its European standing, which related intimately to British institutions, conventions, political parties and the economy.

By the turn of the twentieth century, British institutions and conventions were relatively unchanged in a fast-changing world. There was, however, a gradual decline in the monarch's role and though the House of Lords survived, by the close of the nineteenth century, its powers had diminished. There were also some changes in the House of Commons in terms of character, composition and procedure. However, as parliamentary representation was still not a salaried occupation, both Houses were dominated by the wealthy. The Liberals continued to hope for a change in the system, but the Conservatives maintained control in the final years of the century. Together, they were the parties that mattered; but increasingly the power of labour was waiting in the wings to be incorporated into the political system.

What was the role of the trade unions at this time? By the end of the nineteenth century there were attempts at combination by various organisations on the left of the political divide, but labour and trade union power had remained in abeyance, its potential unrealised until the introduction in the twentieth century of a more democratic franchise.

Taking 1870 as a marker, the maturing British economy had enjoyed many years of industrial expansion, an estimated 3–4 per cent annually for the greater part of the century. The 'workshop of the world' was still the leading industrial nation. Yet, this leadership could not be taken for granted. A change in emphasis was becoming more and more evident, from old industrial processes and practices to the new, especially in the light of challenges from American inventions. This was a period of growing overseas investment and, by the end of the century, 'Free Trade' was no longer sacrosanct, while in South Africa the Boer War triggered new ideas concerning the interlocking relationship between economics, politics, society and government.

In the latter half of the nineteenth century, the urban population increase was greater than in the country, though this trend began to reverse after 1900, as people began moving into the 'suburbs'. By 1890, some of the world's largest cities – London, Birmingham, Glasgow, Manchester and Liverpool – were to be found in the United Kingdom; and at the beginning of the twentieth century, Cardiff, Dublin and Belfast were still growing.[5] Urban conurbations demanded a wide range of social and cultural services which, in turn, generated employment. The dramatic changes in industrial life took their toll in the quality of life of its inhabitants and for many working-class people, life was brutish and short. Infant mortality was especially high in the industrial towns of the North, and in Scotland, inadequate housing in overcrowded tenements facilitated the spread of disease.

London, the great metropolis, remained pre-eminent, and much attention was focused on it. The population spillover into such areas as East Ham, West Ham, Tottenham, Leyton, Walthamstow, Hornsey, Willesden and Croydon could not eliminate deep concern for the deplorable conditions in the 'human rookeries' of London. Two books, evocative of the times, Andrew Mearns's *The Bitter Cry of Outcast London* and Charles Booth's *The Life and Labour of the London Poor*, investigated the poverty and human degradation found there – findings replicated in 1901, in *Poverty: A Study of Town Life in York*, by Seebohm Rowntree. Together, these publications helped to bring a new awareness of the desperation in the cities.

In the last three decades of the nineteenth century, employment in agriculture declined, resulting in an influx of people to the main cities and a movement towards greater democracy in local government – changes which, though not yet clearly evident, contributed to the process of restructuring power in the countryside, which had for so long been dominated by the aristocracy and large landowners. The countryside (and seaside resorts) however remained places of historic interest and natural beauty, to which town dwellers could escape.

Recreation and education had also grown in importance. Games (especially ball games) in the United Kingdom were very popular and football dominated the winter sports scene. Eight years after a Football Association was formed in 1863, the FA Cup competition began. Professional footballers entered the game in the 1880s and the English Football League was formed, setting a precedent for other parts of the United Kingdom. Football Association and various competitions were established in Scotland, Wales and Ireland and international competition between England and Scotland was inaugurated in 1876.

Rugby was next in popularity and gaining ground all the time, while cricket dominated the summer in England where, after

1873, the County Championship attracted much interest. Towering over the game was the striking presence of Dr W.G. Grace, and the Indian Ranjitsinghji, of whom more will be said later. The other ball game that attracted much attention was lawn tennis, which received the boost it needed when the first Wimbledon Championship was held in 1877.

Education and religion were other important aspects of British life. Education from 1870 was not a singular blanket arrangement or system, although in elementary education the three 'Rs' were seen as fundamental in the British school system. Other subjects (geography and science) were, in some cases, also taught, but history was 'little regarded'. In the last three decades of the century, numbers of teaching staff in elementary schools increased, and were accompanied by an overall increase in the number of women teachers. By the 1890s, working-class children were offered some places at the previously elite grammar schools, although the opportunities were woefully inadequate.

In higher education, much change had taken place with the establishment of university colleges in Manchester, Birmingham, Liverpool, Leeds, Newcastle, Nottingham, Sheffield and Bristol. In terms of finance and course structure, some change had also been introduced to Oxford and Cambridge.

Education in Scotland differed from England and Wales, literacy being much higher in the former than the latter. The Scottish system was also more national and the four well-established Scottish universities accepted more university students than anywhere else in the United Kingdom.

South of the border, there was need for reappraisal. In 1876 when Mark Pattison, the Rector of Lincoln College, Oxford, had addressed the Social Science Association, he ignored the fact that few women were admitted to higher education. Not surprisingly the education of women raised other matters relating to their position in society. While, as late as 1900, girls from working-class backgrounds were encouraged to receive elementary education only, girls from the middle classes were beginning to be afforded more opportunity. Nevertheless, there was still a marked disparity between the males and females in higher education, which became increasingly a target for change.

In these last decades of the nineteenth century, Christianity came under threat, but paradoxically, as the historian Keith Robbins notes, 'almost all denominations continued to expand and the churches occupied a prominent place in community life'. Unity seemed impossible among the various churches, as divisions were maintained doctrinally, in church administration and in the approach to worship. By 1900, five main churches had emerged in the United Kingdom: the Roman Catholic, Anglican, Presbyterian, Baptist/Congregational and Methodist, each believing that it held the key to heaven.

What emerged with some clarity from this confusion was that while some working-class people were thoroughly immersed in church activity, the majority of the masses lacked conviction. Many of them were the victims of poverty and deprivation and looked for the more immediate secular solutions, for example, by adopting a more equitable socialist path. But even for those who were no longer 'believers', 'church values' still held a comforting fascination.

For some, like Thomas Arnold, Headmaster of Rugby School, absence of religion could be made good by 'culture' which, in time, incorporated the arts or 'high culture' including music, literature and painting.[6] While Edward Elgar enjoyed success as a composer, and orchestral works were often performed in London, for most of the United Kingdom those who engaged in music-making were amateurs, whose music appealed to people of various backgrounds. Here, mention must be made of the famous black composer–musician Samuel Coleridge Taylor (and his outstanding predecessors George Bridgetower and Joseph Emidy) whose life and work will be discussed later in the text.

One feature of this period was the appearance of working people's choirs in industrial counties. In these close-knit communities, the piano was a common and treasured item in working-class homes and the family were encouraged to sing. Brass bands too were popular and, by 1900, through the artistry of George Robey, music hall entertainment had become more socially acceptable. At this time too, white men were blacking their faces and lustily singing racist songs in music halls. Few historians have bothered with this aspect of British music hall historiography.

Illiteracy prevented the appreciation of the best of English literature. Nevertheless, by the end of the nineteenth century, the works of Shakespeare, Charles Dickens, Walter Scott, Thomas Hardy, Henry James and Robert Louis Stevenson were best-sellers and Rudyard Kipling caught the British imagination with his tales of India. Although the *literati* were concentrated in London, Hardy remained in rural England, while Irish, Scottish and Welsh writers, both poets and novelists, focused largely on the themes of their native land. Few have been as successful in England as the Irish writers Oscar Wilde, Bernard Shaw and W.B. Yeats. Writing for the theatre, on the other hand, was still a minority literary interest, but no less passionate for that, for since Shakespeare's time plays have continued to be written and produced in England, perhaps more than in the other regions of the United Kingdom. All the same, the level of readership remained more or less the same. Thus the literary culture of the United Kingdom was distinguished by clear division, with less than 10 per cent of the population availing themselves of the Public Library services. By the close of the century, a common literary culture in late Victorian Britain was still unrealised.

Earlier, in the world of art, the pre-Raphaelites and Edward Burne-Jones had made an impression, but patronage was erratic. Nevertheless, the solo efforts in interior design by William Morris were profoundly influential beyond the lower reaches of British society. Representative of the architecture of this period was Port Sunlight, which reflected the 'afternoon nap of High Victorian Gothic', as Graham-Dixon described it, 'the Victorian ideal of calm community [which] finally produced: a snooze of the soul given architectural form, a love of retreat and renunciation expressed at the level of bricks and mortar'. In this respect, he felt that the British had 'entered the twentieth century looking backwards'.[7] But this 'looking backwards' selectively, this 'retreat and renunciation', this 'snooze of the soul' seemed also to have affected British historians, who continued to ignore in their voluminous histories of the British

Isles the presence and contribution of black and Asian peoples in Britain and in her colonial possessions.

THE COLONIAL LABOUR PROBLEM

On first landing in India, British and European merchants, instead of finding a country that was industrially and technically backward, discovered that it was at least 'not inferior' to that of the more advanced European nations. India, perceived as primitive, unchanging and mythical in the eyes of early Europeans and those who came after, was largely agricultural, which may have obscured its manufacturing capacity in the eyes of these foreigners. But Indian textiles were to be found in European and Asian markets and its artisans had bequeathed to succeeding generations the art of iron-making which helped to secure a shipbuilding industry along the extensive Indian coastline from Calcutta to Bombay. By the turn of the nineteenth century, Indian workmanship was applied to carvings in stone, and to gold, silver and ivory, among other industries,[8] which flourished and complemented the rural agricultural village communities that had for centuries formed the backbone of the country.

However, this industrial-cum-agricultural structure did not win respect and was therefore unacceptable to British rulers who had set out to create a new Indian economy that would serve the designs and purpose of Britain. To this end, the manufacturing sector was destroyed, at incalculable human cost, changing forever the lives of millions of Indians who were forced to engage in agricultural production – dyes, jute, oilseeds, cotton and wool – for the British market. So, with Indian industries effectively defunct, by 1880, British-made goods flooded the Indian market.

As the first industrial nation in the world, Britain maintained its one-way 'free' trade policy with India by imposing very high tariffs on Indian manufactured goods, especially textiles, the effect of which was appalling inequity. This, in turn, brought about not only predictable unemployment to millions of Indian workers, but also the disappearance of indigenous industrial vested

interests. Surat, Dacca and Murshidabad, India's leading manufacturing centres, were wound down and millions of textile workers tramped the countryside in search of alternative employment
or faced the grim prospect of starvation. By the last two decades
of the nineteenth century, cloth production in India had fallen to
less than 10 per cent of home demand, while imports from
Britain reached almost two-thirds of India's yearly imports.

Presiding over this industrial devastation was Queen Victoria, absentee ruler of India, the enigmatic symbol of Empire,
towards whom India's wealth continuously flowed, a drain of
the subcontinent's life-blood, and the root cause of its desperate
poverty and hunger.

Although the worst excesses of human exploitation endemic
in the indigo plantation system, initiated in 1833, were
tempered following official inquiries, West Indian planters
(having been for so long in command on the slave plantations)
now bought land and so entered a sphere of enterprise in the
East which favoured their masterly inclinations. 1833 had seen
the passage of legislation to free the slaves in the British
Caribbean, a region from which many disgruntled planters now
shifted their operations to the East, where slavery under British
rule was still in existence, thus ensuring near perfect entrepreneurial conditions in the form of a large pool of cheap labour.
This shift in economic interest would, in time, become increasingly significant as Britain amassed even more wealth from its
vast Indian Empire.

Such encouraging returns from India's plantations should not
surprise us, especially when we consider the aggression of
Caribbean and American planters, who also assumed the role of
mentors to their less experienced fellow-planters; nor should we
ignore the long history of struggle in India which, after years of
domination and control, had tested the patience of the Indian
people to the limit. On the subcontinent, as in the Caribbean,
uprisings were widespread, reaching a climax in the Indian
National Uprising[9] of 1857–8, which drew on support from
both ordinary Indian people and those of aristocratic background (including the courageous example of Indian pride
exemplified in the heroic death of Laxmi Bai, Queen of Jhansi)
in a rare show of Indian solidarity.

The revolt was sparked when the British Army brought into service a new gun. This required that the tip of each cartridge be greased with pig's fat and then bitten off before it was loaded. For Indian soldiers, both the Hindus and Muslims, this was a flagrant flouting of deeply held religious beliefs. They felt that there was no alternative but to act. The Uprising which began in Meerut, led to the loss of life at Cawnpore of 400 British men, women and children, a tragedy[10] countered by British forces, whose revenge was swift, brutal and indiscriminate. Thousands were slaughtered, irrespective of age and sex, armed or unarmed, including many who were their own loyal servants.[11] The Bengalis took the lead in Indian nationalist agitation and the upshot was that from 1858, India was no longer governed by the East India Company, but came under the direct rule of the British Crown via Whitehall in London.[12]

So 25 years after the Bill which led to the African slave Emancipation Act, the plantation system took root in India, and the poorest of the country's blighted poor, in desperation, sought new means of survival from the very class of people who had been the cause of much of their misery. Indeed, in 1834, many Indians, under the direction of British capital, faced the drastic prospect of becoming labourers in distant lands.

In the post-Emancipation colonial world, especially in the tropical territories, there was, according to the planters, a 'crisis' of labour on the plantations. Earlier, after the African slave trade was abolished in 1807, Britain, though still involved, nevertheless faced the problem of how to acquire a continuous supply of 'free', but low-cost and easily controlled labour for its slave-less colonial plantations.

One of the problems was the supposed reluctance of 'free' Africans and their descendants to work for wages. How sugar was to be produced without slaves remained the nagging question as the Emancipation Bill was drafted. There was also the planters' welfare to consider once the slaves were free. After the Emancipation Act was passed, the British government not only gave the planters £20 million in compensation, but also provided for an intervening period of Apprenticeship (half-freedom).[13] By the time that Apprenticeship had ended in 1838, plans were already being considered for tapping the labour resources of India by means of indentureship (which had already been introduced in Mauritius in 1834) – a form of labour control which some feared, coming so soon after Emancipation, would become a new form of slavery.

EMIGRATION WITHIN THE BRITISH EMPIRE

As early as 1810, a British Parliamentary Committee had been appointed to consider the practicality and expediency of supplying West Indian colonies with free labour from India, a consideration that was part of the government's wider design of immigration within the British Empire, which meant engaging (often through deception) dispossessed men, women and children.

Accordingly, in 1839, a new body, the Colonial Land and Emigration Commission, was set up to oversee emigration within the British Empire. This mass movement of people was conducted mainly to South Australia, New South Wales, Victoria, Queensland, Van Dieman's Land (Tasmania), Western Australia, New Zealand, the Cape of Good Hope, Natal, the Falkland Islands and Vancouver. The following figures give some idea of the magnitude of these movements: from 1840 to 1872, the total British emigration to Canada was 956,748; to the United States, 4,487,497; Australia and New Zealand, 958,077 and all other places, 175,736.[14]

The need for white settlers to open up these 'virgin' lands was imperative, though significantly, there was no question of non-white emigration to these lands, although all of these places already had an indigenous non-European population. However, before its abolition, the Commission was involved in a new phase of mass emigration, supervising the movement of Indians to Mauritius in those crucial years when the Indian indentureship system was being established. This movement was followed by African, Asian and, most importantly, East Indian (as Indians were officially called) indentured labourers to the West Indies and other tropical British colonies, bonded people destined to fill the labour vacuum created after Emancipation.

The failure of African sources of free labour to satisfy labour requirements (for example, liberated Africans rescued from illegal slavers by the British Navy and the emigration of free Africans from Sierra Leone) forced West Indian planters to intensify their search, to look elsewhere for a cheap labour supply, which became more urgent when the introduction of Chinese labourers failed to meet the insistent demands of the colonial plantations.[15]

EAST INDIAN INDENTURESHIP: THE 'NEW' SLAVERY

Before large-scale Indian emigration, labour in the British overseas territories had been employed in various forms, including slavery, an institution which had its own long history in India. Although the Greek traveller Megasthenes found no evidence of slavery in India in the fourth century BC, Kautilya's *Arthasastra* and Asoka's accounts indicate the presence of slaves in ancient times.[16] People were forced into this form of bondage often through indebtedness or as captives of war. Indeed slavery existed under both Hindu and Mughal rule and persisted long after the establishment of British rule. Indian slavery was different from West Indian slavery though in that the slaves in the West Indies were from Africa, whereas the vast majority of those in India were from the indigenous population.

In 1883 H.E.B. Frere argued in his 'Abolition of Slavery in India and Egypt' that comparing information 'district by district' with the questionable estimates of the total population 50 years earlier, the lowest estimate he was able to make of the total slave population of British India in 1841 was 8–9 million. The slaves emancipated in the British colonies on 1 August 1834, he noted, were estimated 'at between 800,000 and one million; and the slaves in North and South America in 1860, were estimated at four million'. So the number of human beings whose liberties and fortunes, as slaves and owners of slaves, were at stake when emancipation of the slaves was contemplated in British India, 'far exceeded the number of the same classes in all the slave-holding colonies and dominions of Great Britain and America put together.'

Slavery in India encompassed both the non-British territories and the British Protected States. Overall, there were an estimated 16 million slaves, a reflection of the tragic and deplorable condition that persisted in British India long after the African slaves in the West Indies had won their freedom.[17] It was not until 1843 that an Act was passed to abolish slavery in India. No doubt, British officials were fully aware of the historical background and contemporary conditions that had created an enormous pool of cheap labour in India. To say the least, a more attractive source could hardly be imagined, given the labour shortages elsewhere in the Empire.

None the less, it was obvious from the beginning that the importation of Indians would involve problems of organisation and finance, so British planters favoured the proposition that the greater proportion of the financial cost of importing Indian labourers should be borne by the colonial governments.

Now what had hitherto seemed problematic was rationalised. For example, although Hindus saw crossing the *kala pani* (dark water, or ocean) as caste defilement, Indian emigration was regarded by British officials as vital to national progress, a modernising influence on India in the early nineteenth century. Among the first to be trapped into servitude as indentured labourers on the tropical plantations by the recruiters' 'false promises' of high wages and a better way of life were the Dhangars, or Hill Coolies, who were considered to be good workers and therefore preferred by planters. They were largely illiterate, destitute and trusting, unlike later waves of Indians from other parts of India. They were uncomplaining and gained a reputation for being stoic under the most difficult circumstances.

If the passage to Mauritius was testing, the long and dangerous journey to the Caribbean was even more so. Nevertheless the decision was made to undertake these longer voyages, and in spite of warnings from eminent British officials, such as Lord John Russell, of this becoming a new kind of slavery while African slavers were still plying the waters of the Atlantic, 'coolie ships' (as the ships carrying the migrant Indians were called) transported the indentured Indians to the other side of the world. Indeed, the arrival of the first Indian indentured labourers in British Guiana in 1838 on the *Whitby* and the *Hesperus* marked the beginning of a new enterprise concerned with trafficking in human beings. This then was the beginning of the last great influx of cheap and rigidly controlled plantation labour to the Caribbean. Until 1851, however, this migration was not continuous, for having begun in 1838 it was stopped in 1839, before it was resumed in 1845. Three years later, it was stopped again, and when it started once more in 1851, it was uninterrupted until 1917.

The two leading shipping companies operating services to the Caribbean were Sandbach Tinne and Company and James Nourse, preceded by Gillanders, Arbuthnot and Company.[18] There were also a few ships known as 'Outsiders' involved in the indenture traffic from India to Trinidad and British Guiana – the colonies receiving the largest numbers of indentured Indians. Although health and safety standards on board ships had gradually been improving, events in the 1850s were cause for alarm, especially when the mortality rate on voyages to the Caribbean hit a new high among the indentured Indians aboard the *Salsette*. The ill-fated voyage of this ship in 1858 proved that the humanitarian concern in relation to Indian workers, was secondary to the economic concerns of the operating companies.[19]

The sugar colonies were not alone in their demands. From the 1860s, the tea industry also competed for Indian labour, and with the reduction in the supply of Hill Coolies, attention was directed at the 'flotsam of humanity', the teeming millions in the cities of Calcutta, Madras and Bombay. Many had left Bihar for Calcutta, the focal point for vast multitudes of Indians who lived on the margins of survival. Calcutta was also the main port of embarkation for at least the first 30–40 years of organised Indian emigration. Here, the poor and those in a state of semi-slavery (known as *Kamiuti*) sold their limited services. Predictably, their vulnerability was exploited by the recruiters, whose aggressive drive for more and more human hands to maintain colonial production knew no bounds. What had seemed unthinkable before its inception became reality in the years that followed as Indians from a multiplicity of castes, religions and cultures and from various regions of India were drawn together in a confined space as voyagers to the Caribbean and other parts of the British Empire.

Among the early migrants were many from the western districts of British India, Benares and Allahabad. A major 'push' factor was the famine of the early 1840s in Upper India, which resulted in starvation in Bihar. During this decade, the number of migrants grew. Within 20 years British Guiana had a larger Indian population than Malaya where the rubber boom had drawn a considerable number of the labourers from Madras. Fiji also became a significant importer of Indian labour, and while Madras supplied the heavy demand in Natal, emigration from Calcutta showed no signs of slackening.

These mass movements of people from the East brought about an unprecedented geographical spread, so that towards the end of the nineteenth century an Indian diaspora had come into being, stretching far and wide as the planters' demands for labour was satisfied. In the Caribbean, St Lucia, St Kitts, Grenada, St Vincent, Martinique, Guadeloupe, Jamaica, Trinidad and Tobago, British Guiana and Surinam all called on India's reservoir of labour. So too did Fiji, the Straits Settlements, Burma, Malaya, Mauritius, Ceylon and Reunion. In South Africa, apart from Natal, they went to Durban, and in East Africa, they went to Kenya and were employed to build the Ugandan Railway. In all, between one and two million Indians went to the tropical plantations in the years from 1830 to 1870,[20] with hundreds of thousands more to follow until the second decade of the twentieth century.

Coming so soon after African slavery, all was not well. Eventually protest against the indentured system gathered momentum and many aspects of the system were targeted. There was growing concern about the seaworthiness of the ships and the treatment of Indians aboard during these long journeys. Cholera, typhoid and dysentery ravaged the migrants during their voyages and only between a third and a quarter of the Indian migrants ever returned. The right of a return passage was conceded only reluctantly by the colonial administration which, in time, offered grants of colonial land to the Indians in lieu of their passage home. But although many of those Indians who had returned to India did so voluntarily, generations of them laboured and died where they had been indentured. They were little more than wage slaves. Those who did survive deserve much respect for their survival was due largely to their fortitude and resilience. More to the point, they had no alternative. Many saw their voyages as but one stage in a longer journey, the second phase of which was their indenture, the reason for their decision to leave the Motherland. In their alien environment, disease, bad housing, lack of medical attention and malnutrition contributed to an unusually high number of suicides. As in slavery, under indentureship, marriage or 'companionage' was an unstable relationship, for although a wife was a status symbol (representing security and prosperity) the low-status poor man was liable to have his wife taken away by a man of superior status. The shortage of women[21] during the entire period of East Indian indentureship caused much concern and comment, and disputes over women constituted the main cause of murders and suicides.

Apart from the hostility of plantation officials, the indentured labourers also faced antagonism from Creole blacks, not only in the fields, but in the barracks. The ex-slaves saw that the Indians were replacing them on the plantations; and indeed, Indians were used by planters as strike-breakers in Jamaica and other West Indian islands. With the passage of time, both Indians and Africans and their descendants developed stereotyped views, referring to each other as 'nigger' and 'coolie'. Where they complemented Creole blacks economically, as in Trinidad, Indians strove to realise the potential of partnership. None the less, Indian immigration remained a major bone of contention[22] while the indentured system lasted.

Some integration and intermarriage did take place, particularly in the smaller colonies. In general, though, blacks did not welcome Indians into their communities, something that was especially marked in the French colonies. Significantly, the Indians often took strike action on the plantations, notably in British Guiana, Trinidad and Surinam. It has been argued that the rise of protest in the Caribbean reflected the fact that the Indians were becoming conscious of their rights, while on the other hand, the absence of mass protest in Mauritius, Ceylon, Malaya and Natal (prior to Gandhi's efforts) was seen as evidence of successful organisation by the colonial authorities in these territories. Together, this opposition demonstrated the potential solidarity of the Indians. The one factor that gave the 'coolies' an advantage over the slaves was that after five years (or in many cases ten years) their indentureships, their 'wage slavery', would end. It was this expectation, not escape or revolt, which generated the greatest hope during their indentures.

So, the Indian diaspora created by the global demands of British capitalism created an Indian diaspora which settled (albeit uneasily) beside the African diaspora, both representing labour systems (slavery and indentureship) designed and instituted to maintain British (French and Dutch) imperialism, which was opposed by its victims. Emblematic of this spread of peoples was their unrelenting resistance, their struggles to transform the manner in which their lives were governed. In other words, they passionately desired social, economic and political inclusion and freedom, ongoing quests that at an earlier period had its exemplars in Britain itself.

HEROIC PERSONALITIES

William Cuffay

Two of the most heroic figures from the African diaspora whose lives were evocative of freedom from imperial domination were William Cuffay and Mary Seacole. Cuffay, like Wedderburn and Davidson, emerged from the ranks of the English working-class movement and was penalised for his activities and political beliefs. Though his father was a slave in the West Indian island of St Kitts, it seemed that he was one of those rare people from the West Indies, who came to England as a free black man.

Cuffay was born in 1788 in Chatham, where he grew up. He became and remained for the rest of his life, a tailor, a trade through which he became thoroughly immersed in working-class activism. Though not easily taken in by his fellow-activists, he was fair-minded. And even though he was critical of the trade union movement, he was not against the practice of trade unionism. As a tailor, he met and exchanged ideas with other craftsmen and in 1839 came in contact with the Chartist Movement and got to know the popular leaders William Lovett and Francis Place. He supported the People's Charter and became increasingly prominent in London Chartism, speaking at local and national conferences and, at times, criticising the national Chartist leadership. His characteristic intelligence and boldness brought him recognition and growing prominence among his peers, as Chartism was challenged to play a positive leadership role. At the National Convention of 1848, it was agreed to call a mass meeting on Kennington Common and a procession that would take the Chartist petition of about two million signatures to the House of Commons. Cuffay took a militant stand at the Convention and when the Committee for managing the procession was set up, he was appointed Chairman.

News of these deliberations and plans was a cause for alarm to the authorities and the procession was declared illegal by the Commissioner of Police. The queen moved to the safety of the Isle of Wight. Seven thousand soldiers were detailed along the Embankment and gun batteries were deployed at strategic positions, while thousands of police were drafted in to block entry to the bridges across the Thames. At the British Museum, Anthony Panizzi, the Italian-born radical and now the dedicated Principal Librarian at the British Museum, rallied his staff to face the possibility of an assault from the marchers. This impressive show of force had the desired effect. After an interview with the Commissioner of Police, O'Connor, the Irish Confederates' leader and an outstanding spokesman, took action which he felt was appropriate and, at that advanced stage, called off the procession, a decision which was met with predictable anger from the large crowd assembled on the Common. Cuffay was strongly opposed to O'Connor and the platform's abandonment of the procession to Parliament, and drew attention to the stupidity of congregating south of the river with the bridges under the control of the police and military. He regarded the whole Convention as a set of 'cowardly humbugs' with whom he did not ever again wish to be associated.

The defeat was a severe blow, which Cuffay would neither forgive nor forget. Insurrection being preached by a black man in an influential leadership position in England (though not unusual at the time) was anathema to those in authority. But the question arose: Was Cuffay the instigator? In the opinion of one historian, although Cuffay was implicated, the true leaders of the revolutionary attempt at insurrection were others, though Cuffay would not have exonerated himself for his part. None the less, to the ruling classes, he was clearly, and conspicuously, a dangerous man.

The search for Cuffay ended when he was arrested in Bloomsbury, having refused the opportunity to go underground, because of loyalty to his associates. Charged with waging war against the queen, he remained resolute throughout his trial and made a powerful speech before he was found guilty and sentenced to transportation for the term of his natural life. Faced with this harsh judgment, the radical press praised Cuffay's courage and the outstanding literary figures of the time, William Thackeray and Charles Kingsley, regarded him as worthy enough to make reference to him.[23]

When he arrived in Tasmania in November 1849, he was employed as a tailor, until he could no longer work because of failing health. To his credit, he remained a voracious reader during these years far away from London and his Chatham birthplace. Such readings may have helped him come to terms with his exile until 1870, the last year of his remarkable life.[24]

Mary Seacole

Born in Jamaica at the turn of the century, Mary Seacole, known as the 'Nurse and Doctress', was a popular 'mother' figure among the white soldiers and civilians whom she served both at home and in distant lands. She was the child of a mixed marriage, her father being a soldier of Scottish descent. Her mother, a local woman, impressed her daughter in the roles she played as a 'doctress' of high repute and the manager of a boarding house in Kingston.

Mary showed a rare dedication to nursing and, like her mother, she became skilful in attending to the sick and dying of all nationalities in the Caribbean and Central and North America. Her immediate concern, however, was to go to England and on arrival she expressed her determination to serve Britain by putting her nursing skills to good use at the battlefront in the Crimea.

She was a woman ahead of her time, audacious and ambitious and, not surprisingly, British officials were not helpful. But, through sheer persistence, she managed to reach the war zone, where she met Florence Nightingale. Time and again, Mary's heroic work received the plaudits of soldiers, who addressed her affectionately as 'Mother Seacole'. Eventually, after determined efforts, she won over hardened British administrators and was recognised as the 'Crimean heroine'. After Sebastopol was taken, she wrote that the 'great work' had been achieved. However, this was achieved in the teeth of her great struggle against 'official indifference, hauteur and prejudice'. After the war, the publication of her autobiography *The Wonderful Adventures of Mary Seacole in Many Lands* helped to maintain her popularity. But, after her death in May 1881, she seemed to have been totally forgotten in England. Three decades ago, few people knew about her. Thanks to the industry of dedicated researchers of the black experience in Britain, almost a hundred years later, her grave was discovered in Kensal Green Cemetery in a 'complete state of disrepair' and efforts were made to restore the headstone and resurrect her extraordinary life and work.[25] If the 'yellow doctress' was forgotten in England, she is today claimed by black people from many lands, fondly remembered in Jamaica as a home-grown heroine and a source of inspiration to many black women in Britain.

While her struggle reflected the oppression of women generally in the nineteenth century, she was the precursor of an exodus of black nurses (and other servants) who would come to serve Britain in the twentieth century, only to realise the harsh reality of class, race and colour prejudice. But for now, let us return to India to consider it as it was under British occupation, especially in the nineteenth century, and to trace the paths followed by some intrepid Indians who made their way into Britain.

ASIANS IN BRITAIN

Indians: Servants of the Empire

What was a novelty in the early eighteenth century, gradually became a custom that only seemed logical in the age of Empire. After 1858, more and more British men, women and their families of various classes joined the steady stream of travellers making their way back to Britain with an entourage of caring and devoted Indian servants.[26] While some were relatively content, others were deeply unhappy. Nevertheless, either as slave or servant, Indians and Africans were viewed by their masters as inferior, a social standing which remained largely unchanged for such persons.

On arrival in England, many Indian servants and ayahs were treated abominably. Their estrangement often hastened their search for a return passage to India. Few were fortunate, and the many who remained found refuge where they could, often in overcrowded lodging houses, ever-hopeful of re-engagement. Overcrowding was not confined to male servants, but was also the uncomfortable experience of the ayahs.

Over the years, ships owned by the East India Company came and went with increasing regularity, discharging Indian Lascars at British ports, especially in London, where the growing problem of destitution among them and Asian servants added to their numbers as exotic beggars. Indeed, for most Indian servants, coming to Britain with their employers was a hazardous business, as many were abandoned either on arrival or soon after. This disreputable practice had got so out of hand that it was recognised by the East India Company's President and Council which, according to the evidence presented, denounced those Britons who brought Asian servants with them. For their part, the EIC's President and Council admitted that although it had taken steps for the return of 'black' servants to India, several of them had been left destitute in England.[27]

Despite its rhetoric, the Company's humanitarian concerns for the condition of these servants was of less importance than the cost that would accrue to them in dealing with the problem.

And why should they be conscience-stricken, when moral and ethical concerns in Britain were to promote the commerce that would bring the highest profitable returns?

In the years after 1858, when the Company no longer controlled India, the destitution of Indian servants in Britain remained unattended and, predictably, their condition deteriorated. What won them some urgent attention was the fact that ayahs were popular among members of the Anglo-Indian community and on their return voyages to England, these women were almost perfect for the jobs assigned to them especially as 'travelling nannies'. We are told that they not only travelled well, but also gave undivided care and attention to their employers and their children and, through trial and error, became competent nurses. But their job security remained questionable, and those with little or no savings, no guaranteed job and no income at the end of each voyage, were faced with the stark realisation that their last refuge was the Ayahs Home in East London. In fact, it was from the Ayahs Home that British administrators and officers going to India with their families recruited ayahs to assist them on the outward journey. Some ayahs became regular passengers on this route. One grandmother is said to have travelled between India and Britain 54 times.

Joseph Salter, in his capacity as Missionary to the Orientals and Africans in London, devoted much time trying to alleviate tensions arising from the overcrowding and distress among these women.[28]

The Asian Poor

Lascars in the Strangers' Home in London had made their way to Britain as sailors on ships that brought the 'tide of wealth' from India. Many of them were so disgusted by their experiences that they walked away from their ships without collecting the wages due to them because doing so would not arouse suspicion of their intention to 'jump ship'. Bravery and courage may have been elements in making their decision, but closer to the truth was their revulsion at the abuse they received. What could be worse than shipboard incidents that were life-threatening nightmares for some? Joseph Salter was well informed about these atrocities.

In the metropolis, these sailors lived precariously and often they were found to be in great distress. The East India Company absolved themselves of all blame and responsibility for the Lascars' difficulties. It was, however, felt that something had to be done to alleviate their distress, and the Committee for the Relief of the Poor was formed to help them. Lascars needed protection for, knowing little or nothing of the English language and way of life, they were especially vulnerable. It is no wonder then that many Lascars were robbed of their precious pennies and the clothes on their backs by petty criminals and prostitutes.[29] Their physical appearance made them easy targets, and, the insensitive treatment they received and the lack of food in lodging houses made their condition as beggars worse, though those who ran the lodging houses, conveniently and persistently blamed the victims. In 1814, the Society for the Protection of Asiatic Sailors was formed to investigate their unsatisfactory circumstances and when a Parliamentary Committee embarked on a searching inquiry relating to the Indian and Chinese Lascars many of the complaints were confirmed. But the efforts the authorities made did not alleviate the Lascars' plight and as prejudices towards them hardened, they became, as one writer put it, the 'most despised group of aliens' in England, encumbered with such negative attributes as being 'naturally indolent', a people who were 'entirely destitute of moral capacity', possessing repugnant habits. Even their closest allies, their Christian friends, thought they were 'extremely depraved'. Of necessity, many joined the ranks of beggars, and thus engaged in a desperate 'profession' characterised by fierce rivalry and precious little gain.

From 1814, about 1,500 Lascars living in barracks received support from the East India Company, at a daily rate of 1s 6d for their board and lodging, a gesture that was woefully inadequate. An estimated 130 Lascars died there between 1790 and 1810, a death-rate which doubled in 1813. And in the winter of 1813–14 even the Company could not deny the death of at least two Lascars each week. On one exceptionally cold day, nine died.[30] The Company responded to any complaints with predictable aplomb, authorising the deportation of those they regarded as troublemakers on the first available ship. The men's grievances were many, but once again repatriation was an argument used to full effect, and was seen as the ultimate deterrent. However, the threats made, coming so soon after the Sierra Leone disaster, had no real effect in solving the problems of the black and Asian poor.

As in the eighteenth century, in the early nineteenth century racial prejudice in Britain was paradoxical for although black radicals achieved prominence by leading fellow-whites as members of working-class groups in London and elsewhere, discrimination against black and Asian people was pervasive. Salter experienced the force of opposition from white residents when he wanted to open an Asiatic Rest, a meeting place which, in his view, was essential for both Asian and African seamen. As if colour and the 'otherness' of religion were not matters of disablement enough, being educated was fiercely attacked. How audacious that a member of an 'inferior' group should show an interest in gaining knowledge! Thus, race and class prejudices that had taken form and developed among whites in India, were brought back to Britain by returnees.

So the blight of poverty continued to take its toll. Characteristically, the Indians fought back, trying their hand at anything that was within their capability. For many, necessity became the catalyst of invention. Henry Mayhew, who considered Asians to be physically unattractive, devious and callous exploiters of unsuspecting local people, found a remarkably varied group. His portrayal was endorsed by Joseph Salter, who affirmed their diversity and creativity which brought forth beggars, hawkers, music-makers, tap-dancers, snake charmers, conjuring tricksters and some who engaged in 'thought reading'.[31]

Lascars and Indian servants were also to be found in Scotland. Many had made their way there in the late eighteenth century, accompanying families associated with the East India Company on their return to Scotland. Although it is difficult to arrive at a plausible estimate of the numbers of Indians in Scotland in the nineteenth century, Salter's *The Asiatics in*

England gives us a clear picture of the Indian presence in Scotland. He encountered them in Dundee, Glasgow, Perth, Greenock and Edinburgh, and when, in the autumn of 1869, he went to Dumbarton in search of 'wandering Asiatics', he counted 81 of them and says he had 'an interesting conversation' with others in Aberdeen.[32]

Unlike servants, Indian seamen were exposed to the misery associated with their lowly status. They suffered verbal abuse and physical abuse in the form of severe floggings. Many died, while others, barely alive, saw England in a delirium. Ship-board brutality was regarded by Lascars as a hazard that went with their engagement. Even so, there was a limit to human suffering. Desertion was their way out, as soon as their ships reached their destinations. Those who remained with their ships were paid and laid off once the ship docked in Britain. In this way, their service was broken, which meant no additional wage costs for the ship owners until the seamen were re-engaged (often at a lower wage) for the return journey. The other option for these men was to stay in the British ports. Here they had to cope as best they could with the dangers that awaited them.[33]

By the nineteenth century, then, a combination of desertion and prolonged delays in re-employment saw the emergence of groups of Lascars in various dockland areas, congregating in lodging houses, where they sought companionship and solace, until employment could be found. Jhulee Khan used to tap-dance his way around Scotland and England; while another Lascar, a Calcuttan, played the tom-toms on the streets for his 'daily bread'.

The Indian journalist B.M. Malabari, who came to Britain in 1890, travelled extensively and in his notes jotted down what he described as a 'brief holiday'. This was later published as *The Indian Eye on English Life* (1893). Malabari was drawn close to the British people, some of whom guided him through a cross-section of British society to various places and people of interest. Most shocking to him, even though he had seen impoverished humanity in India, was the 'poverty and degradation' he saw among the working people in the cities. He was haunted by the gap between the rich and poor in Britain and was moved to write about the poorer sections of these cities, where many Indians had lived:

> Poor as India is I thank God she knows not much of the poverty as the East End of London ... parts of Glasgow and other congested centres of life. Men and women living in a chronic state of emaciation, till they can hardly be recognised as human, picking up as food, what even animals will turn away from; sleeping fifty, sixty, eighty of them together, of all ages and both sexes, in a hole that could not hold ten with decency; swearing, fighting, trampling on one another; filling the room with foul confusion and foul air. This is not a picture of occasional misery; in some places it represents the everyday life of the victims of misfortune ... And side by side with such heart rending scenes of misery one sees gorgeously dressed luxury flaunting in the streets.[34]

The hardship of the majority of Asians must be juxtaposed with those whose experiences were positively different. Perhaps the most fortunate of all the Indian servants brought to Britain were Abdul Karim and Mohammed Bux, who arrived at Balmoral to serve Queen Victoria herself. But while she was excited by them, she was, of course, mature enough to understand the merits of colour and its colonial gradations (light-brown, brown, dark, black) in ruling her vast Empire. She favoured the lighter-skinned Karim, and recognised the value of language in maintaining her rule. Karim became her tutor, teaching her one of the languages spoken by her subjects in India, Hindustani. 'It is of great interest to me', she admitted, 'for both the language and the people I have naturally never come into contact with before.'[35] Soon she was proficient enough to engage in the real purpose of this linguistic exercise which was simply to welcome, in a few words of their own language, visiting Indian princes and nobles who were, of course, impressed. Thus, she enacted what some 386 years earlier the Bishop of Avila had clearly foreseen when he informed Queen Isabella of Spain that 'language is the instrument of Empire'.

So the British queen's symbolic gesture was not without deeper significance for throughout the Victorian age, since Lord

Macaulay's Indian Education Minute, British officials and writers played the language game by imposing their 'superior' English language upon subject peoples of the Empire, though this outwardly imperious stance was susceptible to Indian influence over the years.

The queen's warm relations with Karim were disapproved of by her family and close advisers, Victorians who possessed an overpowering sense of class, imperialism and the place of 'natives', as depicted in novels and school texts. When she died, Karim's 'papers' were destroyed[36] because, in this Imperial age, he belonged to one of the 'inferior' races. His case was none the less unique, for he and Bux were far better treated by the monarch than the Lascars and servants ever were by the British population at large.

An Emergent Community

The early presence of a few Indians stranded in Britain gradually became a population of servants, ayahs and Lascars, an essentially Asian, integral and ever-changing part of the widening 'black' community. London remained the hub of activity, to which Asians, especially Lascars, gravitated. British perceptions of these Oriental aliens were based upon assumptions of their 'Otherness' and, as we saw earlier, they lived in some of the poorest slums. Their degraded state served as the 'push' factor in seeking an alternative way forward. So when Joseph Salter states that 'a wandering life is an essential characteristic' of the Asiatic, he is only partly correct, for he ignored the cause, while identifying the effect. Salter, nevertheless, meant well; and in his determination to guide the Lascars towards the path of righteousness, he pursued them in London, Birmingham, Liverpool, Manchester, Brighton, Southampton, Peterborough, Sunderland, Durham, Hull, Bath, Bristol, Cardiff, Glasgow, Edinburgh, Leith and Stirling.[37]

By 1868, their dispersal throughout Britain was surprising and little known to many, including the Asians themselves. Slowly but steadily, though, they were gaining in confidence. Salter was impressed and, it seemed that, more than anyone else at the time, he recognised the potential of this early Asian community. Many Lascars took white wives (English, Welsh, Irish or Scottish); and as many of their children married other whites, the darker hues of skin colour faded. These mixed marriages were perceived as offensive to British purists and racists, who regarded the white wives of black and brown men, as 'fallen' women.[38]

Unlike the more numerous servants and Lascars, other Asians of varying backgrounds came to Britain for different reasons. They were mainly from the upper reaches of Indian society – merchants, traders, teachers, barristers and doctors. In a variety of ways their cultural input contributed a new dimension to British life. For the British were afforded the opportunity of learning about and seeing at first hand Indian nobles, many of them exiles whose domains had been wrested from them by their British rulers. Thus, a cross-section of Indian society was visible, and though lacking in numbers and cohesion at this time, it coexisted with other groupings of Britain's non-white and white communities.

Visram has distinguished between two sections among the Asians: a 'visiting sailor community' and the 'resident', who enacted colourful rituals of festivals and burials which became 'part of the British social scene', a trend consolidated before the last decade of the nineteenth century with the erection of Britain's first mosque in Woking, where there was also a cemetery for Parsees and their Religious Society of Zoroastrians.

A large number of Indian students and academics had, over the years, gone to Scotland to further their British education. Jane Cumming Gordon was the first Indo-Scottish child admitted to the country. Her Scottish father, George Cumming, was in the service of the East India Company. Jane was followed by John Campbell, the child of a Scottish father and an Indian mother, who went to Scotland to be educated at Tain and Aberdeen universities. Inspired with the desire to help the needy after graduation, he went back to India around 1830 to do missionary work in Bengal.

By the nineteenth century, there were over 50 students from India (most of them descended from Scotsmen serving in India) studying at Scottish universities, among whom was Josiah

Dashwood Gillies, who studied medicine at St. Andrews University in the mid-1850s. On his return to India, he practised as a doctor in the employment of the East India Company, where he experienced the harsh reality of racial prejudice and discrimination from his white colleagues.

Wazir Beg, a native of Bombay, regarded as the first Indian to study in Scotland, was registered as a medical student at the University of Edinburgh in 1858–9. Thereafter, the number of Indian students rose. Gopal Chandra Raj, admitted in 1869, became the first Indian medical student at the University of Glasgow. Medicine was the main interest of these ambitious youths and, as their numbers grew, the Edinburgh Indian Association was established in 1883 to meet the students' various needs. From a membership of six at its inception, there was steady growth until 1900 when the Association claimed an estimated 200 members. The student body then had its own accommodation, a homely meeting-place, which was used as the venue for debates and for holding social and cultural activities, and where Indian food was served.

In Glasgow too, the number of Indian students continued to rise and the Glasgow Indian Union was founded in 1911. After graduating, many students stayed in Scotland, and it is interesting that of the Indian students who came to the United Kingdom in the period from 1890 to 1910, no more than half of them went to England. This trend though was to change as the numbers in Scotland began to decrease slowly, especially after the first decade of the twentieth century.[39]

In the last two and a half decades of the nineteenth century, another rare class of Indian was to be found in the person of Aziz Ahmed, who visited Glasgow in the 1880s. He was a well-educated Christian convert who, with his Scottish wife and children, lived in Glasgow, where he lectured on Islam and related topics, and wrote for various Indian publications. For some unknown reason (perhaps because of his writings) the Glasgow police were suspicious of him and consistently monitored his activities, but could find nothing against him. A generous and caring man, he gave invaluable assistance to unlettered, impoverished seamen, who felt a deep sense of isolation because of their inability to speak the English language.

An integral part of the Indian presence in Scotland at this time were the oculists (eye surgeons), three of whom (Munshi, Nabi Baksh and Din Mohammed) had come to Scotland in 1892 and made their homes in Edinburgh. Alas, their adventure as 'eye surgeons' failed and, having no means of gaining a livelihood, they sought refuge in a poor house, where they stayed for several weeks before the Edinburgh parish authorities paid their passage back to India. But such failures among the Indians in Scotland before the end of the nineteenth century can be compared with the historic success, south of the border in England, where Dadabhai Naoroji became the first Indian to be elected Member of Parliament, timely news which lifted hopes amongst the Indians in Scotland, as the twentieth century beckoned.

Another group within the Asian community were professionals – linguists, teachers, doctors, lawyers and businessmen, representatives of the higher classes of Indian society, who began arriving in Britain from about the last third of the eighteenth century. Among them were linguists such as Monshee Mahomed Saeed, Syed Abdullah, Ganendra Mohan Tagore, Aziz Ahmad and Sake Dean (or Deen) Mahomed, perhaps the best known of this professional group of Indians, whose background is most enlightening.

Dean Mahomed

Dean Mahomed (or Mahomet) was born in 1759 in Patna, Bihar, the second of two sons of a family which is said to have had a tradition of service to the Mughal Empire. Indeed, there seemed to have been a history of the male members of his immediate family serving in the armed forces. So it was not surprising that when Dean Mahomed was about eleven years old, he was prepared to follow his father and brother, who had joined the English East India Company's Army in Bengal.

From 1769 to 1784, he was a loyal servant of the Company, years which he recounted in his *Travels*, an autobiographical narrative of his early life written many years after he had left India. As a child and youth, he came to know the Muslim elite, who had served the ruling power of Patna. Now, it was the all-powerful East India Company, who had conquered the Province, to whom this youth gave his allegiance. His induction into the Company's Bengal Army was through an Anglo-Irish ensign, Godfrey Evan Baker. This relationship was fortuitous, for in the 15 years they knew each other in the Army, Dean Mahomed graduated from being a 'camp follower', to 'market master' and subaltern officer, while Baker became a captain and enjoyed all the independence accompanying that status.[40] When Baker resigned his commission Dean Mahomed chose to travel to Ireland, the land of his master. Soon after his arrival in Cork, Dean Mahomed met and married an Anglo-Irish woman with whom he found much valued companionship.

From the distance of the strange homeland of his patron, India loomed ever larger in his mind and he saw the relationship of things and people more clearly. Such thoughts were too powerful to be contained in mere conversation or to be carried in his head. He felt bound to express himself in a more public manner. His years of association with Captain Baker and other Europeans, and his continuous use of language opened up a new world for him, the world of writing and within ten years of leaving India he had completed and published the *Travels of Dean Mahomet, A Native of Patna in Bengal ...*, and thus became the first Indian writer to publish a book in English.

Travels was a significant publication, not least because it gives the reader an Indian's perspective at a time when all other writings on India were by Europeans in the form of histories, memoirs, journals and letters, a body of literature which was supplemented and amplified by their fictional records of the lives and travels of Asians.[41] Though imitative of European authors, *Travels* is distinguished in giving us an informed Muslim Indian's viewpoint. This makes Dean Mahomed's book a special travel narrative, through which we get insights into India's cities, countryside, social divisions and the diversity of Indian society, as he travelled from region to region. He describes his Muslim inner circle and the uneasy relations with other Indians; and, as he rose among the ranks of the East India Company's Army patrolling the Ganges, he becomes an agent of British rule in India. While many thousands of Indians agreed with him, the vast majority took a different view of the British conquest of India. As an ambitious man and as a Muslim, faced with Hindu rulers, he chose the dominant British side, even though this was a time when racial division between whites and non-whites in India was especially rigid. Few Indians were allowed to enlist in the Company's European corps and Dean Mahomed made the most of the opportunity to do so. The need for men like him, an opportunist, was all the more viable given that a relatively small number of British officials administered some 30,000,000 people in Bengal and Bihar.[42]

In the years that followed publication, he had the responsibilities of a wife and a family, and dissatisfied with the limitations placed upon him, he sought horizons beyond the confines of Ireland. So, in 1807, he moved to London. The capital offered not only greater flexibility for self-improvement, but also restrictions, especially for a man with a growing family. During his years in London, the ever-resourceful Dean Mahomed did many jobs, for example, he worked as a 'medical practitioner', then as a proprietor of a coffee house and restaurant, specialising in Indian cuisine, until a shortage of money prompted him to seek other avenues for his cumulative experience and varied talents.

At the age of 55, he left London for the fashionable seaside resort of Brighton where, in 1814, he inaugurated an Indian Vapour Baths and Shampooing Establishment, and practised as a therapeutic masseur. After an inauspicious start, the success of his 'cure' for muscular maladies and his herbal remedies attracted the attention of sections of high society and, as 'Shampooing Surgeon' to the king, he was responsible for overseeing the Royal Baths at the Pavilion.

With the fame of this enterprising Indian spreading, *Cases Cured By Sake Deen Mahomed*, written testimonies of his patients, was compiled. Then *Shampooing*[43] was published, its third edition appearing in 1838, a fitting historical moment, and a year coincident both with his success at the very heart of the Empire and full emancipation of the African slaves in the British colonies. Mahomed's achievements were, to say the least, extraordinary for he managed to turn the

negative perception and attitudes of the British into positive
acceptance of his medical services. But, as the Victorian era
gained momentum, he found it increasingly difficult to
maintain his role and position in British society.
When he retired in 1843, he was succeeded by one of his two
sons, Arthur. After Mahomed's death in Brighton on 24
February 1851, his pioneering example was followed by his
grandson, Frederick Akbar Mahomed, whose outstanding work
in the medical profession won prizes and honours beyond the
reach of his contemporaries. Thanks to Sake Dean's ambition
for both himself and his family, Frederick's early 'private'
education had set him on a course of excellence, to the extent
that, when he died in his mid-thirties, something of his
grandfather's greatness was echoed by a Cambridge Professor,
who regarded the magnitude of this loss as 'great' in both the
national and international contexts.[44] Following in Frederick's
wake, several Indian doctors not only practised their profession
with distinction, but also, like Sake Dean Mahomed and his
children, married white women.

Dean Mahomed lived in England for almost 60 years,
inventing and reinventing himself, as he played different
unstereotypical roles to suit the changing social and economic
environment. In his way, he was continuously reimaging
Britain and, no doubt, Britons were also trying to place him, as
he dared to try new things. He opened the first Indian
restaurant in London, thus initiating a gradual Indo-British
culinary process which, a century later, would become an
integral part of British cuisine. While much of Sake Dean
Mahomed's achievements have been overlooked since his death,
his writings and life should be celebrated, and their meaning
made clear and understood for the years during which he lived
in India, Ireland and England, as the British Empire extended it
boundaries and might.

With strong and growing trade links between Britain and India,
a few Asian businessmen-cum-political activists came to form
another rare strand of the community, men who came to
Britain initially to represent their companies' interests, a
connection which, in many cases, had direct political implica-

tions. This was the case with Dadabhai Naoroji, of whom more will be said later.

Nevertheless, in spite of their undoubted achievements white perceptions and attitudes towards Asians did not change. Indeed negative images of them remained strong, though perhaps less so for Indians from the highest reaches of society.

Although Indian nobility graced British society with their opulent presence, Vagdama, quoting Rudyard Kipling, noted that the 'responsibility for governing India has been placed by the inscrutable design of providence upon the shoulders of the British race'. This was a popular view in Britain and underscored British condescension towards Indians, including the hundreds of princes who ruled the subcontinent prior to the arrival of the British. Once the conquest was in progress, only those Indian rulers who accepted British rule were allowed to retain their rank.[45]

Among the indigenous rulers and members of the nobility were Duleep Singh, Princess Gouramma and Nawab Nazim.

Duleep Singh

Duleep Singh was born on 4 September 1838. His father, Ranjit Singh (who founded the 'Sikh nation'), became Maharajah of the Punjab in 1843. Six years later, the British brought the Punjab under their domination and Duleep Singh lost his inheritance including the precious Koh-i-Noor diamond. He was permitted to keep the title of 'Maharajah', but his finances were withdrawn by the East India Company, which relentlessly pursued the accumulation of vast wealth.

Under the care and tutorship of a Scotsman and ardent Christian, Dr John Login, Duleep Singh made an extraordinary leap of faith and became a Christian. After his conversion the East India Company cleared his visit to Britain. The queen-empress was pleased with this impressionable boy and was convinced that it was only due to Duleep's conversion that he was able to cure himself of the 'natural indolence' so characteristic of 'all easterners'. When he came of age in 1857 (that

traumatic year in Indian history) the East India Company gave
him control of his severely restricted affairs and granted him an
annual income of £25,000, a sum Duleep found inadequate,
and he requested a further £10,000 a year.

Duleep Singh, who had become owner of Elveden Hall on the
borders of Norfolk and Suffolk, was a local socialite, mixing
with British nobility, and was sportingly and fondly known as
the 'Black Prince'. Such a life-style had its costs, and while
financial difficulties continued to preoccupy him and as his
debts rose, he reflected more and more on India and his distant
childhood in the Punjab which was once his forebears' domain
and all too briefly his. Eventually, he rededicated himself to
Sikhism and attempted to return to India, in an attempt to
regain his birthright. He was stopped at Aden. Frustrated and
still a long, long way from home, he spent the rest of his life in
Paris, where he died in 1893.[46]

Princess Gouramma

Princess Gouramma was born at Benares in February 1841 the
youngest of eleven children. Two days later her mother died.
Her father, the ex-Maharajah of Coorg, regarded her as his
favourite child, the 'fairest of the flock'. When she converted to
Christianity at the age of 13 and became Queen Victoria's
god-daughter, the event was recorded in the *Illustrated London
News*. A marriage between Duleep Singh and the Princess was
considered, but did not materialise. When she married Colonel
John Campbell, a widower 30 years her senior, Victoria saw a
'brilliant' future ahead of her. Tragically, like her mother,
Princess Gouramma died, after giving birth to a daughter. She
was just 23 years old.[47]

Prince Nawab Nazim

Prince Nawab Nazim came to Britain in 1870 to plead with the
British authorities for an increase in his allowance. He, too, was
a favourite of the queen and after settling in north London, he

was censured by the upholders of certain social standards in India for his fall from grace to a meaningless life, in particular his marriage to a lower-class white woman, which was perceived as an unforgivable disgrace. Like Duleep Singh, Nawab Nazim had over-spent, but not, as he argued, because he was careless with money. Eventually, he received £8,000 pounds a year, which he welcomed, but was debarred from re-entering India. In 1880 he left England and made his way to the city of Kerbala.[48]

Ranjitsinghji

The most famous Indian in nineteenth-century Britain was 'Prince Ranji'. Cricket dominated the summer in England and towering over the game was the imposing figure of Dr W.G. Grace. In this period, cricket transcended colour and religion, and the Indian player, Ranjitsinghji, the Maharajah of Nawana-gar, made a striking and historic reputation in English cricket. He was adventurous and exciting in his strokes, wielding his bat 'like a scimitar' which brought him great acclaim. As a batsman he was second only to Grace. Charles T. West, one of the leading composers and lyricist of popular songs of the day, immortalised him in the song 'Ranj'.

I sing a glorious hero bold, his name well known to fame;
A man of might in friendly fight, in our fine old English game;
A Prince of our Indian Empire, the willow he wields with ease,
And with practised skill a right good will, he scores his centuries.

(Chorus)
Ran-ji-tsinh-ji
All the way from Inji.
Right well he plays, and earns our praise,
Ranji, Ranjitsinhji;
'Cuts' for three, and 'smacks' for four,
Soon to the century mounts his score,
And loud the crowd then shout and roar
Bravo! Bravo! Ranji!

The song was enormously successful and two years later, West penned another melody: the 'Ranjitsinghji Waltz'. Such was Ranji's fame that in 1899 the magazine *Cricket* revealed in the lines of a 'ditty' that there was some uncertainty about his return to play for Hove, in Sussex, after visiting Australia, a concern expressed in the endearing song, the 'Sussex Welcome to the Wanderer'.

Ranji was the first hero in this sport from the colonial Empire,[49] and the first player ever to reach a score of 3,000 runs in a season. It should be remembered that he also accompanied the England team on their tour of Australia. Ironically, while British newspaper headlines proclaimed that Ranji, the brown-coloured Indian, 'saved' England, black men in Britain were parodied and devalued, as images of them in the form of caricatures came into vogue in British music halls, on the dramatic stage and in the exalted world of classical concerts.

BLACK PERFORMERS AND 'BLACKFACE' (MINSTRELSY)

Samuel Coleridge Taylor

Samuel Coleridge Taylor, the son of an African father and an English mother, was born in central London on 15 August 1875, and grew up in Croydon, where he was introduced to the rudiments of music at St George's Church. He was good enough to be admitted to the prestigious Royal College of Music, where he met the respected music teacher, Charles Stanford, who became his mentor and life-long friend. Here he won a number of prizes for composition, including the coveted Alexander Prize, the first black man to do so. As he strove to realise his musical potential, he met many talented pupils, including Vaughan Williams and Gustav Holst, though none could match his musical accomplishment and achievements.

About this time Coleridge Taylor composed the 'Ballad in A Minor', which catapulted him to the front ranks of the RCM students and brought him fame. Among those who attended concerts at the College was the ever-curious Auguste Jaeger, a German enthusiast, who exclaimed when he heard Coleridge Taylor's 'Ballad': 'I have long been looking for a new English

Composer of real genius, and I believe I have found him.' This opinion found further justification in Coleridge Taylor's other compositions, including his famous work, 'Hiawatha's Wedding Feast'. Soon Jaeger was on intimate terms with his discovery, and did all he could to advance Coleridge Taylor's career. Indeed in his capacity as musical adviser to the music publisher Novello and, as critic to *The Musical Times*, Jaeger brought to bear an attitude which may aptly be called critical enthusiasm. The beautiful songs which Coleridge Taylor published in his early twenties all came under Jaeger's influence and when the time came to publish 'Hiawatha's Wedding Feast' it was at Jaeger's insistence that the publishers issued it, in spite of their own emphatic assertion that 'they did not expect to sell a copy of it'.

As his work reached more people, Coleridge Taylor became more self-assured and fell in love with a fellow-musician, Jessie Walmisley, whom he married.

At the age of 23, Coleridge Taylor came to the notice of Edward Elgar, who recommended that he be commissioned to write works which he himself could not undertake. But there was much opposition to this rising black star. A symphony by a 'nigger' was too much for the German Hans Richter. Nevertheless, Elgar's strong recommendation was confirmation of the young man's musical genius.

Thus far Coleridge Taylor had little to do with the 'nigger' question, and a significant moment in his life and work was meeting Paul Lawrence Dunbar. This African-American, son of a slave and a poet, had some influence over Coleridge Taylor and urged him to write about the dispossessed, 'your people, write of yourself'. He championed the music of Dvorak and moved closer to 'erotic' compositions. And increasingly, as more of his music was published and performed, his admirers came from far and wide, and included a Mrs Hilyer, a visiting African-American woman, who was advised by Frederick Loudin (on a tour with the Fisk Jubilee Singers) to call on the now famous black British composer. So impressed was she that on her return to America, as a member of the Treble Cleff Club, she and the ladies of this organisation formed the Samuel Coleridge Taylor Choral Society, and she wrote to the composer declaring her pride in doing so, before inviting him to visit the

United States. He was deeply touched by this response to his work and assured his African American admirers that as a 'great' believer in his African ancestry, he never lost, as he put it, 'an opportunity to remind my friends here of it'.

In 1904 he performed his 'Hiawatha's Wedding Feast' for the first time in America and met President Roosevelt, a visit which was as memorable as it was an eye-opener. He also met the respected African-American leader, Booker T. Washington, who told Coleridge Taylor that he was 'a source of inspiration to us all'.

On his return to England, he was appointed a Professor of Music, but being relatively poor, he had to continue at a gruelling pace – writing, composing, teaching and conducting, travelling up and down the country with little rest. His pauses, though rare, were intense moments of thought and reflection as to the direction of his work and life. There were indications now of a greater willingness to express strongly held views. Indeed after his composition 'Tale of Old Japan', he did some 'political' work, which was perhaps understandable in the circumstances, for he and his children were the targets of racists, who saw him as a 'clever little nigger'. Such attacks on his person, combined with overwork, brought about a darker, drearier vision; and when he heard his music played over the public address system at Victoria Station, he felt his life was finished, that there was no future for him in England, because he was black.

Fortunately, his American friend Carl Stoeckel was enthusiastic about Coleridge Taylor making a second visit to the United States, and when he did so, his success was such that he was nicknamed the 'African Mahler'. He had achieved much, yet his long cherished hope to visit Germany and have his works performed there, still eluded him.

And although it was memorable, his American tour was nevertheless a punishing schedule of concerts, social gatherings and meetings with VIPs which, predictably took its toll. On his return to England, at the age of 37,[50] he collapsed at Croydon Station and spent his last hours in a delirium, muttering: 'I'm too young to die, I'm too young to die.'

Samuel Coleridge Taylor was the most popular conductor/composer of his day, and came to accept with pride his African heritage. This 'Apostle of Colour' was consistently true to his art; and though largely unrecognised by British society he enriched the world with the legacy of his music.

Another striking musical feature of this period was the popularity of music hall entertainment, especially 'Burnt Cork Minstrelsy', in which white men impersonated black men.

'Turn about an' wheel about an' do jis so
An' ebery time I turn about I jump Jim Crow'

According to the Englishman Harry Reynolds, an ardent practitioner of Minstrelsy, these two lines of a song sung in African-American dialect, with all its racial implications, caught the attention of the actor/comedian Thomas Dartmouth Rice in Cincinnati in 1830. He does not seem to have attained any noticeable degree of eminence in his profession, but had an eccentric personality and during the progress of a play, the leading actors frequently complained that Rice, playing only minor parts, was constantly the focus of attention, because of his mannerisms. Furthermore, he possessed what many of superior artistic abilities lacked, namely tact and shrewdness, and he kept his wits about him for anything that might be turned to professional and profitable use.

In his autobiography *Minstrel Memories* (1928), Reynolds described Rice as the man who developed and popularised burnt cork minstrelsy, the theatrical presentation of white men blacking up to represent black men in music halls in both the United States and in Britain. After two years in Pittsburg, Rice visited Philadelphia, Boston and New York before sailing to England, where he met with 'high favour in his novel characterisations'. On his first appearance at the Surrey Theatre on 9 July 1836, he introduced his famous song 'Jump Jim Crow', which became the 'rage' everywhere. For the rest of the nineteenth century through to 1909, as one London daily newspaper noted, 'nothing of any consequence seems to have arisen to take its place'.

Nevertheless, there seem to have been few burnt cork comedians in London and provincial variety theatres, no successors to the popular black-face artistes, E.W. Mackney,

G.H. Chirgwin (the white-eyed 'Kaffir') and Messrs Brown, Newland and Le Clerq. Among the white-faced burnt cork minstrels was Sam Redfern, the 'Negro delineator', who was regarded as perhaps the 'most versatile' of the 'musical niggers', but whose performances were never quite predictable. Eugene Stratton was another black face minstrel/musical comedian, who poked fun at black people through cameos of 'Negro characterisations' such as 'The Old Nigger', 'The Idler' and the 'Whistling Coon', not to mention his 'impersonation' of a 'Negro horse thief'. Stratton won many hearts and, as Reynolds tells us, his rise to fame came through his songs 'The Whistling Coon' and the 'Dandy Coloured Coon', which placed him 'firmly on the pedestal of fame'. G.H. Elliott was another top black face music hall act. Known as the 'chocolate-coloured coon' he was by far the 'greatest exponent of coon song and dance' in England. His portrayals were so convincing that Reynolds was moved to say: 'As a vocalist Elliott, with his well-trained, musical and resonant voice, can get more out of a coon song than anyone. He idealises the coon with his love songs to the moon and other things and when he vocally expresses his passionate desire to return to Idaho or Dixie, he so hypnotises his audience that they become imbued with the same desire.'

Previewing the tour of Haverley's Minstrels and Callendar's Minstrels at two London theatres, a cartoon by Alfred Bryan entitled 'A Shower of Blacks' shows four well-dressed Englishmen, three of them top-hatted and one bowler-hatted, being showered by miniature black figures in dancing and banjo-playing poses. But when Haverley's Coloured Minstrels (black men playing themselves) eventually appeared on a tour of Britain in the 1880s, their success was less than they had hoped for.[51] If one deduces from this that the British public was more in tune with white men blacking up (a very thin disguise indeed) than with the real black performers, then such a deduction is not only accurate, but also reveals that racial prejudice and negative images of black men persisted in popular British music hall performances, precursors of the once immensely popular twentieth-century stage and television version, the Black and White Minstrel Show.

Ira Aldridge

The African-American actor Ira Aldridge played Othello on the London stage, becoming the first black man to achieve world renown as a Shakespearean actor – an achievement all the more rare because it challenged preconceived ideas and deeply held beliefs about the inferiority of the black man vis-à-vis white men, both as a man and as a performer. Apart from the role of Othello, he played Lear, Macbeth and Shylock, roles never before attempted by a black man who, ironically, had to 'whiten' up to portray characters considered to be the preserve of white men.

Aldridge was born on 24 July 1807 in New York, the son of a preacher, a man of education and of good social standing in the black community. Ira attended New York's Free School, well known for its pro-Abolitionist reputation and where exemplars for those aspiring to leadership were in abundance. His sights were, however, elsewhere: on the New York theatre. His hero in the acting world was James Hewlett, an African-American actor. At this time too, the African Theatre opened in New York City and after his first acting part in *Pizzaro*, Aldridge quickly realised that if he was going to make it, he would have to leave America. Still in his late teens, he travelled to England and in 1825 made his British debut as Oroonoko in Thomas Southerne's play *The Revolt of Surinam, Or a Slave's Revenge*, adapted from Aphra Behn's novel. His dark colour was promoted and may have been good publicity, but reviewers' perceptions were another matter. *The Times* did not like his performance because the 'shape of his lips' made him incapable of pronouncing English words properly. *The Globe*, on the other hand, was encouraging and disagreed with *The Times*. The London press did not, however, take too kindly to Aldridge's blackness and so he tried the provinces. It was about this time that he met and married Margaret Gill, a respectable English woman, a union which seems to have generated a spirit of renewal as he set about doggedly learning his profession, while touring major northern English venues, the Scottish cities and Belfast.

Steadily gaining in confidence, he played a range of roles including Othello, which earned him the description of being an 'actor of genius'. His blackness and the actress Helen Tree's whiteness drew racial poison from newspaper critics, however.

Unhappy that the West End had denied him the opportunity to perform, he left England for a tour of no fewer than a dozen Continental capitals where his performances received outstanding praise. Now he returned in triumph to London and performed in the West End. He had made the role of Othello his own, challenging even the great English actor, David Garrick. Single-handedly, he extended the bounds of the theatre by performing across Europe, where few people (especially English actors) ever visited. While he was on tour in Poland, doing what he enjoyed and did best, he died in Lodz in August 1867, just a year short of his sixtieth birthday.[52] Throughout his life he fought bigotry and racial prejudice to become an African-American artist of world renown, and fittingly his legacy lived on. Sixty years later, in 1930,[53] his daughter Amanda, a singer, teacher and composer, was on hand to assist the next African-American to play Othello in London, Paul Robeson.

The successes of Samuel Coleridge Taylor and Ira Aldridge were achieved against heavy odds in a century which not only saw emancipation of the African slaves, but also the introduction of their replacements, the indentured Indians, who laboured under a 'new' system of slavery. But as the nineteenth century progressed, the questions of race and colour, on which colonial exploitation was based, were uppermost in the minds of African and Indian nationalists. The black intelligentsia from both the African and Indian diasporas stepped up their challenge to those in power on these questions and demanded the fundamental right of colonial people to govern themselves.

So, in addition to those who excelled as performers in the arts, there were also the penetrating works of rare individuals, African and Asian intellectuals who wrote, spoke and dedicated their lives to the anti-colonial struggle.

RESISTANCE: THE AFRICAN AND ASIAN INTELLIGENTSIA

The Early Pan Africanists

In Britain, from the emergence of black and Asian communities in the eighteenth and nineteenth centuries, there was a gradual tendency towards a counterpoise to British racism, committed responses best illustrated in the narratives of free black men and women. In Equiano's *Interesting Narrative* and Cugoano's writings one can trace the roots of the Pan African tradition. But, it was only in the nineteenth century that the Pan African idea, put forward by Delany and Edward Blyden, achieved some clarity and form in Britain, when the Pan African Association came into being on 24 September 1897, with Henry Sylvester Williams as Honorary Secretary, a role which he continued to play (and in which he was supported by the Indian nationalist Dadabhai Naoroji) until the first Pan African Conference was called in London in 1900. Before him, however, were the notable spokesmen Celestine Edwards and J. Albert Thorne, both West Indians, who dedicated their lives to the advancement of the 'black race'.

Celestine Edwards came to Britain from Dominica, where he was born in 1857. He was a strong believer in Christian fundamentalism, the brotherhood of men and the cause of temperance. As the first black editor in Britain, working on the magazines *Lux* and *Fraternity*,[54] he blazed a trail for other Pan Africanists such as Sylvester Williams, Duse Mohammed Ali and J.E. Taylor.

J. Albert Thorne was no less passionate about his ideological involvement, being concerned with the 'preliminary stage' of Pan Africanism, spanning the years from 1894 to 1897. He was intent on establishing a colony of West Indian families on the banks of the Zambezi, a project which, it seems, had much influence on Marcus Garvey. Born in Barbados in 1860, he was the youngest of 13 children, a family experience from which he derived much benefit. When he came to London in 1884 he made friends easily, some of whom were highly placed in society. But Thorne was acutely conscious of his racial background and developed a deep respect for learning. Towards the end of the 1880s, he entered the University of Aberdeen and graduated with the degree of Bachelor of Medicine and Master of Surgery. 'African colonisation' remained an important theme for him, and as Robert Hill suggested, it is highly likely that Thorne was influenced by Blyden's thoughts and writings on Christianity, Islam and the Negro race. It was also likely that he was influenced by the pioneering work of Dr James Johnston, the Scottish missionary. Nevertheless, given his awakened racial consciousness, and against the background of problems endemic in the Pan African triangle, he wrote with a sense of deep understanding to Bishop Henry McNeal Turner (the African-American AME Zion Church leader, who was not only involved in religious activities, but also in black politics) being a central figure in the campaign for black emigration to Africa:

> The first great lesson we have to learn, I think, is unity. It does not matter whether we are born in Africa, in the United States of America, in the West Indian islands or in any other part of the world. It is enough that we are all members of the African race, whose past history has been the same, whose future is also identical, and whose present, though it may differ in a few individual instances, nevertheless is, in the main, beset by the same racial disabilities.[55]

This constituted the essence of the ideology of Pan Africanism as the racial vanguard of the African diaspora.

Henry Sylvester Williams

In Thorne's absence, his idea of an African homeland remained to be acted upon. Among those in the African diaspora, it seemed that there had to be a 'son of Africa' committed to redeeming the good name and humanity of the African and his people as a whole. The circumstances were propitious for just such a person to emerge, for in response to James Anthony

Froude's Negrophobe travel book *The English in the West Indies* (1888), J.J. Thomas, a Trinidadian schoolmaster wrote *Froudacity, West Indian Fables by James Anthony Froude Explained*.[56] But this well-stated argument was not enough, for while many had thought of the idea, few had acted on behalf of the African peoples until Henry Sylvester Williams, who became aware of this need while he was a student in London.

Williams was born in north Trinidad in 1869, where the villagers were mainly of African descent. Slavery had been abolished for just 36 years and people were still alive while he was growing up, who had experienced the 'middle passage' and others who had come to Trinidad as 'recaptives'. In Williams's young mind, Africa and his Africanness were real. The African form of worship, African drums and dances formed part of Trinidad village life. All of this, however, was being increasingly undermined.

British colonial rule had the effect of making Trinidad (and other West Indian colonies) less African, less French and more English. And for some, like Williams, Africa and Africans did not go unnoticed in Trinidad at this time. The fact that he knew there were African princes in the land of his ancestors raised many urgent questions, which drew him closer to Thomas's work. Thomas was clearly preoccupied with Africa (the 'cradle of our race') and felt, as others before and after him, that Africans and their descendants in the Western Hemisphere would be better off in Africa. Thus the back-to-Africa and Pan African vision of Thomas had a major influence on Williams, who, in turn, developed and set the idea in motion, through much deliberation and devoted organisation.

After teaching in Trinidad, at the age of 22, Williams went to the United States (an unusual move at the time for a young black colonial) where he took an interest in issues relating to Afro-Americans who were discriminated against, denied equal rights, terrorised and lynched. He was also concerned with the increasing disenfranchisement of black people in the South. And it is more than likely that, given the wide publicity surrounding it, he was aware of Bishop Henry McNeal Turner's back to Africa plan.

Such factors as racial barriers and the lack of congenial work ended Williams's study in the United States and he moved to Canada, where in 1893 he registered at Dalhousie University as a student in the Faculty of Law during the 1893–4 season. By 1896 he was in England where he pursued his ambition to read for the Bar, by enrolling in December 1897 at Gray's Inn. Here he delivered his first address as Honorary Secretary of the African Association, which he had founded. Having forged this link of black brotherhood, it seemed he felt free to enter the bond of inter-racial marriage, and at the age of 29 he married a white woman, Agnes Powell, in spite of her father's disapproval.

The African Association was established on 24 September 1897, the purposes of which included encouragement of 'a feeling of unity and to facilitate friendly intercourse among Africans in general'. Though its membership had to be drawn from British subjects, the Association aimed at protecting its members' rights by appealing to both the British and colonial governments to redress their wrongs.

The Association's activities spurred the call which was issued as early as 1898 for a Pan African Conference in 1900. However, Williams had, in fact, already conceived the idea of a world conference of black people in 1897, well before the formation of the African Association. He was fully aware that his plans could only materialise if he could get 'representatives of the race' to come to London. Accordingly, he reasoned that those black people who were going to the great Exposition in Paris might be induced to combine their trip with a visit to London for the Conference. And how fortuitous that proved to be for the Pan African movement.

The first Pan African Conference was opened on 23 July 1900 by Bishop Walters, whose address dealt thoughtfully with the 'Trials and Tribulations of the Coloured Race in America', thus setting the tone of the Conference. 'For the first time in history', he said, 'Blacks had gathered from all parts of the globe to discuss how to improve the condition of the race; to assert the rights of blacks and to organise them so that they might take an equal place among nations.'

After the Conference, the organisation and administration of the new Pan African Association was Williams's main task. He worked diligently for the Association and his efforts to spread the message took him to the West Indies and the United States, where branches were formed. At the meetings he addressed, much-needed subscriptions were collected to fund *Pan African*, the monthly magazine which he hoped to publish in London. Indeed, the first issue of *Pan African*, with Williams as its editor, was published in October 1901, but folded after six issues.

He continued to prepare for the Bar and gave public lectures on the status of the African in the British Empire. Later he became involved in municipal politics, serving on two standing committees, dealing with legal, parliamentary and housing matters, which did not deflect his interest in, and devotion to, African affairs. But after a spell of 'protecting Liberian interests' he discontinued his role as a black spokesman in England and returned to his native Trinidad, which was still very much a white-dominated colony of the British Empire. As it was, Trinidad and Africa were focal points of interest during his organisational work and representations, but furtherance of the ambitious cause of Pan Africanism from the more familiar, restrictive setting of colonial Trinidad was most unlikely. Nevertheless, he continued to review the local and international situation. He had much time for reflection. According to his biographer, Williams 'perhaps prematurely, popularised the vocabulary of black grievance, coined a useful phrase "Pan Africanism", challenged conventional notions regarding Africa and called for a new sort of British Empire'.[57]

There was no doubt in Williams's mind (and he never failed to remind himself of this) that black people were the equals of other human beings, and there was no finer example of this than himself, a colonial who had influenced W.E.B DuBois, the distinguished African-American scholar and writer, who identified colour as a crucial and divisive factor. Williams, like Edwards and Thorne, at that crucial stage in black history, regarded Pan Africanism as the racial vanguard of the African diaspora. Overall then, these early beginnings, initiated in the nineteenth century, led to the dramatic developments in Pan Africanism that were to come in the twentieth century.

EARLY REPRESENTATION AND RESISTANCE FROM THE INDIAN EMPIRE

Given its 'history of resistance' the quest for Indian freedom extended beyond the subcontinent to Britain itself, a location which afforded to those Indian colonials who opposed the Empire new perspectives in their campaigns. Here, at the centre of the Empire, they found many British sympathisers, which gave them added confidence in their advocacy of the social and political progress of the Indian people.

Among the first of these Indian voices to address the British Parliament and people was Rajah Ram Mohun Roy, who became known as the 'father' of Indian nationalism. Roy's representations contradicted misleading views of the British rulers in India, who wrote extensively and said much about India and Indians. Not surprisingly, many thoughtful and oppressed people listened and sympathised with Roy and Dwarkanath Tagore (both Bengalis), who also believed in the importance of establishing an organisation to promote Indian aspirations in Britain.

The inauguration of the British India Society in July 1839 was encouraging as its Anglo-Indian membership emphasised that the continued well-being of Britain was underscored by its dependence upon India. The Society not only sought concessions for the East India Company, but also activated the 'Friends of India' and significantly lodged in the public mind the need for political change in the subcontinent.

Twenty-six years later, another group, the London Indian Society, was formed to mobilise and communicate Indian interests in England. Among those closely associated with the Society was Dadabhai Naoroji. Soon this body was overtaken by the East India Association, whose views were liberally expressed and in which Naoroji also figured prominently. As President, he steered the Association towards greater unity among Indians in England and a better understanding of the issues that concerned India; and having shown his interest in, and understanding of, the Irish Home Rule Movement and Irish politics, he, in turn, sought the help of Irish politicians in communicating the

Indian nationalists' message to British Members of Parliament. These approaches indicated the political direction in which these nationalists were moving, for it was clear to them that it was not enough to continue attending meetings and making speeches. Now they declared their candidacy as MPs, but such parliamentary dreams as they had were shattered when the courageous Lalmohun Ghose failed to become the first Asian to win a parliamentary seat as the Liberal candidate for Deptford in 1883. He was followed by the Conservative candidature of R.R. Singh, who also failed. But such failures were, it seemed, necessary prerequisites for the success to come. Let us now follow some of the thoughts and actions of three leading Indians at this time – Dadabhai Naoroji, Mukherjee Bhownaggree and Syed Ameer Ali.

Dadabhai Naoroji

Dadabhai Naoroji came to Britain as a representative of the Cama Company in 1855. He was the only child of Parsee parents, and one of the first graduates from Elphinstone College in Bombay, the first Indian appointed as Professor of Mathematics and Natural Philosophy at Elphinstone and founder of the London Zoroastrian Association for the well-being of Parsees in the capital. He championed the cause of countless of his Indian 'brothers and sisters' on a range of issues, educational, social and political, for which he campaigned throughout his eventful life.

The devaluation of Indians and the plunder of India by Britain were among his main concerns. In arguing his case, he identified the imbalance of trade between Britain and India and the drain of an estimated £30–40 million each year from India. And what was worse, the wealth that came to Britain, he added, was not for the benefit of the workers, but for the ruling elite.

Naoroji was also determined to see more Indians employed in the Civil Service. In order to achieve this, the existing restriction, he argued, should be relaxed. Underpinning his argument, he emphasised that he was not advocating radical change, but reforms in the Indian Judiciary and the Legislative Council.

Naoroji won much admiration and benefited from the support of a few distinguished Englishmen whose names carried much political weight. These included John Bright, Sir William Wedderburn and the socialists H.M. Hyndman, Keir Hardie and Ramsay MacDonald. Among Naoroji's concerns was the fact that, with the emergence of the Indian National Congress in 1885, he felt it was tactically necessary to twin the Congress in Britain with the British Committee of the Indian National Congress, a move which was aimed at rousing the English working classes to an awareness of England's debt to India. Through the pages of *India*, the Committee's journal published between 1890 and 1921, he guided the Committee's commitment to Indian reforms.

Nevertheless, the question remained: How was he to secure the desired goals? He realised that for all its merits, his effort thus far to educate the British public had been of limited value, a shortcoming which pressed him to seek election to Parliament, for within it there was much 'ignorance and apathy' about Indians. He was diligent and steadfast in his ambition to bring for the first time in Parliament a true representation of the millions of people who had made India the British Crown's 'brightest jewel'.

So after much thought and discussion, in 1886 he canvassed support as a Liberal candidate for the Holborn constituency in London, which he lost. But victory came when he stood as the Liberal candidate for Finsbury Central, which, unlike Holborn, was a 'working-class constituency'. Naoroji thus became the first 'black' Member of Parliament. The outstanding feature of this election was the fact that white working people were not only willing to listen to what he had to say about India and Indian affairs, they also respected him for being an honest man, the agent through whom messages from both the Indian and British working classes were communicated to the higher councils of government. Post-election euphoria did not blind him, however, for he was not unaware of his hysterical enemies among his fellow Liberals and in the Conservative Party, one of whom tagged him a 'Baboo from Bombay', while Lord Salisbury referred to him as the 'black man' in Parliament.

Naoroji's colour was an issue which the press made much of, inflaming the xenophobia among Britain's masses, an attitude which was also meted out to Ira Aldridge who dared to assert his humanity above mere colour considerations. The *Bristol Times* and *The Times* went beyond Naoroji's colour and talked of his racial inferiority and therefore his unsuitability as a representative of his English constituents.[58]

Naoroji was a man of broad outlook, a nationalist who favoured Irish Home Rule, and when he was initially accepted as a candidate for Holborn, his long residence in England and his knowledge of English politics were his main planks. As Visram claimed, he assured his constituents that their interests were his primary concern, though he made it clear that matters relating to India would not be neglected.

However, for all Naoroji's political skill, the British public at large had doubts about his new status as a Member of Parliament and, once again, his colour and race were invoked to discredit him. This was, however, easier said than done, for Naoroji was no ordinary Indian, but one who was formidable enough to meet the challenge of parliamentary representation; and in doing so he took every opportunity, as he said he would, to inform the House of Commons of India's concerns vis-à-vis British interests. Fortunately for his British constituents, throughout his political career, at a time when British racism had reached new heights he remained a man worthy of his 'race'. And though not lacking in confidence, he may nevertheless have been heartened to have had confirmation of his ability and stature when, before the end of the century, another Indian, Prince Ranjitsinghji, had single-handedly extended the bounds of Anglo-Indian relations by winning plaudits from a section of England's sports-lovers. How paradoxical this might have seemed to Naoroji, who had lost the elections of 1895 and 1906, when he stood as an Independent Liberal Candidate. To his credit, he remained an optimist about India, even though his passionate work as a reformer was not successful, as he had hoped. He retired to India in 1907, but the outbreak of the First World War reactivated his interest as he urged Indians to support an Imperial Britain in what he perceived to be the 'common cause' of liberty, an approval which contrasted sharply

with the views of a younger generation of Indian nationalists.
When his long life ended at the age 92,[59] a new phase of Indian
nationalism and nationalists had already been born, and
weaned on a passionate new radicalism.

Mancherjee Bhownaggree

Mancherjee Bhownaggree, another reformer, became the
second Indian to enter Parliament when he won the Bethnal
Green North East seat as a Conservative candidate. Like
Naoroji, his father was a Parsee. They were, however, unlike
each other in various ways. Bhownagree's father was rich and
his political allegiance was Conservative, a matter which was
of more than passing concern among members of the Indian
National Congress.

Born on 15 August 1851, Bhownaggree was educated at
Elphinstone College and Bombay University and did editorial
work on *The Statesman*. He arrived in England in 1881 to study
law at Lincoln's Inn and five years later, after his appointment
as a Judicial Councillor in India, he reformed the Law Courts
and the police, in conformity with British practice, thus
declaring his partiality and respect for British institutions. He
not only promoted women's education and women's rights, but
also as an author of a conservative, elitist persuasion, he wrote
on topics such as the East India Company's Constitution and
Queen Victoria's writings. Unlike Naoroji, he had a high profile
and was fully accepted in British society, receiving many
prestigious honours from those whom he tried to emulate.

He seemed destined to come to England and, when he did so
again in 1891, it was to take up permanent residence. Oppor-
tunists to the bone, the Conservatives soon recognised his
political potential in relation to their Indian Empire and set out
to exploit it, indeed to capitalise on it. For one thing, Bhownaggree, a 'sound imperialist' alternative and an acceptable voice
of India in Britain, was the best counterpoise to Naoroji's
'extreme' views on India. Not surprisingly Bhownaggree's
victory at the polls again in 1900 served to enhance his
conservative profile. But failure to regain his seat meant a loss of

his personal following and ended his political life. Thereafter, he proved to be a willing and useful agent for the India Office. Perhaps Bhownaggree's most enduring legacy was his donation of a gallery at the Commonwealth Institute in London, which bears his name.[60]

Syed Ameer Ali

Another dimension of Indian nationalism was presented by Syed Ameer Ali. While Indians (Hindus, Sikhs and Parsees, for example) hitherto tended to present India's case in more general terms, Ali's focus was more specific, his main concern being to safeguard his fellow Muslims' interests in India from the domination of Hindus, thus clearly articulating his position on intercommunal tension which was potentially damaging to Indian nationalist aspirations. He too, thought of British rule in India as being of 'vital necessity' and did not see an early end to it.

He was born in Orissa on 6 April 1849 and although his family was poor, he was able to complete his college and university education before winning a scholarship which enabled him to come to England in 1869 to enrol as a law student. On his return to India, the subject he chose to teach at the Presidency College was Islamic law. He later became the distinguished Tagore Law Professor at Calcutta University and was appointed as a High Court Judge in Calcutta. He returned to Britain in 1904 and was invited to sit on both the Privy Council and its Judicial Committee, the first Indian to do so.

Ameer Ali's challenge was to seek a separate identity for the Muslims in India. It was he, as Visram noted, who brought about the 'political awakening' of the Muslims in India. Impressed by Hindu organisations and the benefits they conferred on Hindus, in his late twenties, he inaugurated a Muslim political organisation, the National Muhammadan Association. For a quarter of a century he travelled the subcontinent encouraging, educating and organising Muslims, and soon more than 50 branches of the Association were established. By the first decade of the twentieth century, the Association was the political organisation through which India's Muslims declared their independence from other sections of the country. Ali spoke against the prejudice that existed and time and again advocated separation from the Hindus, rather than integration.

During his retirement in England, he closely followed his co-religionists' political progress in India and helped to found the All-India Muslim League in 1906. The need for Muslim solidarity was vital in advancing their claims. Indeed two years later, when an AIML branch was set up in London, Ali accepted its Presidency and co-ordinated activities between London and India. High on the League's agenda, and a vital element in its strategy, was the need for support from the British public. In pursuing this objective, when he was not speaking, Ali wrote extensively for newspapers and journals about the position of Muslims in India.

With time, his conviction that separate Muslim representation in India was the only way forward grew stronger and a move in this direction eventually came with the Government of India Act of 1909, which confirmed the importance of winning support from both the British Parliament and public. Like Naoroji and Bhownaggree, he denounced the ill-treatment and general plight of the indentured Indians (among whom were many Muslims) in South Africa; and he continued to expound on the law of Islam and history, pronouncements which reached appreciative audiences when he graced the Mosque at Woking with his Chairmanship. When he died, *The Times* recognised his refined taste, historical sense and versatility, and his rare ability to combine Eastern values with those of the West.[61]

In addition to the Muslims' representations for a separate identity, there was a more general radical movement of Indian students in London, essentially young men impatient with the delaying tactics of the British Raj. If the older Indian nationalists were accommodating to British rule in India, this new group of intellectuals wanted nothing short of Indian home rule.

It was time for the British to go, they argued. Unlike their westernised predecessors, who were susceptible to British influence, these young men looked to India (not the West) and gained inspiration from its history, religion and culture. Pride in their Indianness was the foundation upon which their resistance to alien rule was built, a challenge which had echoes among Africans and their descendants in the diaspora, who, in the last half of the nineteenth century, excelled not only as performers in the arts, but also as the foremost thinkers among the colonial peoples.

According to one estimate, in the last third of the eighteenth century, there were approximately 10,000 black people[62] in Britain. Intermarriage with members of the white population meant a degree of absorption, especially after Emancipation, when there was no large influx of black people into Britain as chattels.

Although there were many 'high achievers' in Britain's black communities (in addition to those mentioned above) including the merchants George W. Christian, Charles Heddle and Thomas Lewis Johnson, the vast majority were working-class, to be found in the docklands of British seaports such as Cardiff and Liverpool.[63] As in the eighteenth century, more and more African, Afro-Caribbean and African American students made their way to Britain. Among them were medical students like the Sierra Leoneans, James Africanus Beale Horton and William Broughton Davies and two African Americans, Ewing Glasgow and Robert M. Johnson.[64] Others, like John Mensah Sarbah, Joseph Casely Hayford and J. Egerton Shyngle, came to study law. This led them to develop ideas about their identity in Britain and, as a consequence, to mass working-class move-ments vis-à-vis the Empire. Amidst the problems arising from 'race' and racism, some like Richard Akiwande Savage gravi-tated towards political activism which served them well in later years when they embraced the cause of African nationalism. Another eminent black person in the nineteenth century was Edward Wilmot Blyden, who held high office as the Ambassador of Liberia at the Court of St James. Others, like Duse Mohamed Ali and J.R. Archer (who was born in Britain), would, at the beginning of the twentieth century, make their mark as champions of black rights.[65] Educated black men had also turned their learning to good use by setting out their nationalist arguments in a number of books, articles, pamphlets and journals,[66] which challenged the prevailing views of the colonial rulers. So, gradually in the closing years of the nineteenth century, much questioning and intellectual work had already been done to ensure that Henry Sylvester Williams's organisational skills would bring about the successful first Pan African Conference of 1900, which was, as Shyllon put it, not only 'climactic', but also 'forward looking'.[67]

Before the First World War, outstanding black personalities and leaders and the small, dispersed Asian groupings did all they could not merely to survive, but to add uniquely, in their various ways, to British life. Although in some cases important contributions were recognised, racial prejudice prevailed: an implacable force that was at once sobering and instructive. More immediately, overcoming it was not so much their concern, as was their survival, because of war and the rumours of war to come which forced certain adjustments upon them that were not of their own making, but very much to do with the economic, social, political and cultural stresses and strains within Imperial Britain and in her relations with the outside world.

PART TWO

BRITAIN AND EMPIRE (1900–62)

BRITAIN: AN HISTORICAL OUTLINE (1900–56)

By 1950, Britain had been through two world wars and the process of decolonisation was moving apace, making Britain less great than it was at the beginning of the century. It is therefore important to consider developments within Britain as well as relations between the Empire and Europe until the end of the 1950s.

The Boer War had revealed that Britain was not a leading military power in Europe. And the Great War, which broke out in 1914, left the people of Britain deeply scarred. 'Virtually anyone who was alive in the interwar period', wrote David Childs, 'was marked in some way ... Some 745,000 men from Britain had been killed ... about 1.7 million were wounded and 1.2 million of them received disablement pensions.'[1] In the aftermath of war, Winston Churchill felt there was a need for a Ministry of Defence, but few agreed, perhaps because of the widespread belief that the Great War would not be repeated.

Earlier, the rivalry among European states had left Britain detached from Europe, its links tenuous. Prior to 1917, in international dealings outside the Empire, Britain remained isolated; and before and after the 1914–18 war there was no resolution as to Britain's role in Europe. Predictably, the Bolshevik Revolution in 1917 incited Conservative antagonism and it seemed that antipathy towards closer ties with Europe was reinforced. However, in spite of the Peace Treaty of Versailles and the setting up of the League of Nations, there were disturbing ideological movements as the fascist leader Mussolini rose to power in Italy in 1922. Meanwhile, Britain maintained a steady, predictable course between its European concerns and its leadership as an Imperial power.

Positive efforts were made to hold the Empire together. Although it was recognised that the transition from Empire to

Commonwealth would be gradual, ties were being strengthened. Indeed in the decade after 1922, over 150,000 people from Britain emigrated to Australia, Canada, New Zealand, Kenya, Rhodesia and South Africa.

Within the Empire, India remained a 'special case'. Support from the Indian National Congress had grown and the All-India Muslim League added its voice, but the idea of Indians engaging in 'responsible' government in their own country was still unacceptable to the British rulers. Agitation and unrest in India continued and, after the Amritsar Massacre in 1919, the protests and marches were maintained, with Gandhi at the forefront. When the Congress proposed its version of a 'Commonwealth of India' in 1928, the British authorities were unresponsive, preferring to talk about a Trusteeship for India and Africa. British Liberals, in particular, persisted in criticising the tragedy of Amritsar, while upholding British rule as preventive of such atrocities in the colonial world. This ambivalent approach would persist as the century wore on.

Closer to home, in the interwar years, there was much movement in the reshaping of the United Kingdom. In Ireland, Sinn Fein showed no interest in calling off its violent campaign and wanted no part in the proposed Dublin Parliament. Finally, after a cease-fire arising from an agreement reached in 1921, the Irish Free State was established. This was an historic moment in the British Isles. The loss of one of the former constituent 'nations' it seemed had the effect of strengthening the bond between the other parts.

But, if the idea of greater democracy in the British political system was anticipated by large sections of the British people, it was an 'idea' that was less problematic for Liberals than the Conservatives. Less sure of itself was the Labour Party, which was beset with disharmonious personalities. The trade unions, to whom the Party was linked, needed to resolve both their legal status and the 'position of their funds', issues that were resolved by the Trade Disputes Act (1906) and the Trade Union Act (1913), which permitted unions to have a separate 'political fund'.

The Representation of the People Act of 1918 increased the electorate, thus bringing into the system the potential power of the working-class vote. Postwar support for the Labour Party was dramatic; and after a brief period in government in the early 1920s, the 1930s Depression would encourage sections of the population to give the Labour Party the vital support that would be needed in the future.

The question of 'Free' Trade as far as the British colonies were concerned, worked to their disadvantage. This might explain, as Robbins put it, why 'It was unfortunate that opposition to Free Trade was so closely linked to enthusiasm for Empire'. But if in 1915 the 'sacred principle' of Free Trade was 'breached', with disruption of the international economic order as a result of the war, the Gold Standard was held in abeyance until such time when a return to it was possible. This promise, though, could not be kept and Britain abandoned the Standard in September 1931, a time when the economic and industrial outlook was more grim than bright.

In the first 30 years of the twentieth century, town and countryside retained their differences in ethos and outlook. Education, academic and vocational training were contained in a system that was lacking in coherence. There was, however, much interest in religion and sport.

Church attendance was falling and even though the divide between 'church' and 'chapel' remained, the decline in religious observance had the effect of bringing about better relations among the Protestant Churches. There was a tacit agreement that the Church of England should survive.

Sport had come to play a more central part in the United Kingdom and international competition became a focus of participation and interest. The 1908 Olympic Games were held in London and in 1911 the first Indian cricket team arrived in England, a visit followed by the inaugural tour of a West Indies cricket team.

The postwar years saw robust participation in sport generally. There seemed to be a clear social distinction between those who played rugby and football, the former coming largely from the middle and upper classes, while the latter attracted the 'masses'. Developments in football gave the game unrivalled status, for although the Rugby League Cup Final was also played at Wembley, it did not generate the same sense of occasion as the Football Association Cup Final, the winners of which received the Cup from the king. Home games between England and Scotland, and Wales and Ireland, kept the pulse of British football beating at a feverish pitch. Walter Tull, one of the first black players (of whom more is said later) made his first appearance in British football.

While cricket maintained its 'Englishness', professional players from abroad were contracted to play English League cricket. The most famous player in the Lancashire League was Learie Constantine, the great all-rounder from Trinidad. As a black man, he had gained unprecedented fame in England, but at the time players did not earn a fortune.

The idea that democracy would not only threaten but destroy civilisation and the arts was strongly opposed by the economist J.A. Hobson. In literature, there were several eminent magazines, including *New Age* and *Criterion*, and among the poets, there were Rupert Brooke, Wilfred Owen and T.S. Eliot, who had arrived from the United States in 1915 and had written *The Waste Land* in 1922. It was, however, the Irish poet, W.B. Yeats who perhaps enjoyed the greatest critical acclaim at this time.

Among the pre-war novelists of note were Kipling, Joseph Conrad, H.G. Wells and James Joyce, whose *Ulysses* caused a furore in British literary circles on publication. The postwar years saw the rise to prominence of Virginia Woolf, D.H. Lawrence (his *Lady Chatterley's Lover* was banned) E.M. Forster, P.G. Wodehouse, Dorothy Sayers, John Buchan and Evelyn Waugh, whose novels of the United Kingdom and the British Empire found a ready readership. In Scotland, Hugh MacDiarmid made a name for himself and J.M. Barrie created the ever-popular *Peter Pan*, which thrilled audiences throughout Britain, while in Wales, poetry and poets were more successful than novelists.

If, as one historian suggested, Kipling was the novelist of the Empire, Edward Elgar with his 'Land of Hope and Glory' was the 'musician of Empire', a contemporary of Vaughan Williams, Gustav Holst and Samuel Coleridge Taylor. Music hall stars and songs were popular, and by the end of the war, jazz, Negro spirituals, the musicals of Kern and Gershwin, Gracie Fields, William Walton and others contributed to the mix of joyous musical styles.[2]

British art remained self-contained, though it was perhaps better than previously. Augustus John, Stanley Spencer, Wyndham Lewis, Paul Nash and Jacob Epstein were profoundly affected by the First World War. Lewis and Nash had served at the Front where, as Graham-Dixon noted, the war had 'the immediate effect of stopping up the imagination'. It was a scenario in which the 'small and stifling taste of the Bloomsbury set could persist. There was a general meek return to old genres and manners ... as if they were attempting to restore order in a disturbed world.'

Architecturally, the one work of genius of the period came from Charles Rennie MacIntosh of the Glasgow School of Art. Such innovation was, however, not to be found among British artists of the 1920s and early 1930s whose modern art, as in the case of Stanley Spencer, was 'not avant-garde but rear-guard ... not vehement, ambitious to inflame the world with visions of hectic change, but benevolent, mild and cautious'. So it was that a good deal of British art at this time 'preferred the female principle to the male as if British artists ... could not bring themselves to admire or reincarnate aggressive masculinity in their work'. Spencer's contemporary, Henry Moore, was influenced by Pablo Picasso's 'brave' drawings of the 1920s, but was also influenced by images of the pre-Columbian Americas and Africa, as depicted in the art of the Aztec and Toltec 'sculpture and the masks of ... Nigeria'.[3]

Overall, though, the arts, which inspired so much passion and interest in those involved, had yet to reach a wider British public.

Radio, television and films were among the great innovations of this period, and together and with increasing sophistication they informed the British public on a wide range of subjects; as more and more, Britain and its relations abroad became familiar and the world seemed a smaller place. Nevertheless, a 'common' culture remained an idea, because the United Kingdom was still divided by class and region and cultures – 'high', 'middle' and 'low' in turn – which reinforced the divisions.

DEVELOPMENTS FROM 1930 TO 1956

There was much talk about peace in relation to the British Empire in the immediate post-1931 years. And while the major European powers were sceptical of this relationship, the well-informed British leaders monitored the rise of Adolf Hitler and Nazism. Italy's invasion of Abyssinia was also cause for alarm in Britain. But Britain's commitment to the Second World War brought only partial involvement with other European states, and significantly it was during the war that Churchill advocated setting up a Council of Europe. Britain's independence could not, however, be maintained and when the postwar offer of Marshall Aid was made by the Americans, Britain accepted it with gratitude. Nevertheless there was also a sense that Britain should continue to play a major role in world affairs. A strengthening of Communism in Eastern Europe led to Ernest Bevin's 'consolidation of Western Europe'; and American ties with Europe were confirmed in 1949 with the formation of NATO. Just a few weeks later, the Council of Europe was formed. However, the Conservatives' return to power in 1951, with Churchill as prime minister, did not bring the country any closer to Europe, and European planners pursued their policies without regard to Britain. The balance of power in world politics had shifted dramatically: the Communists dominated Eastern Europe, while in Western Europe, several countries pursued the goal of a Common Market. After the Suez Crisis, Britain's exclusion from Europe seemed all the more implausible.

These decades were especially dramatic in Britain's relations with its colonial Empire. The presence of Mohandas Gandhi in London for the Round Table Conference in 1931 to discuss India's future was an historic occasion. The Indian leader had suspended his campaign of civil disobedience, but the British National Government felt it could not meet his demands. When, in 1935, full self-government was granted to the Indian Provinces (with the proposition of setting up a Federal Assembly) Conservatives' voices were raised against it. But what had given offence in theory turned out differently in practice. Britain committed India to the Second World War, which satisfied

Conservative die-hards, but not the Indians. This was, however, a masterful piece of political engineering by the British, who knew the momentum for Indian self-government could be delayed only in very exceptional circumstances. The war was just such a circumstance, and Stafford Cripps assured Gandhi that full self-government would indeed be granted after the war. The leaders of the Indian National Congress and the Muslim League surprised the British by calling for immediate self-government, and Congress resumed the campaign of civil disobedience. Their bold and simple demand now was that Britain should 'quit India'. The British would have none of this and when Gandhi and Nehru were imprisoned, millions of people responded by rioting – a clear signal to the British government.

Yet again, global war proved costly for Britain and it was the official duty of the new Labour government to do what had for so long been unthinkable – transfer power into responsible hands in August 1947. When the British eventually left the subcontinent, the independent states of India and Pakistan emerged, a long-awaited and joyous occasion, but one which was not without tragic consequences for millions of people who felt bound to cross the border in both directions.

Having left India, if there were any doubts about Britain's postwar military capacity, the Suez Crisis finally laid them to rest. In the years after 1956, Britain could not stem the rising tide of decolonisation and had to come to terms with the prospect of dealing with the postcolonial world.

In the early years of the period under review, National Governments were considered to be more representative than one-party governments. But, after the war, the Labour Party's rise was meteoric, and they formed the immediate postwar government, which nationalised key sectors of the economy. By 1951, however, they were in opposition to the Conservatives. The 1950s saw the abolition of food rationing, full employment and the erection of over a million homes, as Sir Anthony Eden was succeeded by Harold Macmillan.[4]

Although the United Kingdom had come through the depression (and recovered well enough) there were hidden weaknesses. If full employment concealed 'evidence of overmanning' as Robbins noted, 'similarly, fear of unemployment was a partial explanation for restrictive practices in industry and demarcation disputes between trade unions concerned about long-term security and traditional wage-differentials'. By the mid-1950s it seemed clear that endemic in the recovery was a resistance to change, for instance, the automation of industry, so vital to the United Kingdom's competitiveness in the international marketplace.

How united was the United Kingdom in these decades leading up to mid-century? Compared with previous years, this was a time, it was argued, when good relations were enjoyed by different regions. The so-called 'Irish Question' had been settled, and in Northern Ireland, the government was consolidating its position. High unemployment in the inter-war years had been accompanied by sectarian riots in Belfast. After the war, in 1949, the Republic of Ireland (formerly the Irish Free State) left the British Commonwealth and the people and Parliament of Northern Ireland were assured by the British government that they were integral to the United Kingdom.

Although Scottish self-government was aired in Stirling in 1930 with a Scottish Office, administering four departments and a Minister of State to the Scottish Office, Scotland was securely bonded within the rest of the United Kingdom. Welshmen, on the other hand, were not shy of asserting the importance of Wales as a 'nation', through their language, literature and traditions. Almost 20 years after three Welshmen, Saunders Lewis, D.J. Williams and Rev. Lewis Valentine, had shown their commitment to their 'nation', support was canvassed for a 'Parliament for Wales' by the Welsh-speaking Plaid Cymru. A Minister for Welsh Affairs and the investiture of Cardiff in 1956 as the capital were not enough to satisfy Welsh-speaking people. On the other hand, in England with all its tightly structured and evident divisions, there were no signs of withdrawing from the rest of the kingdom which, for all its diversity, remained united.

Between the 1930s and the 1950s more people took to the roads: an estimated 30 million holiday-makers visited the coasts each year. But just past mid-century, there was an even clearer shift from rail to road as the motor car, motor cycles and coaches afforded greater flexibility and convenience.

Population pressure in the large cities such as London and Glasgow justified the planning of new towns, which spawned new communities and attracted much comment, but on the whole, they did not ease the difficulties of London and other urban areas. Increasingly, agriculture was juxtaposed with the ever-expanding towns and conservation. What seemed 'irreconcilable' then (as indeed now) was how best to plan the environment so that some balance could be struck between the town and the country.

In terms of education, the 1930s were years of intense discussion, and before the decade ended more than half of the United Kingdom's elementary schools were reorganised and secondary education was investigated. In British universities there seemed to be, according to Keith Robbins, a lack of 'an agreed sense of direction and purpose'. Broadly, however, there was much educational change and in spite of differences in 'structure and ethos' in the four regions, the general trend tilted towards a unified structure.

In sport, after a decade of competition, between 1929 and 1939, the United Kingdom football teams resumed international competition with European countries and both England and Scotland participated in the 1950 World Cup which, in 1954 became a televised event.

Rugby retained its non-professional status and cricket gained in popularity. In 1932, C.L.R. James, a young writer and sports journalist at the time, had arrived in England from Trinidad and soon began writing for the *Manchester Guardian* as cricket correspondent, on the recommendation of Neville Cardus. He would continue to write on cricket for many years and eventually produced one of the greatest books on cricket, the politics of the Caribbean and himself, *Beyond a Boundary*. Almost two decades after James arrived in Lancashire, the West Indian cricket team toured England and won the series, their first Test Match series victory which, once and for all, placed Frank Worrell, Everton Weekes and Clyde Walcott among the world's greatest and best-known batsmen. The spin bowlers Sonny

Ramadhin and Alfie Valentine, were immortalised in song. For black people in England, the Caribbean and elsewhere in the Commonwealth, this cricket triumph was one to savour and, as James demonstrated, it went far beyond the sport: 'What do they know of cricket, who only cricket know'.[5]

Lawn tennis was also boosted through royal patronage and Wimbledon gained in popularity as the most prestigious tournament in world tennis. The Empire Games attracted deserved attention, being well attended by black and Asian athletes and in 1954, the Englishman Roger Bannister ran the first recorded four-minute mile.

Sport was still largely leisure, though there were some professionals by the early 1960s. Television cameras were by now ubiquitous, an intrusive eye recording most events, and it was in this period that the most famous sportsman of his time, Muhammad Ali (formerly Cassius Clay), was introduced in the boxing ring to the world. Few then though could have imagined the global impact of sport in the decades to come.

In this period, literature was not lacking in diversity, giving rise to modernism in British and the emergent colonial and postcolonial literatures. In poetry, those with established reputations included Robert Graves, Cecil Day Lewis, Louis Mac-Niece, Stephen Spender, W.H. Auden and Dylan Thomas. Among the best known novelists were Somerset Maugham, P.G. Wodehouse, Virginia Woolf, Evelyn Waugh, Graham Greene, George Orwell, C.P. Snow and Anthony Powell. The Caribbean-born writers resident in England, V.S. Naipaul, Sam Selvon and Jan Carew, had already completed their first novels. The outstanding playwrights were Sean O'Casey, Christopher Fry, Terence Rattigan and Noel Coward. In all, they constituted a formidable array of British literary talent.

On the music scene, the best of British talent was seen and heard. Michael Tippet, Benjamin Britten, Peter Pears and Vaughan Williams were well aired and featured prominently at the various concert halls; and symphony orchestras were formed in England, Scotland and Wales. Dance band music was very popular and although 'serious' classical music and 'popular' music remained distinct, in general, there was a shift in direction towards 'mass culture' as wax recording and record players became more widely available. The traditional patterns though persisted. The transition in American popular music was also in evidence in Britain, from the popular crooners Bing Crosby and Frank Sinatra to the rock'n'roll of Elvis Presley and a gallery of superb African-American singers and entertainers of different styles, including Paul Robeson, Fats Waller, Bessie Smith, Billie Holliday, Ella Fitzgerald, Nat King Cole, Harry Belafonte, Sammy Davis Jr and Winifred Atwell, the Trinidad-born pianist, whose spirituals, honky-tonk, blues, jazz, calypso and folk musical styles were important influences in the evolution of the modern British pop scene.

In the world of art, while Henry Moore and Barbara Hepworth continued to work on monumental sculpture, Graham Sutherland, Ben Nicholson and L.S. Lowry joined Paul Nash and Stanley Spencer among an outstanding group of British painters. But there was another distinctive group of painters, which included Robert McBryde, Robert Colquhoun, Lucien Freud and Francis Bacon. From the 1930s to the 1950s, according to Graham-Dixon, these artists were immersed in 'mother nature', evoking a 'mood of wistful, quiet pastoralism'. Painting from nature, the rural scene was redemptive and the fact that 'nature and the natural world' have preoccupied the 'British mind' for some four centuries is a reminder of its history, a preoccupation which is not rooted in painting, but in the 'radical theory of the Reformation – not in art, in other words, but in a tradition of anti-arts'. The artist Richard Long exemplifies this attitude to nature best in the twentieth century. If the 'early Protestants preferred God's creation to the feigned creations of men ... the real world to false images of it', Long leaves us in no doubt of his 'preference for the unformed over the formed, for nature over culture'. But Long's work ultimately 'discovers the common ground' which links it to the other end of the spectrum, to its 'apparent opposite: another iconoclastic, realist art', an art 'not about the land', but about the city. Painting the city in all its drabness had passionate adherents in Walter Richard Sickert and William Coldstream. Then came John Bratby's work in the 1950s and Lucien Freud's stark evocations of the urban environment of the dispossessed and migrants. But of all these twentieth-century British painters (whose creations fall within the 'tradition of disaffected realism') Francis Bacon was regarded as the greatest.

He did not so much deal in 'grand narrative' as in the opposite. He was not only an iconoclast, but also a 'babooner-ist', the latter powerfully depicted in his triptychs. He centred the marginal and responded to the horrors of the Second World War. In the 1930s and 1940s, he stayed in Paris where he painted 'pictorial equivalents to the literature of alienation'. If Sartre's existentialism of *Being and Nothingness* was evocative of Bacon's work, that other prominent literary figure, Samuel Beckett, was spiritually closer; and if his paintings express a randomness and isolation, a 'volatile process' reflecting man's evolution from birth to death, then paradoxically, it is from just 'such grimness' that a 'form of strength and great sense of beauty is won', his portraits underscored by 'a savage, joyous vigour and carnality which communicates not gloom but celebration'.[6]

Images on film were no less celebratory of the art of film-making. Cinema-going had become an integral part of the lives of millions of people in the 1930s. But while the war lasted and in its aftermath, the film industry was beset by financial problems,. Having enjoyed great success, Michael Balcon's Ealing Studios were sold to the British Broadcasting Corporation and from about the mid-1940s cinema audiences continued to fall. Four years later, television provided another medium through which news, current affairs, sport and entertainment programmes were projected, and what emerged from both media was a core of unrivalled British documentary film-makers, some of whom had worked on stories which included images of black and Asian people in film and television, a topic that will be considered later. In terms of culture, one of Britain's foremost venues was (and remains) the South Bank in London, with the Festival Hall as its centrepiece.

Artistic celebration was counterpoised however by a 'spiritual crisis' in the Christian churches by the mid-1950s.[7]

It is perhaps worth reiterating that for the decades under consideration, and those earlier, white British historians have said little about the story of the black and Asian presence in many of the aforementioned areas of British life. It is within this historical context that we shall resume the narrative of the black and Asian experience from the turn of the century to the end of the 1950s, a period when the culture of British racism (having evolved from 'plantocracy racism' through 'pseudo-scientific' racism)[8] appeared in new guises during the declining years of Empire, a time when W.E.B. DuBois's prophetic remark that the problem of the twentieth century is 'the problem of the colour line' had a depressingly true ring.

3 RACISM, EMPIRE AND LABOUR

Imperialism's culture was not invisible nor did it conceal its worldly affiliations and interests ... One of imperialism's achievements was to bring the world closer together and, although in the process the separation between Europeans and natives was an insidious and fundamentally unjust one, most of us should now regard the historical experience of Empire as a common one.[1]

The huge profits that poured into Britain from the Empire in large part helped the British nation to maintain the status quo, for the 'Imperial question' was a 'bread and butter' question. The extension of the British Empire in the last third of the nineteenth century continued into the twentieth century. A further 1.5 million square miles were acquired through the imperialist war of 1914–18 so that by the eve of the Second World War the British Empire's protectorates and dependencies contained approximately one-quarter of the world's population, representing most of the world's major religions and imposing its own cultural standards upon different peoples and cultures. The era of industrial capital gave way to the era of finance capital, with Britain retaining its hold as the great colonial exploiter. This exploitation was vital to Britain's well-being and, in the face of a rising challenge from British workers, Cecil Rhodes said in 1895:

I was in the East End of London yesterday and I attended a meeting of the 'unemployed' I listened to the wild speeches which were just a cry for 'bread', 'bread', 'bread', and on my way home I pondered over the scene and I became more than ever convinced of the importance of imperialism ... My cherished idea is a solution for the social problem. In order to save the 40,000,000 inhabitants of the United Kingdom from a bloody civil war, we, colonial statesmen, must acquire new lands to settle the surplus population, to provide new markets for the goods produced by them in the factories and the mines. The Empire, as I have always said, is a bread and butter question. If you want to avoid civil war, you must become an imperialist.[2]

But imperialism means war and Britain had for centuries proved its military might. Following the end of the Boer War and, as indicated earlier, after the First World War, Winston Churchill felt there was need for a department of government for defence.[3] While Europe was on the brink of taking dramatic political turns, Britain maintained a steady, predictable course between its European concerns and its leadership as an Imperial power. Indeed, positive efforts were made to hold the British Empire together, for fear that it might dissolve.

The vast majority of the Empire's population were colonised, non-white people, the mainstay of an Empire that had to be kept under control. To ensure this, British rulers adopted a brand of racism more sophisticated than the cruder plantocracy version, which was widely disseminated through literature and in the education system, which together inculcated in young minds the idea that black and Asian peoples were innately inferior to the white Britons who ruled them. Especially in the nineteenth century, this myth underscored the thoughts and literature[4] of influential Britons, thus perpetuating the belief that Asians and Africans were incapable of self-government. Not surprisingly, racists abounded from the last third of the nineteenth century and, as Philip Curtin notes, 'virtually every European concerned with Imperial theory or Imperial adminis-tration believed that physical racial appearance was an outward sign of inborn propensities, inclinations and abilities'.[5] Thus racial differences informed much of what passed for British colonial policy.

In India, British rulers, not shy of their superiority, expected and demanded of their colonial subjects a devoted sense of inferiority tantamount to the 'qualities of a good hound'.[6] Either as loveable pets or occasionally elevated to the status of obedient school children, this Imperial perception of Indians justified their exclusion and the paramountcy of white supremacy, which had a profound believer in the Prime Minister, Balfour, who led the British government at the beginning of the twentieth century.

So the intertwined relationship between Britain and her colonies bred superior/inferior perceptions and attitudes on the part of the British ruling elites, who were determined to infiltrate every field of intellectual endeavour, starting with the very young in school, both at home and abroad. In British schools, history books reflected the 'British' version of Other (colonial) peoples, who were portrayed as uncivilised and, in India, Lord Macaulay, the historian and politician who had earlier issued his famous Minute on Indian Education, set the standard for generations of aspiring Indians.

It was, however, the effect on children at home that generated special interest. More cool-headed observers felt obliged to comment. J.A. Hobson, the author of *Imperialism* (1902), noted the 'persistent attempt to seize' the British school system on behalf of imperialist designs and warned that by capturing the childhood of a country and poisoning its 'early understanding of history by false ideals and pseudo-heroes ... to feed the always overweening pride of race ... to fasten this base insularity of mind and morals upon the little children of a nation and to call it patriotism is as foul an abuse of education as it was possible to conceive'.[7]

If this was the problem in Britain, imagine how much more detrimental this would have been for the children of the 'victims of racism', who peopled the Empire. As previously, school texts and history books[8] in particular, published in the first decade and a half of the twentieth century, continued to propagate the essential Imperial idea that the guidance of the British and other Europeans was necessary. In this literature, there was hardly a hint of recognition of the human agency of those whom they governed so cavalierly. Such paternalism underpinned the trade, commerce and profitability of the British Empire, which was always a target of counter-aggression from the subject peoples, who had become enmeshed in a long-standing and deeply involved relationship.

THE ABOLITION OF THE SYTEM OF EAST INDIAN INDENTURE

Change in the Indian indentured labourers' circumstances came only with the change in sugar production. The shift towards fewer estates and larger central sugar mills resulted in the movement from an estate-based population to a rural smallholder or peasant population. Mohandas Gandhi was right in identifying Lord Curzon as the first Viceroy of India to recognise that the indentured Indians were mere helots of the Empire. Gandhi's own efforts in South Africa helped to highlight some of the problems of the Indians as important politically. And though they represented opposite ends of the political spectrum, both Gandhi and Curzon called the system into question.[9]

Thereafter the movement to abolish Indian indentureship gathered momentum. In South Africa, Indians were on the march; in Mauritius, they were moved to periodic protest; in the Caribbean, the only political movement was that of Creole blacks who campaigned for self-government in such organisations as the Trinidad Workingmen's Association, which was opposed to further Indian immigration as a threat to wages and living standards. In British Guiana, the People's Association, a black organisation, protested against taxation levied to promote immigration. It was against this background of colonial resistance to indentured labour that the Sanderson Committee began its work.

Elsewhere in the Empire, the abolition issue proceeded towards a resolution in the inter-war years, reinforced by Gandhi's earlier struggle against oppressive laws in South Africa through his mass campaign of *satyagraha*, in which the majority of participants were indentured and ex-indentured Indians.

The news quickly reached Whitehall and Delhi, provoking a response from the principal administrators. In an extraordinary speech, Lord Hardinge stated that the Indians in South Africa had violated 'as they intended to violate, those laws, with full knowledge of the penalties involved ... In all this they have the sympathies of India – deep and burning – and not only of India but of those like myself' who had feelings of sympathy for India.[10] The British Cabinet considered his recall from India, but desisted for fear of an Indian backlash. Against this background of events, the McNeill and Chimman Lal Report on *The Condition of Indian Immigrants in The Four British Colonies: Trinidad, British Guiana, Jamaica and Fiji and the Dutch Colony of Surinam* was being considered.

While Gandhi (who was preparing to return to India) recognised the importance of the Viceroy's intervention, with Indian independence in mind, he attached greater importance to *satyagraha*, his method of 'passive' resistance. By 1915, Indian feeling about emigration was still only partly aroused and in January, Gandhi returned to India, where several organisations were founded especially to fight 'coolie' emigration. From his subcontinental base, Gandhi continued to speak out against indenture. Finally, in 1917, Indian indenture officially ended, though many Indians were still bound by their indentures in the sugar colonies. Two years later, all indentures were terminated in British Guiana, though still outstanding was the fact that the indenture system, as a working reality, had to be cleared away once and for all. In theory at least, the labourers were now free and many returned to India only to find that industrial conditions there, after the famine of 1920, were unfavourable. They experienced great difficulty in obtaining employment, and many found themselves strangers in the country; more powerfully, many of the India-born came to realise that their long residence overseas had rendered them unfit for the old social conditions.[11] Strangely, the now familiar bounds of the plantations offered the only hope. So the Indian diaspora, both during and in the post-indentureship phase, achieved a settled, permanent foothold alongside the African diaspora, their historical experience of Empire more or less a common one. Thereafter, Indians continued to emigrate, but their concern was not with the colonies, where the Indians remained the labouring poor. Instead, they looked towards East and South Africa, where Indians were trying to establish

themselves as urban middle-class communities. Their attention was directed especially to East Africa, Kenya and Uganda.

The first major threat to the status of overseas Indians emerged
in Kenya, where the white settlers plotted to force the hand of
the British government and where the Indians were now mostly
traders. Despite protest and non-cooperation, the East African
Indians were forced to accept an uneasy middle position
between the Europeans and the Africans.

In the 1920s, the Indian community in South Africa came
under attack as legislation eroded their rights; those who left the
country could not return, and dependants were denied entry.
They were also profoundly affected by the Class Areas Bill of
1925, which confined Indians to separate residential and
commercial areas. The Indian government and politicians
protested loudly, yet they could do little to confront South
African racism. Motilal Nehru told the Indian Congress in 1928
that the best way to help Indians overseas was to act 'to gain our
freedom here' (that is, in India).[12] Clearly colonial exploitation
was far from over, though it would be tempered by grudging
concessions to an already impoverished labour force. How did
this colonial labour dimension relate to the British labour
movement? And how did British politicians respond to workers'
needs after the debacle of the two world wars? Let us consider
the second question first.

BRITISH LABOUR AND IMPERIALISM

Twentieth-century British politicians, including Winston
Churchill, Lord Cranbourne and Ernest Bevin, were unanimous
in echoing Rhodes's concern that the Empire was the essential
economic base which would, if maintained, save British workers
from starvation. They believed that the exploitation and degradation of colonial workers were indispensable in safeguarding
the standard of living of certain sections of the British working
class. Implicit in this argument is the fact that the British
economy was dependent on colonial revenues for much of its
well-being. Concentration on foreign investment, as opposed to

industrial renewal and neglect of home investment, would have serious repercussions, at least in the short term. But while the British ruling elites could amass huge profits at the expense of, starvation-level standards of living in many Caribbean colonies, Africa and India,[13] attention was deflected from the increasing lack of industrial and agricultural investment in Britain. There was every reason for optimism that British workers would continue to benefit from colonial exploitation. However, the good times were evidently curtailed, as prior to the First World War, nearly 40 per cent of British imports were no longer paid for by exports. This import surplus rose dramatically and although initially it was covered by income from overseas investment (such as financial commissions and shipping), later even overseas income could not cover the unpaid imports, resulting in a net deficit in the balance of payments.[14]

If imperialism means forceful aggression, then the imperialist basis of the British economy was clearly founded on an unstable dependence on colonial exploitation which was bound to lead to violent reaction. The disturbances or 'riots' (an emotive word, though at times an appropriate description, which was more often than not deliberately used in the records to suggest insubordination on the part of the colonised) as they were called in India, Africa, Trinidad, Jamaica and elsewhere in the Caribbean, during the decades before the Second World War, were symptomatic of the weakness of British Imperialism.

On the question of the British labour movement's attitude and policy towards the Empire in the 25 years from 1899 to 1924, given that 'labour' concerns were primarily about the organisations and functions of a group of people and not a doctrine, Labour parties can be doctrinally collectivist like the British Labour Party after 1918, or individualist, like the South African Labour Party. When, therefore, we look for something 'distinctively labour' in Labour's imperial policy, we can expect it to be doctrinally neutral. But significantly, and paradoxically, British Labour had consistently backed labour movements and parties in the Empire, whether they practised racial discrimination, as in South Africa, or civil disobedience, as in India. This was a distinctively 'Labour' approach in a period when there was very little criticism of the Empire from the ranks of British labour. On the other hand, British labour opposed all attempts by governments or businessmen in the Empire to encourage anti-trade union labour and strike-breaking. But this doctrinal neutralism adapted itself poorly to Labour's status as a national party. It comes as no surprise, therefore, that the strong 'socialist' element in Labour's imperial policy has been more lasting and has produced a more coherent set of attitudes.[15] It was only after 1918 that Labour's policy for the Empire became distinctively non-socialist, though it remained crucial to the economic interests of British workers. Repeatedly, contradictions appeared in the speeches of Labour ministers who believed in combining the philanthropic aims of Empire with the goals of economic exploitation. In this, the true relationship of the British and colonial working classes was revealed, the legacy of Labour Imperialism. It is in this context that we must look at the experience of black and Asian workers (the casualties of Empire) prior to, between and immediately after the two world wars, particularly those people who had settled in the port communities of Cardiff and Liverpool.

THE CONSEQUENCES OF EMPIRE: CARDIFF AND LIVERPOOL

Over the centuries of British trade with Asia, Africa, the Americas and the West Indies, many blacks and Asians were employed on British ships which left Bristol, Liverpool and London, the main ports where black men had come and gone and indeed settled. By the turn of the twentieth century, Cardiff had become a port with a sizeable and well-established non-white, multi-racial community,[16] located principally in the Bute Town dockside area. The mildness of the climate and the availability of work at the end of the First World War attracted many black seamen. However, in spite of trade union insistence that all seamen, irrespective of colour, should be paid at the going rates, black seamen engaged in the West African trade from Liverpool received a lower rate of pay than white seamen. More generally, because crews signed on at non-British ports earned far less than crews in Britain, the wage gap was wide enough for wage manipulation, thus placing black seamen at a great disadvantage.

If times were hard for white seamen, they were even harder for those who were black and/or Asian. With the closure of the war industries, demobilisation of white soldiers and the consequent laying up of ships, West Africans, Asians and West Indians found it difficult to survive. To add to their distress, the ship owners, shipmasters and the trade unions adopted the provocative employment principle of 'our own people first'. Tensions between black and white men rose, and it was against this background that serious racial riots broke out in Cardiff in 1919 with echoes of a similar predicament among black people in other British ports.

It was difficult to avoid the charge that racial prejudice was the determining factor in the Cardiff docks. For regardless of the views of the problem taken at the National Union of Seamen's headquarters, a few of the local officials exploited the opportunity to encourage black repatriation. They aroused public animosity by citing the black community's expense to the public rates and in this connection, the *Western Mail* and *South Wales Echo* reported George Reed, Secretary of the local branch of the union, as saying that thousands of impoverished black men had unrestricted entry into Cardiff. He, like the government officials of the day, had no doubt that if these men were going to be displaced, they should be repatriated.[17]

The citizens of Cardiff were warned by the *Western Mail* that

Morality and cleanliness are as much matters of geography as they are dependent on circumstances. The coloured men who have come to dwell in our cities are being made to adopt a standard of civilisation they cannot be expected to understand. They are not imbued with moral codes similar to our own, and they have not assimilated our conventions of life. They come into contact with white women, principally those who unfortunately are of loose moral character with the result that a half-caste population is brought into the world.[18]

This was a burden which the newspaper concluded it could not tolerate, ignoring the fact that there were many adults in the Tiger Bay area of Cardiff who had been born there and had become grandparents there. For these people, there was no going back. Cardiff was their home. Many continued to be philosophical, drawing some consolation by reasoning that if peace had brought the indignities attendant upon unemployment, poverty, prejudice, violence and desperation to the 'black' community, the Second World War offered the hope that things could not get much worse. In the deepening distress of wartime, there was always a glimmer of hope, often eloquently expressed through one or two role models. Though a fading memory, let us pause and ponder a true British multicultural hero, Walter Tull, one of the growing number of people of mixed black and white parents in Britain, a man whose life was brief, but none the less memorable.

WALTER TULL

Walter's father had come to Britain in 1786 from the Caribbean island of Barbados and had met and married an English woman from Folkestone. Though Walter's grandfather was a slave, his father used his relative freedom to good effect. He became a joiner and, as a devout Christian, he attended the Methodist Church in Folkestone. Walter was one of six children and was just seven when his mother died; a tragedy compounded two years later with the death of his father. The care and responsibility of six children was too great for Walter's stepmother, so he and his brother Edward were sent to London in 1898, where they were admitted to the Bethnal Green Methodist orphanage.

Both boys learned well the lessons taught to them. In time, Edward established a thriving dental practice in Glasgow, while Walter, who was apprenticed as a printer, also excelled in the field of sports as a footballer, playing the game as an amateur for Clapton, before signing as a professional for Tottenham Hotspur in 1908, the second black professional footballer in Britain. (The honour of being the first went to the goalkeeper Arthur Wharton of Darlington and Preston North End.) Unlike Wharton in goal, Walter Tull was free to roam in attack, the first black 'outfield' player, mesmerically weaving his way forward and goalwards. Soon his ability and superior skill attracted growing interest, not least in the press. His rising star status was recognised by *The Daily Chronicle*, publicity which, it seemed, had a positive effect on him.

Not surprisingly, Tull's sporting life as a professional took him to the most revered soccer venues in Britain and in 1909 he travelled with his team to play Bristol City. And there in the former slave port, members of the home crowd hurled unsporting racial abuse at him during the game, using language that was described as being 'lower than Billingsgate'. Such unprecedented behaviour in the premier British professional sports arena was a shocking experience for both Tull and his team mates. How much this incident affected his career is indicated by the fact that in the next season, he played only three times and the following year, he was sold to Northampton Town. Were 'Spurs' glad to relieve themselves of an awkward problem that was likely to go on recurring and thus ignore the issue of racism on the terraces, rather than confront it as unacceptable behaviour? As far as they were concerned, it seemed that the price of Tull's departure, a 'heavy transfer fee', was adequate compensation and that was the end of the matter, honourably settled. But this was not the end of the talented Tull, who soared in Northampton Town's ratings, having played 110 games for the first team and regarded as 'probably their biggest star'. As it was, his star quality was not lost on those who were most knowledgeable about the game. In 1914, he was sought by Glasgow Rangers, but before he could sign up, the outbreak of the First World War robbed football fans north of the border of seeing him display and further develop his dazzling athleticism, his rare sporting skills.

Although it may not have been obvious at the time, his approach to sport and to life was guided by certain Christian principles. Indeed, the time had come for him to move on from the playing fields of Britain to the European battlefields of the First World War. Underlying his calm exterior was a depth of character which would be tested in the extreme when he joined the Middlesex Regiment's 17th Battalion. Two years into the war, he had conducted himself with distinction enough to become a sergeant. How did this happen to the boy from the orphanage? Confronted with the continuous hellish bombardment of the enemy's guns, exploding shells, the noise, the dead and dying all about him, he nevertheless ventured forward. However, his daring led him to contract 'trench fever' which got him out of the war zone because he was certified as an invalid and brought back home.

But, as soon as he was fit and well again, he took another unusual and ambitious step by joining the officer cadet training school in Scotland.[19] If 'Negroes' were forbidden from assuming 'command' as officers, how did this man do it? One explanation is that he had enough charisma to warrant recommendation to the school by no lesser persons than his superiors. So on behalf of Britain, in 1917, Tull was sent to the Italian Front, where he again displayed characteristic qualities such as 'gallantry and coolness'. The following year he was in France, engaged in the second battle of the Somme. Here, the fighting was fierce and relentless; not yet 30 years of age, he was killed. Although he was eulogised by his fellow officers as 'popular', 'brave' and 'conscientious', courageous, friendly and faithful, his passing was largely ignored by British society and, as a consequence, his monumental efforts and unusual achievements remained obscure, hidden for several decades.

THE TIGER BAY COMMUNITY

Originally known as Bute Town, Tiger Bay was the name given to the fast-growing and colourful port area of Cardiff by Portuguese seamen who regarded the approach to the docks as like coming into a 'Bay of Tigers'. So, in its unique way, it proved to be down the years, as other descriptions, usually negative, were imposed upon this part of the town. Soon it was viewed as being 'exotic' which became synonymous with being foreign. The growing presence of British Commonwealth sailors and seamen added to the Bay's cosmopolitanism and, it seemed, a corresponding fear gripped the white population, who became more and more judgemental and xenophobic about the place and its people.

Many street names in Bute Town: Angelina, Nelson, Sophia, Maria, Frances, Henry, Christina, Patrick and of course, Bute Street, for example, are familiar, and so too are the Glamorgan Canal and the Pier Head Building. These streets became legendary during and after the First World War and the 'First War of Tiger Bay', as the racist attacks during the 1919 Cardiff riots were officially called. Since then the people of various cultural backgrounds have settled down to normal life. Through the good and bad times, they have helped each other and, given the constraints, lived lives as full and law-abiding as people anywhere else in the United Kingdom. Yet Tiger Bay continues to have a bad press and a bad name; a place more to be feared than respected. Insiders, however, those born and bred in Tiger Bay, tell another story.

Children growing up in the 1940s like Neil Sinclair remember the seaport, the seamen and the streets of the community. The songs they sang were especially haunting, recalling days past, yet ever-present in the collective memory. Since the last quarter of the nineteenth century, black Caribbean, African, Asian and Middle Eastern peoples have been visiting Tiger Bay where many married local women and settled down. So intermarriage between black men and white women, though few and far between in the nineteenth century was, by the turn of the twentieth century, much more in evidence, though the impression was given by official investigators at the time of the Cardiff riots and long after that the city had a problem in the form of 'half-caste' children, the result often of loving and lasting unions between non-white seamen and 'fallen' white women. Thus many Afro-Celtic families were already well established before the Cardiff 'Crisis' of the 1930s.

Though a sense of community grew stronger in the 1940s and 1950s, times were often hard and those with some ambition or talent had to look elsewhere to earn a livelihood; others left the Bay for various parts of Britain and the wider world. The connection between the Bay's seamen and the different ports that they had visited meant an infusion of new ideas and experiences, which enriched the community. By the 1950s, as a new generation reached their teens, old Loudoun

Square became a central meeting place for residents, where the song 'Tiger-Bay-ee' was often sung.

Naturally, the Tiger Bay youths of the 1950s came to reflect upon their past: to re-run memories of powerful images in the films they had seen starring Paul Robeson (a regular visitor to the Bay), especially in *Proud Valley*, which was shot on location in Wales. These young non-white people were proud to see a black man filling the silver screen at the local church-cum-cinema. Indeed, many of the extras for Robeson's film *Sanders of the River*, made at Elstree Studios had come from Tiger Bay. And then, of course, there was J. Lee Thompson's film *Tiger Bay*, made in the 1950s and starring Horst Buckholst, in which Neil Sinclair (who later wrote The *Tiger Bay Story*) appeared as a boy. In all, these films brought Tiger Bay to the attention of the world.

Music also excited strong passions in some youths among whom were a few female singers, including Shirley Bassey, one of the brightest prospects who came to London, recorded popular hit songs, travelled the world and achieved well-deserved international stardom.

Nevertheless, Tiger Bay and the Bute Docks remained home for many, an unusual diversity of people, who inhabited the areas known as 'Up the Bay' and 'Down the Docks': an array of peoples – Spaniards, Portuguese, Africans, West Indians, Indians, Maltese, Arabs, Somalis, Italians, Greeks, Turks, Chinese, Malays, Ukrainian, Estonian and Scandinavian, among others.

The fact that these men had local wives added to the cultural diversity of this extraordinary square mile, characterised by Arab butchers, the Indian restaurants, the Greek and Italian coffee shops and milk bars, social clubs, dance halls, pubs, shops, markets and the sheer profusion of colour and variety[20] of this unique and vibrant community.

In the inter-war period, the black presence in Liverpool, deeply embedded and intertwined with the local culture and politics over the centuries, had conditioned the attitude of white people in the city, because their collective experiences were so inextricably linked with West Africa, the slave trade, slavery and the African diaspora. Here, too, there was high unemployment

among the black population; and after the First World War, the
area suffered from the severe effects of the depressions of the
1920s and 1930s. Black workers were usually the last hired and
first fired, until the onset of the Second World War brought a
change in many black workers' position, as the wartime demand
for munitions generated demand for skilled labour on Merseyside. Some of this demand was filled by West Indian volunteers
and, once again, in wartime, the government found a way of
exploiting black labour.

So it was that amidst the circumstances of war that hundreds
of West Indians volunteered to come to Britain under a scheme
of development and welfare relating to the West Indies, organised by the Ministry of Labour and the Colonial Office, with the
object of increasing war production, a scheme that was legitimised because it was regarded as contributing towards the relief
of unemployment in the colonies. No doubt, the West Indians
were so ravaged by poverty and joblessness at home that they
felt there was little or nothing to lose by 'going away', though
there were those who enlisted for British service because they
felt a sense of loyalty to the Empire. British officials welcomed
their efforts, including those of a number of courageous women.

Until recently, with the publication of *West Indian Women at
War*, little had been published on black women's contribution
during the Second World War. Joyce Croney, Nadia Catouse,
Esther Armaegon, Gwen Jones, Connie Mark, Lillian Bader,
Odessa Gittens, Marjorie Griffiths, Louise Osbourne and
Camilla DuBoulay-Devaux, among others, should be remem-
bered and celebrated for their heroic work in the Auxiliary
Territorial Service. These West Indian women knew well the
dangers of war, but they also experienced the ugliness of racial
prejudice in Britain. In moving accounts of their lives, we get a
new dimension of the black war and postwar experience in
Britain and the Caribbean. 'The recruitment of women into the
Army had a significant impact on the Armed services, society
and the women recruits themselves,' wrote Ben Bousquet and
Colin Douglas. 'The British military establishment, with its
entrenched sexism, was sent into a state of virtual apoplexy ...
black women had to deal with not one form of discrimination,
but a cocktail of prejudices.' Indeed, the stories of these women

confirm the insidious presence of British racism in the Second World War.[21]

In the aftermath of war, the continued presence of black workers on Merseyside led to a policy of keeping them in gainful employment. Not all those who came were skilled, which meant there was much flexibility and on-the-job training. But the persistence of racial discrimination, more often than not, mirrored their experience. Futile official and employers' attempts at arguing the contrary only masked the truth for there was enough evidence that discrimination in employment against black people was a fact.

For both the government and private employers, black workers had become a cause for concern now that their colonial war contribution had been made. On the other hand, black workers had set themselves certain standards and were very sensitive about work which was 'unpleasant and below their dignity'. They were prone to interpret being given such work as an example of prejudice and discrimination against them, a theme that would rankle wherever they happened to be employed. For their part employers did little to improve the situation and justified their prejudices often by exploiting differences between the available groups of workers at their command.

How did these West Indians fare in their relations with the British trade unions, which were now in their postwar ascendancy? At about this time, trade unionism was still in its infancy in the West Indies so for many West Indians this was a new experience, which was met with a variety of responses. While some became active, holding office in the Amalgamated Engineering Union (AEU), for example, the majority of them were apathetic.

Before the scheme ended in 1946 many changes in employment were introduced, with the result that there was greater flexibility between contingents and among different firms. At the end of the scheme some private employers had taken on one or two West Indians, but the hard experience for this group of workers, generally, in the immediate postwar period was redundancy and loss of earnings. From 1946, unemployment remained a central issue in Liverpool and the Northwest, while Merseyside was 'above the average' for Britain as a whole. The policy of setting up new industries in the area did not move fast enough to compensate for the decline in employment.[22]

With no future in Britain, many considered the prospect of returning to the West Indies. Sir Frank Stockdale, who said at the beginning of the Scheme that it would make 'a small contribution towards relieving unemployment' in the West Indies, seemed to have forgotten the serious implications of the war and the prospect of repatriation. If the global conflict had offered opportunities for workers from the West Indies to escape from unemployment, low wages and poverty to the relative security of the war effort in Britain, repatriation was cold comfort, the sad realisation for many who had returned home to familiar impoverishment. As expected, many of these repatriated workers found themselves as part of an influx of West Indians who were compelled by circumstances to make their way back to Britain in 1948[23] and thereafter. From the volunteers of the West Indies, we turn now to the war contribution of the Indians.

INDIANS BEFORE AND AFTER THE TWO WORLD WARS

Indian soldiers in Britain during Victoria's reign, especially on major royal occasions, provided a sumptuous display of the majesty and splendour of the British Indian Empire. Eventually, there was a shift from the symbolic to the real, and Indian soldiers were called upon, not only to defend India, but to serve the wider interests of Britain in colonial conflicts in places as far apart as China and Egypt. But it is significant that the British were careful in not allowing Indians to shoot at the white opposition in the Boer War, essentially a war between white men and conducted far from Britain. This limited engagement on the part of the Indians was not to last, for when the First World War began in Europe, Britain could not afford to forgo the potential force of the vast Indian Army.

Before 1914, the Indian Army, estimated at 155,000, was commanded by 15,000 British officers; and among the most loyal of the Indian soldiers were Gurkhas, Jats, Pathans, Rajputs and Sikhs. But, although many were outstanding combatants, they could not join the ranks and authority of European officers; to achieve the status of 'commissioned officer', Indians had to wait until the First World War had ended.[24]

Their wartime contribution was, however, not only financial, but also made in terms of manpower and services. What surprised many was that at a time when Indians were vehemently protesting and campaigning for India's freedom, the Raj had managed to rally support for its cause, not just from Indian princes, but also from Indian nationalists such as Bannerjea, Naoroji and Surendranath. For their part, India's Muslims, represented by the Aga Khan, assured the British of their loyalty; and on behalf of those students and Indians resident in Britain, Gandhi informed the British government of their willingness to make their contribution as responsible members of the British Empire.

The British had perceived and treated the Indians like children for so long that many people (not least the Indians themselves) were curious to know if the British government would now allow Indian soldiers to fight at the battlefront. They did not have to wait long. Without consulting the Indians, Britain committed India to the war and any lingering doubts about India's support were dispelled by the end of hostilities in 1918, when an estimated 1.3 million Indians constituted the Indian Army, a phalanx of recruits second only to the British troops.

While the war lasted, the need became so desperate that Britain had no alternative but to send Indians to the front. Some of them, overwhelmed by so novel and profound an experience, felt they had to record their thoughts of service in Europe. They were especially surprised in turn by the extreme temperatures and changeable weather, the lack of food and the incessant, fearful and ever-deafening sound of guns and exploding shells, and the stench of disease and death. Instances of mistrust of the British authorities were also recorded; as was the Indians' discomfiture with the disruption of their religious observances and their attitude towards the dead. The horrors of war in the trenches left indelible impressions, as they shot and were shot at by white men.

Some Indians were hardened, others were philosophical in their predicament.[25]

Arising from the chaos and carnage, Indian doctors were drafted in to care for the Indian wounded, in England. But although the war had brought into being good relations between Britain and India, the more discerning British government officials were only too aware of the simmering tensions and agitations in India. And how right these men proved to be, as deeply ingrained attitudes surfaced in Britain, reflecting the alleged superiority of white people over black and brown peoples. It was felt that white women should not be allowed to get too close to 'inferior' dark men. Sexual relations between Indian soldiers and British women had to be avoided, indeed discouraged, for if Indians became familiar with British women, such relations could have harmful effects on continued white rule in India. (The idea of 'race' and colour would also come into play in the relations between black and white American soldiers and British women in the Second World War.) The erection of walls at the Kitchener Hospital during the First World War to prevent Indians from mixing with whites was a physical manifestation of the mental barriers that racism had failed to accommodate.

These varied impressions of the war, England, the British people and Europe by Indian soldiers were conveyed to their correspondents in India, and whether they intended it or not, certain barriers were breached. Many openly expressed both their appreciation and 'kindness' of the English people they had met and their own reservations about the ruling elite. They were also deeply impressed by European technological advances and the availability of education for children. Moreover, the profoundly sad experience arising from human conflict had a healing effect and generated a sense of accommodation of the existing differences between Indians of various regional, tribal, religious and caste backgrounds who, of necessity, lived in amity. Uppermost in the minds of most Indians though was the nagging question: How would Britain respond to India's call for freedom after the war?

With the wartime experience still fresh in their minds, there was a resurgence of nationalist feeling; and more and more the imagery and words they frequently used in letters were evocative of being 'servants' and 'slaves'. Instead of making them less assertive, the war had deepened their resentment of British rule in India. The barbarism of white rule which the Indians had experienced was a matter which Englishmen could not be proud of, especially when they persisted in accusing the Indians of barbarous behaviour, a myth which they had so carefully and masterfully constructed over the years. In combat too, the Indians proved their worth. Whatever else the Great War might have done for Indians, there was little doubt that they could not any longer continue to be appeased by the temporary palliatives of fine words and mere reforms. They would accept nothing short of Indians deciding their own future.

Some two decades after the First World War, the Indians' worst fears were realised as Britain was again engaged in global conflict. Its enemy, as before, was Germany, though this time, the country was under the direction of the dictator, Adolf Hitler. Again, India's loyalty (by no means unanimous, but no less genuine) was to be tested as Europeans squabbled with each other for world pre-eminence and national security. The rise of fascism was most alarming to Britons, whose considerable interests were threatened; and with the outbreak of the Second World War in 1939, the Viceroy of India ignored Indian leaders and forced India once again to make wartime sacrifices, an attitude which confirmed the worst fears of many Indian nationalists. Many were reminded that almost 20 years earlier, Indians had gone to Britain's aid, serving progressively in a wide range of activity, so that by the end of hostilities, an estimated 2.5 million Indian troops were deployed around the globe: in Europe, in keeping the Japanese at bay in the East and in the Middle East.[26] A European-inspired global conflict had once again engulfed the peoples of the Empire, and Indians, regardless of their nationalist pride and gender, came forward to defend Britain's interests, if need be with their lives.

Amongst the most unusual of the decorated Indians was Noor Inayat Khan, an extraordinary Indian woman of truly outstanding ability and courage. Born in Moscow in 1914, the daughter of Inayat Khan, she was one of four children. Life was tough for the Khan family when they moved to England, but their belief in Islam saw them through the worst times. The family then went to Paris, where Inayat Khan pursued his work for the Sufi religious persuasion and when he died, seven years later in India, Noor had just entered her teens. She would have been by then, and in the years that followed, deeply respectful of, and impressed by her father's learning – his knowledge of music, religion and literature. She not only studied music, but also took a degree at the Sorbonne in 1938 and demonstrated her versatility in the arts by writing music and short stories. But this relatively tranquil period was interrupted when the family was forced to flee from France to Britain in 1940, and Noor volunteered for service in the Women's Auxiliary Air Force. She adopted the name 'Nora' and learned to operate as a wireless operator. A few months later, she joined the Royal Air Force Bomber Command where her 'intelligence work' became more complex and demanding. As a wireless operator in the War Office, her fluency in French and knowledge of France qualified her for work across the English Channel in assisting the French Resistance.

This was her first return visit to France. Yet the context of that time and place was never forgotten. She was much concerned with the movement for freedom in India and fully aware that Nazism and Islam were strange bedfellows and found this period of her life to be more uncertain than ever before. The security she had hitherto known had been replaced by harsh reality. Soon after her arrival in Paris, she narrowly escaped the Germans, but refused to return to England. This was the moment of truth; her life and work were now in Paris, where she continued to elude the enemy. Eventually, in 1943, she was captured by the Germans and, as her interrogators found, she was stubborn. A month after her capture, she was taken to Germany, where she was executed. Her service, courage and bravery were not unrecognised. Two years later, the George Cross[27] was posthumously awarded to her, an honour symbolic of one woman's contribution amidst monstrous forces that surrounded her short life.

But for the moment, though fascism may have been defeated, India was still unfree.

What was the experience of Indians in Scotland between the two world wars? The end of the First World War saw the return of soldiers and many Lascars to their small port communities, especially in Glasgow. But these seamen (and other black workers) found it difficult to stay employed, largely because, as in Cardiff and Liverpool, white workers and their trade unions were opposed to competition from Asian and black workers for the few jobs. It was felt therefore that these 'alien' workers should, as it were, be blacked. And so the National Sailors and Firemen's Union and the National Union of Ship Stewards, Cooks, Butchers and Bakers called for a ban on the employment of aliens, who had so valiantly laboured and fought for Britain in the war.

Hitherto, the Indian seamen had not seen this side of their white co-workers. White aggression led to violent and ugly scenes in Glasgow early in 1919, as riots broke out and black men were hunted down. This was racism, and for the 130 black seamen in Glasgow at this time, the future seemed bleak, a plight their fellow blacks in most parts of Britain also experienced. Perhaps the most depressing aspect of this confrontation was the collusion of the British government with employers and the trade unions which denied alien black workers their eligibility for 'out of work donation'. For Indian and black seamen, their contribution in the defence of Britain now aroused mixed, even bitter feelings. Many Indians thought it best to seek a living elsewhere. Some went back to India, others left for England, but most of them stayed in and around the ports of Scotland, hoping for the tide in their lives to turn.

Insecure, both individually and as a group, they fought a deepening sense of disorientation, and perhaps this was enough to discourage the settlement (at least until about 1920) of Lascars and ex-servants in Scotland. They preferred door-to-door peddling, a pattern of employment which began to change in the early 1920s, as more Indians made their way to Scotland from India. These newcomers were neither seamen nor ex-servants, but migrants in search of a better life than they had had in India.

The exodus was caused by the lack of jobs in industry. As a result, by 1920, millions of landless peasants were without a livelihood. The stark alternative was emigration. Many opted for relocation to different parts of the subcontinent, while others went to various British colonies. But with immigration controls operating in certain Dominions and colonies, the best prospect for the Indian migrant, as a British subject, was to take advantage of the open-door policy of immigration from the British Commonwealth in Britain.

So, it was against this background that an influx that had started in the nineteenth century, continued into the first quarter of the twentieth century. Before the mid-1920s there were 'no settled' Asian communities in Scotland and such groupings as there were that approximated a settlement, first appeared in Scotland around this time in Glasgow, where an estimated 20–30 Indians were accommodated in four houses which they owned. This was a significant achievement, and from then on there was a gradual rise in the number of Indians, a pattern which provided the conditions for further emigration and the settlement of Scotland's Indian community.[28]

Among these early migrants was Nathoo Mohammed, a man who was central to the growth and development of the Asian community in Scotland. Born in the village of Kot Bedal in the district of Jullundur in 1892, Nathoo's Muslim parents were small farmers. He did not get the opportunity of attending school, but had a strong sense of enterprise and responsibility, especially after he married and began his own family. He left his village for Bombay, where he was engaged as a Lascar on a British ship, a job which he did for over a year before he decided in 1919 to move on, to take the chance of making a living in Glasgow. When Nathoo arrived there were few Indians, and no 'settled' Indian community, only a transitory population, with many beggars among them. He was encouraged, however, by the fact that he was not alone; there were an estimated 130 black seamen in Glasgow at the time and it is possible that Nathoo got to know Indians who had been in Glasgow before the First World War.

Soon he was engaged as a hawker, but on the advice of a Jewish warehouseman, he became a pedlar. Not content though, he expanded his enterprise by becoming a wholesaler and a respected man within his community.

From the early 1920s when the small Indian population in Scotland was still a mixture of Lascars, ex-servants and students, Nathoo acted as a catalyst for both the existing group and a new influx of Indians, which did much to consolidate Indian settlement in Glasgow and elsewhere in Scotland. The steep increase in the Indian community was largely due to Nathoo's visit to India, where he 'inspired and encouraged' fellow Punjabis to come to Scotland. And, as they came in, he provided them with 'help and hospitality'. Thus an Indian 'chain migration' got under way[29] which led to the population of pedlars being dispersed to Edinburgh, Dundee, Aberdeen and the islands, and soon the Indian pedlar became a familiar sight in most parts of Scotland.

Although Edinburgh was one of the main attractions for Indian visitors to Scotland, by 1929 there were only an estimated five or six Indians in Edinburgh, who were not students, a population that had barely risen by the outbreak of the Second World War. Edinburgh did not welcome these 'dark strangers' and, the 'reserved and snobbish' attitude which the Indians faced did little to foster the growth of an Indian community in the inter-war years.[30]

Nevertheless, the few Edinburgh Indians did not lose contact with their more numerous compatriots in Glasgow. Regular weekend trips between the two cities and business updates and gossip kept the Edinburgh Indian residents fully informed. And when Bal Krishnan returned to Edinburgh from India as a married man in 1939, his was probably the first family to emerge among the settled Indians. Krishnan's wife was more than likely the first Indian woman to join the armed forces in the war.

Beyond Edinburgh, Dundee was the destination of a few pedlars who could not make a living in Glasgow. What made some areas more attractive than others was initially an Indian contact in the new town or city and, in this respect, Dundee was no exception, a city that had a long-standing connection with

India. This link was maintained in the early years through the intrepid Lascars, whose presence paved the way for those of higher status, such as J.D. Saggar, one of the earliest residents and general medical practitioners in Dundee. He was born in 1898 in Ludhiana District in the Punjab and, after graduating as a doctor at the University of St Andrews, he decided to take permanent residence. Through his professionalism, skill, good manners and personality, he won the 'confidence and respect' of the local white people. If he was politically responsive to the times he lived in, he was no less so socially, and in time, was joined in Scotland by two younger brothers, one of whom, Dhani Ram, followed the same profession and also won the respect of the citizens of Dundee for his sensitivity to the needs of the community. By the late 1930s, nearly half a dozen houses in the Hill Town district of Dundee were occupied by Indians.[31]

THE DEVELOPING COMMUNITY

In the inter-war years, the flow of newcomers from India persisted as relations and friends joined their contacts in Scotland to the extent that by the end of the1930s, there were 175 pedlars occupying 21 houses in all.[32] In Glasgow the community was concentrated in the Port Dundas district, where although housing was deplorable, the rents were low, as they were in the Anderston area and the slums of the Gorbals, the latter attracting residents from the Port Dundas tenements when these were demolished in the late 1930s.

As the economic recession of the hungry 1930s began to bite, Indian pedlars felt the sharpness, and many went back to India disappointed. This had a dampening effect on those Indians who desired to migrate to Scotland. With little or nothing on offer in Glasgow, many moved to the countryside and the 'fishing towns' of the north and north-east. Thus, community gave way to dispersal, which proved to be, as Maan claimed, 'quite beneficial all round'.

Towards the end of 1933, it became apparent that change for the better was on the way. It was not long before this was transmitted to villagers in the Nakodar and Jagraon areas in the

Punjab, thus generating a wave of migrants of greater magnitude than previously, including many who had returned to their homelands. And the further dispersal of Indians to Wick, Thurso and the Outer Hebrides, Stroma and Stornoway eased the pressure of overcrowding in Glasgow. Thus these migrants were doubly unfortunate in experiencing British imperialism not only from outside, but also from within.

Few would disagree that their lives in this cold land were, for the most part, dreary and monotonous. But the boredom these energetic young men may have felt was, at times, broken when newcomers arrived from India or when one of them visited his Indian village. The small community looked forward to the arrival of newcomers, who could bring personal messages, presents and news from home. Likewise, messages and presents were sent back by visitors to India.

At this time too, there was a more confident and growing sense of community. A marked feature of this was the strong feeling of brotherhood, of belonging, which seemed to override, it was said, all other considerations such as caste and religious differences.[33] It was a significant shift away from custom to find that Hindus, Muslims, Sikhs and Untouchables living in the same house considered their Indianness to be more important than their differences, especially when they were all treated as 'alien', by individuals and institutions of the host society. So it was more and more common to find Hindus and Muslims helping each other in the depressed 1930s in Glasgow.

Generally, it would seem that these Indians were treated tolerably and inoffensively, but while some of them felt 'Johnnie' was a nickname they could cope with, 'darkie' was always offensive. Most Indians were emphatic about not experiencing 'any racial prejudice, abuse or discrimination' and regarded the people of Scotland as a whole to be friendly and helpful. Their problems, it seemed, were of another kind, and given time, were recognised as being within their control.

Illiteracy and the inability to tally their sales accurately were difficulties which, in the short term, as pedlars they could not overcome. As a consequence, they endured unavoidable frustrations and humiliations. But this, they reasoned, was better than being idle in India. Not all the Indian pedlars, however, were

illiterate. By the late 1930s at least two ex-students had joined
their ranks and with the growing size of the community in
Glasgow, such expertise as they offered to their fellow-pedlars
was invaluable. An outstanding example of this was the
unselfish contribution of S.M. Joshi, described by one Indian as
a 'godfather and guide to his countrymen as long as he lived'.[34]

In 1938, most of the estimated 200 Indians in Glasgow were
Muslim Arraiens from the Punjab. The others included Sikhs,
Jats, Untouchables, Bhatra Sikhs and just 'one or two Hindus'.
The fact that there were so few Hindus was predictable for, prior
to the Second World War, the Hindus were the dominant group
in India and there was therefore little or no incentive for them,
especially those who had jobs and families, to migrate. Moreover, Hindus were reluctant to travel overseas for 'caste and
religious' reasons; obligations that were inapplicable to the
Muslims and Sikh groups. Muslims and Sikhs were often not as
well educated as Hindus and therefore occupied, in the main,
the lower rungs of the socio-economic hierarchy as farmers,
soldiers, peasants and labourers. For many, a new start abroad
was an opportunity to help themselves and their families. Thus
before 1939 an Indian community had come into being in
Scotland, and with it the formation of an Indian Association,
through which they gradually reclaimed and strengthened
essential social and cultural practices that had lapsed. Their
original intention was not to settle in Scotland, but to make
money and return to India in much the same way that many
West Indians thought of their migration to Britain. But the
demands that survival had made upon them over the years were
so overwhelming as to transform their world view; and in the
uncertain years between the wars their cumulative inventiveness and creativity brought about their own 'little India' in
Glasgow.[35]

Hard as their lives were before the Second World War, with
the outbreak of hostilities they felt deeply concerned for their
safety, and for some, it was all too much: they decided to return
to India with the minimum of delay. Such good fortune,
however, was not shared by the majority of Indians in Scotland.
Those who had penetrated the remoter parts now made their
way back to Glasgow, and those in Dundee and Edinburgh did

not venture out much. For those who were rejected as soldiers, there was employment to be found in the war-oriented factories at Bishopton and Hillington; and soon these labourers settled down to a new mode of work and the added compensation of a regular income.

If it was not evident before, it was now clear that the hostilities in Europe had brought about a greater degree of consolidation to the Indian community in Glasgow, where by 1940, about 400 Indians had settled, out of a total Indian population of 450. The problems arising from their concentration in the notorious Gorbals prompted a new-found desire not only to survive, but to do better. This led to the formation of the Muslim Mission in 1940 (to serve the religious and recreational needs of the Scottish Muslim community) and the Sikh Association, the following year.[36]

If the peddling trade was set aside during the war, it afforded the Indians invaluable experience for they were drawn into establishing connections with the Scots, whom they could no longer avoid meeting in their daily activities, either economically or socially. No longer could the Indians use the barriers of language and differences in culture and religion. Wartime had its own agenda and now Indians engaged in close social relations on the factory floor and elsewhere. And what may have earlier been perceived as a liability was now seen as an invaluable asset, for at this time their trust had deepened their understanding of each other and they often became good friends. Furthermore, their ability to communicate more effectively in English had, in many cases, improved markedly, as a result of the prolonged and greater amity with the Scots who, in turn, also benefited.

So from the turn of the century, through the inter- and postwar years, there was an increase in the black population in Britain, which comprised a heterogeneous group of people who were, in spite of growing cohesiveness, still largely disorganised. Often they sought representation for their grievances from the existing black organisations, few of which had any real grassroots credibility. The middle-class black intelligentsia, more concerned with the ideology of Pan

Africanism, did not ignore the questions of racial discrimination against black people generally. At this time, a major concern of black people was coming to terms with their role as low-paid workers in Britain. But, for the many Afro-Asian leaders, this was subordinate to the more pressing concern of colonial freedom.

4 AFRO-ASIAN CHALLENGES (PRE-1962)

After the First World War, John Alcindor succeeded Henry Sylvester Williams as leader of the African Progress Union,[1] as the movement of black intellectuals, especially in London, evolved.

At the beginning of the war, the black communities in Britain comprised labourers, domestic workers, artisans and sailors. During this disruptive time, black people were drafted in to do a whole range of work for the war effort; and the entry of a few black and Asian students to the universities of London, Cambridge, Liverpool, Glasgow and Edinburgh continued.[2] By the end of the war, there were an estimated 20,000 black people in Britain,[3] a presence which was unacceptable to the returning white soldiers and sailors, especially in the port communities.

In spite of the shipping depression, it was said that some black seamen in Cardiff earned good money and through hard work and thrift a few of them were able to occupy apartments and houses, while others held dockside jobs and married local white women. After demobilisation, however, white ship owners and shipmasters adopted an employment policy of 'our own people first' which increased tension between blacks and whites. Eventually, the ugly mood of white racists was expressed in unprecedented violence as the mixed non-white population in Cardiff was attacked in what came to be known as the race riots of 1919.[4] Similar disturbances, as mentioned earlier, occurred in Liverpool and Glasgow.

But, such negative perceptions and attitudes were countered by an ever-growing impulse among black people in Britain and in the diaspora to learn more. Thus, the flow of black students persisted during the interwar years and, significantly, black munitions workers, volunteers and soldiers came to help Britain during the Second World War. The arrival of some 10,000

African-American troops in 1942 provoked in some white people strong feelings of fear and insecurity and the view that these black men should be kept at a distance from local white people was denounced by the *Sunday Pictorial* which stated that 'There is – and will be – no persecution of coloured people in Britain'.[5]

Paradoxically, while black American troops were welcomed by some in Britain, their fellow white Americans discriminated against them. In effect, the American fighting forces in Britain constituted an Army which was segregated by race, a well-thought through and strictly implemented policy.[6]

The British government found itself in a dilemma. Tom Driberg, the Labour MP, said in Parliament that discrimination against black American troops was unfortunate and asked Winston Churchill if he would 'make friendly representations to the American military authorities asking them to instruct their men that the Colour Bar is not a custom in this country'.[7] But, although others like the Communist MP Willie Gallagher had also commented on the issue, white American officers were adamant in asserting their white superiority, not only over black Americans, but also over West Indian troops in Britain.[8] Thus, the Colour Bar remained a central issue.

Indeed, in the 1930s and 1940s, there was a sense of urgency in dealing with the questions of race, colour and colonial freedom among black intellectuals in Britain, ideologues who increasingly adopted radical Pan African views, which, as the Great Depression deepened, they expressed forthrightly in London's black press.[9] In so doing, they were pursuing a process which dates back to the early nineteenth century. As it was, the writings of these decades were to prove invaluable in educating people of the African diaspora, as the bankruptcy of Empire became more evident after 1945.

So from the turn of the century, black radicalism was in the ascendant and a keen sense of national identity clarified the fact that political freedom was not enough; economic and cultural self-sufficiency were also of primary concern. From this composite of approaches the urgent need to 'educate, organise and involve the masses' towards the ultimate goal of self-government and national pride through Independence crystallised. Among the chief advocates engaged in consolidating the disgruntled factions in Asia and Africa were Shapurji Saklatvala, Krishna Menon and George Padmore. But first, let us turn our attention to Indian nationalism and to the committed discourse and actions of one of the earliest of the Home Rule League activists, Joseph Baptista.

INDIAN NATIONALISTS IN BRITAIN IN THE TWENTIETH CENTURY

Since Raja Ram Mohun Roy's representations in the nineteenth century, many outstanding Indians have helped to generate a growing sense of nationalist feeling among the Indian people. Less well known is Joseph Baptista, who is regarded by some as the 'father' of the Indian Home Rule Movement in India. In the 1870s, he was one of a group of 'angry young men', middle-class agitators. Working closely with B.G. Tilak (a central figure who helped to generate growing nationalism among the Indian people, and a co-founder of the Indian Home Rule League in 1916) Baptista proved to be an able coordinator. Significantly, while Baptista and Besant were setting up their Home Rule Leagues, Gandhi was hoping to establish a new socio-economic order in India based on truth and love; a sage, saint-like approach to the 'establishment of the Kingdom of God on earth'. It was against this background that Baptista, later known as 'Kaka' (uncle), emerged as a leading figure of the Home Rule Movement in Britain.

Born on 17 March 1864, he was educated first at Bombay University and then at Cambridge University, and after being called to the Bar at Gray's Inn, he was appointed Professor at the Government Law School in Bombay. It was on his return to India in 1899 that he realised the potential for organisation in Bombay and was drawn towards Sir Phirozeshah Mehta and Tilak, particularly the latter. According to his biographer, Baptista could, with justification, lay claim to have been the first Home Rule advocate in India. There was no doubt that he harboured a strong desire to free India and in 1900 he suggested to Tilak that a Home Rule League should be formed. To his credit, he was among the first to see the possibilities of British Labour Party connections in fostering the cause of Indian nationalist aspirations.[10]

When he arrived in England in 1917, his appeals to the Labour Party resulted in the Party pledging itself to support the principle of Indian self-determination. And as the awareness of nationalist feeling in India increased, Baptista never lost sight of the importance of the support he received from British Labour Party and the working classes. His mission in the metropolis was, if anything, perceived as worthy for as the war took its toll, many in Britain were beginning to become aware of the Otherness of those millions of people in the British Empire, who had for centuries contributed to Britain's well-being, yet had been denied their histories and cultures that have so continuously and profoundly shaped British culture.

Having declared his position as a foreign agitator, it would have been unthinkable if Baptista's movements in Britain were not to be monitored by the security forces. Indeed, he reported to Tilak that the police were in attendance at all his lectures and had passed on their reports to the government. Yet, he was possessed with an enthusiasm for his mission which seemed boundless. Outside London, his lecture tour took him to Glasgow, Dundee and parts of Lancashire and Hull, where Labour Party leaders rallied to the cause of India. For his part, Baptista felt it was fortunate that he was in England, 'otherwise there would have been nobody to take India's side'. For the rest of his stay in Britain, his concentration on political work ('one mad rush') was spent largely attending social functions and holding political discussions with Indian and British friends. As the war came to an end, he returned to India, having done more substantial work in Britain than any of his predecessors.

After Tilak's death, in a new crucial phase of the movement for Indian freedom, Gandhi joined the All India Home Rule League and became President, thus ending his splendid isolation. He explained that the causes he wanted to promote through the Home Rule League were Swadeshi, Hindu-Muslim unity with special reference to the Khilafat and linguistic redistribution of the provinces; and he was especially careful that he should not be misunderstood. He felt that the Home

Rule League had to match the changed political situation in India. Thereafter, the League was renamed Swarajya Sabha, and among those who opposed this move was the Muslim leader M.A. Jinnah. With time, as the Swarajya Sabha lost its identity, it was absorbed into the Indian National Congress and, as the Home Rule Movement lost credibility, the prestige of Baptista also declined.

Tilak's demise was an irreparable loss to Baptista, who believed in working with, rather than against, the British. But the leadership of Gandhi led to the rise of Gandhism and the eclipse of Baptista in Indian politics. This was the turning point in Baptista's political career; and as growing radicalism encroached upon the centre ground of Indian nationalist politics, he dissociated himself from unconstitutional methods which were increasingly employed in the cause of political progress. He died on 18 September 1930,[11] leaving the struggle for nationalist freedom to others.

SHAPURJI SAKLATVALA

One of the most devoted and militant nationalists to visit England was the Parsee Shapurji Saklatvala, a tireless worker in the cause of workers everywhere, an activist who immersed himself in trade union and political struggles on both sides of the imperial divide. In both respects, Saklatvala was more radical than Baptista and Gandhi. His work in Britain as a Communist Member of Parliament and at grassroots level far exceeded that of Joseph Baptista or indeed any other Asian before him.

Saklatvala was born in Bombay on 28 March 1874, at a time when British domination and control of Indians had become increasingly forceful. Human degradation and the suffering of his fellow-Indians had bothered him and in spite of his privileged birth,[12] he was drawn to the labouring masses. To forestall growing militant nationalism in Bengal and elsewhere in India, British repression had become a disturbing trend which was not lost on Saklatvala, and following this transitional stage in Indian politics, he came to England.

His development from Capitalism to Communism reflects a spiritual and intellectual journey. From a wealthy family background, he was able to make a passionate commitment towards finding means to end the poverty and misery of the masses in India. As he told Robin Palme Dutt, the prominent socialist, there were four stages in his spiritual odyssey: first, he sought in religion the key that would unlock the door to a new awakening and advance of the nation; second, he turned to science as a means of helping the Indian people; third, he felt that in order to end Indian poverty, industrial development was necessary, hence the establishment of his family's concern – the Tata Iron and Steel Company; and finally, to climax his spiritual pilgrimage, he entered the world of the National Liberal Club in England, but soon found among its members a narrow outlook and snobbish hypocrisy. It was in the wake of his confrontation with Morley, then Secretary of State for India, that he moved towards British working-class politics. This shift though was the culmination of a gradual process.

After a brief spell of work in Tata's Manchester office, he came to London, where his family made him a life-member of the National Liberal Club. It ws hoped that Saklatvala would become 'respectable' by meeting 'friends' of Indian freedom. Among those whom he met was Lord Morley of the Morley–Minto Reforms of 1909 (drawn up 'to rally the moderates' in the face of militant nationalism), which created divisiveness rather than unity among Indians. And so, given this liberal bankruptcy and hypocrisy concerning the true interests of the Indians, in 1910, he left the Liberal 'mausoleum' and entered British working-class politics through the Independent Labour Party,[13] an association which also proved unsatisfactory. As an internationalist, he was disappointed by the Party's shift from a Marxist orientation to being anti-Marxist. His belief that India's oppression was directly related to British imperialism was strengthened in 1917, when the Russian Revolution marked a new dawn, heralding new possibilities in international politics.

In 1920, the Communist Party of Great Britain was formed and militant activities in the trade union movement were pronounced. According to one observer, it is no exaggeration to claim that Saklatvala was a product of the British working-class movement. His unselfish commitment drew him closer to trade union organisers and soon his popularity grew among rank-and-file workers. Not unexpectedly, his career took a new turn when he successfully contested the Battersea North seat in the general election of 1922 and was again elected in 1924. During both terms as a Member of Parliament, he worked closely with Scottish ILP members and maintained his broad outlook, emphasising the interconnection of the workers' struggle in different parts of the Empire; and naturally he sought to rouse support for the workers and peasants in India. He was now well placed to do so, for he was not only a member of the Home Rule League, but also of a number of worker-oriented bodies in Britain and abroad, a multiplicity of activities (especially his association with the League Against Imperialism) that were perceived by British government officials as subversive.

Consequently, like Baptista, Saklatvala's movements in Britain were monitored, though he was much more closely watched. In addition to being a 'black' Communist MP in Britain, his political career had always been controversial. Nevertheless, he remained undeterred and during this turbulent period, he played a full part in the many political and industrial disputes, notably in the 1926 General Strike, when he was arrested and charged with sedition. His home was raided[14] and he was imprisoned in Wormwood Scrubs, experiences which seem to have strengthened his resolve.

After he moved to England, he returned to India three times, but it was his last visit that was especially memorable. He received a hero's welcome from most of the Indian nationalists. But when he returned to Britain, the authorities were at him again. India became a no-go area, being excluded from the list of countries for which his passport was valid. And as he found out, his real enemies, ironically, were Labour members such as Wedgwood Benn, Secretary of State for India and Arthur Henderson, Foreign Secretary, who upheld the ban on his entry into India when the Labour Party was returned to office in 1929. Unfortunately for Saklatvala, at this time, the political divisions on the Left had hit a new low; and although he contested parliamentary elections again, he was unsuccessful.

Nevertheless in the last years of his life, he kept up a gruelling schedule, speaking at meetings across the country, especially on unemployment, and he visited the Soviet Union for the third time. On his return to Britain, he was back on the hustings in Scotland, even though his chances of winning were remote. Unbowed and stubbornly pursuing his own brand of radicalism, Saklatvala continued to address meetings until two weeks before he died from a heart attack on 16 June 1936.[15] Saklatvala's work was invaluable and although he did not live to witness Indian Independence (which came just over a decade after his death) others, no less passionate than he was, did.

KRISHNA MENON

In the interwar period, Indian nationalism took a new turn, as nationalists demanded nothing short of an 'India for the Indians', full control of Indian affairs and departure of the British rulers. And, as before, this struggle in India had its advocates in Britain, among them the radical Vengalil Krishna Menon, of whom the world was unaware until after 1947. As the biographer T.J.S. George noted, he 'burst into the limelight with dramatic suddenness', when he was just past the age of 50 and 'full of eccentricities, volatile, fantastic and whimsical', a man with a capacity to generate hate or adoration, never indifference, inspiring a few, infuriating many and embarrassing all.[16] So what was he up to for half a century?

Born in Malabar on 3 May 1896, Krishna Menon was fortunate in having a 'prosperous family', who were able to afford the best education for him. From the Municipal School in Tellichery he attended the Native High School in Calicut, then moved to Presidency College in Madras, which he left at the age of 20 and proceeded to the Madras Law College. These years of instruction served as a process of elimination for him, and soon he was drawn to his abiding interests that were social and political, as they related to his populous country which, in spite of its huge riches, was blighted by poverty, degradation and helplessness. Foreign domination was hardly helpful and was never accepted by this unusual young man whom one biographer has described as having walked the earth 'as though it belonged to him'.[17] He came to know Annie Besant's Theosophical Society and joined the Home Rule League, an involvement which, in retrospect, seems logical.

He was 28 years old when he arrived in London, eager to learn all he could about the teaching profession from his chosen course of study, at the end of which he gained a Diploma. He seemed then to have been no different from many Indian students in London. But such qualifications as he desired and had come to Britain for, were, in the 1920s (as well as before and after) in British India of vital importance, if a young Indian was to stand any chance of making progress. His intention to complete his course and return home in six months was, to say the least, a miscalculation. He found much to detain him in London, where he remained for over 20 years.

In England, between odd jobs, usually teaching, he oriented his life in a relentless pursuit of further education gaining not only his teaching Diploma, but also a first degree at the London School of Economics, followed by an MA and an MSc from the University of London, before he was called to the Bar in 1934.[18] These academic successes were all the more gratifying because they were courses sandwiched between the hours of earning his living, so common among students from abroad. His high expectations, though, were sadly unrealised. For one thing, he could not have had a successful practice because most of his clients were poor. But, while his altruism was undoubted, as an explanation for his failure in his chosen profession, this was only partly true. The main reason was racism.

He soon came to learn that academic success was no guarantee of making a living, so he turned to something he had done more as a stop-gap than as a consuming interest. He was drawn to journalism as the 'London correspondent' for a number of Indian publications. But British officials unanimously disapproved of his brand of journalism and he may not have been aware of those who monitored his transmissions to India, for he pursued his literary work with characteristic passion in the capacities of editor and publisher, with engagements at the publishers The Bodley Head and Selwyn and Blount, as editor of the Twentieth Century Library series and as general editor of Pelican Books, at its inception, when a series of titles addressing social and political issues were launched. Underscoring such work, however, was his main preoccupation, 'freedom and determination' for India.[19]

His engagements took him all over Britain. As branches came into being and groups to the left of the Labour Party rallied round, the Commonwealth of India League in Britain became the official voice of the Indian Congress Party. One of his major triumphs was the arrival in India of three Labour MPs on a fact-finding mission, which issued a damning document portraying the deplorable conditions in India. Although those who read it were appalled, it was a view which the British government did not share. Indeed official high-handedness in relation to Indian affairs was to reappear when the Second World War was declared and Indian troops left the subcontinent 'without prior consultation' with Indian leaders.

Menon's political sympathies and progressive stand on India had not endeared him to British government officials, who were only too aware of his political track record in Britain: his membership of the Labour Party, his election as a Labour Councillor in St Pancras and in devoted work on the various Council committees, his adoption as a Parliamentary Labour candidate for Dundee, his championing of the causes of the St. Pancras Library and Arts Festival, and service in getting improvements to air-raid shelters during the bombing of London. Although British officials were not pleased, his high profile was a major cause of restraint in taking action against him. His position was further strengthened when, fortuitously, in 1945, the Labour Party endorsed India's demand for self-government; and having resigned as a member of the Party in 1941, because of its failure to endorse Indian self-government, he regained his membership of the Party.

After the war, in the weeks before India gained Independence, Menon was instrumental in maintaining links between leaders of the Indian National Congress and Viceroy Mountbatten, who was impressed by Menon's invaluable work as an adviser.[20] Independence in 1947 was, for Menon, not an anti-climax, for having previously been a 'special representative' of the Indian government at the United Nations General Assembly between

1946 and 1947, he was a rising star in the firmament of Indian politics and went on to become India's High Commissioner in London for the next five years. Such tenacity and loyalty as he displayed in the service of his country were exemplary and while others might have felt a change in life-style was appropriate, it seemed that Menon continued to live modestly.

His two main concerns were Indian Independence and service, in a number of capacities, to the people of St. Pancras and Camden in London. His work in Britain has been nothing short of monumental, and those best placed to appraise his contribution honoured him. Like George Bernard Shaw he was an 'adopted' son of the Borough of Camden; a statue of him was erected by the India League in Fitzroy Square.[21] He never married and died in New Delhi on 5 October 1974.

For Indian nationalists, midnight on 15 August 1947 was their hour of triumph. They had, at last, won their Independence. The departure of the British from the subcontinent saw the birth of two new political entities – India and Pakistan – an outcome which, just two years after the Fifth Pan African Congress in Manchester gave added impetus to African nationalists, whose hopes for freedom burned ever brighter, as a direct result of the extraordinary leadership of a number of black people, especially of men like Harold Moody and George Padmore.

LEADING PANAFRICANISTS IN THE TWENTIETH CENTURY

Dr Harold Moody

In the wake of the Cardiff race riots of 1919, colour prejudice was to rear up time and again in Britain. Discrimination against black people was a fact, a cause of uncomfortable tension that would not go away. By the mid-1920s feelings against the heterogeneous dockside groups (all conveniently categorised as 'black' and therefore without individuality) were so strong that instead of being entirely disorganised and demoralised, they were drawn together as a community, but lacked representation in the forums of society where it mattered. But gradually and though beleaguered, the wider support that they had been without for so long was, it seemed, now forthcoming as feelings of racial pride stirred many, not least Dr Harold Moody, who founded and became the first and only President of the League of Coloured Peoples.[22]

This unusual Jamaican, who had risen from the ranks of the comparatively few black students in Britain in the early years of the century, felt there was a need for an organisation which would bring together not only students (as the West African Students Union had done) but also people from as wide a range as possible. According to Ras Makonnen, the Guyanese-born Pan Africanist, the LCP group was an extension of the English charitable tradition, being inter-racial, involved in 'mild protest' and in harassing the 'goody-goody' elements in Britain.

The aim of this black group was to bring the black races together. 'Coloured' was the description of black people in these years and could well explain why Dr Moody included it in the name of his organisation. Women such as Una Marson (a writer and playwright), Stella Thomas, Christine Moody, Sylvia Lowe, Dorothy Clarke, Amy Barbour James and Viola Thompson, played important (though largely hidden) roles in the League's social and cultural affairs, and by the mid-1930s C.L.R. James, Louis Mbanefo, Arthur Lewis, Learie Constantine and Peter Blackman, among others[23] (representing the Caribbean and Africa) had also become associated with the organisation.

What was beyond question was the fact that the 'Colour Bar' in Britain was all-pervasive, permeating every level of British society. Those who suffered from it, individually and culturally, had no recourse but to seek solidarity with other groups on common issues. If the League was the only organisation able to bring any degree of co-ordination to, and respect for, the black workers' experience in Britain, to understand its true nature, it is necessary to review the life of Harold Moody.

Moody arrived at London's Paddington Station, as a 22 year old in September 1904, and found lodgings in the top garret of a house in St Paul's Road, Canonbury. From that moment he became progressively aware of his colour for he was not spared colour prejudice in London. Years later, he reminisced that the 'Mother Country' had not given him a warm welcome.

Born in Kingston, Jamaica on 8 October 1882, Harold's mother exerted a profound influence over him. Although she was denied the opportunity of scholastic achievement, she was a quick learner, an ability which her son inherited. Indeed, during Harold's schooldays, she insisted that he should make friends with those of lighter skin than himself, and that he should promote feelings of 'race distinction', even though race and colour were especially oppressive in the old British colony. Mrs Moody was very religious (as were most black women in Jamaica at the time) and it was no surprise that her son became a devout Christian. Naturally, she tried to get the best education for him and succeeded magnificently as Harold was prepared to become a medical student in London, a rare ambition for a black youth at the time in colonial Jamaica. Before he left the island, one of his friends asked what was his greatest ambition, to which he replied: 'To do something for the Race'.[24] In this, he was, of course, echoing the thoughts of fellow-West Indians Blyden, Edwards, Thorne and Williams for whom the idea of racial advancement was paramount. Few white men, at the time, in spite of the centuries-old commercial and trading intercourse between them, understood the intensity of this sense of pride among black men.

In London, Moody realised how little he knew of Jamaican history and culture. There was no doubt that he was English in education and upbringing, but in temperament he was not. He pondered the question: Where did he really belong? His sense of purpose kept him on course. As an activist, he became a popular speaker at students' meetings and was honoured with election to the Presidency of the College of Christian Union. From King's College, he went to King's College Hospital, where he did his clinical training and ignored the colour prejudice he knew existed among fellow students, a situation which demanded a certain strategy: not of confrontation, but of perseverance, coolness and courage which eventually paid off with unrivalled academic success.

As a qualified doctor, he travelled back to Jamaica in 1912 and on his return to London that same year, he began his medical practice at Peckham, where he was conspicuous as a black man with few (if any) black patients. It would have been an extremely awkward and trying time for him, getting to know and to win the confidence and trust of his white clients. For both doctor and patients this was a new relationship, contrary to custom and practice, something Moody had to come to grips with. Indeed, when he married a white nurse, Olive Tranter, the families on both sides were unhappy. Twenty-five years later, he recalled:

> I have always held that marriage is an individual, private and personal matter concerning only the two contracting parties with which no one has the right to interfere as long as the parties are of age and independent. This does not seem to be the general point of view of the English people ... I see no reason why two persons, more or less equal in their education and social opportunities, who believe that they love each other sufficiently to overcome any differences of temperament and to contract marriage should be prevented from entering upon such a contract.[25]

After nine years in England, Moody had gradually built up an established practice, and had settled down with his wife and four children to family life. Though this might have been enough for most men to be getting on with, it was not so for Moody, who spent much time and energy on the work of Clifton Congregational Church, where he first made contact with the people of Peckham, whose deep affection he had aroused by demonstrating his versatility in combining both his medical practice and various religious duties. It is just as well that he had that warm experience, for when in July 1919, he and his wife and children had set out on a holiday to Jamaica, they were barred from visiting the beach, when their ship called at an American port. This instance of colour discrimination moved him to write in his diary that it is character and not colour that is the thing of ultimate importance. 'I will not and shall not apologise for my birth.'[26]

In Jamaica, he travelled beyond Kingston, roaming freely round the countryside, an experience which brought a clearer vision of his responsibility and a commitment to fight for his beloved people, through the Christian faith. He took pride in his heritage and vowed to work for the betterment of his 'race'. Appropriately, this visit precipitated the defining moment from which his life's work would derive.

On his return to England, he wasted no time. He saw church activities as being important in addressing the issue of race and no one could deny his work for the Colonial Missionary Society, through which he persisted in raising issues connected with the rights of black people. Soon, his home became the hub of activity and fellowship, and often the place of call for many foreign students. No doubt, they reminded him not only of his own arrival, but also the unforgettable and salient experiences associated with it. Somehow, these students gave him strength and, conscious of the need for co-ordination of the existing, but disparate British organisations, he explored the possibility of forming one umbrella organisation. To this end a committee was set up and when they met on 13 March 1931 at the Young Men's Christian Association in central London, it was decided to form the LCP. Recognised as the League's leader, Moody was elected as its president.

As the League developed, Moody, unlike some of his more radical associates, became more concerned with the immediate problems of black people in Britain, rather than with winning colonial freedom. Black nationalism was not his central goal, as it was for the Pan Africanists. Many of the League's activities were concerned with the difficulties facing black students in London. This in itself was not enough though. In Moody's view, it was paramount that the League's existence and activities should be addressed to the widest audience if it was to grow into a viable and effective organisation. The idea of producing a periodical on a regular basis was therefore important, but financing such a venture was a challenge. Eventually, the first number of *The Keys* appeared in July 1933 as the official organ of the League. The name of this publication is associated with the African Dr Aggrey, who said that the fullest musical harmony could best be expressed by the use of both the black and white keys of the piano. In its explanation the League spelt out in the first issue of *The Keys* that the name symbolised what it aimed to achieve, namely more opportunities in jobs and housing for coloured peoples and greater harmony and co-operation between the black and white races.

Moody imposed his strong personality upon members of the LCP. As his responsibilities grew, so did tensions and conflicts with members of his Executive Committee, many of whom were pragmatists and Marxists. It seemed that the growing responsibilities of his more or less autocratic leadership had become too much for him and three years after the League's formation, he informed readers of The Keys in October 1934 that because of the great demand made upon his time and his money, he felt constrained to offer his resignation as President, effective from March of the following year. He appealed to the Africans and West Indians to stop bickering among themselves, to forgo all 'petty jealousies' and 'childish petulance' and co-operate with each other for the good of the race. 'How can the Englishman respect us', he asked, 'if we do not respect ourselves?'27

So what had hitherto seemed to be a harmonious group, was in truth shot through with discord. If Moody could not change his autocratic style of leadership, neither could his critics change their oppositional, critical stance. Although the cleavage in the Executive remained, Moody was unable (indeed unwilling) to depart from his post and in April 1935, The Keys announced that, having reconsidered his decision, Moody would continue as President. With this administrative matter settled to his satisfaction, Moody's main preoccupation was the attitude of black people to world conflict. The Italian attack on Abyssinia precipitated mass meetings in London and the League had no hesitation in calling for the 'complete freedom' of Africans from any domination whatsoever.

Other League concerns included measures undertaken by the colonial governments in St. Vincent and the Gold Coast, for example, which introduced powers of censorship, actions that compounded the already deplorable living conditions in the West Indies, where riots broke out in many islands. These disturbances (as the riots were called) were investigated by a Royal Commission to which the League made its submissions on the need for change and development in the region, so devastated by centuries of a monocultural past. While Moody and the League hoped for radical recommendations from the Commissioners, events in Europe pushed its peoples further to the brink of war, which darkened the prospects for people of colour wherever they happened to be, but especially in Europe.

With the outbreak of the Second World War, the League, short of money, found that it could no longer publish *The Keys*, which was succeeded in October 1939 by *News Notes*, a monthly newsletter. Although the war was a time of hardship for black people in Britain, Moody felt that the League's championing of certain causes should be restricted. But when the offensive term 'nigger' was aired by the British Broadcasting Corporation in 1940, Moody was quick to denounce it and demand an apology for this unfortunate relic of slavery.[28] The Colour Bar was still a live and provocative issue in Britain and political power had become increasingly a central part of his vision for a better world.

Another aspect of Moody's multidimensional contribution was his extensive writing: letters to *The Times* and other leading British newspapers, occasional articles for various periodicals and the publication of many of his sermons. He edited and wrote regularly for the League's journal and, apart from his autobiography *Negro Victory*, he was the author of four booklets: *Youth and Race*, *Christianity and Race Relations*, *Freedom For All Men* and *The Colour Bar*.[29]

He guided the League over many years on a range of issues, spanning the Cardiff 'crisis' of 1935 and the outbreak of war. He had no choice but to deal with the 'crisis' as best he could, a period of 'extreme depression' in the shipping industry, when the National Union of Seamen supported a Bill introduced to the House of Commons, which restricted the number of non-white men that could be employed on British ships. This resulted in unemployment among non-white seamen, the effects of which was a 'crisis' that became 'one of the most important events in the history of race relations in the British Isles'.[30]

Moreover, Moody was confronted with other matters of significance, notably his handling of the League's problematic relations with other more radical black groups in Cardiff and elsewhere in Britain, such as the Negro Workers' Association (a

black workers' social and welfare organisation), the West
African Students Union (representing the interests of African
students) and the International African Service Bureau (a radical
Pan African organisation). This was a period demanding leaps of
the imagination from the black brotherhood which held discussions, laid plans and generally harboured high expectations.

With Moody's death in 1947, a unique organisation and
personality were lost, and not surprisingly, in retrospect, his life
and work begged comparison with other black leaders. In one
fundamental respect, Moody and Garvey (both Jamaicans)
shared a firm belief in the advancement of the black man. But
although Garvey was a charismatic leader, Moody was not. As
Sam Morris, General Secretary of the League from 1945 to
1953, noted: 'if Marcus Garvey could be called a visionary,
which he was, the name could no less be applied to Dr Moody'.
Both possessed leadership qualities, which afforded them
dominion over their rivals and members within their groups.
There is little doubt that Moody was the League, for just over a
decade after his death, the organisation he had led and
dominated petered out.[31] Before he died, the effects of the
Depression and the consequences of the war had profound
effects, shattering old ties and creating new and often unacceptable conditions in the British colonies that were in need of
urgent and fundamental redress. And among those who were
opposed to Moody's moderate black leadership (at least in terms
of delivering colonial freedom) was the pre-eminent radical Pan
Africanist, George Padmore.

George Padmore

George Padmore was the adopted name of Malcolm Ivan
Meredith Nurse, who was born in Trinidad in 1902, just a year
after fellow Pan Africanist C.L.R. James. Malcolm did not show
any unusual academic ability during his early years of schooling
and was not distinguished as a reporter for the *Weekly Guardian*
in Trinidad. It was not long, however, before a characteristic
trait emerged, namely, his inability to accommodate the arrogance of authority, which was abundantly evident in his

relations with the English editor of the newspaper, Edward Partridge. Repeated confrontations left an indelible impression on the young Malcolm.

Like so many boys in colonial Trinidad, he felt he could improve upon the very basic education he received, and decided to go abroad. In 1924 he went to Fisk University in the United States to study medicine, but other interests – law, political science and journalism – distracted him. His intelligence, sense of self and awareness of his colonial past shed much light on the issues of the day. Soon he was enmeshed in university politics and met a number of foreign students, including the Nigerian Benjamin Azikiwe. Contact with young men from Africa had a profound effect upon his developing racial consciousness and spirit of nationalism. The activities of the racist Ku Klux Klan in the American South posed even greater challenges for Malcolm, who abandoned his degree course and left the South for New York, where he re-entered university life. But yet again, he was forced to leave his law studies uncompleted and move on to Howard University, where he became a Communist Party activist and changed his name to George Padmore.

His outspokenness became increasingly pronounced towards the end of the 1920s, as he engaged in Communist politics on behalf of Afro-Americans and Africa. (At this time, many American intellectuals gravitated towards Communism, without arousing suspicion of their allegiance to their country.) But Padmore's attention was turned more and more in the direction of colonialism, African affairs and the depredations of imperialism. His disenchantment with Communism reached a head in mid-1934 when he was expelled from the Communist Party. This was a significant juncture for he no longer believed that Communism could deliver decolonisation and the elimination of racial prejudice,[32] and, as he argued for black 'Negro' unity along race, rather than class lines, he indicated his willingness to work with W.E.B. DuBois, the distinguished African-American scholar and Pan Africanist.

The black unity that Padmore hoped for remained elusive. Nevertheless his sense of injustice was so deep-rooted that only one direction concerned him: to develop a black brotherhood in London that would eventually free their fellow colonials. Among the capable black men around at the time who, in various ways, helped to bring about a sense of camaraderie and bonding in London were C.L.R. James, Eric Williams, Ras Makonnen and Jomo Kenyatta, whose contributions were, time and again, brought together by the more militant tendency of George Padmore, who not only spoke at countless meetings, but also wrote many articles and books, among them *How Britain Rules Africa*, *Africa and World Peace*, *The Gold Coast Revolution* and his last book *Pan Africanism or Communism?*

In the volatile world of black groups Padmore managed to bring a few of them together. And with the able assistance of Kwame Nkrumah, he pressed on with Pan African organisation which gained momentum, and became more and more radicalised during and after the war. By 1945, Padmore's credibility was such that he was able to convince the veteran DuBois and other black leaders of the timeliness of a Pan African conference. And so in August 1945, the black brotherhood in Britain gathered in Chorlton Hall, Manchester, where they deliberated, passed resolutions[33] and eventually made their way back to Africa, the United States and the Caribbean.

Following this historic Congress and coinciding with the end of the Second World War, DuBois, who was elected International President, returned to America with a deep sense of having participated in a momentous event. He had no doubt that there was a new 'colonial abroad'.[34] For Padmore, the Fifth Congress, largely ignored by the British press, had profound implications which would herald a new dawn in Africa.

After advising Nkrumah to return to the Gold Coast, Padmore did a two-hour interview with Ho Chi Minh, with whom Padmore had a relationship close enough for him to become the 'unofficial guardian of Viet Minh interests in London'.[35] Nevertheless, African affairs remained his consuming passion and intellectual concern. In 1946 and thereafter, he lectured often on Imperialism, Africa and the West Indies, and launched a newsletter entitled *The Colonial Parliamentary Bulletin: A Monthly Record of the Colonies in Westminster*, which was produced at his Cranleigh Street flat in London, where he lived with his English partner, Dorothy Pizer. At this time, he was optimistic that the Labour government would be more vigilant in dealing with racial discrimination in Britain. In particular, he blamed white American officers and troops for the unacceptable wartime racial conflict which his Pan African Federation was determined to eliminate.[36]

After the Second World War, Padmore became more focused on West Africa. He continued to relate the struggle in Britain to Africa, and surprisingly in December 1946, he joined forces with the League of Coloured Peoples leadership at an anti-colonial meeting. A few months later, he denounced Creech Jones, the Colonial Secretary, for the growing unrest in East Africa, but maintained his links with British MPs sympathetic to colonial affairs, men like Leslie Hale and Fenner Brockway.[37] Dr Moody's death in 1947 ended an uneasy alliance between the two Pan African leaders, one a 'moderate', the other the pre-eminent 'radical'. But in spite of their differences, Padmore's respect for, and recognition of, Moody's contribution to Britain's black community and colonial freedom were evident when he attended the LCP leader's funeral, as the Pan African Federation's representative.

In his roving and multifaceted role, Padmore was always available to meet African officials and leaders like Benjamin Azikiwe who visited London. Meanwhile, agitation on the Gold Coast moved apace, as Kwame Nkrumah roused the masses to action. After the ensuing riots, Padmore condemned the colonial police violence and said that the 'spectre of Pan Africanism is haunting the "dark continent"'.[38]

Between 1948 and 1957 he spoke tirelessly and wrote voluminously. 'Is Imperialism Dead?' he asked in 1950, and finally in this crucial decade, he visited his ancestral homeland, West Africa. He regarded Nkrumah 'as the embodiment of the hopes which international socialists had for renascent Africa' and claimed that the Gold Coast had 'gone down a road all Africa would follow'.[39] Failing health did not dampen his enthusiasm for the first Gold Coast general elections. Eventually, in 1957, Padmore witnessed the winning of Ghanaian Independence and in the autumn of that year, he was appointed Nkrumah's adviser on African affairs.

Amidst the euphoria of transformation of the Gold Coast colony into independent Ghana, Padmore was disturbed to learn that there was considerable opposition to his presence in the new nation. Yet his fervour and high hopes for the cause of Pan Africanism drove him on. In 1959 he attended a meeting of the national leaders of Liberia, Guinea and Ghana in Saniquelle, Liberia, where he became a victim of dysentery which compromised his already fragile health. He returned to London for treatment, but died three days after being admitted to University College Hospital. Richard Wright, the celebrated African-American novelist, wrote of Padmore as the greatest living authority on African nationalist movements, who not only understood these movements and their leaders, but whose life embodied their movements, aims and ideologies.[40]

After a funeral service at Golders Green Crematorium on Monday, 28 September, Padmore's ashes, at Nkrumah's request, were flown to Ghana, where they were interred at Christianborg Castle. Moved by the loss of his mentor and friend, Nkrumah, the first black African Prime Minister said of Padmore when they first met:

> We both realised from the beginning that we thought along the same lines and talked the same language. There existed between us that rare affinity for which one searches for so long but seldom finds in another human being ... our friendship developed into the indescribable relationship that existed between two brothers.[41]

In death, Ghanaians began to institutionalise Padmore, but the man who, for most of his life, had moved with an uncompromising sense of his own dignity in the white man's world, traversing the physical and intellectual Pan African quadrangle and beyond in a journey from the periphery to the centre, from Communism to Pan Africanism was soon forgotten.

Interestingly, none of the leading Pan Africanists was born in Britain, which perhaps helps to explain their heightened sense of the African diaspora. By the late 1950s, almost all of them had left Britain just as a new unprecedented wave of migrants began to enter the country. These audacious ideologues who had appropriated the 'standard' (Queen's) English as the means through which they articulated their subversive nationalist aspirations, returned to the colonies to fulfil the pledge they had made: to educate, organise and mobilise the masses.[42] As they expected, the postwar colonial world had not changed. In fact, the social and economic problems were of massive proportions. In Britain, however, the reverse was true. But this postwar economic boom would give rise to a brand of British nationalism that would have adverse effects on black and Asian newcomers in the decades to come.

NEWCOMERS (1950–62)

In conditions of postwar prosperity, at the invitation of the British government, waves of new migrants (largely from the Caribbean) landed in Britain in search of jobs and a better life. Yet again, the British economy demanded and got cheap black labour, at a time when the British working classes vacated low-paid, low-status, dead-end jobs at the base of the employment structure. This substitution of black for white labour would in time weaken working-class solidarity and increase the racist tendencies of white workers, who would increasingly become an integral part of the growing middle classes in postwar Britain.

The new migration into Britain in the postwar years from 1948 to 1962 aroused much controversy, comment and tension. From the point of view of those who were colonised, the exodus was extraordinary. The Jamaican poet Louise Bennett, in 'Colonization in Reverse', wrote:

'What a joyful news Miss Mattie,
I feel like me heart gwine burs'
Jamaica people colonizin
Englan' in reverse'.[43]

Another West Indian, the novelist and writer V.S. Naipaul, who came to England in the 1950s, noted that this emigration was part of a larger movement of peoples between continents and cities such as London, which were to change, becoming less national and more international as a result: 'They were to be cities visited for learning and elegant goods and manners and freedom by all the barbarian peoples of the globe, people of forest and desert, Arabs, Africans, Malays',[44] he wrote. But the treatment meted out to these 'barbarian peoples' who came to London was an experience so shocking that many could never forget it. Soon the cumulative experience of the arrivals had the quite unexpected effect of galvanising the various peoples, especially the West Indians, who had hitherto been so entrenched in their island identities, into a broader perception of themselves. 'No Barbadian, no Trinidadian, no St Lucian, no islander from the West Indies sees himself as a West Indian', George Lamming observed, 'until he encounters another islander in a foreign country.' In this sense, he regarded most West Indians of his generation as being 'born' in England.[45]

Housing, Employment and the Trade Unions

The newcomers went mainly to London, Liverpool, Manchester, Cardiff, Birmingham, Bristol, Nottingham, Bradford, Leeds, Leicester, Wolverhampton and other towns and cities in England; to Glasgow and Edinburgh in Scotland, and a few to Dublin and Belfast. In general, this period of migration was characterised by a greater number of people from the West Indies than Indians and Pakistanis.

In many cases, West Indian, Asian and African migrants joined family and friends who had preceded them. West Indians encountered a number of difficulties, especially in Nottingham and the Notting Hill area of London, where they faced an increasingly virulent resentment and opposition to their 'foreignness'. Repeated calls for black repatriation were made with unprecedented urgency, as more people from the West Indies or Caribbean (of African, Asian and European descent) arrived.

Sea transport was the cheapest and therefore the most popular means of travel. 'Goin' to Britten' became a well-known phrase and a new line of enterprise for local businessmen and travel agents; and while West Indian governments did not encourage emigration, most of them permitted it. Indeed, in one case, the government was actively involved: the Barbados government assisted migrants to find both jobs and accommodation in Britain. The number receiving such aid was small and generally West Indian migrants made their own arrangements. It is significant that warnings of housing and unemployment difficulties did not deter prospective migrants, for those who eventually made the trip were determined to succeed, regardless of the shock of initiation.

On arrival in Britain, the authorities did not ignore these 'dark strangers', for whom the help that was on offer (an initial gesture of goodwill) became increasingly politically motivated. According to an official estimate there were in total about 210,000 black people, less than 0.5 per cent of the total British population.[46] Though similarly small in relative terms to the black population of London in the late eighteenth century, the circumstances of the late 1950s, presented a 'new situation' of a 'black' population that was growing, that was more heterogeneous, that came to Britain 'voluntarily' and was 'free'.

Many migrants from India and Pakistan also found employment in London, Birmingham, Wolverhampton, Bradford, Leeds and Cardiff. The influx to Scotland was mainly to Glasgow and Edinburgh. Among those who had come to Britain were a growing number of Pakistani and Sikh pedlars, whose lack of English restricted their job mobility. Instead, they conformed to the fundamental requirements of their prospective employers, especially in the Midlands, where there was an overwhelming need for manual and preferably cheap labour. Physically strong and impressive, the first groups of Sikhs laboured and settled down, and from these wage-earning bases remittances were made to their families in India, who were prepared to join their relatives and friends in the postwar years of prosperity in Britain. This was the 'pull' factor.

The 'push' factor in this phase of Indian emigration was the establishment of the two independent states of India and Pakistan in 1947, which led to horrific communal violence, loss of life and uncertainty, particularly in the Punjab, as millions of Indians moved out of what is now Pakistan into India, while millions of Pakistanis moved in the opposite direction, an upheaval which dislocated an estimated 15 million.[47] This in turn led to a scramble for scarce land. Hardship intensified and the people naturally sought alternatives and those with families and friends in Britain made known their need for refuge and help. Two of the most populated areas of the Punjab were the districts of Jullundur and Hoshiarpur, from where many migrated to Britain to fill the vacancies for unskilled labourers in factories of one sort or another. Sikhs, in particular, were no strangers to migration both within and outside India; they were not inhibited from travelling overseas by the Hindu taboo of crossing the seas (kala pani), which automatically meant caste defilement and therefore a loss of caste status in Indian society.

The clash over Kashmir also led to the displacement of people, who were pressed to flee across borders within which they felt safest. And like Jullundur and Hoshiarpur, population pressure on Mirpur was relieved by the departure of Pakistanis, many of whom left via ships bound for Britain. In the years leading up to 1950, some jumped ship and became factory hands. Such newcomers, like their West Indian counterparts, were tuned in to the migrant network from which they gained support. This migrant flow was continuous, though not great. All the same, it reflected a variety of backgrounds – from the skilled and well-educated to the unskilled, unlettered manual labourer. By the mid-1950s the number of Indian and Pakistani migrants was just around a quarter of those from the West Indies. After a decrease in the last two years of the 1950s, the number of arrivals rose again in 1960.

Unlike the situation in the West Indies, where historically Europeans imposed themselves upon the African slaves and their descendants, in India, the British had little social intercourse with the Indians, a social distance which added to the British mystique and through which the British maintained the sense of awe they inspired, especially among older Indians. Nevertheless, Indians were quick to recognise that Britain and its inhabitants were foreign, alien, aloof, which was unhelpful in narrowing the gap between white Britons and themselves. Thus Indian and Pakistani workers emigrated to Britain not just for a mix of socio-economic and cultural reasons like West Indians, but purely for economic gain. And like West Indians, many Indians and Pakistanis often had to take an indirect route to Britain. In short, administrative controls in these countries were inhibiting factors in emigration to Britain. The rumour that legislation would be passed to restrict entry into Britain led to a rush which saw a rise from 8,400 migrants in 1960 to 48,850 the following year and a further increase just six months into 1962.[48] This dramatic growth in immigration was characterised by more male migrants than female. In 1961, in Bradford, the ratio of Indian men to women was three to one. But although the first immigration ban was passed in 1962, it did not stop the flow of migrants. None the less in the pre-1962 period, Asian immigration was characterised by two stages, divided by the year 1960. Prior to this date, Asian immigration was not even a third of the influx from the West Indies, while after 1960, it rose sharply to reach West Indian levels, and this larger Asian presence boosted their confidence although direct contact with a friend or relative remained crucial for all newcomers in both periods, as they tried to adapt to living in industrialised cities and towns.

The partition of India was celebrated by Muslims and Hindus in Scotland. However, harmony between these two religious groups proved hard to achieve in India, especially in the period immediately after Independence. And in the extraordinary circumstances of mass displacement and confusion in the subcontinent, many were determined to take flight to Britain to join the relatively small population of an estimated 600 Asians in 1950. The rise thereafter was dramatic, doubling in the succeeding five years. This decade not only saw an increase in the number of families, but also a change in the number of Asians becoming pedlars. Fewer newcomers were prepared to undertake the great sacrifices that peddling entailed and many sought jobs as wage-earners in the postwar prosperity. At this time too, there were many educated and economically well-off Asians whose attentions were directed away from peddling. In spite of this change, peddling retained its pre-eminence as the most popular occupation of South Asians in Britain at least until the end of the 1950s, which saw a larger number of Asians go to the factories and mills of Bradford and Birmingham than those who went to Scotland. But by the end of the decade with economic recession and factory closures, large numbers of Asians from England went to Scotland to take jobs, thus adding to the Asian populations in the three areas previously mentioned, which totalled some 4,000 in 1960.[49]

Throughout the United Kingdom, the birth of migrants' children and the gradual settlement of families, marked a feeling of permanence, a new beginning and a new awareness among black and Asian people of their place in British society.

Housing

'After all these years of paying rent, I had the ambition to own my own property in London, no matter how ruinous or dilapidated it was', so argued Moses, the central character in Sam Selvon's novel *Moses Ascending*. 'If you are a tenant, you catch your arse forever, but if you are a landlord, it is a horse of a different colour.'[50]

From the outset, employment and housing were the two main concerns of black migrants in London. In the four years prior to 1958, housing was as serious a problem as unemployment with which it was related. Soon enough, it was found that mutual help within the migrant community was the only solution.

West Indian newcomers to London initially tended to spend one night at least with a friend or relative. While few of them arrived without an address, temporary accommodation had to be found for some, who stayed in Salvation Army hostels. Others were assisted by welfare officers who met them on arrival. Similar arrangements were made for nurses and for Barbadians who came to Britain under their Government's Scheme. The West Indian Welfare Officer, employed by the London Transport Executive, was charged with finding accommodation for workers recruited by the Executive, but although few of them have been helped in this way, the vast majority found rooms through personal contacts and sheer determination.

Perhaps the main benefit was the help that newcomers received from those who had earlier established themselves, compatriots whose houses became 'hostels'. Unofficial 'reception centres' of this kind were to be found in North Kensington,

Camberwell, Brixton, Islington and Hampstead.[51] The scattered locations of these centres (most within a radius of 6 miles from Charing Cross) avoided the creation of a 'coloured quarter', as migrants frequently tried to get better and permanent accommodation as close to their first bases as possible, an inclination underscored by a sense of belonging encapsulated in the often repeated phrase 'we all in the same boat now'. Another element in the location of these 'first bases' was that of chance, as in the case of settlement in Brixton. When, for example, the first large group of West Indians arrived in 1948, the Colonial Office, seriously concerned about them (not least because this was an unforeseen problem!), directed that they be temporarily accommodated in Clapham Common Underground Station, which had been used as a wartime air-raid shelter. Creech-Jones, the Colonial Secretary, wrote to Councillor Jack Simpson, Mayor of Lambeth, whose borough was close to Clapham Common and asked if some welcome could be arranged (as though the West Indians were not migrants, but guests) but Simpson with an entertainment allowance of £600 for the whole year, said he could entertain only 40 Jamaicans. So, on the afternoon of Wednesday, 3 June, in a room over the Astoria Cinema in Brixton, a representative group of Jamaicans were invited to tea by the Mayor. Local officers and two Members of Parliament were also present. In expansive mood, Colonel Marcus Lipton, Labour Member for Brixton, told the men that they should regard Brixton as their second home. The Mayor offered his best wishes and commented: 'When I heard of your coming here I was moved. A journey like yours does not take place without good reason.' Afterwards, the disoriented West Indians were treated to a free cinema show and on their return to the air-raid shelter that evening, the 40 men described the reception to their friends. As Joyce Eggington recorded, they 'spoke with enthusiasm, joyous that a few people had taken the trouble to make them feel welcome ... In the unknown and perplexing vastness of England, the Jamaicans now felt they could be sure of one place. Brixton was friendly. In Brixton they could make their homes.'[52] And so they did. In years to come, Brixton would, in the popular imagination, become synonymous with black settlement and black culture in Britain.

After this welcome, most of the men were employed locally, which was an added incentive to stay in the district. And even though this was the beginning of postwar migrant settlement, these areas offered accommodation to the mass of migrants who constituted a low-income group. In the main, West Indians could not find accommodation in the working-class districts of the East End and the southern riverside boroughs where, because of the stability of the population and tenancies, there was no room for subdivision. The ranks of the white working class were effectively closed and the newcomers at that time were not eligible for the new municipal flats and houses built by the London County Council and the Metropolitan Boroughs. Middle- and upper-class districts such as Hampstead, Chelsea, Westminster and South Kensington, among others, were not available to most West Indians. Many old streets and squares had become fashionable and expensive, as office blocks, stores and hostels competed for space. Meanwhile, the scarcity of residential space was not effectively dealt with by the policy-makers, whose objective was to discourage population as reflected in the patterns of development that followed. West Indian newcomers were therefore shunted into restricted areas with poor accommodation, neglected patches of London, which had been in the process of 'decline and social downgrading'. Some accommodation near Portobello Road and Paddington Station was 'forbidding'.[53] Depressing though these conditions were, among the more enterprising West Indians, necessity brought invention, especially in relation to rooms inhabited by families. Many applied themselves industriously to the task of transforming their drab surroundings in an effort to make them more pleasant and colourful: in a word, habitable. But for all their native inventiveness structurally some lodgings could only be temporary and as such, presented an even more depressing prospect.

As London expanded, often decay and rejuvenation were juxtaposed, contrasts that were especially pronounced in North Kensington, where the facades of some houses indicated that migrants were the occupants; and the condition of the streets and the surrounding spaces revealed 'an important aspect of the so-called "colour problem"'.

Since Charles Booth's *New Survey of London Life and Labour* in the 1920s, there had been a rapid deterioration in this area, with gaps along streets of terraced housing, the so-called 'streets of transition' where a large number of West Indians found rooms, adjacent to bombed-out sites, which formed part of the environment. And at the margins of these zones were Notting Dale and Kensal New Town, areas of transition since the late nineteenth century that had become 'rotten parts' of the Royal Borough in the twentieth century, districts notorious for their poverty, overcrowding and crime. Some rooms in these areas were described as 'slum basements', which warned of the dangers of rheumatism and bronchitis and, as expected, parts of North Kensington figured weekly in the police news.[54] By the early 1950s, Kensal New Town had the highest rate of overcrowding in London, some five times greater than the average for the whole of London.[55]

Increased immigration made the 'zones of transition' more dense and, as a consequence, housing conditions deteriorated and rents increased. Several migrants sharing one room was not uncommon, and in the limited living space, they slept, cooked and ate, staying indoors (except when the weather was warm) for most of their free time. 'Double-rooms' were often little more than box rooms. One of the first West Indians to write about the black experience in Britain, the Indo-Trinidadian Sam Selvon in his novel *The Lonely Londoners*, coined the phrase, a 'two by ten room'.[56] And such washing facilities as there were more often than not had to be shared. In these cramped conditions, West Indians, so used to the warmth of the sun and the outdoor life, found their rooms claustrophobic and depressing. They often felt homesick.

Soon there was a sense of inevitability that it would be just a matter of time before this 'rack-renting' was exposed, even though black tenants were threatened with violence to prevent them from seeking a rent reduction at a rent tribunal. These 'shark' landlords plagued migrants, exploiting their real fears of homelessness. Regardless of the difficulties, many West Indians took pride in making their rooms as comfortable as possible. Significantly, some who were relatively better-off bought their own homes, a source of great pride and achievement.

As prejudice and discrimination reduced their chances of better accommodation, the migrants' complaints were, in time, echoed by many observers, as they competed for the limited available amenities with their white counterparts, many of whom were themselves badly housed. This rapidly became a source of bitter contention as the physical and social constraints which they felt were attributed to the black newcomers. As *The Times* reported, working-class white people, suspicious and sensitive, resented their black neighbours because they lowered the standing of the neighbourhood.[57] Not surprisingly, negative images of black people were strongest where housing conditions were worst. As irritations proliferated and hardship accumulated, disputes between black and white tenants and landlords spread, and for what seemed like an interminably long period, strained relations characterised the migrant zones, as increasingly, black people looked to each other for assurance and support.

How, in these early days did a black newcomer become a landlord? As we saw earlier, becoming a house-owner, rather than a rent-payer, was Moses's dream in Selvon's novel. Usually a number of people pooled their savings to raise the deposit to purchase a house. Once they had possession of the house, rooms were let to relations and friends, to new arrivals and 'refugees' from other lodgings. The accumulated rent was ploughed back into buying another house, and so on. In this way, a chain of ownership was formed and fortuitously for the landlord concerned, black migrants tended to favour black landlords rather than white, though at times, the rents (a 'colour tax') charged were higher. White tenants, on the other hand, particularly in North Kensington, blamed their higher rents on the migrants, while white landlords invested in housing in the zones of transition, hoping that their investments would be rewarded by profits accruing from 'rack-renting' black tenants, whose options were few. Soon it became known that such landlords had encouraged their West Indian tenants to behave in 'an anti-social way to dislodge sitting tenants so that higher rents could be charged'.[58] Thus, the few West Indians who cooperated in this practice incurred an unfavourable and lasting reputation, which their detractors were not slow to exploit.

Few could help the West Indian migrants. One manager of a small London estate agency, said that he had as many as 200 West Indians a week asking for rooms, but could only help about seven in that time.[59] But if xenophobia in housing was pervasive, the job market for West Indians was as bad and a major site of racial discrimination.

Employment

The world of work was also an extraordinary experience, especially in London. Sam Selvon, in a vivid passage from *Moses Ascending*, depicts the lot of a group of black workers, whose alarm clocks ring earlier than the rest of the population, and who make their way in the early hours of the day, lucky to be breathing the 'freshest' air before their working day began. In Selvon's words the black cleaner ' is manager of all the offices in Threadneedle Street, he is Chief Executive of London Transport and British Railways, he is superintendent of all the hospitals, he is landlord of all the mansions in Park Lane and Hampstead ... He ain't reach the stage of scrubbing the floors of Buckingham Palace ... He should realise that if it wasn't for him the city would go on sleeping forever.'[60]

The Colour Bar when recruiting West Indian workers was relatively disguised, though discrimination and prejudice on the grounds of race and colour in employment were entrenched. For those who found jobs, many experienced a 'new chain of frictions'.

Into the second half of the twentieth century white Britons (the English in particular) had an entirely different attitude towards black people in the workplace as opposed to them in their vicinity, never mind as marriage partners. For it seemed that while many white people were prepared to work with black people, they were reluctant to accept them as neighbours. And while some white men praised black people as workers, the vast majority perceived the black male as shiftless and lazy, living off national assistance or the earnings of prostitutes. West Indians were aware of this attitude among their white co-workers, and soon it was clear that employment, and the attendant indignities in securing and enduring it, were the hard reality for colonial workers.

The prospect of a large West Indian workforce in British industry with its implications for race relations was anticipated. In order to avoid incurring a 'black problem', the British Transport Commission first proposed that Italians should be recruited for the railways, a proposition that was opposed by the National Union of Railwaymen. Thereafter, the Transport Executive found it expedient to focus attention elsewhere – on Ireland and then the Caribbean. For the Executive the difficulty was not in employing blacks (they had already employed a few though not many in the 'operating grades') but deciding at what level. When the decision was eventually taken to employ them in the operating grades a recruiting team was sent to Barbados and an elaborate organisation was set up on the island.[61] The British invitation to black workers could not, on the face of it, be more genuine and public.

When the recruits travelled to London, they were, of course, unaware of the realities that awaited them. London Transport had filled its recruitment needs by employing about 4,000 black workers, who after two days' training started work in the lowest grades, though ever hopeful of promotion. Two years later, some had become bus-drivers, train-guards and booking office clerks and, in a few cases, station foremen. Those in junior supervisory posts were in charge of both white and black workers, but they were only a token few.

If the employment of migrants by London Transport was exceptional, elsewhere they were received with hesitation or treated with antipathy. Employers' views of black workers were more or less the same and while some gave good references to West Indian workers, others regarded them as slow and careless. There was a tendency to exaggerate the employability of black workers.

The diversity of the migrants' backgrounds, aspirations, attitudes and responses indicated a richness and variety of experience. Encouraging though they were, the few success stories had to be weighed against the reality of hardship and failure of the majority, for whom there was no room at the top. Another aspect of the newcomers' experience was occupational downgrading to a variety of low-paid jobs in London.[62] Women seem to have had some latitude, though not much. A considerable number of them (including many Indo-Caribbean women, and others of Portuguese and Chinese descent) went into nursing, some were eventually employed as doctors, as teachers and journalists or as black-coated workers, while others worked as skilled manual workers and less securely in the world of entertainment. There were barbers, tailors, cleaners, laundry men, shop-keepers and café-owners and a few businessmen, whose establishments were, in the main, patronised by West Indians. Nevertheless, it soon became apparent that only a few West Indians were in middle-class and skilled positions. The Conservative government was determined to keep blacks and Asians out of the Civil Service,[63] and many had no choice but to accept positions inferior to previously held 'white-collar' and skilled jobs, and accept a drop in status to that of the lowest ranks of the unskilled.[64]

The grievances of black people in the workplace posed a challenge to the trade union movement, which proclaimed its belief in equality and the brotherhood of working men. This was unequivocally emphasised in a General Council statement at the Trades Union Congress held soon after the racial riots in Nottingham and Notting Hill in the summer of 1958.[65]

Many unions and branches submitted resolutions denouncing discrimination. But there was no united approach on the colour question among the local branches of any one trade union and ambiguity persisted within the labour movement in the late 1950s. It has been suggested that the attitudes of white workers and trade union branches to the 'colour problem' was most pronounced in the Midlands and the North, where memories of the Depression were still vivid and xenophobia strong. The fear here was that black workers would cut overtime earnings and that employers would use them as a source of cheap, sweated labour and, in the event of strikes, as 'blacklegs'. This had been, and would become, a recurrent argument used by white workers against blacks, a time-worn traditional prejudice towards the foreigner that was rooted in the fear of economic competition that arose from the racist legacy of imperialism and colonialism.

In London, the attitude towards the recruitment of blacks was dramatised in the public transport services. Indeed there were few initial difficulties when black people joined London Transport, though in several provincial cities, there were unofficial strikes or threats, when Indians, Pakistanis and West Indians were recruited to work on the buses. Regardless of assurances, 'tolerant' white people, among them trade unionists, supported discrimination.[66] The 1950s therefore saw relations between blacks and Asians, on the one hand, and between blacks and whites, on the other, become distinctly troubled in the workplace. In fact, during the 1950s, colour prejudice, whether ambiguous, concealed or open, led to discrimination primarily in housing and jobs and tended to be self-perpetuating. This had disastrous effects on the lives of both the West Indian and Asian newcomers to Britain. Yet no serious consideration was given to the tensions that had, by this time, already accumulated beyond the workplace.

THE RIOTS OF 1958

Ten years after the SS *Empire Windrush* arrived in England with hundreds of West Indian migrants, some 2,000–3,000 black people were living in Nottingham, a considerable number of them in a 'decaying' district. It was here, in The Chase, a public house, on Saturday, 23 August 1958, that a fight took place between two men, one black, the other white, before closing time. In so intemperate an environment, the fighting spread quickly. Attacks led to counter-attacks and several men were stabbed, while dozens were injured. Reinforcements were called in to aid the two or three policemen who, at first, attempted to pacify the hostile crowd that had gathered. The fire brigade was also notified in case the 'ugly riotous crowd' started fires. And, as was the case in Cardiff earlier in the century, several injured black men were taken away by the police 'for their own safety'.[67] Just under two hours later, order was restored and by midnight the crowds had dispersed, leaving many unanswered questions.

The events were not a case of 'spontaneous combustion' – tension in the area had been running high for a long time as black people (who, according to the Assistant Chief Constable of Nottingham, were generally 'very well behaved')[68] were beaten up by 'Teddy Boys'.

Unlike the Nottingham disturbances, during the London riots the main confrontations occurred outside the black settlements and significantly the assailants were from white housing estates. A climate of menace and fear pervaded the neighbourhood, as random assaults and 'nigger-hunting' became part of the pattern of violence directed against black people, who faced attacks by individuals as well as by gangs of white youths. Fascist slogans such as 'Keep Britain White' and 'People of Kensington Act Now' were chanted by racist agitators and the White Defence League and the Union Movement held meetings opposing the black presence in Notting Hill. The rising tension eventually led to violence. For a while black people stayed at home and stood their ground as best they could, before they came out and demonstrated their disgust, resistance and solidarity in Notting Hill.

As news of the riots flashed around the world, three leading West Indian politicians, Norman Manley, Carl La Corbiniere and Hugh Cummins, arrived in London for talks with the British government and meetings with the besieged West Indians in the affected areas of London and Nottingham. Whatever goodwill there was previously towards West Indian migrants now seemed to have vanished as nine white youths were found guilty and received 'severe' sentences. The press in Britain and the United States expressed concern about the causes and advanced various explanations. However, the 'colour problem', which was at the very heart of the matter, remained a vexed issue. On reflection, it was clear that the Notting Hill trouble-makers were acting out tendencies that were pervasive in British society. Indeed, the 'rabble' were 'shouting' what others were 'whispering'.[69] This was, perhaps, the lesson of the 1958 riots, which revealed not two but several divided nations. But if government practices and policies had brought about inner city decay and subsequent black immigration, was there a political solution? And what were the reactions of responsible officials to the riots?

Britain's 'colour problem' hit the international headlines and was followed by soul-searching national reports, comments and reactions. The media did not shirk its responsibilities, and white commentators who sought a balanced view were, more or less, at one in censuring the Notting Hill 'hooligans'.[70] *The Times* pontificated on a 'family of nations' and British race relations were debated within political parties, the trade unions and churches. Colour prejudice could not be denied. Yet British opinion leaders, protected by the rigid class system (and perhaps genuinely ignorant because they were simply not interested) persisted in viewing racial discrimination as 'un-British'. But the tide of world history was against the former Imperial powers, as the strains of this phase of decolonisation became dramatically evident in skirmishes and, increasingly in violent confrontations in Africa, Asia, the Caribbean and the Americas, countries whose peoples' history and culture had hitherto been so intertwined with Britain's. Moreover this anti-colonial proc- ess was advanced through consolidation of labour and the formation of political parties as the struggle for Independence intensified.

Meanwhile, among the British intelligentsia, a polarisation of opinion emerged in the debate on race, colour and immigration as some politicians called for both the deportation of Common- wealth migrants convicted for criminal offences, and for immi- gration control.[71]

Predictably after the Nottingham disturbances, two local MPs asked for just such control, while other parliamentarians joined in the chorus for an immigration 'quota'. Together they were able to bring enough pressure to bear to get a response from the government. It was abundantly clear to many that since the demand for restrictions referred not to the migrants who were white, but to those who were black and Asian, immigration control was a polite term for a Colour Bar. However, some seemingly sensitive spokesmen were at pains to lay such anxieties to rest. Indeed the Conservative Party Conference in the autumn of 1958 resolved to revise the immigration laws of entry 'irrespective of race, colour or creed', palpably a red herring. But the Conservatives were not alone in promoting such self-delusion; immigration was an issue that cut across party lines. While the Labour Party took a firm stand, convinced that any form of British legislation limiting Commonwealth immigration would be disastrous to Britain's status in the Commonwealth, the Liberal Party denounced racial discrimination and rejected any restriction. The parties feared that legislation against colour would jeopardise the unity of the Commonwealth.[72] They were right for the forces of disintegration had already been set in motion.

Political debate on immigration control did nothing to diminish tension in some parts of North Kensington, as the 'Keep Britain White' campaign persisted and was complemented by the spiteful jibes and activities of the fascist leader, Oswald Mosley. Underlying such confrontational displays were the deeper rumblings from an environment characterised by decay and social discontent. On the night of 17 May 1959, racial hatred claimed its first victim, when Kelso Cochrane, a 32-year-old West Indian carpenter was killed by a gang of white youths. The police thought robbery was the motive, but black people in the area believed that Cochrane was killed because he was black, an unprovoked murder which increased 'race tension'. The upshot was that much of what was submerged now came to the surface, as Notting Hill and its environs were again in the spotlight, and the White Defence League referred to Cochrane as 'this manufactured martyr'.[73]

Cochrane's death became a symbol of the need for black unity. At his funeral, people felt the need to show their sense of outrage and solidarity. And so they did, as some 800 marched behind the coffin from the church in Ladbroke Grove to Kensal Green cemetery. In the wake of the murder, much attention was focused on the causes and symptoms of tension: a housing shortage, crowding and blight, casual employment and inadequate policing. In all, they were symptomatic of the general malaise, manifestations of social disorder and violence, both mental and physical. At root, government policy was inadequate and, as was the case during the 1940s in Liverpool and in 1958 in Nottingham, it was said that on the whole, black people were distrustful of the police,[74] charges that would have a familiar ring in the decades to come.

As the general election of October 1959 approached, the fascists kept up their menacing anti-black propaganda, and now agitated to 'Keep Hampstead White' because a black doctor, David Pitt, was the Labour Party's candidate in that constituency. He was heckled with racist slogans while he was speaking in Hampstead Town Hall.[75] Pitt lost in Hampstead, but the fascists were ecstatic, having won several thousand votes.

Even as the extremist organisations continued to preach racial hatred, some activity was directed at bringing about the integration of the non-white minority, through what was meant to be a counterpoise to the 'Keep Britain White' lobby, the 'Keep Britain Tolerant' groups. So it was that in the wake of the sad events of 1958, social, educational and welfare activities came into being as never before.

Some West Indians became more trusting and friendly with their neighbours, while others joined churches (which would more and more become the place where they would gather and build community strength), political parties, trade unions, student bodies, sports, jazz and social clubs; and throughout London, much goodwill was expressed through a number of socially-oriented groups whose programmes reflected their cosmopolitan and inter-racial nature, much of which were evident at dances, socials and lectures, though they were short-lived.

The black churches were especially helpful to West Indians, and in education and welfare, community spirit was to be found more readily. Indeed, there seems to have been a real determination among black people not only to assist in the adjustment of newcomers into the migrant community, but to extend the frontiers of racial integration in relation to the rest of London's population.[76]

Informal contacts were made through meetings held in basement rooms, street corners, markets, cafés and barber shops. Bed-sitting rooms and barber shops in particular served as community centres where West Indian newspapers were read and discussed, all the latest news and gossip were heard, and one could get information about new arrivals, possible job vacancies and accommodation, threats of unemployment and the announcements of meetings and dances. Migrants also met in their own licensed clubs and in shopping centres such as Brixton Market, Finsbury Park, Camden Town and Portobello Road. Although small at this time, the various black communities were 'alert, active and connected' and able to exercise some influence. One of the organisations strengthened after August 1958 was the Association for the Advancement of Coloured People, which had benefited from being presided over by Mrs Amy Dashwood Garvey, who ran a hostel and club in North Kensington. This was a case where one leader worked at several levels. Since publication of *The Keys*, there had been a communications vacuum. What had become obvious to the more committed and campaigning leaders was the absence of a journal disseminating information about the black experience in Britain. Claudia Jones, a rare woman and radical activist from Trinidad, had recognised this and became editor of *The West Indies Gazette*, a monthly publication which, in its first issue of March 1958, proclaimed that West Indians in Britain formed a community with its own special wants and problems which 'our own paper alone would allow us to meet'. And so efforts were directed towards the furtherance of British–West Indian unity. By 1960, with a total circulation of 15,000 copies, the *Gazette* gradually began to establish itself. Less successful were *Link* and the *Anglo-Caribbean News*.[77]

The *Gazette* was therefore not only timely, but also a vital medium of communication within the black community and, as the black population increased, the *Gazette* played an even more important role through its advertisements, which included announcements of various meetings, steamship travel to and from the Caribbean, information about West Indian shops, clubs, restaurants and services in London; and, significantly, organised the first 'Caribbean Carnival' in Notting Hill in January 1959, a cultural event that continued to grow in scale and spectacle over the years and through which it was hoped to bind even closer West Indians in Britain. In its Carnival brochure, the *Gazette* called for an 'Independent United Democratic state of West Indians in the British Commonwealth' and for the unity of West Indians and other coloured people in

Britain. Of paramount importance was the fact that it stressed friendship with the British people, based on equality and human dignity, irrespective of race, colour or origin. This was, as the succeeding years of the Notting Hill Carnival have shown, a sound basis for social expectations from which celebrants could proceed. Black migrants rallied around the journal, which became the recognised medium through which people gave and received goods and services, underscored by an encouraging measure of goodwill, as the horizon of the community expanded and was mirrored in the 'Anglo-Caribbean Diary' section of the *Gazette*. With the arrival of more Asians and Africans, this feature was renamed the 'Afro-Asian-Caribbean-UK Unity Diary',[78] which noted that 'black' encompassed all non-whites, thus broadening the scope of the column. This was a timely development for although racial discrimination continued to be ignored, immigration control was once again a contentious issue in British politics.

With the Conservative Party's victory at the polls in 1959, its 'restrictionist lobby', which argued for no less than stringent control of black immigration, became even more vociferous. Migrants took note and warned families, relatives and friends abroad that Britain was likely to cease its open-door immigration policy. As a consequence, the large numbers of migrants who came to Britain, described as an 'unarmed invasion', boosted the West Indian population from 16,400 in 1959 to 49,000 in 1960, to the great displeasure of the anti-immigration lobby.[79]

The black presence has always raised fears (more imagined than real) among white racists in Britain. More often than not, deportation and repatriation of black people were considered as necessary measures. Now the black presence and immigration had again become a preoccupation, in some quarters. Race permeated British politics. On this matter, the Commonwealth Relations Office and the Colonial Office stood opposed to the Home Office, and the British government was faced with the problem of administration in the event of control, since the majority of black migrants at the time were from the West Indies and, as such, were citizens of the United Kingdom and the Colonies. Therefore any change in the legal definition of

British citizenship would have courted the charge of racism by the affected Commonwealth countries. To complicate matters further, the process of Federation in the West Indies was already underway. Once federated, it was the British government's hope that, like India and Pakistan, West Indian emigration would be controlled at source.

As the 'open door' policy on Commonwealth immigration became threatened, more attention was paid to the settlement of blacks and Asians already in Britain. But settlement was, and continued to prove, uncomfortable for the migrants themselves, particularly in view of Sir Cyril Osborne's statement that England 'is a white man's country' and he wanted it 'to remain so'.[80] So the debate continued.

However, the fear of control had its own dynamic, generating a sharp increase in the number of migrants and those who had 'beaten the ban' (that is, the Immigration Act of 1962) now joined the ranks of earlier migrants. For these people, the sense of displacement and alienation was profound. And from their various and often modest places of abode, during the first five decades of the century, many to their great credit, sought to express themselves artistically on the stage and through technological advances made in the modern mediums of film and television.

IMAGES OF BLACK PEOPLE IN FILMS AND TELEVISION (PRE-1960)

Among the earliest images of black people on film was their appearance in *The Wandering Negro Minstrels* screened on 9 March 1896 at the inauguration of the Cinematique in London's Leicester Square. Their brief on-screen performance of singing, dancing and playing musical instruments was none the less historic.

Black performers also began to appear in shows such as *In Dahomey*, which was staged in London's Shaftesbury theatre in 1903 with the African-Americans Bert Williams, George Walker and Pete Hampton who, as a singer, made several recordings and added a film appearance in 1909 to his credit.

This new art form, Stephen Bourne noted, attracted growing interest and at the beginning of the twentieth century, several American productions featuring African-Americans were shown in Britain, provocatively named silent films such as *The Dancing Niggers, The Lightfooted Darkey, Dreamland Adventures, The Ugly Golliwog, Stump Speech, Sambo, Nigger Courtship, Bertie's Baby, Keeping it Dark* and *Slavery Days: The New Master*.[81] And at a time when boxing and entertainment were among the main areas of black/white contact, not surprisingly, Jack Johnson and Tom Molyneux,[82] the most famous African-American boxers of their day, were remembered in moving images.

In Edwardian Britain, non-American black people appeared in British-made films. Though best known for his advocacy of Pan Africanism, Duse Mohamed Ali, also a literary agent and theatrical impresario, helped black playwrights and actors such as Ernest Trimmingham from Bermuda, who was identified as the first black film actor in Britain when he appeared in the 1912 series of silent films entitled *The Adventures of Dick Turpin – The King of the Highwaymen*. Seven years later, he played Pete in *Jack, Sam and Pete*, before his last film appearance in the ironically named *Where the Rainbow Ends*. Thereafter, he acted on the West End stage, before his death in 1942, at the age of 61.[83]

Though black entertainers were numerous in British music halls and London night clubs, as actors they were not highly regarded. White British opinion was divided and the lack of seriousness on the part of British film-makers in their approach to black Caribbean performers continued to be far more problematic for them than it was for African-Americans.

The towering presence of Paul Robeson in British films in the 1930s was the single greatest contribution by any black person to British cinema. His popularity in Britain and internationally was unsurpassed. While honouring Robeson, Sidney Poitier said: 'There would need to be a ceremony like this every day for the rest of our lives for us to ever begin to be aware of the impact he had on the role of blacks in the [film] industry.'[84] However, although he was one of the twentieth century's greatest artists, his rise to prominence was not easy. His films in particular, were 'mainly poor', as David Shipman claimed in *The Great Movie Stars: The Golden Years*, nor were his films important except for his 'presence in them'.[85]

A measure of Robeson's disenchantment with some of his film portrayals was demonstrated in his anger following the completion and screening of *Sanders of the River*, which glorified the British Empire. Two notable and distinguished black critics of this infamous film were Marcus Garvey and Dr Namdi Azikiwe, who were joined by *The Keys'* film correspondent. Garvey had no doubt as to what art should represent. In his view, black 'creative artists should not only identify with the struggle of their own people but ... their work should be a direct contribution to this struggle'.

In spite of criticisms from both blacks and whites, the overall value of Robeson's role in the film industry cannot be underestimated.

Apart from films, Robeson also made numerous appearances in documentaries, interviews and concerts on British television and radio, from the beginning of the Second World War until his death in 1976. Since then, yet more has been spoken and written about him as new generations were (and are) exposed to images of this 'conscience of America'.

Before Robeson came to Britain, many black men became 'film extras', a truly precarious means of earning a living. Among those so engaged were Joseph Bruce, Napoleon Florent and members of their families, Jomo Kenyatta (then a student), Ernest Marke, Anthony Papafio, the Conner family of Canning Town in London, and many black people from Tiger Bay in Cardiff. All these people could be seen as African extras in various productions, including Robeson's films. Other black men and women who appeared on film were Cleo Laine, Norris Smith and Ras Prince Monolulu. And, of course, there were the nameless few, such as the unknown black 'extra' who, as a chained prisoner, evoked a haunting, compelling image in David Lean's film of Charles Dickens's *Great Expectations*.[86]

Many African-American performers, who had their first appearances during the Harlem Renaissance, came to Britain where their recordings, music hall and club performances won them much acclaim. Earlier shows featuring Bert Williams,

George Walker and Florence Mills in *Shuffle Along* and *Black-birds* had also enjoyed success. Images of Jocelyn Bingham could be seen in Phototone Reels and Ellis Jackson, the versatile African-American entertainer, played his parts. In 1930 Johnny Nit tap-danced his way on Broadway and in the short film *Sugar and Spice*, to be followed by other outstanding black dancers, notably Bill 'Bojangles' Robinson. Another rare and unforgettable talent was the choreographer Buddy Bradley, a 'genius of dance' and acknowledged as such by the likes of Fred Astaire, who prompted Jessie Matthews to recruit Bradley for her popular musical *Evergreen*. As a choreographer in the 1930s, Bradley collaborated with Matthews on many films and worked on radio and variety shows for television. But significant as his contribution was to dance on film, he has received scant recognition from film historians and commentators. Though John Kobal mentions Bradley's work in conjunction with Matthews, Bradley is omitted from David Shipman's and Colin Larkin's books.[87]

Another hugely popular African-American to come to Britain was Elisabeth Welch. Born in New York City in 1904, she had a long and glorious career on stage, in British films and television, appearing often with the most distinguished black performers of her time, including Robeson.

Black Music on Film: 1930s–1950s

Black rhythms and black music generally, though new and exotic sounds when set against conservative British taste, proved to be irresistible to British film makers. Black singers and dancers who come to mind are Turner Layton, 'Buck and Bubbles' and the Nicholas Brothers, among others. Then came Mabel Mercer, Leslie 'Hutch' Hutchinson (singer-pianist), Reginald Foresythe (pianist-composer and bandleader) the jazz greats Louis Armstrong and Fats Waller, Ken 'Snakehips' Johnson and the trumpet player Leslie 'Jiver' Hutchinson. Though the appearance of black musicians in British films was rare, in the early years, a few performers can be identified, namely Leslie Thompson in *A Night in Montmartre*, pianist

Fela Sowande in *The Lisbon Story*, Ray Ellington in *Rhythm Racketeer* and, in the 1940s, *Walking on Air* and *Paper Orchid*, Freddie Crump in *King Arthur Was a Gentleman*, Cyril Blake in *At the Havanna* and Edmundo Ross and his popular band, especially in the 1940s, in *Night Boat to Dublin* and *Here Come Huggetts*.

Black music also reached the medium of television. The inauguration of BBC television saw the appearance of the African-Americans Buck and Bubbles in a Variety Show broadcast from Alexandra Palace in November 1936. In the prewar years of television transmission, celebrities featured were Nina Mae McKinney, Johnny Nit, Adelaide Hall, Valaida Snow, Leslie Thompson, Albert Hunter, the Mills Brothers and Fats Waller, among others.

By 1947, when the BBC was again operational after the wartime disruption, the singers Todd Duncan, Josephine Baker and Dorothy Dandridge made appearances. So too did Edric Connor, the West African Rhythm Brothers, Leslie 'Jiver' Hutchinson, Cyril Blake and His Calypso Band, Reginald Foresythe, Ray Ellington, Ida Shipley and Coleridge Goode. And after a gap of five years, Katharine Dunham and her black dance troupe performed before the cameras. This was encouraging, as indeed the succeeding years were to show, especially after the coronation of Elizabeth II in 1953, which triggered a dramatic rise in the number of television viewers. A new channel, ITV, began broadcasting two years later, and offered more popular shows such as *Sunday Night at the London Palladium*, which brought unprecedented exposure to black performers like Winifred Atwell, Cleo Laine, Shirley Bassey, Eartha Kitt, Duke Ellington, Sarah Vaughan, Harry Belafonte, Nat King Cole, Lena Horne, Billie Holiday and Paul Robeson in the 1950s. But as Pearl Connor (wife of Edric) recalled, African-American performers were preferred for parts in British films and television, which should have been offered to established black British actors. 'We suffered a lot because of this bias,' she said, though there was no lack of determination among these actors to prove their worth.

Though black performers were hard to find in ballet, opera, jazz, classical music and dance, they were becoming more in evidence in rock-and-roll, West Indian folk and calypso and African music and dance. Alas, few of these broadcasts have been preserved for posterity. As Stephen Bourne found, such programmes, 'transmitted live', had 'disappeared forever'. But from what still exists of black entertainers in these early years of British television, we are afforded 'fascinating glimpses'.[88]

As far as black actors and actresses were concerned in these decades, the outstanding black performers on British film and television screens included Robert Adams (actor), Edric Connor (actor-singer) and Winifred Atwell (pianist). All three came from the Caribbean, and did their best to promote positive images of black people on the stage and on film and television screens.

Though appearances of black women on British television were rare, soon after the Second World War, Pauline Henriques and Connie Smith (followed by Nadia Cattouse, Sylvia Wynter, Isabelle Lucas and Cleo Sylvestre) were among the first to face the cameras. The vehicle for Pauline's first dramatic appearance was Eugene O'Neill's *All God's Chillun Got Wings* and she reflected on how 'tremendously exciting' it was for her. She identified 'very strongly' with her blackness and thought of the play as a 'very important thing' for the BBC to have undertaken. 'After all', she pointed out, 'it was the 40s and a very different world then for black people. I think the BBC pioneered something in giving us a play of that stature to act in.'

Born in Kingston, Jamaica on 1 April 1914, Pauline came to England in May 1919 and lived in St. John's Wood, London, where she received an 'English education'. In the immediate postwar period, however, she was able to find employment both as an actress and broadcaster on radio with the BBC Caribbean Service, a time when she met and worked with the writers George Lamming and Sam Selvon, who were engaged in the successful programme *Caribbean Voices*.

Pauline also acted in radio plays by Sylvia Wynter, Andrew Salkey and Jan Carew.

Earlier, in 1950, her confidence was given a boost when Kenneth Tynan cast her as Emilia in a theatre production of *Othello*, which toured England, Scotland and Wales. But while this was an important achievement for her as an actress, she felt she 'could do better'. However, with ever-diminishing opportunities, she could not rely on the acting profession to make a living. So, faced with desperate times, she turned to social work, which would occupy her for the next 40 years.[89]

For her part, having left New York in 1894 to come to Europe, Connie Smith arrived in England in 1895 (after touring Denmark and Germany) and played the music halls doing the 'cake walk', which was well received by her audiences. She was a variety performer and successful 'character actress', and after the war, on both the BBC and ITV, she made no fewer than eleven appearances. Astonishingly, she returned to the stage in 1956 at the age of 80, when she joined the Royal Court Theatre Company and performed in *The Crucible*, *The Member of the Wedding* and *Flesh to a Tiger*. According to Pauline Henriques, she 'underplayed everything' until she died in 1970 at the age of 95.[90]

Nadia Cattouse was born in Belize City, British Honduras, on 2 November 1924 and came to Britain in 1943. After serving her time as an ATS volunteer during the Second World War, she trained as a teacher in Glasgow in 1949, before returning to her homeland. Soon she was back in London to further her studies at the London School of Economics.

At this time, she realised that acting and singing were much more than just 'fun'. She accepted an invitation to join a variety show and made her television debut in 1954 in *Halcyon Days*, followed by appearances in *The Runaway Slave*, *Caviar and the General* and *A Man from the Sun*. In 1958, while rehearsing *The Green Pastures* for the BBC, she vividly remembered the effect of the race riots on rehearsals. The violence had already started and, as they rehearsed in a schoolroom, Nadia, sensitive to the issue, noticed that a crowd of white youths had gathered outside the building. 'The BBC were informed about this and they were concerned that we were in danger,' she recalled. 'Decisions were quickly made and a bus arrived to get us out. The entire cast were asked to get on it [a bus] whether we lived in Notting Hill or not. The next day the BBC found us an alternative room in Ealing.' She too found work on BBC radio and in the 1960s she enjoyed popular acclaim as an international folk singer and radio presenter. Thereafter, she went on to make several television appearances.[91]

Sylvia Wynter was both an actress and a writer, who was born in Jamaica. In the 1950s, she appeared in eight television plays for both the BBC and ITV and wrote several plays for BBC radio.

Isabelle Lucas, in pursuit of her ambition, came to Britain in 1954 from Canada, where she was born in 1927. Although she was a diligent student of opera at Covent Garden and Sadler's Wells, it was clear that there were no opportunities for black singers in this sector of the entertainment business. Nevertheless, Isabelle remained undeterred. In the 'scramble for any work', she sought and found many televised roles.

Cleo Sylvestre was born in the year that the war had ended and grew up in Central London. Following the steps of her dancing mother, Cleo took tap and ballet lessons and her breakthrough in films came in 1953 with *Johnny on the Run*.[92]

Before proceeding further let us consider the neglected but important larger British historical background spanning the period from the 1956 to the early 1990s, against which the following chapters of this history of blacks and Asians is set. What in fact was the state of Britain (the United Kingdom) in the postwar years, when these hopeful migrants started to arrive and settle down?

PART THREE

THE EMPIRE WITHIN (1956–98)

AN HISTORICAL OVERVIEW OF THE UNITED KINGDOM (1956 to the Early 1990s)

Although India, Pakistan, Ceylon (Sri Lanka) and Palestine had gained Independence by the mid-1950s, key parts of Asia, Africa and the West Indies were still under colonial rule. But not for much longer. Two decades later, most of these territories were no longer controlled by Britain. In effect, the British Empire had been dismantled. This process of decolonisation was accompanied by a movement towards ever closer ties with Europe, until Britain and the Republic of Ireland became members of the European Economic Community.

While West Africa achieved Independence with little difficulty, the same could not be said of East and Central Africa. The Mau Mau rebellion in Kenya was contained by 1956, but the position of the whites and Asians was uncertain; and although the idea of federation had gained currency a few years later, uniting Tanganyika (Tanzania), Kenya and Uganda foundered. The Federation of the West Indies also failed. Nevertheless, the irrevocable movement towards decolonisation saw Malaya, Guyana (formerly British Guiana), Trinidad and Tobago and Fiji, among others, become Independent by the early 1970s. What emerged from the new circumstances was a Commonwealth of Independent States, which retained what many of them perceived as valuable links with the United Kingdom.[1] Internal tensions apart, the Commonwealth remained a viable and desirable organisation. In 1965, a Commonwealth Secretariat was established, and a Canadian became Secretary General of the Commonwealth. Later, the first non-white person to hold this post was an Indo-Guyanese, Sir Shridath Ramphal, an appointment which was as symbolic as it was real, reflecting the changed (and ever-changing) circumstances. Unity remained elusive as war broke out between member states, notably the Nigerian Civil War and the war between India and Pakistan in 1971. Such deep rifts raised doubts about the future of the Commonwealth in Britain, thus strengthening the arguments of pro-Europe politicians in various British governments. Ties with the former Empire could not, however, be severed cleanly for there were still many supporters of the Commonwealth. So it was that by the 1970s, Britain's 'unbroken decline' since 1870 ended with the disappearance of what it had come to rely upon for so long, its Empire.

Loss of Empire revealed a more streamlined Britain in terms of its overseas commitments and resources. In defence, Britain had formed a close alliance with the United States and, both economically and politically, there were improvements in dealings with Western Europe. But, despite its decline as a world power, the United Kingdom was fortunate in having a complex network of international connections that made it 'just a little more than an offshore island'.

Disunity within the United Kingdom had become evident by the mid-1970s. There were, as usual, the sceptics and the moderates, among commentators. Regionalism and nationalism became divisive forces and significantly were coincident with the dissolution of the Empire. The importance of this point demands elaboration. 'The chronological coincidence could not be accidental', for, as Robbins noted, the United Kingdom 'only made sense (if repugnant sense) in an age of Imperialism. Since Britain no longer rules the waves, there really was little need for Britain to exist at all'.[2]

It was a sign of the times that Scotsmen who had served in the British Empire loyally channelled their energies and attention towards the creation of a new Scotland, separate from the rest of Britain. Culturally, politically and economically, many Scotsmen were strongly opposed to the label 'British' being applied to them. 'English ignorance' has no doubt contributed to the rise of this regionalisation and its accompanying discontents. The English were prone to think of Britain as being synonymous with England, a common assumption as the history taught in schools and universities tended to perpetuate this fallacy.

The dominance of England has obscured for too long the rich local histories and cultures of Scotland, Ireland and Wales. Indeed, the progress of the English language was such that it squeezed Celtic to the margins of the British Isles, so that with few exceptions, English and English-based historians have tended to view British history from an English perspective. Separate assemblies for the Scots and the Welsh, it was thought, were therefore not the solution. And until the recent referendum on Scottish devolution, previous attempts at separation of the Scottish and Welsh nations have failed. But although the United Kingdom has remained a political entity, the underlying tensions arising from cultural diversity disturbingly persist.[3]

Repeated civil disorder and violence in Northern Ireland had, in particular, by the end of 1974, claimed well over 1,000 lives. Alarmingly, this figure continued to rise and predictably there was much talk of peace as the troubles hit the headlines in Britain and stayed there for years, 'troubles' within which 'paradoxes abounded' and evolved into a very complex issue to which, it seems, there is no easy solution. It should be borne in mind that Irish men and women have long been settled throughout the Kingdom. Indeed 'New Irish' immigration was much higher than that of any single group of new Commonwealth migrants. In 1969, for instance, an estimated 750,000 migrants from the Irish Republic, and thousands more from Northern Ireland, came to England. The New Irish did not settle in the depressed areas of Liverpool and Glasgow, where there were old-established Irish populations, but in London (especially Kilburn) Bristol and Birmingham. Though like the Poles, Jews and Italians, the Irish were unlike the newcomers from the Caribbean, India and African, who were 'highly visible' because of their colour.[4]

The rise of Plaid Cymru in the 1960s and early 1970s and the alliance of the Welsh Labour Party MPs Michael Foot and James Callaghan had given Wales a higher profile and encouraged its aspirations to be regarded as a 'nation'. In Scotland too (where, in 1967, there was a Scottish National Party election victory) nationalism was in the ascendant. But in England, if the question of identity was not pronounced, it was elevated to the forefront of 'coloured' immigration, an issue that brought forth increasingly strident comments as the black migrant population in England and Wales reached 595,100 in 1966, a figure which rose in the succeeding decade.[5]

English identity became more defined throughout the century, but perhaps more widely and seriously after the Nottingham and Notting Hill race riots. Then followed the first Immigration Act, the 1964 White Paper on immigration policy, the Kenyan Asian crisis and the Race Relations Act of 1968, among other legislative concerns. Enoch Powell became the most strident anti-black and Asian immigration voice, a man who saw no peaceful future for race relations in Britain; and who often emphasised England and Englishness. His solution was to send black and Asian people back from whence they came. But, of course, there was no going back. These distinctive migrants were here to stay. There was much talk about integration, rather than assimilation. A liberal-minded Home Secretary looked forward to 'equal opportunity accompanied by cultural diversity in an atmosphere of mutual tolerance'.[6] Such optimism, however, had to be tempered by the circumstances of the day, a 'time when the cultural and political identity of the indigenous communities of the United kingdom and their economic prospects looked more uncertain' than it had been for some time.

The 1950s was a time of leadership change in both the main parties, with Hugh Gaitskell heading the Labour Party and Harold Macmillan initiating the 'Macmillan years'. Conservatives did not inspire the nation, but rather, as *The Times* declared, 'brought the nation psychologically and spiritually to a low ebb'. Macmillan was succeeded by Alec Douglas-Home, and Harold Wilson became leader of the Labour Party and faced Edward Heath, his Conservative counterpart, who had replaced Douglas-Home.

Politically and economically, the period was one of unease. The anti-trade union Conservative government created a tense climate of 'us and them', which was aggravated by incomes policy. Wage restraint and the reform of industrial relations dominated much of the political scene. A pay freeze in 1972 and the possible introduction of a three-day working week was the government's response to the potentially damaging and disruptive action of various sections of the workforce. The oil crisis, though, placed the miners in a good bargaining position. The tension between them and the government was so acute that Prime Minister Heath felt the only way to resolve the 'crisis' was to go to the country in 1974. He misjudged the mood of the people and lost the election, leaving a Labour government to deal with thorny issues relating to the miners, other trade unionists and their leaders, and industrial relations generally.[7]

When Margaret Thatcher became leader of the Conservative Party she set about the task of reducing what she and right-wing Conservatives perceived as the all-too-powerful role of the trade unions. Her far right political philosophy could not be more different than the beliefs and ideological orientation of the foremost trade union leaders (Lawrence Daly, Hugh Scanlon, Clive Jenkins and Tom Jackson) who were associated with the British Communist Party. Thus, the battle lines were drawn. As unemployment rose, Cabinet government gave way to autocratic prime ministerial government[8] which, aided by the medium of television, suited the Conservative leadership.

In the world of sport, not only did England win the coveted Jules Rimet World Cup in 1966 at Wembley, sport in general took a new turn. Football, in particular, attracted hitherto unimaginable audiences thanks to the medium of television, which made it possible for an estimated 400 million people around the world to watch this historic match. But after a long and euphoric celebration, 12 years later, England failed to qualify for the World Cup. And even though Scotland did, England fans were unable to hide their disappointment. In fact, it was difficult to suppress for long the game's dark side. Time and again in the twentieth century, football hooliganism had reared up and, as it spread, racial abuse could be heard on the terraces of football grounds across the country. Yet no one could doubt the genuine passion and interest of the millions of fans whose desire for more football seemed unquenchable. This, in turn, generated the need for more exciting professional footballers, including foreign players, and transfer fees and salaries rocketed. It was, however, the growing incidence of racial abuse[9] and violence on the pitch that aroused the most heated debates and emotions.

More recently though, a chorus of black and white fans and administrators have come to regard such unsporting behaviour as intolerable, so much so that after repeated campaigns, especially over the last two decades (and as more and more black players have entered the British and European game) a Football Task Force, headed by the former Conservative MP, David Mellor,[10] was set up with the aim of eradicating racism from football. This determined move is not surprising, for while a black player, Paul Ince, has twice captained England, there are far too few black managers and no Asian professional footballers to date in the premier league. Why? Racism has been an evil in British football not only in Tull's (and later in Clyde Best's) time, but even more so today. Famous players subjected to alleged racism include John Barnes, Ian Wright and Stan Collymore, not to mention those who are less well known and the hundreds of unreported cases.

Against this background, the opening of the Walter Tull Memorial Garden was regarded as a fitting tribute to an extraordinary man and British patriot, whose unselfish sacrifice and courage in peace and war ennobled his life and work, and should serve as a reminder to white Britons of a debt of gratitude, which they owe to men like Tull, an Englishman of a darker hue.

Although Rugby Union did not escape the focus of the television camera lens, it retained much of its amateur status. But the international fame of black star players did not make them immune to the seductive powers of big business barons who saw in the game much room for investment and a good return. Off the field celebrity status as television presenters for the rugby player Jeremy Guscott (and the footballer John Fashanu) could hardly be spurned.

In cricket progress was, at first, slow. Finance was the main difficulty for the County Cricket Clubs, so much needed changes were introduced to make the game more attractive and economically viable. The demarcation between amateurs and professionals was abandoned, and by the late 1960s, overseas players from the West Indies and India were playing for English counties. Not since Ranjitsinghji in the late nineteenth century and Constantine in the twentieth had non-white cricketers played county cricket in England. Several years elapsed before English fans were afforded the excitement of watching Garfield Sobers at the crease each summer, during his successful years at Nottinghamshire. He was a crowd-pleaser, an elegant stroke-player, who naturally drew large crowds and, in turn, generated national and international interest in the game, so that when the touring teams came to England or England went abroad, something resembling patriotic fervour was heightened as the pent-up energies of hundreds of thousands of English people were released. Such was the nature of the most English of English sports.

But as international competition intensified, the cricket teams arising from the former colonised peoples in the West Indies, India and Pakistan, proved that they were among the best in the world. As if to underscore their successes, C.L.R. James's classic *Beyond a Boundary*[11] was confirmed by the game's most respected commentators as the greatest book on cricket. The Trinidad-born James, already an outstanding Caribbean historian, a novelist, culture critic and writer, became internationally known as the years passed.

Lawn tennis was not far behind. Wimbledon remained the Mecca of the game and it was here that the world's greatest players (including Arthur Ashe, the first black player to become Wimbledon singles tennis champion) assembled to compete for the highest honours; and here too television cameras brought to millions of homes a ball by ball commentary of the worst and best, the memorable moments of each tournament.

In athletics, following in the wake of Herb McKinley, Arthur Wint and MacDonald Bailey were such black British track and field athletes as Linford Christie, Colin Jackson, Tessa Sanderson, Fiona Lewis and Daley Thompson, who made their mark, flying the British flag both nationally and internationally.

In all, each sport had its best ever champion, as standards were raised ever higher and the media hype intensified. Increasingly, black sportsmen and sportswomen were setting new standards. But of all the great champions of the twentieth century, the man most people regarded as the greatest of them all was the heavyweight boxer Muhammad Ali, a hero not only for black people, but for whites as well, an icon of the twentieth century. Such is the power of sport in modern times.

Different definitions of British culture had been proposed including those of Raymond Williams and Richard Hoggart, who wrote about the same time in the late 1950s. In his *Culture and Society* (1958)[12] Williams identified the main problem as arising from 'the incompatibility of increasing specialisation with a genuinely common culture ... in a context of material community and by full democratic process'. Hoggart, on the other hand, in his *Uses of Literacy* (1957)[13] considering the impact of the mass media on the 'assumptions, attitudes and morals' of the working class in the north of England, saw a merging of the classes. He was concerned that a 'faceless' culture would arise thereafter. Adding his weight to the argument, C.P. Snow, lecturing on the Two Cultures, pointed out the separation in British society and culture of 'the scientist and the non-scientist', a 'serious intellectual divide' which characterised the age.[14]

In this period, British society came to be seen as post-Christian. Whatever confusion there was among Christians, in the mid-1970s, as black and Asian migrant population grew, Islam and Hinduism became religions in the ascendant. Mosques and temples appeared in accordance with such religious beliefs, thus making British society more pluralistic than it had been hitherto. Christianity had, for long, been synonymous with British society, but with the large migrant communities, this could no longer be guaranteed.

In the world of music, the United Kingdom, and London especially, attracted the world's attention, as a wide range of styles were played in the various concert halls, from classical to pop. The Proms, broadcast live by the BBC, continued to enliven classical interest, while American influences dominated popular music tastes. The Beatles and the Rolling Stones dominated the British rock scene[15] and did fantastically well around the world. But blues, jazz, soul and rock were followed in Britain and the rest of the world by the Jamaican superstar, Bob Marley and his brand of reggae. Young people of all ages and ethnic backgrounds flocked to his concerts and listened to his recordings, which aroused in many young black people a search for roots and routes to where they were. Thereafter, other cultural paths were pioneered and new musical creations gained a following, including hip-hop, bhangra and jungle. So culturally and musically, black and Asian youth were recreating and reinventing themselves, as and when this became necessary, which was often.

The stars of British painting in the 1950s and 1960s were John Bratby and David Hockney. And 'pop art' had added its iconographic input. Such 'pop' as Britain produced was not in art, but in music, not Salvador Dali, but David Bowie, not Dadaism, but the Sex Pistols. Succeeding Hockney and Bridget Riley were Patrick Caulfield and Howard Hodgkin, whose works evoked the 'power of colour'.[16]

From the early 1970s new freedoms were enjoyed by British artists, but their liberation was 'not always entirely liberating'. Nevertheless, a 'new spirit' in British art schools promoted an openness to unconventional images which brought the works and attitudes of modern British artists closer to their fellow artists abroad. But if the British 'visual tradition was originally broken into fragments by the Reformation: a moment of severance from the rest of the world', it had become 'fragmented by the opposite: a moment of joining up with the rest of the world'. In spite of the difficulties, historically the British artist has shown that he or she is 'well equipped to cope with adversity'.[17] Amongst those who had experienced the depths of adversity were the artists whose 'Other Story' (more of which will follow) was showcased, for the first time, at the Hayward Gallery in London in 1989.

British films continued to reach large audiences at home and abroad; and British film-making began to reflect some of the social concerns of the 'angry young men'. British literature and the media served the varied tastes of an increasingly literate and better informed public. Novelists from the working and middle classes abounded, among whom in the former category were John Braine, Alan Sillitoe, Keith Waterhouse and David Storey; and in the latter, Graham Greene, Angus Wilson, William Golding, Malcolm Lowry, Iris Murdoch, Muriel Spark, Margaret

Drabble, John Fowles, Anthony Burgess and John Le Carre. Colin MacInnes was the first among white writers to address the presence of black people in London during the 1950s in his novels *City of Spades* and *Absolute Beginners*.

Poets included John Betjeman, Philip Larkin, Ted Hughes, Peter Parker and Seamus Heaney, whose achievement in winning the Nobel Prize for Literature has, once again, placed the spotlight on Irish literature and the ongoing process of reinventing Ireland. The mass of British readers showed a preference for historical romance and detective stories. But more and more literature from immigrant/exiles in Britain began to appear, for example, poetry from the Indian Dom Moraes and the Jamaican James Berry; and novels by Caribbean writers – Sam Selvon's *The Lonely Londoners*, *Moses Ascending* a lesser known work about West Indians and family life in these early years of immigration *Because They Know Not* and of course, the works of Jan Carew, Andrew Salkey, C.L.R James, Wilson Harris, George Lamming, Shiva Naipaul and his celebrated brother V.S. Naipaul. More recently, a new generation of poets has emerged, including Jean Breeze and Linton Kwesi Johnson, whose work reflects the hard experiences of the black unemployed and working people. A number of young novelists, including Salman Rushdie, Ben Okri, Merle Collins, Buchi Emecheta, Hanif Kureshi and Caryl Phillips are among the best known in contemporary Britain.[18]

There was rapid progress in radio and television as changes in organisation and structure brought Britain closer to a 'comprehensive' culture.

THE THATCHER YEARS

The political scene in Britain saw the rise of Margaret Thatcher and the decline of Labour from the mid-1970s. When Thatcher came to power in 1979 increasing output and reducing public expenditure and unemployment were among her main priorities. Her first three years in office brought no reversal to the United Kingdom's continuing industrial decline; and to compound the economic malaise, social tensions erupted in unprecedented riots in Britain's most deprived inner city black and Asian communities.

James Callaghan's resignation as leader of the Labour Party came as no surprise to many and Michael Foot became his successor. There were, however, four individuals in the Party who were not content to be followers: David Owen, William Rodgers, Shirley Williams and Roy Jenkins, broke away to form the Social Democratic Party. The 'Gang of Four', as they were called, in alliance with the Liberals, gained electoral success and for a while, they engaged in high-profile challenge of the two main parties. But Thatcher's resounding second victory at the polls in 1983 left the other contenders considerably weakened, and from that year a 'Conservative ascendancy' was initiated. Thatcher now set about her goal of dismantling the trade unions generally, but more particularly, the National Union of Mineworkers, led by Arthur Scargill. Eventually she had her way, the miners were defeated after some of the ugliest scenes of police violence seen in Britain and trade unions were banned at GCHQ, in Cheltenham. Few had any doubts that she was indeed the 'Iron Lady', who was 'not for turning'. After leading the Conservatives to a third victory in 1987, it seemed that Thatcher and 'Thatcherism' could go 'on and on', but her turn came, just past mid-way of her third term. In 1990, she was forced to step down as party leader and John Major, then Chancellor of the Exchequer, replaced her.[19]

Towards the end of the 1970s it was felt that a new culture was needed to stem the British decline. To do so, much emphasis was placed on British 'enterprise'. Thatcherism was an attempt to do this, and many felt that such a culture change had been achieved. The cost of doing so was deregulation and denationalisation, which transformed huge sectors of the economy to the detriment of the worst off in society. And apart from 'Yuppies' and well-to-do shareholders, not much had changed in British culture. Thatcher's liberation was an imposition rather than a democratic process; and throughout her premiership, economic recession, very high rates of unemployment and the alarming increase in the number of people sleeping rough in London have certainly brought change of a subcultural kind, the fall-out of her political swing to the far right. On balance, however, through Thatcher's hectoring, anti-social style of leadership, the idea and practice of 'enterprise' is today more acceptable in Britain than it was in the mid-1970s.

Throughout the Thatcher years education was a contentious issue, especially the school curriculum. A pluralistic approach was thought preferable to 'state education'. A general reorganisation had become necessary by 1988, when a 'three-tier' system was introduced. And in higher education too, there was organisational change, with the redefinition of the purpose of a 'university' and the renaming of many existing polytechnics. While the number of students increased, so too did the problems of obtaining and repaying grants and loans. With such competition and difficulties, careers advisory officers did not encourage working-class black and Asian students.

Determination was not lacking on the part of the Conservative Party to revitalise the education system, by introducing 'enterprise'. But here, as in other sectors, where they tried to implement it, resistance was prolonged and acrimonious, and may well become one of the more lasting legacies of Thatcherism.

Was Thatcher xenophobic? Or was she just a combative politician who was over-protective of her country's interests? Britain's relationship with the European Economic Community during her years of leadership was often tense and unfriendly. One got the impression from her dealings with the EEC that it would have been best if Britain was out rather than in. But the clock could not be turned back for by the mid-1970s two out of three people had voted to stay in the Community, thus giving a clear signal to policy-makers and politicians that Britain's future was in Europe.

The sense of superiority which the English felt in earlier centuries towards other parts of the British Isles, and then in relations with the subjects of its widely-dispersed colonial Empire, was now being exercised in Thatcher's approach to Europe. Often, she gave the impression that her voice alone was the voice of Britain; and being the astute politician that she was, she invoked nationalism (jingoism and xenophobia) to rally support for her cause. Conveniently, or otherwise, the interconnectedness of things eluded her. The glory and grandeur of 'British' history was pristine, separate from the history of Europe. But the history of both areas had evolved since the British voters' endorsement in 1975 and before. Relations between them have been reflective of intertwined histories, which even Thatcher could not deny. But, in spite of these realities and arguments, she found support for British sovereignty, whenever proposals for 'closer Union' were put forward, so that those who were sceptical of European unity were made even more so. Instead of encouraging an understanding of Britain as part of Europe, sections of the media impressed upon the minds of the British people the separation, rather than the abiding relationship (for better or worse) between the two regions. Subsequently, history texts, cultural differences and the complexity of their relations were juxtaposed widening the gap of understanding, rather than narrowing it and perhaps, in the future, even of bridging it.

On the other hand, it seemed that the Labour Party's attitude under Neil Kinnock's leadership was to be cautious, to keep as many options as possible open. Fortunately, the Party's well-known socialist sympathies made for easier relations with the European Community's socialist President, Jacques Delors, who was anathema to Thatcher.

Predictably, Thatcher's reluctance to agree to Britain joining the Exchange Rate Mechanism of the European Monetary System was not endorsed by John Smith, the Labour Shadow Chancellor.[20] So Britain struggled on independently negotiating 'opt outs' and exclusion of the 'Social Chapter' (which the Labour Party was committed to) as agreed by other members at Maastricht.[21] Whatever actions a British government may or may not take in the future, it is unlikely to inhibit the momentum of the European Community, an indication that the government might as well be positive about its role so that it can affect the policy-making process.

But indications were that Thatcher was not alone in her xenophobia. Policy documents from the European Commission show that there has been an alarming increase in racism and xenophobia within Europe. And although this was unlikely to bother her, others were (still are) deeply concerned.

So if politically Britain was a 'problem' in Europe, what was its status in the world, now that it no longer had its Empire? Was Britain a world power? Its membership of the United Nations Security Council and its nuclear capability brought Britain ever closer to the United States; and relations with the Commonwealth helped to maintain Third World links, which otherwise were more or less redundant. Mrs Thatcher was no sentimentalist in her attitude towards the Commonwealth. So much of a realist (opportunist, some might say) that her dealings were brutally direct, as in her handling of issues such as the Rhodesian crisis (which after a meeting under her Premiership at Lancaster House in 1979, ended the long-standing illegal white minority rule in Rhodesia) and her support of South Africa's Apartheid regime, both of which were unpopular with the member countries of the Commonwealth. She recognised that the Commonwealth was of little value to Britain, even though Hong Kong was then still a matter to be resolved in the future.

If there was a need to reinforce her political power, the Falklands War could not have been more opportune. British sovereignty and commitment to the Falklands Islands was a matter of little concern, until the Argentine's armed invasion.[22] In response, after a relatively restrained approach, Thatcher became convinced that there was no alternative to engaging in all-out war. The prospect of success was tantalising. After three weeks of fighting, the complete British victory elevated the Prime Minister's and the country's political standing and prestige, for a while at least, both at home and abroad, as world economic affairs moved unpredictably in erratic twists and turns characterised by rapid technological change.

While British 'enterprise' culture made much progress, it should be considered in the wider enterprise context. For most of the 1980s, for example, British investment was highest in the United States, compared with the European Community. The end of the decade, however, brought a change that was favourable to the European Community with the imminent implementation of the Single Market, a reflection of the instability of international markets in the last two decades.[23] Over this period, much had happened, and quickly, to change the world. Communism had collapsed in Eastern Europe and the Soviet Union, and German reunification had necessitated new approaches to foreign policy.

Whatever unity there was in the various regions of the United Kingdom from 1975 to the early 1990s, it has been suggested that this can be linked in political terms to the Thatcher phenomenon. Paradoxically, she emphasised unity, but both at home and abroad, it was the 'national interest' that concerned her. In her pursuit of this, she was determined to crush what she perceived as actual or potentially divisive elements in British society. Yet socially, she failed to bring the 'classes' into a closer relationship to effect her desired unity. Instead, her political actions tended towards separating, rather than uniting them. She believed in the 'individual' rather than society.

Moreover, the image she projected of the regions (Scotland, Wales and Ireland) was of 'Englishness' and 'English' history, not Scottish or Welsh history. Therefore, her perspectives on what concerned the people of these regions of the United Kingdom were at variance with those who lived and worked there.

In Northern Ireland, too, division was (and still is) endemic, and violence had for years been a daily occurrence. Politics could not be separated from religion, culture and identity. Integration of the various 'communities' as one diverse entity seemed unlikely then, as now. So too was integration with the Republic of Ireland.

The presence of British troops, tit-for-tat murders between Catholic and Protestants, the planting of bombs in the provinces and in London by the IRA and the disturbing number of deaths in 'peace-time' Britain have continued to polarise the two communities. So divisions, both locally and in the United Kingdom generally, have persisted beyond the Thatcher years. The consequence was a 'Society under Stress', which generated 'other divisions', a legacy of Thatcher's 'enterprise culture'. 'Those very incentives and deregulation initiatives of which the government was so proud', as one authority put it, 'served to deepen divisions of wealth, health and welfare. These, in turn, were related to poor skills, poor opportunities and the breakdown of family life in the form of accelerating divorce (from which the Royal Family was conspicuously not exempt) and illegitimacy rates.'24

Accompanying these manifestations were a rise in crime, a policing crisis (even though more resources were allocated to this work) and the emergence and spread of a fashionable 'drug culture' among the young. Other social trends at this time included a marked decrease in the number of smokers and an encouraging and positive public attitude to desist from drinking while driving.

Among the most blighted areas of the poor were the inner cities, where unemployment and congested housing fostered crime and violence. Not surprisingly, for the dispossessed poor, with seemingly no way out of their degradation, rioting was largely a desperate expression of their disadvantaged position from which they were expected to compete in an 'enterprise culture'. Increasingly the streets of the inner cities were littered with cardboard boxes or discoloured sleeping bags and rags assembled about the bodies of the homeless, comprised of a cross-section of people, many of whom were both the young and prematurely old. In addition, the elderly were disregarded and the young were sexually exploited. It would seem implausible, as some have argued, that these problems should be blamed simply on Thatcherism, which was opposed to the 'welfare state'. As it turned out, welfare was not safe with Thatcher and the Conservatives. Predictably, a cost-benefit analysis of the NHS led to new practices, for example, the National Health Service Trusts and fund-holding GPs, all of which, the British public was reassured, would provide a better service at less cost. Many, though, believed that such a 'service' would be difficult to deliver. So the nation's health and social cohesion became issues that were divisive and highly contentious, a neat approximation of Thatcher's legacy.

THE MAJOR YEARS

When John Major succeeded Mrs Thatcher at the age of 47, he became the youngest prime minister to serve Britain in the twentieth century. He was a relatively unknown politician. Was he also, like the 'Iron Lady', not for turning? Which way was he likely to turn?

He won his first victory at the polls as prime minister in 1992, an election which saw the re-election of the four black and Asian MPs. Significantly, though, John Taylor, the black Conservative candidate for Cheltenham (a candidacy which aroused strong controversy in the local Conservative Association) lost this relatively 'safe' seat to the Liberal Democrats. Any white person it seems would do; being a 'black' man was one likely interpretation of his defeat. Another feature of the 1992 elections was the rise of women actively involved in politics. The number of women candidates who won seats in the elections rose from 41 in 1987 to 60 in 1992 (an indication of things to come, as women became assertive about their contribution and role in society), the Labour Party winning 37, the Conservatives 20, the Liberal Democrats 2 and the Scottish National Party 1.[25]

Women also figured prominently over the decade from 1982 to 1992 in the media, advertising, publishing, the Civil Service, the NHS and the legal profession; and more women were entering higher education. By 1992 women comprised 44 per cent of the British labour force, a percentage higher than any other country in the European Community.

While there was a paucity of women academics, there were a number of prominent women writers – Beryl Bainbridge, Anita Brookner, P.D. James, Pat Barker, A.S. Byatt, Angela Carter, Maureen Duffy, Iris Murdoch and Fay Weldon, among others. And in the 1980s and 1990s, writers in English from India, Africa, the Caribbean, the United States and Canada, expressed themselves in their various works, through different Englishes that have enriched the English language. This development (of long gestation) was recognised when Rabindranath Tagore and, more recently, Wole Soyinka, Derek Walcott and Toni Morrison were awarded the Nobel Prize for Literature. Though 'standard' English had its supporters in Britain, the challenge from without was unmistakable and relentless, as English became increasingly less British and more global, a reflection of Britain's loss of hegemony as an Imperial economic power, and the consequent spread of competitors in international trade and commerce.

Moreover, in the transitory period from the 1980s to the 1990s, the Labour Party lost a general election, yet again. Why? According to David Childs, 'Labour urgently needed to persuade reform-minded voters that it had a practical alternative to Thatcherism and the Liberals.'[26]

This is the wider context in which the various groupings of the semi-skilled and unskilled migrant workers sought work. They formed the nucleus of what would evolve and become a much larger body than ever before, a majority of men and far fewer women, who were either in or were available for employment in Britain. Significantly as this period brought us towards the closing decades of the twentieth century, the cumulative influences of race and Empire, stubbornly lingered on, especially at the lower levels of British society, where it was starkly evident during the many ongoing struggles of blacks and Asians in the 'Empire within'.

5 THE MIGRANT WORKERS' STORY

In several ways, migrant labour in Britain differed from other Western European countries. Under British capitalism, the shortage of labour from the mid-1950s was made good through Britain's continuing relationship with the Commonwealth, a 'legal legacy' which is central to the presence of black and Asian migrant labour in the country in that as Commonwealth citizens these workers had the right to live and work in Britain. Thus they were, comparatively speaking, better off than other migrant workers in Europe, such as Turks and Greeks in Germany, for example, who are legally 'alien'.[1] In the context of full employment during the 1950s and the early 1960s, black labour served as replacement labour for socially undesirable jobs vacated by white indigenous labour. There was also evidence that the concentration of black labour in manual work was being reproduced, in part, because of racial discrimination. The prospects then (as now) for those fortunate enough to be employed were discouraging.

Historically, the evidence shows that governments, politicians, neo-fascist political organisations, the mass media, employers, institutions representing the labour movement and sections of the British working class have all acted upon and articulated racist beliefs, and in so doing have identified black and Asian workers as an excluded category.[2] It is against this background that migrant workers and their children have been racially categorised. Thus perceived and located, a whole range of racially biased forces came into play, inviting individual and concerted responses from the various black and Asian communities, who were (and are) unanimous in their rejection of urban squalor and deprivation.

Hitherto, much has been taken for granted about these communities and perhaps it is appropriate here to correct at least one generalisation before proceeding further. Historians have had much to say about the inflow of Caribbean migrants, who are generally regarded as people of African descent, without identifying the Indo-Caribbean people among them, who constitute a smaller, but distinctive and significant, part of the 'Caribbean' migrants in Britain.

THE INDO-CARIBBEAN PRESENCE IN BRITAIN

Anthony Trollope wrote much that was detrimental to African slaves, while defending the powerful West Indian planters. Nor did he shirk in his opinion about the East Indians who replaced the slaves on the plantations.[3] Like their fellow African labourers, the 'coolies' had only one contribution to make, according to Trollope, and that was to provide the labour necessary for the plantation economy. As bonded labourers, these Indians were caught in a cycle of poverty and indebtedness to their employers and often, like the African slaves, they were engaged in strong resistance against their oppressors. Yet the experience of indentureship strengthened the resolve of the majority (approximately two-thirds) to remain in the Caribbean and make their homes there. Since abolition of indentureship, the Indians have made invaluable contributions to the economic, social, political and cultural activities in the British, French, Dutch and Spanish colonies.[4] Yet, until very recently (and even today), far too few people outside the Caribbean knew of their presence there! For far too long, in Trinidad, for example, they were obscured at the margins of society.

Increasingly, in the post-indenture period, as East Indians gained access to primary and secondary education (especially after the 1960s) many of them went abroad to study medicine, law and other subjects, while thousands (like other West Indians) migrated to Britain in search of a life that was better than they had known in the Caribbean.

So hidden has the Indo-Caribbean presence in Britain been that it prompts the question: How well do people in Britain (including Afro-Caribbean people) know them? The common assumption held by whites, Asians and Africans alike was that Indo-Caribbean people were either from India, Pakistan or

Mauritius. These assumptions have been a continuing source of irritation, not because the people from these countries are unworthy, but because many Indo-Caribbean people feel robbed of their identity, which is so subsumed that it needs more than mere explanation. As Vertovec notes, in Britain, they have been 'overlooked, miscategorized and misunderstood' by whites, Asians and also Afro-Caribbeans. And Nanan has found that in certain social contexts this group is 'neither West Indian, Asian nor British'. Their double exclusion created the necessity of setting up their own 'networks to survive'.[5]

In the literature concerned with womanhood in Britain, Indo-Caribbean women have been overlooked, perhaps because so much has yet to been done in this area of research. The total Indo-Caribbean population in Britain, estimated to be between 22,800 to 30,400, there is agreement that many Indo-Caribbean women were an integral part of that wave of Caribbean women who came to Britain to be trained as nurses. Since the recruiters were not too particular about the gradation of skin colour, they were all banded together as 'West Indians'. But they were neither Asian nor Afro-Caribbean and their insistence that they were Indo-Caribbean people was consistently ignored, when not sneered at by high-caste Hindus from India. For many Indo-Caribbean women, being thus sidelined was a truly oppressive and unacceptable experience.

More generally, however, there is a paucity of literature dealing with women in migration and, disenchanted by the attempt to redress the balance, Karran quoted Morokvasic, who saw migrant women confined to the role of 'dependants, migrants' wives or mothers, unproductive, illiterate, isolated, secluded from the outside world and bearers of many children'.[6]

The emigration of Indo-Caribbean people to Britain in the 1950s was, as we saw earlier, preceded by East Indian emigration to the British colonies in the nineteenth century. A significant feature of this emigration was the sex-ratio imbalance, a pattern which was, more or less, set from the inception of this traffic. Of the 396 Indian indentured labourers carried by the first two ships, only eleven were women, and in the years 1865–1917, the ratio was approximately 43 to every 100 men. The implications of this were profound. No doubt there were many women who (like some men) were deceived, 'kidnapped' and generally pressed into accepting indentureship. But this image of female scarcity should not imply negative images of these women migrants, for we are reminded that instead of 'being docile, dependent, subordinate characters', they were women who, given the social and economic circumstances in which they found themselves, had no choice but to assert their independence and take control of their lives.

The traumatic experience of the long voyage and the circumstances of the plantations modified much of the old traditional caste and religious practices. But although these women were not unduly concerned with gaining equality and independence, conditions on the plantations favoured their important role in the Indian family, particularly because they identified their oppressors as being the indentured system (rather than their men) which exploited both men and women and, indeed, their children.

Plantation labour may have frustrated but did not prevent the retention and re-creation of Indian culture in the Caribbean. Instrumental in this as the 'keepers of culture', Indian women established in the new plantation society, so far as possible, traditions and cultural practices of the homeland. They improvised, as circumstances demanded, and in time they were able to consolidate certain core values upon which the Indian family depended, not least their roles of mother and wife. But while she kept her family together, the Indo-Caribbean woman contributed to the 'socialisation and reproduction of the labour force'. And because of this pivotal role both in helping to maintain indentureship and her scarcity value, she was vulnerable to violence and murder committed by Indian men, who were often provoked by the illicit sexual relations between Indian women and European overseers and managers, relations that aroused deep-seated feelings.[7]

East Indian indentureship was also a source of racial tension between East Indians and the recently freed Africans and their descendants. As a poorly paid labourer, the Indian was perceived as undercutting the rate for jobs. The planters, well-versed in the divide-and-rule strategy, did nothing to ease these potential and dangerous tensions, and over time, both groups developed negative images of each other, making the prospect of closer relations and inter-marriage less likely. All the same, the sexual attractiveness of the Indian woman has been immortalised in song by calypsoists. There was, however, a darker side to this sexual fantasy, which was 'dramatised' in Guyana during the pre-Independence struggle when the Indo-Guyanese woman felt the full impact of Afro-Guyanese male aggression amidst bloody inter-racial confrontation, a conflict which left much racial bitterness among the Indo-Guyanese in Britain, who were forced to migrate.

Indo-Caribbean history and culture has tended to be subsumed in Caribbean and British discourse thus further obscuring their presence in the region, even though they are an integral part of Caribbean culture. For many Indo-Caribbean people living in Britain, their sense of unbelonging was real enough, a daily lived experience. And, as if conspiring against them, there has been a tendency among many Jamaicans, Trinidadians and Guyanese, to keep the 'Indian' side of their parentage or ancestry silent, while loudly proclaiming their 'Africanness'. This partiality widens the gap between the Indo- and Afro-Caribbeans, and aggravates relations between them.

Part of the problem has been the lack of assertiveness on the part of Indo-Caribbeans themselves. Many men, who have been emigrating to Britain since the 1950s, have found jobs in factories, London Transport, the Post Office, Inland Revenue, the Civil Service and, after many years of part- and full-time study, as lawyers, doctors, dentists and university lecturers. The vast majority of these men, it should be remembered, did boring, badly paid, dead-end jobs in which their prospects were, to say the least, grim and depressing.

Perhaps the best that could be said about their situation is that the employee had a job, something he did not have or might not have had in the Caribbean. Though this was not always true, the employer found it convenient to harp upon it when it suited him, emphasising his importance and devaluing his foreign worker. But he knew little of his Indo-Caribbean employees, who were not short of skill and inventiveness.

To date, there has been no serious study of Indo-Caribbean men's migration to Britain, and much more needs to be done in relation to Indo-Caribbean women who, in most cases, migrated to Britain as 'workers and students', single women, whose period of training as nurses was a lonely and financially unrewarding experience. Some wives did follow their husbands, as was the case of Shan Jagdeo, who came to England in 1959 from Guyana. Within a few weeks of her arrival in London, she found a job in an engineering factory and soon became involved as a trade union representative. The multi-ethnic, multi-gender experience of life in the multi-racial Caribbean served her in good stead in her dealings with workers, who came from diverse backgrounds. The speed with which she took to this industrial activity reflected the denial of opportunities in Guyana, because of gender and race discrimination which, in effect, had made redundant the high level of literacy she undoubtedly possessed. Although many male Indo-Caribbean students had gained their degrees at various English and Scottish universities, the myth of the illiterate Indo-Caribbean woman needed to be uncovered, and Iris Sukdeo, another Guyanese, proved beyond any doubt the capability of her 'sisters', when in 1969, at the age of 29, she became a Doctor of Philosophy at the University of Sussex. Moreover, the Trinidad-born Lakshmi Persad achieved the distinction of being the first Indo-Caribbean woman novelist.[8] In many other professions and at various levels of British society, Indo-Caribbean women continue to play their parts.

Indo-Caribbean men have also struggled to better themselves, many of them working and studying, usually part-time. But, far too often, circumstances dictated the end of their ambitions. Such failures, however, made the successes among them all the more dramatic, profound and therefore worthy and joyful achievements. Though 'controversial', Roy Sawh, has been one of the most effective, courageous and consistent public speakers, a tireless campaigner in vocalising (often in the open air of Hyde Park) the oppression of African, Asian and Caribbean peoples in Britain.

Moreover, Indo-Caribbean migrants, for the last four decades, have made important contributions in many aspects of Caribbean community life, disproportionate to their relatively small numbers. Self-recognition was the prerequisite for general acceptance, first by the 'Caribbean' community and then by the larger British public. Such a 'reassessment or restatement', as Goulbourne noted, is necessary for it is 'not enough to reconstruct an equally incomplete picture in order to correct past injustices'.[9] So as part of the 'Caribbean' community in Britain, Indo-Caribbean people too have become integral, actively engaged at various levels in the defining Afro-Asian struggles of the 1960s through to the 1980s.

STRUGGLES AT WORK: FROM THE 1970s TO THE 1980s

If, as Knowles contended, 'one cannot agitate successfully without widespread grievances',[10] for black and Asian workers in British industry during the 1960s, 1970s and 1980s, there was no shortage of discontentment. These were years of rapid changes in industrial organisation, the growing size and complexity of production units and their greater interdependence (through multinational corporations) and the rate of technological change demanded planning and co-ordination from the centre. So the strong feelings generated by strikes (be they unofficial or unconstitutional), though essentially a management problem, were very much a concern of government. Indeed, it was within this context that black workers took action in these decades.

While some firms openly practised discrimination against black and Asian workers, others, the more 'enlightened' managements, adopted the 'soft glove' technique, a less confrontational, though no less mean-minded and acrimonious approach. Nevertheless, both types of employers faced the problem of increasing productivity and profit, on the one hand, and the resistance of black and Asian workers who were drawn into questionable schemes to achieve these shifting targets, on the other. Thus prolonged exploitation predictably led to strong reaction.

One of the first 'immigrant' strikes took place in the mid-1960s at Courtaulds Red Scar Mill in Preston over management's decision to force Asian workers (among them, a few

West Indians, who were crammed into one area of the labour process) to man more machines for proportionately less pay. The strike was significant. For the first time in the industrial struggle of Asian workers, the black movement made a well-publicised intervention during which two West Indians, Roy Sawh and Michael De Freitas (Michael X), of the Racial Adjustment Action Society (RAAS), made statements. While Sawh called for a separate union of blacks (inclusive of Asians), De Freitas later said that although he was against white people he was 'not for separate unions'.

When the strike ended, there was no shortage of views from the press and public. While John Torode championed the cause of a union-led educational drive for its Asian workforce to avoid strikes, Paul Foot regarded the strike as a necessary action in bringing about improved communication between management, unions and migrant workers.[11] But the striking revelation was that although the industrial action was fought by the migrant workers (with crucial support from the wider Asian community and in particular, the Indian Workers' Association) they failed to win against their unyielding employer, because of the lack of official union support.

Almost a decade later, Asian workers again took strike action against their employers, Imperial Typewriters in Leicester, and questioned the practices of the Transport and General Workers Union chief negotiator, George Bromley, a Justice of the Peace, stalwart of the Leicester Labour Party and one of the 'lieutenants of capital'. Referring to the tensions between Africans and Indians, Bromley ignored the tension that existed between whites and blacks as a direct result of a large National Front presence in Leicester and, concerned as he was about Communists, believed the strike was being led by professional agitators who, he argued, were intent on changing society by infiltrating and taking over the trade unions.

When the Asian workers did eventually turn to their union for help, they soon realised the true nature of the union's role. Bromley reminded them of the need to keep the company a going concern. 'You are ill-led,' he wrote to the strikers, 'and have done nothing but harm to the company, the union and yourselves.'[12] The Asian workers disagreed. They had struck because of a deep feeling, not based on preconceived ideas, but through hard experience accumulated over a long period of economic 'wrong-doing' and racial exploitation. As the strikers gained support from the factory workers, their collective power and resolve strengthened. Sensing the strikers' implacable resistance to its malpractices, the company's response was positive and predictable. The first of the strikers were notified that they would be sacked if they did not return to work and, in the ensuing deadlock, third parties intervened. Tom Bradley, the local MP and President of the Transport Salaried Staffs Association, tried to get the workers back in the factory. 'I told the strike leaders they were getting nowhere by walking the streets,' he said, 'and urged them to adopt the proper procedure by returning to work and resuming discussions under an independent Chairman.'13 This was nonsense for, after many months of complaining, their reasonable 'discussions' through the proper procedure had got them 'nowhere' in the factory.

But whereas an 'ordinary' strike would have collapsed within days because of an initial lack of commitment by workers or a lack of union support, or both, the strikers at Imperial responded with a strength and creativity which would help to shape the struggles of black and Asian people for much-needed change in the workplace. Free from the so-called unprogressive traditions of British trade union bureaucracy, and newly proletarianised after leaving East Africa and the Indian subcontinent, the Asian strikers brought certain qualities to their struggle: a spirit, an approach and willingness to adopt an effective and appropriate tactic. No half-way measures would suffice in situations that had become desperate. Overall, such was the experience of migrant workers that it provided lessons not only for the trade unions, but also the wider labour movement.

The TGWU, supposedly an organisation of the working people in fighting against capitalist exploitation, was exposed as a vehicle for the further accumulation of capital. This had also been the case in earlier disputes: for example, at Woolf's and Rockware Glass in West London in 1965, Malmic Lace, E.E. Jaffe, Jones Stroud, British Celanese and Harwood Cash in 1973, Perivale Gutterman and Coventry Art Castings. In this TGWU dispute, the strikers saw the union's actions as complicity with the employers, a clear demonstration of race emerging as a major and divisive issue within the British working class. The outlook was bleak, as the strikers were left to struggle on, while the wider trade union and labour movement remained largely deaf to the appeals of these courageous Asian workers. Ironically, just a few years later, a black man would assume the highest elective post and become leader of this powerful union.

GRUNWICK: THE STRIKE

If black and Asian migrant workers had been exploited in small firms and factories because the trade unions were either weak or simply not allowed to exist (and where they did, they were incapable of giving support) then the Grunwick strike proved most revealing. Grunwick Processing, founded by A. Grundy, George Ward and John Hickey, first began processing, developing and printing black and white films in 1965. Eight years on, it had not only expanded, but also merged with Cooper Pearson and three years later it boasted a workforce of nearly 500, mainly migrants. In fact, by the summer of 1976, almost all the Mail Order department staff were East African Indians, who spoke predominantly Gujarati.[14] A large number of them were women.

Traditionally, and in the British popular mind, among other attributes, these women were regarded as 'passive', always obedient and subservient to their husbands. Among them were a number of East African Asian students, some of whom worked in the Mail Order department. Together, this migrant workforce laboured to procure increasing profits for the firm, with no adequate current or forthcoming financial reward. In this sense, Grunwick was no different from other sweatshops, and in spite of Managing Director George Ward's complacency, the workers' grievances were more deep-seated than he cared to admit. Their concerns included long hours of work, 'compulsory' overtime and aggressive management. Indeed, it was the unfair dismissal of one of the employees which triggered a walk-out by three others, and much thought and heart-searching among the main actors and those implicated. The firm's questionable practices were debated by more and more workers, including Jayaben

Desai, a remarkable India-born woman, who came to inspire and symbolise the determination of the strikers to win their workplace rights. She and her son, Sunil, joined the original four strikers at the gates of Grunwick. Mrs Desai was quick to grasp the relevance of trade unionism to the dispute and sought the support of union officials. Predictably, the company was opposed to having a trade union operating as part of its organisation. On the other hand, APEX (the union involved), Brent Trades Council and the Trades Union Congress were unable to introduce trade unionism in the company, in spite of unprecedented mass picketing, regular media coverage and political interventions.

Jayaben Desai had not bargained on a long, drawn-out struggle, which would take its toll physically, mentally and spiritually, when she walked out of Grunwick's Mail Order department on 20 August 1976. After a 15-month picket in all weathers, facing police violence, victory seemed as distant as ever. As a final act of spirited protest in line with the Gandhian technique of passive resistance, she was joined by three Asians on hunger strike on the steps of the TUC headquarters, a 'strike' which met with the displeasure of both APEX and the TUC, not the support that they had hoped for. And for good measure, two other Asians who had joined the hunger strikers, had their membership in APEX and strike pay withdrawn. As non-union members, they were powerless to act and now their struggle for trade union recognition had been bitterly disappointing, for they were disciplined, not just by their employer, but also by the police, and even their own union!

There was more disappointment to come. On 14 December, the House of Lords supported Lord Denning's defence of Grunwick in the Advisory Conciliation and Arbitration Service (ACAS) appeal. The strikers' strident voices were heard over months, but now it seemed there was little to shout about. Christmas 1977 was not a happy time. The winter and the turn of the New Year were bleak times. An attempt by the Strike Committee to renew mass picketing in April 1978 failed and the strikers and their union drifted further apart. Finally, on 14 July, the Strike Committee, nearly two years after it began its work, announced the end of the bitter Grunwick strike.

In retrospect, and once again, this strike demonstrated the assertiveness of Asians to confront both the union and management so that they could have legitimate workers' rights. These workers, like those before them, did not take action against the company simply because they wanted to belong to a union. Indeed, they voted with their feet because they were no longer prepared to tolerate the abuse, exploitation, low wages and unbearable conditions in their workplace. They were determined to fight the 'slavery of it all'. And when Jayaben Desai said that the treatment she and her co-workers received was 'worse than the slaves in *Roots*', she was echoing a common historical experience. The worrying aspect of the strike was that rank-and-file militancy was at odds with the trade union spokesmen. 'What we are witnessing', *Race Today*, the campaigning black journal, noted, 'is a takeover bid for the independent movement of Asian workers by the left-wing of the labour movement, whose immediate interest is to keep the union kite flying'.[15]

Trade union activists like Arthur Scargill and Jack Dromey saw the Grunwick struggle as symbolic of the fundamental right of a worker to belong to a trade union. In this respect, the Grunwick strikers have been likened to oppressed workers of an earlier era, the Tolpuddle Martyrs and the East End Match Girls. This was not the tradition from which the Grunwick workers came. The emotional appeal to defend unionism succeeded in getting the support of thousands of white workers to the Grunwick picket lines. But this did not mean that the white workers were there to support a strike by Asian workers. The white workers were there simply on the issue of 'defending the trade union movement'.

In effect the strategy that the Grunwick strikers had subsumed themselves to was a denial of their own history. From the beginning of the walk-out, they had been led to believe that mobilising white workers had to be their prime goal. Fourteen months later, with no victory in sight, the strikers had no recourse but to appeal to black workers in other parts of the country for support. Thus, the history of black and Asian workers in the twentieth century, and their experience of trade unions in Britain, had forced them to create their own methods and means of struggle. As all previous black movements had done, the activities of black and Asian youth and workers had propelled race to the forefront of the struggle (and racism as a daily lived experience) and thus laid the basis for a powerful national and international linkage of Afro-Asian struggles, a source that remained untapped during the Grunwick dispute.

While the strikes prior to the 1980s demonstrated the courage and determination of militant Asian women in the private sector, simultaneously their 'sisters' from the Caribbean were waging a hard struggle against their taskmasters, mainly in the public sector.

CARIBBEAN[16] WOMEN: NURSES AND ANCILLARY WORKERS

For many women from the Caribbean, who had migrated to Britain, of particular relevance to the changes in their lives were the patterns of employment and control over their assets and economic resources.

In London, isolation from relatives, alienation from the rest of society and loneliness and boredom in the confined spaces of their homes, was alleviated at work, which provided the opportunity to meet and mingle with people and to take every opportunity to acquire new skills. This economic process, it was argued, could engender a greater sense of independence.[17]

In the early 1970s, and for the first time, black and Asian nurses came out on strike in support of their demands for more pay, a necessary action which was interpreted as being contrary to the myth that women administering to the sick, the young and the old should not behave in this 'unprofessional' manner. Seen in historical perspective, this strike was the manifestation of a long struggle.

Nursing, the 'caring profession' nurtured in the traditions of the family and in waged employment in Britain and her former colonies, brought many Caribbean women, who were conditioned to think in this way, into the British hospitals and the Health Service generally. A Health Service catering for all, and not just for those who could afford it, brought about a massive recruitment of low-paid workers, whose conditions of employment were unchallenged. However, in the 20 years leading up to the first nurses' strike, the class composition of nursing changed. What had been a vocation for middle-class women in the nineteenth century, was now a job for women, many of whom were from the Afro- and Indo-Caribbean communities, and from other postcolonial migrant groups.

Overseas student nurses, mainly from the Caribbean, Hong Kong, Mauritius, Malaysia and Ireland, were a major source of cheap labour for the British Health Service, their numbers increasing each year, from 6,000 in 1959 to 19,000 in 1970.[18] Their desire to train as nurses was not always the main reason for their decision to come to Britain, but having arrived, they were contracted to the NHS to work for at least five years. They were prepared to work hard and tolerate initial slights, exploitation and racial harassment in the hope that things would improve. But the evidence shows that they were misled. Many were directed to take the State Enrolled Nurse (SEN) training and qualification, instead of the State Registered Nurse (SRN) qualification. The former qualification was, at the time, of no use to them outside Britain and, at best, it guaranteed a trained, but low-paid workforce on the ward. 'When you are interviewed', said one nurse, 'they ask you if you want to do the course in two years or three, and all of us said we would like to do the two-year course. It's only when you get here that you realise if you do two years, you will be an SEN.'[19]

Black women were predominantly employed in the lower grades, serving doctors, 'professional' nurses and, of course, patients. So discouraging were their promotion chances that few black nurses entered the NHS as a vocation, and as a result, they brought to light the real nature of nursing, thus undermining the hierarchical structure of the Health Service, which relied so much on their 'wanting to be part of it'. With the recent changes in the Health Service, however, their numbers have dwindled considerably, evidence enough to support the case that for many of these women, the time had come to reappraise their 'profession'.

With low pay, bad working conditions and unsociable hours of work, the dissatisfied black nurses, as a matter of course, sought alternatives, one of which was agency nursing, an attractive proposition and a 'force for change' at the time, in the National Health Service. No one was left in doubt as to the preference for agency nursing. In the early 1970s, both the number of nursing agencies and agency nurses rose with married women especially attracted to this kind of work, because of its flexibility and locations in London, jobs closely associated with the teaching hospitals that were heavily reliant on agency nurses.[20] But even within this area of employment, there was division and discrimination. Some agencies operated a dual pay scale: one for white nurses and a lower one for black nurses. A black nurse who was told never to discuss her wages said: 'I did and I discovered that Australian nurses were getting more.' A Jamaican nurse who started as a nursing auxiliary and later trained as an SEN, explained why she was doing agency work:

> Most of the night staff are black. Night nurses are black because they have children and it's more convenient for them to be at home in the days to see after their children. If you work days, you're not there to send them off to school, you're not there to receive them when they come back, and you have to get somebody to look after them. With nights, you can actually put them off to bed before going to work. I support the strike whole-heartedly. Nurses are saying they won't work with agency nurses and I think they're being silly, because number one, they should find out why nurses have to go to the agency, because in my case it's not because I wanted to but because I was forced to ... I can't do without working.[21]

The divide-and-rule strategy was therefore operational among migrant workers and among these women workers, racism and sexism were brought into play, creating schisms so that the profitability of capital could be maintained. In their representations, the Black Women's Group, concerned with matters relating to work and the black community, argued that the agency nurse was the first to refuse to be tied to the hospital structure, thereby confronting the blackmail that faced all nurses. The unity necessary to make a fight was expected to come only when NHS nurses joined with agency nurses to raise these issues, and they made known the fact that black nurses had been accused of not participating in the struggle – accusations that were based on the racism inherent in the hospital hierarchy.

In the early 1970s, for the first time, hospital and night cleaners too came out on strike and in their protracted confrontation, they demanded more money, shorter hours, modern equipment and, distrustful of white trade unions, the right to have their own union. This workforce comprised a large number of migrant women, a substantial percentage of them West Indians. Five black women auxiliaries (hospital ancillary workers) were elected by their colleagues to represent them on the negotiating team which had talks with the government during the 'pay beds' dispute at Westminster Hospital, where management decided to close 48 beds in NHS wards while the private wards remained open. The auxiliaries went on a work-to-rule in protest. The representation of these women marked a new stage in the lives and struggle of Caribbean women in Britain and smashed the myth that Caribbean women of that generation were non-participants in militant action: 'My first experience of strike action was in 1972,' said one of them.

> We did not stay out very long. We wanted more money. At that time we worked in the hospital, scrubbing and cleaning. You came to work at 7.00 am and went home at mid-day, back again at 2.00 pm and left at 7.00 pm and at the end of the week you had ten pounds in your hand. It was a wonderful experience striking. We marched and shouted. From 1972 to today we have had to fight for everything we have since won. Now we no longer work the split shift, but we work harder than before because after 1974 they introduced the bonus system – where before there were four of us to a ward, now there are only two.[22]

These disenchanted women were representatives of people from the Caribbean who came to Britain during the early years of postwar immigration, part of a 'defeated and demoralised' section of the Caribbean working people who had arrived in a 'hostile' country to be employed in the worst jobs with the lowest wage. They were crucial in laying the foundations for the black community which has since evolved, often displaying remarkable control as well as a capacity to fight whenever necessary. This was a continuation of their struggle in the Caribbean, and for many years, their disenchantment and revolt as part of the British working population has been muted, underplayed and ignored, a tendency rooted in the past.

They also brought with them the tradition of 'rebellion and resistance'. For most of the women who took strike action, it was their first experience as wage earners in a modern industrial economy; a paradoxical experience, new, yet in some ways familiar. Dirty, boring, badly paid and low-status employment was their common lot regardless of their former colonial economic and social status. Moreover, they were, in many instances, the breadwinners of extended families, often including their children in the care of relatives in the Caribbean.

So, well before the beginning of the 1980s, young black women had upheld the tradition of resistance and rebellion, courageously embraced by their mothers, fathers and other colonial forebears. In the late 1960s, hundreds of young women were attracted to, and had participated in, the Black Power movement in Britain as black and Asian youth simultaneously came out in open revolt. There was a characteristic boldness in their confrontations with the police, school authorities and employers, and also with their parents, whose conservatism could not accommodate the views and actions of their progressive children, a new generation brought up and schooled in Britain. The differences between Asian and black children and parents seemed incalculable, as new ideas brought about increasing instability, a reflection of which was the large number of young black women in state-funded hostel accommodation.

But if in the closing years of the 1970s the 'power and significance' of black women had grown, by the early 1980s, with a new Conservative government, their circumstances changed for the worse. When Norman Fowler, Secretary of State for the Social Services, announced the government's proposals that ancillary work in the NHS should be taken over by private companies, this directly affected an estimated 70,000 black workers (mainly women), a third of the total workforce in catering, porterage, washing-up, laundry and other cleaning jobs.

For nine months they were on strike, picketing and voicing their opinions forcefully, as they waged a tenacious struggle which won them support from thousands of workers, both black and white. Some powerful unions showed concern and even the TUC gave its backing. At last others had recognised their plight. They all believed that they would win the pay rise they demanded and this belief sustained them in their prolonged strikes.

The workforce was united, morale was high, public opinion and moral authority were on their side. And as the days passed more nurses joined the strike. Of crucial importance was the militant support they received from miners and print workers. On 22 September 1982, when over 120,000 workers took to the streets of London, the common interests of the nurses and ancillary workers were undoubted. But such overwhelming support was not enough and eventually a two-year pay settlement was reached after which the strike was called off. The TUC had withdrawn its leadership in the dispute and the hopeful Caribbean women workers felt betrayed.[23] Yet again, black workers vented their anger over the leadership of the TUC and the union.

With implementation of the Conservative government's policy of privatisation of the NHS the number of nurses and ancillary workers dwindled alarmingly and has since become a subject of heated debate. Into the 1980s and the years to come, the continued exploitation of Caribbean women would generate and reflect a rising militancy and solidarity with other sections of Britain's black and Asian workforce, caught up in disputes in the motor and textile industries.

At Ford's assembly plants, a major sector of industrial production in the British economy, there has been a strong sense of solidarity among Asian and West Indian workers, who regard the relationship between work and community as indivisible. Not surprisingly, in 1981 when Britain's inner cities were shaken by uprisings, Ford's workers felt their own industrial vulnerability. Indeed, three of Ford's plants were located in the troubled areas: Halewood in Toxteth, the Langley truck plant in Southall, where many Asian workers lived, and Dagenham, whose many workers came from Brixton and other London areas affected by the summer revolt. These workers struck for long overdue improvements in terms of pay, working hours and pensions, action which brought them up against Ron Todd, their union's chief negotiator in the dispute.

To say the least, his performance on behalf of TGWU members left a great deal to be desired. Although there had been an increase in the number of Asian shop stewards representing line workers, there were ongoing hidden struggles in Ford's southern plants, which often took the form of 'sabotage',[24] struggles not exposed to public scrutiny, but their cumulative effect was evident in the growing conflict within the relevant unions.

Overall, as the confidence of black and Asian workers grew through struggles at work and in their communities, many of them progressed towards independent cultural organisation. Let us, however, briefly appraise the postwar experience of black and Asian workers and the British Trade Union Movement.

AFRO-ASIAN WORKERS AND THE BRITISH TRADE UNION MOVEMENT

A black worker, when asked whether he had taken his case of alleged discrimination to the union, said, 'The union? Man, that is for white people.'[25] The vast majority of black workers in Britain would agree. On the other hand, the unions, essentially defensive working-class organisations, especially in their heyday from the 1960s through to the early 1970s, used their official powers to defend themselves against criticism from black and Asian workers. But having put into perspective the general problems of black and Asian workers, how did the white unions and black workers see each other? There are no straightforward answers in the complex interrelationship between the various groups of black workers and their unions. Pakistani workers, for example, posed special difficulties and questions as to what their attitude to unions was and their reasons for joining or not joining were put to nearly 200 of these migrants. In these years, the majority of Pakistanis were employed in the textile industry, with a smaller number in transport and engineering. One study showed that, on the whole, West Indian workers were more highly organised than Pakistanis, the West Indians being free of English language problems with which the Indians and Pakistanis were faced when they came to Britain, and that Indians, especially in the Bradford area, were helped by Sikhs in the Indian Workers Association,[26] an amity and co-operation between Muslims and Sikhs that was precious to both communities at this time.

Another matter of importance in the relationship between black and Asian workers and the trade unions was the question: Were they 'workers' or 'immigrants'? This question needed to be addressed because union officials often stressed the differences, cultural and otherwise, that existed between migrant workers and others. Union officials stressed some of the difficulties caused by the language barrier: migrants joining and then becoming disillusioned by the lack of effectiveness of the union; migrants' distrust of the union and frequent job changes; lack of understanding of the purpose of unions; and apathy and objections to the political levy. Taken together, these reasons heaped all the blame on the migrants themselves and begs the question: were the unions blameless?

The prejudices that existed were inescapable. Some union officials, more affected than others, believed that migrant workers (particularly Pakistanis in Bradford) worked long hours because this was their preference. Closer to the truth was the fact that the majority of these employees worked 'no overtime at all', and many of those interviewed said that they were not interested in working long hours, for health reasons. So, migrant union membership and the questions of overtime and long hours were confused, serious issues which reflected the union's inability to gain the desired improvements in its members' standard of living.

How were these disadvantaged workers recruited? Usually, it was found that they were approached by friends, instead of the shop steward, a clear indication from the migrants' point of view that the central actors in the unions were not interested and it was on such evidence that their opinion of the union was based. Moreover, the unions were not forthcoming in representing the migrants' case, so powerfully demonstrated in the disputes mentioned above. The implication of this failure was that migrant workers on the shop floor were likely to act collectively, to give themselves a much-needed voice.

In conclusion, the Bradford study clearly revealed that trade union officials knew yet, from the evidence, cared very little about the special difficulties of migrant workers. Significantly, few of those officials questioned appeared to distinguish between the various nationalities of migrants: Pakistanis, Indians and West Indians (Afro-and Indo-Caribbeans) among others, who were, more often than not, lumped together. While some migrants identified cultural and linguistic differences, on the whole, they regarded their claims as legitimate and reasonable, as workers who wanted to improve their industrial position like other less well-paid workers. But even when migrants became members, few played an active part in the union and, overall, emphasis was on the widespread disillusionment among migrants, thus highlighting discrimination in the trade unions, which, in turn, often gave rise to mistrust and discouragement.[27] Finally, unilateral action by migrant workers proclaimed an extension of the bounds of British industrial relations, thus giving credence to acting outside the trade union framework, as they wrestled with a number of urgent workplace concerns.

The problem of racial discrimination which loomed so large in the 1980s and beyond, had become, in many ways, more distressing. In the report *Britain's Ethnic Minorities*, considerably higher rates of unemployment were found among ethnic minority groups than among the white population, 13 per cent and 7 per cent respectively, spanning the years from 1988 to 1990.[28] According to another report, these rates could be even higher. In fact, *Race and Unemployment* showed that ethnic minority unemployment was almost 19 per cent in London, about 20 per cent in the North-West and the West Midlands and over 23 per cent in Yorkshire and Humberside.

In the main, black workers (except the well-qualified) were concentrated in low-paid jobs. Afro-Caribbean and South Asian men earned about 15 per cent less than white men, but Indians and African-Asians earned more than Afro-Caribbeans, and Pakistanis and Bangladeshis less. There was little difference between the earnings of ethnic minority and white women. But if women as a whole were concentrated in the low-paid sectors of the economy, there were two significant differences (as far as the statistical evidence was concerned) between ethnic minority and white women covering the years 1989–1991: first, in the clothing, footwear and leather goods sectors, 5 per cent of ethnic minority women were in employment, compared with 2 per cent of white women; and second, in the medical, health and veterinary services, 15 per cent of ethnic minority women worked compared with 9 per cent of white women.[29] Moreover, some local surveys, such as Leicester City Council, found that male South Asian workers received about 80 per cent of the earnings of white workers, and both black and Asian workers continued to work in low-paying industries, namely textiles and the service sectors (hospitals, hotels and catering and retail distribution).

As the 1990s approached, unions were hard-pressed to adapt to the dramatic technological changes and work practices. On the issue of low pay, for instance, one union said: 'It is in the interests of all our members that black workers in our trades and industries should be members of and active in our union. Without that input, challenges on low pay, equal treatment and rights at work will never be successfully met.' In addition to low pay, overall, ethnic minority workers (especially Pakistanis) were also identified as being more than likely to do shift work.

Most encouraging, however, was the fact that from the 1980s some progress was evident among well-qualified African-Asian and Indian men, who were as likely as white men to be engaged in professional jobs, a trend which indicates a movement towards closing the gap between the two major groups. But in spite of this, the evidence indicates that ethnic minorities experienced discrimination, their relative positions reflecting different cultural backgrounds, class structure, skill and the length of their residence in Britain. Put simply, while black and white workers continue to address the issue of racism in the workplace, black and Asian workers have often organised in groups within their unions to give added force to their disenchantment.

Much attention has been focused on equal opportunities in the past, and this remained a preoccupation into the 1990s. Time and again, while the concern was expressed that no well-organised workplace should lack a good equal opportunity policy jointly agreed by the employer and union, such policies have tended too often to be too general. None the less, some of the more recent agreements, of necessity, make a more specific commitment on race equality in terms of recruitment, training and promotion, while others incorporate not only the employer's commitment to ensuring that the composition of the workforce should reflect a cross-section of the local community, but also state how this could be achieved. The Commission for Racial Equality (CRE) was staunch in its espousal that the 'most reliable and efficient way of monitoring the effectiveness of an equal opportunity policy is to carry out regular analyses of the workforce and job applicants, by ethnic origin'. Indeed, both the Commission for Racial Equality and the Trades Union Congress have provided guidance on 'monitoring' and so too have local councils such as Leicestershire County Council and Manchester City Council.

Recruitment and training in employment have posed great challenges to employers. It was found that one-third of private employers discriminated against black people by denying them an interview, while granting one to equally qualified members of the white community. Equality of opportunity in recruitment and training, a core area of concern, was closely monitored by the CRE.

Black women occupied a highly disadvantageous position in the labour market at the end of the 1980s: 12 per cent of black women, compared with 7 per cent of white women, were unemployed. Pakistani and Bangladeshi women were most severely affected – double the rate for all ethnic minority groups and over three times higher than the rate for white women. There was also a high incidence of shift-work being done by Asian women – 15 per cent compared with 10 per cent for white women.[30] Homeworking was also more prevalent among Asian women, especially in areas like West Yorkshire and Leicester (more will be said of this later in relation to the 1990s).

For their part, some unions took bold steps to make racist behaviour a disciplinary offence within their own organisations and in the workplace, and insisted that racial discrimination should be included within a disciplinary code, thus indicating the seriousness of their approach. A number of other unions provide guidance for their memberships on a definition of harassment, and how to prevent and deal with it. Because racial harassment is a form of racial discrimination, it is employers' responsibility to confront such acts, as and when they arise, for failure to do so is tantamount to their endorsement.

Another (relatively new) area of interest in this decade related to the fact that a considerable number of black and Asian workers in Britain have close ties with their families abroad and their desire to return there periodically is a natural and reasonable inclination. Therefore, the idea of extended leave agreements was put forward to give workers the right to be absent from work for an extended holiday. This would be beneficial to all workers, it was argued, regardless of colour, an opportunity which should be given once every 5-10 years, so that individuals could visit other countries and broaden their experience and interests.

There were also the cultural and religious needs of black and Asian workers to consider, for where they conflict with work requirements, employers, as the CRE recommended, should give due consideration to the practicability of facilitating such needs, including prayer time, religious holidays and food. Importantly, the health of many black and Asian workers (especially sufferers from sickle cell anaemia and thalassaemia) needed to be addressed. Though most common among people of African and Caribbean descent, sickle cell anaemia can also affect people from India, the Middle East, Palestine and the Eastern Mediterranean, while thalassaemia, though prevalent amongst people of Mediterranean descent, can also affect people from India, Pakistan, Bangladesh, North Africa, the Middle and Far East.

Measures to prevent discrimination in employment were written into the law, appearing on the statute book as the Race Relations Act of 1976, which encompasses acts of victimisation on racial grounds, the disallowance of positive discrimination and the taking of a case by someone who has been discriminated against, to an industrial tribunal. The CRE was more or less in agreement that the Act was right, though believed changes were necessary to deal more effectively with certain forms of discrimination.[31] Much depended at this time on the momentum induced and maintained by rank-and-file workers and the organisations to which they belonged and through which they channelled their grievances in the 1980s.

Earlier in the 1980s, change, though inevitable, was slow, almost imperceptible. Indeed, with rising unemployment, black and Asian workers were still largely employed to do what was described in the previous decade as 'shit work', the site of many unpleasant confrontations with managements. One of their more protracted struggles in the 1980s was in the textile industry, a large employer of Asians, and an industry in which 'dirty jobs' and bad working conditions prevailed. In Bradford, the wool textile industry was fortunate in having cheap labour, but as a group, these workers were victims of the racist attitude of those in their union. Moreover, technological change had brought with it a paring down of the industrial structure. Many small firms went out of business. This meant a reduction, not only in the workforce, but also in the demands made upon it by increased productivity targets. Paradoxically, technology meant more work, but fewer workers. The introduction of new machinery and techniques resulted not only in speeding-up processes, but also in redundancies, with adverse effects on the trade union movement, the implications of which were closely monitored by black and Asian workers.

With the publication of the TUC's *Black Workers' Charter*, and the *Workbook on Racism* and the formation of the Black and Asian Workers' Trade Union Solidarity Movement in 1981,[32] some unions could no longer ignore the problems that black and Asian workers have been consistently identifying and called special conferences to address issues of race and race equality. Consequently, a few unions have initiated ethnic monitoring procedures and, by the early 1990s, Afro-Caribbean and Asian workers had a higher rate of union membership than their white counterparts, Pakistanis had a lower rate than whites, while Bangladeshis registered a very much lower rate. Among workers of all ethnic backgrounds, union membership was highest among the older people; men were more likely to join a union than women.

As leader of the TGWU (Britain's largest union, until UNISON was formed) Bill Morris was (and still is) regarded as the outstanding example of a successful black trade union official, though this achievement should not obscure the Herculean efforts and unrivalled achievements of black, Indo-Caribbean and Asian rank-and-file representatives, who have for decades given voice to a multiplicity of grievances, often becoming targets of employers, who see them as 'troublemakers'. According to the Labour Research Department, though nine unions had black full-time officers, they still amounted to a 'very small' proportion of union officials. And of 21 unions canvassed, ten had a national committee specifically concerned with race equality. But by 1993, only NALGO had an officer at national level who was engaged in race equality. Nevertheless, expectations were high. Thirteen unions had adopted 'specific measures' and initiatives to enlarge their black membership. Other initiatives include training courses for both members and officials on tackling racism, and the TUC had issued a guidance note on race monitoring and the unions. While these initiatives have helped, there is still a good deal of concern that more blacks and Asians could become members, and there is much room for black members becoming more involved in their unions.

More specifically, Afro-Caribbean, African and Indian women have higher rates of union membership than whites. And according to the Labour Research Department, by the early 1990s, some unions were concerned that structures should properly reflect the interests of black women and ensure that they are represented at all levels of the decision-making process. Indeed, the TGWU have national officers responsible for race and women, whose aim is to work together as an 'equality team'. Apart from basic rates of pay and hours of work, a number of other issues relating to women still need to be negotiated with employers, including job access, job security, leave, child care and upgrading.[33] Taken together, the evolutionary process has put a new spin on the approach of the TUC. But this once powerful umbrella organisation has not been as decisive on the question of 'race' as it might have been.

Prior to 1973, the TUC General Council was enmeshed in established government machinery dealing with race but economic recession brought paralysis to the British economy and had adverse consequences for the trade union movement. Moreover, after the 'winter of discontent' (1978–79) and the advent of the Conservative government and its monetarist policies, the trade union movement was further weakened, to the dismay of its leaders – a weakness reflected in the lack of TUC influence on government policy-making[34] into the 1980s, when the attention of black and Asian people shifted to protecting themselves from physical attacks from racists. By this time, there was no doubt as to the extreme right's stridency and the National Front's provocative and intimidating racist marches. Years of 'Paki-bashing' and the murder of young Asians in the previous decade, the growing concern over racist policemen at the Grunwick picket lines and violence against blacks and Asians up and down the country, gave urgency to the need for anti-racist support in fighting NF-led racism.

Overall then, into the 1980s with the passage of the Nationality Bill, the much sought 'support' of the whole trade union movement was clearly not forthcoming. And in these trying days, 'separationist solutions' seemed the only alternative as the TUC, in desperation, took initiatives to fight racism among rank-and-file trade unionists.

In spite of the TUC's deliberations and such steps as it had taken, black workers were still dissatisfied, for no real progress had been made in terms of their pay and working conditions. After the miners' strike in the 1980s, the systematic dismantling of the trade unions, and a shift to the culture of enterprise in Britain, brought about by the anti-labour philosophy of the Conservative government, the attainment of ethnic minorities' rights, as workers and as citizens, seemed more remote than ever.

Yet, in spite of the liberal slogan 'White labour can't be free while black labour is in chains', the vast majority of black working people remained firmly shackled under the pressure exerted from all sides within the British capitalist system. This finally gave rise to the founding of the Black Trade Unionists Solidarity Movement, a group of activists who came together 'to begin a united movement of all blacks and Asians in Britain, to pressurize the existing institutions, and fight for our rights'. They were no longer willing to acquiesce. They wanted to control their destinies, through membership which was open to people of Asian, African and Caribbean descent, employed or unemployed. Disturbances in Brixton, Southall and other parts of London showed that blacks and Asians were no longer prepared to accept unemployment, bad housing, police provocation and the institutional and individual racism inherent in British society.[35]

What is interesting about this development is that many militant black trade unionists clearly saw the link between their workplace struggle and their efforts at community survival. Thus, they have clearly stated their intention to organise and work within the trade union movement. In other words, they want white workers to recognise and act on the real, day-to-day problems of racism and sexism, so that together they can achieve some rapprochement. But so far, the black and Asian initiative has met with only marginal response, trade unionism appearing more and more as a negative expression, a dirty and unacceptable label to the generation which has grown up in the last two decades.

Nevertheless, the fact remains that, historically, the vast majority of trade unionists have been complacent about black workers and slow to act. The Annual Reports of the Trades Union Congress, prior to the mid-1980s, confirm this. Since then, the TUC has launched a number of initiatives and campaigns (essentially educational) against racism. In fact, the final decades of this century reveal the depressing conclusion that discrimination at the workplace remains alarmingly and unacceptably high.

6 MIGRANTS IN TRANSITION AND AUTHORITARIANISM (1960-89)

When the Pan African ideologues left Britain following the Fifth Pan African Conference, there was a vacuum of militant black leadership in Britain.[1] Even while they were in England, these radicals were more concerned with developments in the oppressed colonies (from whence many of them had come) than they were with the plight of black and Asian people in Britain, as indeed Moody was. With the exception of Claudia Jones, the leadership that emerged during the 1950s and 1960s was middle-class and conservative. Not only did this contrast sharply with the radical Pan Africanists, it also tended to mislead unsuspecting black migrants in these early years into believing that multiracial organisation and integrationist arguments were the best means for improving their disadvantaged positions. But soon enough, with further deterioration of the black migrants' status as 'second-class' citizens, the prospects for their children appeared no less depressing than they were for them, and naturally, they sought a way out of their predicament.

The Nigerian-born writer Buchi Emecheta, who came to England in 1962, tells in her novel *Second Class Citizen*,[2] the story of Adah, a woman from the Ibo tribe, who comes to England to live with her Nigerian student husband, and discovers that life for a young Nigerian woman in London in the 1960s is grim. Rejected by British society and thwarted by her husband, who expects her to be subservient to him, she is forced to face up to life as a second-class citizen. In the United Kingdom, there was no kingdom of heaven for Adah, and indeed for Emecheta herself. But the unremitting oppressiveness of Adah's circumstances necessarily provoked the great desire to survive. Ultimately, it was her courage and resourcefulness which kept her and her children sane and eventually allowed her to remake her life.

But unlike the Pan Africanists, potential and actual black and Asian leaders had to wrestle with the problems endemic in the permanency of their fast-growing communities. They had few options and faced the prospect of continuing as they were: going through the motions of leadership, rather than tackling the root of the problem – white racism. Many attempts to organise and integrate black migrants were made, but time and again, they were refused entry into many areas of British social life. Historically, their exclusion had highlighted linkages between blacks in Britain and others in the diaspora. In effect, one sustained the other. And now in the second half of the twentieth century, the struggles elsewhere, especially in the deprived inner city precincts of the United States, were evocative of disadvantages in Britain. Black nationalism (preached by the Pan Africanists to end colonialism abroad) had been translated into Black Power, a cry from the American ghettos which triggered deep responses among black people in Britain by the close of the tense and violent 1960s, when Black Power and black autonomy were increasingly being applied to the struggles waged by the black communities 'colonised' in the metropolis.

Ghanaian Independence in 1957 was the first example of 'Black Power' in Africa, of the black man's right and ability to govern himself, contrary to earlier British propaganda. At last, it seemed that the African would be free of foreign domination and this victory was powerfully symbolic for black people in other colonies, in the United States and Britain.

In 1966, after the historic Meredith Mississippi March, Stokely Carmichael and the concept of Black Power caught the imagination of thousands of impoverished African-Americans and in following the leaders who had preceded him, he too was acutely conscious of Africa. 'The reality of black men ruling their own nations', he wrote, 'gives blacks elsewhere a sense of possibility, of power, which they do not now have.'[3]

From 1965 to 1971, Carmichael's writings and public appearances as a spokesman chart his evolution as a 'revolutionary activist and theoretician'. For him, Martin Luther King's movement for civil rights, in itself a good thing, was too central a 'buffer' position between white liberals, on the one hand, and embittered young black people, on the other. He had no doubt where he stood. Clearly and uncompromisingly in favour of Black Power, Carmichael was unruffled by the strong opposition with which this slogan was greeted. Indeed he warned that the student SNCC 'should listen and represent the needs of the community and nothing else'.[4] He cited colour as an oppressive factor which was employed to devalue and denigrate black people. But now, he suggested that those who led the charge against such oppression should use the colour 'black' as a positive means of self-liberation. To this end he advocated the destruction both of racism and exploitation.

Given the social, economic and political problems, the context of black ghettos in American cities confirmed in Carmichael's mind that Black Power was necessary; and such 'power' could only be attained through independent black organisation. Black Power, he insisted, should not be confused with black tokenism. It was therefore appropriate in Carmichael's view that black people should move towards Pan Africanism.[5] The message in the 1960s and 1970s was the need for a new black consciousness.

Into the post-Black Power phase of the depressed 1980s, organisations representing new identities and a new generation had emerged as an integral part of black British and Asian communal responses, especially among the youth of both communities.

ASIANS: MOVING ON (PRE-1970s)

It should be borne in mind that the people in Britain who formed the Indian, Pakistani and Bangladeshi communities came from agriculture-based economies and deeply religious backgrounds from which their values and attitudes are derived. For Hindus, the land is vital. Thousands of villages dot the landscape, and the seasons of planting and reaping are marked with some form of thanksgiving.

Life, in spite of the demarcations of religion and caste, has historically been oriented through the joint family, a form of organisation designed for human survival, particularly in agrarian societies such as India and Pakistan. This family structure is dominated by an authoritative male member and the central-ity of community which underscores the process of socialisation (emphasising the interconnectedness of families) deeply embed-ded in the minds of the peoples of the subcontinent, so that when one comes of age, the sense of family becomes an integral part of life.

Within the family, the father's authority is unchallenged. The mother also shoulders her responsibility which is largely concerned with raising the children and tending to household chores. Indian women, however, are not all passive. On the contrary, the Indian woman tends to be assertive in her own domain. The institution of marriage confirms and consolidates these values, through relations between families, rather than between two people engaged in a love match. Such practices among Asians have been transplanted into Britain.[6]

These agrarian societies are characterised by the high pre-mium placed on mutual exclusivity in marriage, the approach to sex-related matters being largely undemonstrative and under-stated. And the need for places of worship have given Asians in Britain a rootedness in their past, traditions that give them confidence from which they could invent new strategies of survival in a foreign land.

South Asians have a healthy respect and desire for education, to which is linked the authority of the guru and his legitimation through the hierarchical structure of Hindu philosophy, incor-porating a number of deities, gods and goddesses headed by a 'Supreme Being' and lesser beings who are also worshipped. Such a system is reflected, to some degree, in the relationship between the teacher and those who are being taught. It is against this historical background that one can better judge the difference in the respect shown by Asian and British children to their elders. But gradually these traditional patterns of behav-iour have been questioned as new ideas and change began to enter the rural villages from which it had become so necessary for thousands to escape. And what a dramatic contrast their arrival from such rural places to highly industrialised Britain must have been. Industrialisation apart, there was also the complex historical, social, economic, political and cultural nature of British society itself to contend with; a society, as it were, denatured, which had become highly industrialised, urbanised and secular,[7] with a greater emphasis on the individual rather than the community. Expectations of the early Asian migrants, from a white British point of view, were high. But being unable to bridge the differences in values that separated them from their British hosts, Asians found themselves further alienated. Something had to be done and thus a two-way process of integration began, with virtually no one having any illusions about the task ahead. Economic change had a major impact in effecting adjustments in the Asian migrants' behaviour. Unlike work in agriculture, industrial employment was more oriented to time and production; and in certain respects, the approach to life was less casual and seasonal. For all these newcomers, work and life in Britain appeared to be robotic. But time and space gradually put the Indian subcontinent in perspective and brought acclimatisation and familiarity with their family responsibilities and British surroundings. In many cases, changes in dietary and religious observances were made to suit the circumstances. Much attention was focused on finding homes which would ultimately house their families still in India. Once these conditions were satisfied and the families had arrived, the home became the hub of activity within the burgeoning Asian community.

Many Asians made rapid economic progress, but socially, they tended to remain securely attached to their Indian, Pakistani and Bangladeshi communities. With the support of their wives, these Asians and their families practised their religion devoutly, though they could not entirely ignore the British culture and environment within which they now lived, worked and brought up their families. There were signs of change among Asian women who began to modify their dress styles. And as their male children began wearing western styles in trousers, shoes and hair-fashions, when they did protest Asian parents were more accommodating of change than previously, though many felt that a line had to be drawn with their daughters, especially when they reached their teens, an age when girls were not expected to adopt the styles, attitudes and practices of their British counterparts. Parents expected their daughters to be dutiful, to keep themselves sexually untouched until they were married. The thriving sex industry, it seemed, did not interest most Asians as much as marital fidelity and family values, the cornerstones of their cultures, which were regarded as bearing a higher morality than the decadence which they perceived in British society.

Asian children were also deeply affected by their displacement, the predicament of being caught, as it were, between two cultures. Confused though they were, as they grew older, the pattern which emerged among them was the adoption of a mixture of western culture and behaviour, and the traditional values and attitudes of their parents. But whatever differences there were between the older and younger generations of Asians, adult Indians, as Hiro noted, brought up and educated in India, were not as exposed to British values, Christianity and Western civilisation as were their children, whose proneness to compromise was likely to lead them to discard aspects of what constituted the essence of their hereditary culture.[8]

YOUNG ASIANS

Confused as many of them were, Asian youths had to come to terms with themselves and with British society. Muslims were loud in their protests and campaigned for exclusion of their children from classes during Christian scripture lessons and, from the 1970s, tended to emphasise the differences between Islam and Christianity. Hindus, on the other hand, did not feel so threatened, because they were pantheists, whose beliefs did not preclude other prophets and gods. Hindu and Sikh youths, comparing their belief systems with Christianity, were more inclined to stress the similarities.

However wayward their thoughts might have been, Asian youths retained in essence the dietary code established by their traditional religions. And in terms of language, depending on background, while they spoke Punjabi, Urdu, Gujarati and Bengali, the entire household strove to speak English more effectively, not least because of its economic pay-off. Asian youths, having grown up speaking English, could alternate between English and Hindi thus clarifying their perspective on, and improving their understanding of, both cultures. With their growing knowledge and cross-cultural familiarity, Indian films, music, song and dance were complemented by an appreciation of Western popular music. Remarkably, much of the conflict at home was defused and relations between Asian youths and their parents tended towards a degree of synthesis, which was informed by the cultural and racial alienation of the wider society.

Asian parents were positive role models for their children. Asian women had, in many cases, to seek employment to supplement their family incomes, and among Asian youth, there was a shift away from arranged marriages to a more liberal accommodation which did not preclude romance.

So for the children of the 1950s, and also those who came later, there was a 'psychological transformation' as they grappled with the two cultures. Sooner or later, they had to confront 'race' and colour prejudice and, at times, violence. 'Paki-bashing' and 'skinheads' were terms that entered the vocabulary of racial prejudice and violence in Britain, as an alarming number of law-abiding Asians were murdered in cold blood – acts of terror that deepened Asians' sense of racial difference. Some in authority conferred (either deliberately or unwittingly) respectability on such criminal behaviour. Enoch Powell, a Conservative politician, had spoken his mind, thus galvanising his supporters, but also alerting Asians and blacks to their enemies. Young Asians felt imperilled, but completed their education, which, they hoped, would enable them to find well-paid jobs, rather than striving for academic excellence. Such realism must be commended, and as they created new spaces beyond their parents' vision, they began to re-invent themselves, and necessarily so, for it seemed the only way to get out of certain time-worn stereotypical moulds. But, for the vast majority there was a worrying gap between their expectations and the directions in which they were pushed by Youth Employment Officers and other career advisers. To their credit, many fought against lowering their sights. With the marked increase of British-born and educated Asians (as was the case with the African community),[9] the 1970s was a period of important change.

ASIANS: POST-1970 DEVELOPMENTS

Two fundamental problems confronted second-generation Asians, according to Bhiku Parekh: 'how to sustain self-esteem, and how to negotiate a way between their own and British culture'.[10] Unlike their parents, British-born Asians are more tied to Britain and therefore feel more strongly about defending themselves in British society. The devaluation of Asian cultures and identities by white people was met with a sense of pride by most Asian youths, and in their perceptions of the British, poorly educated working-class Asian migrants behaved with deference to white people, the legacy of their 'sense of inferiority and insecurity' in India, while their children, having been in close and regular contact with white people and educated and socialised among them, tended to be more forthright and assertive in their response to prejudice.

East African Asians were also, in their way, less tolerant of prejudicial treatment as they had shown during the industrial action taken at Mansfield, Leicester and Willesden. The celebrated dispute with the Grunwick company, owned by an Anglo-Indian, revealed the importance of class over race, and left no doubt that while a 'substantial minority' of Asians were of a social class closely associated with the Conservatives, the majority of Asians were militantly in step with trade unionism (albeit a more progressive brand) as a means towards achieving equality at that crucial and pivotal site of migrant struggle, the workplace. It is significant that, at this time, such actions coincided with white British working-class solidarity with ethnic minority groups and the anti-racist movement generally. Indeed, it was a time when Asians and blacks realised that the level of prejudice among white people in Britain was not uniform.

Another group of Asians, young Bangladeshis, came out on the streets to demonstrate in the late 1970s. These radicalised Asians added strength to white left-wing groups which at times supported the Asians' cause, groups to which some Asians gravitated. This politicisation marked the degree of discontent among young, articulate Asians, who were determined to oppose fascism and, as a consequence, formed their own organisations. The attitude of members of these new groups was striking. They had little respect for the middle-class leadership of earlier organisations who had been prone to acquiesce to white liberals. This 'middle-class' Asian leadership, drawn from the business and professional classes, contrasted sharply with the working-class or lower middle-class youth leaders. More than that, as Asian-Britons they were more assertive in demanding their rights. The distinction between the generations was further emphasised when Gurdip Singh Chaggar was murdered in Southall.[11] Following this savage attack, the older community leaders were content to leave the matter in the hands of the police. But the Asian youth leaders, often desperately unhappy with the police, felt it best to initiate and maintain their own defence strategies.

Street demonstrations attracted much publicity which, it seemed, the older leaders wanted to avoid and this, in turn, excited greater political interest among Asians, as reflected in a rise of almost 10 per cent in Asian voter registration over the 1970s, a political consciousness that was evident during the 1979 Parliamentary elections, when the National Front provocatively pressed forward their right to hold a meeting in the heavily populated Asian community of Southall. Young Asians were incensed and through the Southall Youth Movement (SYM), they demonstrated, along with anti-Nazi organisations, their strong opposition to the National Front. While the support they received from the Anti-Nazi League was exemplary, the SYM could not surrender their leadership role to others. Moreover, it is significant that unlike their fellow anti-racists in the Afro-Caribbean inner city communities, these Asians operated in a community that was 'materially prosperous and socially cohesive' and were therefore prepared to defend themselves against racist attacks.[12] Put simply, the uncompromising message from these Asian youths was that they would stand their ground.

In Scotland long-settled Asians and others had been working towards tolerance and coexistence between cultural traditions and diverse faiths: Hinduism and Sikhism among Indians; Islam among Pakistanis, Indians, Bangladeshis, Malaysians,

Turks, Iranians and Arabs from the North African states;
Christianity among Afro-Caribbeans, Africans and Indians; and
Buddhism and Taoism among the Chinese.

Christians felt a strong sense of belonging and their accommodation in Scotland seemed thus far to be unproblematic,
especially for those from the Caribbean, where the cultural
heritage was more European than the others. Clear guidelines
were (and are) followed by Muslims. The believer in the Quran
has certain obligations, social and dietary regulations and the
observance of important Islamic festivals. Hindus do not rely on
one holy book, but draw on several works of scripture: the
Vedas, Upanishads, Puranas, Bhagavad Gita, Mahabharata and
the Ramayana, among others. Hindus also participate in social
and dietary traditions, and celebrate important festivals. Sikhs,
too, follow a distinctive belief system which venerates one
all-powerful Creator, condemns the worship of idols and images, and rejects the caste system. Sikhs must also observe
social and dietary regulations and celebrate the birthdays of
Guru Nanak and Khalsa. Devotees of Buddhism and Taoism
engage in their many festivals, which unite the Chinese people
across Britain.[13] This religious and cultural diversity has, over
the years, added to the changing multicultural mosaic of
evolving Scottish communities, especially in Glasgow and
Edinburgh.

BLACK YOUTH

By the early 1970s, in England and Wales, much attention was
being directed at black youths, mainly those of Afro-Caribbean
descent, for it was becoming clear that the second generation
were failing in the education system. In other words, they were
low achievers, and had a high and disproportionate incidence of
unemployment and 'alarming levels' of homelessness.[14]

Young black people not only faced a bleak future, but also
found themselves associated with criminality. In spite of being
among society's most vulnerable people, they were perceived as
the most threatening. Not surprisingly, they found themselves
over-represented in the main categories of crime, including

mugging, which cast the archetypal mugger as black and the helpless victim as white. Against this scenario of racially directed crime, black youths were seen as a social problem and the state took appropriate action. Consequently, the 'sus'[15] law was introduced and heavy sentences were imposed by the courts. (More of the relationship between black people and the police will follow.)

So for the West Indian youth, the education system posed a particular problem, especially for those with a low self-image. Such a child must also face a selective process which generated an even greater sense of inadequacy and, in turn, this tended to reinforce teachers' stereotypes of West Indian children, whose needs the British education system failed to address. As a result, they were drawn more closely to their own black culture, thus relegating school, as it were, to a secondary position. Rastafarianism was, it seemed, opportune, bringing greater self-esteem to black school children categorised as 'remedials' and 'low streamers'. The idea and practice of Rastafarianism reached them by way of reggae music, through which a political message is transmitted. And soon 'Babylon', Ras Tafari and the teachings of Marcus Garvey became more and more meaningful as a lived experience. Garvey taught black men and women to see beauty in themselves, a message which he regarded as a rallying call to the oppressed and disaffected. Black youth took heed of his message and through the distinctive music of Bob Marley, added force and meaning were given to the message, refocusing attention on their immediate environs.

Their separation from the mainstream of the British education system led to strong social solidarity among black working-class children, who expressed themselves in the popular arts and sports. Outside school, the police, perceiving the alternative lifestyles of black youth as disruptive and therefore unacceptable, persisted in their harassment of the young, who seemed even more threatening than those who were steeped in 'Englishness'.

So the pressures of racism pushed more marginalised black British youths towards Rastafarianism and opposition to their containment in what they perceived as Babylon. Black music became an important starting point in that it brought insight, when there was little or none on several broad issues. Thus a process of learning was set in motion and the acquisition of knowledge generated further questioning, with a consequent movement away from their parents' British-based culture and traditions. In effect, their music helped them along on their journey to Jah; and from the inner city communities in Britain, a warmer, powerfully revealing and more attractive, imagined Africa beckoned. The quest for the 'true self', the 'I and I' and their African roots was paramount.[16]

Their acceptance of Rastafarianism has brought about marked changes in consciousness. In a word, integration was (and is) for the Rastaman, unworkable. Not all young black people were Rastas and, of those who were, not all were male. Among the women, there were accomplished and innovative musicians, such as Judy Mowatt, who expressed art and culture through her songs in a distinctive 'feminist' interpretation, which complemented that of her male brethren.[17]

BLACK PEOPLE AND THE POLICE

The Harringey Community Relations Council has noted that the proportion of black people arrested for 'sus' declined from 47 per cent in 1977 to 10 per cent in 1978. These figures do not bring us any nearer to a fuller understanding, unless 'sus' is seen in the context of relations between black people and the police.[18] 'Sus' created growing resentment within the black communities, and incidents revealing malpractice have made relations with the police worse. Examples given by the Institute of Race Relations include disregard of the Judges Rules, inadequate investigation of racial attacks, abuse of the power to enter homes, harassment of juveniles to admit guilt and the swamping of areas where black people have settled by Special Patrol Groups.

Black people's hostility towards the police must, therefore, be seen in historical perspective. During the 1960s and 1970s there was a steady increase in the number of complaints against the police, and from the evidence given by members of both the black community and the police organisations, relations between black youths and the police were particularly unsatisfactory. With little in common, each was wary of the other. By the 1980s, this had become a matter of serious concern. In fact, this was a period characterised by a high incidence of police harassment as at the Notting Hill Carnival, where tensions rose and tempers flared, thus serving notice to an unsuspecting public of a deepening crisis among black youth. An indication of the extent of their alienation was contained in a pamphlet entitled *The Fire Next Time*. The choice they faced was a stark one: as it was, their life chances were few and untenable. They were hard put to find a way out and, more often than not, they were confronted by the ubiquitous presence of the police.

In using the 'sus' charge, the police refuted the allegation of bias on their part against black people. Yet, they were trapped in their own way of thinking which, more often than not, linked black youths with crime. Even the former Commander of the Metropolitan Police, David MacNee, felt bound to state that law and order in London 'are now firmly linked to matters of race',[19] a message which would be echoed by one of his successors.

By September 1981, as unemployment approached three million, there were no signs that the economic recession would 'bottom out'. For the jobless, the forecast of mass unemployment was gloomy. To cope with such an eventuality, a highly authoritarian regime was necessary. Mass unemployment had been anticipated during the 1970s, and instead of finding jobs, by the end of the decade, the black unemployed found that the police force was ready to put down any potential trouble as tension mounted in the inner city areas. For their part, the police were invested with greater powers as their numbers increased in England and Wales to a record of 117,423 in 1990. This was not surprising since Britain had proportionately the largest prison population in Western Europe, about 44,000 in 1982,[20] a figure that would rise in the succeeding decade. Furthermore, the British had been engaged in 'civil war' in Northern Ireland, for over twelve years, a marathon exercise of peace-enforcement, which would have the side-effect of providing good training for controlling and disciplining the country's black communities. Thus the growing social and political problems, which necessitated the transition from relatively 'liberal' democracy to 'authoritarian' democracy, was reflected in two significant steps: first, in certain communities, the police force was strengthened, thus altering its role and image; and second, the security services were reinforced and new techniques of surveillance were introduced.

Given the experience of surveillance and security in Northern Ireland the development of computerised record-keeping systems in policing was not unexpected. The 'most secret' change, however, involved the military, in dealing with public order situations. This was evident in the winter of 1977–78, when the Army was brought in during the nation-wide firemen's strike. An estimated 20,000 troops were deployed. Thus the Army was substituted for a workforce to bring about the much desired defeat of the strike.[21]

Largely hidden from public view, these moves, legitimised through the media, marked the emergence of 'authoritarian' democracy. And as expected, the police force was at the forefront. Gone was the postwar image of the 'friendly bobby', the police had acquired a new image. In 1977 riot shields were in evidence for the first time in mainland Britain, for instance, at Lewisham during battles between the police and anti-fascists at a National Front march, and later at the Notting Hill Carnival.

Amidst the general circumstances of recession, the police regarded the maintenance of public order as their primary task. Characteristic of their strategy was a tendency to 'over-react' and 'over-police' in an aggressive manner. Consideration was also given to a 'third force', a paramilitary police. In fact, they were preparing to face their biggest enemies, the disadvantaged, harassed and impoverished black and Asian communities. Such force not only had sophisticated riot control equipment (water cannon, CS gas and armoured personnel carriers) but also specially trained marksmen to deal with riots, demonstrations and strikes, all those actions that were likely to disrupt the profit-making schemes and activities of those elites who owned and controlled the country.

At least in theory, the separate roles of the Army and the police were to be maintained. In practice, however, from this time on, the role of the 'ordinary' policemen would change. One approach was the creation of the Special Patrol Groups (SPGs) in the major cities. Like the London SPG, they were to be trained in riot control techniques. But why? Clearly the state was worried about the effects of the deepening economic recession on the disadvantaged black communities, and from here on, in certain 'black' areas, police tactics assumed a war-like footing, reminiscent of Northern Ireland.

A notorious example of 'third force' policing was seen at the Red Lion Square demonstration in June 1974, when one of the protesters was killed; and again in April 1979, at an anti-National Front demonstration in Southall, when a member of the SPG allegedly murdered Blair Peach, a white school-teacher. But, it seemed, local SPGs alone were unlikely to contain violence on the streets, which necessitated the added assistance of Police Support Units as policing black and Asian people, already an expensive exercise, became even more costly.

The police were faced with the paradoxical situation of having to reconcile two incompatible demands – 'to police the community in the normal everyday sense and to act as Britain's third force'. What more could then be said about community policing? John Alderson, Chief Constable of Devon and Cornwall, stated that the 'era of preventive policing is phasing out in favour of a responsive or reactive police'. In his opinion, the trust and confidence the community placed in the police was the main casualty, with the police and the people likely to meet only in conflict. This 'fire brigade' policing in Britain's major cities was likely to lead, Alderson argued, to policing more in keeping with an 'occupying army'.[22] The other aspect of community policing of concern at the time was the role of the police officer on the beat – a fast-diminishing presence.

Insensitivity in their relations with the black community led to calls for a systematic programme of police education on ethnic minorities and for a departure from the use of 'strong arm' tactics which arouse hostility to the police presence, as in Southall, and more recently, in Brixton and Bradford. The intervention of the SPGs did not inspire mutual trust and co-operation between local groups and the police. Although there has been much criticism of the specialist police units, commanding officers McNee, Anderton and Jardine singled out such units for praise. By contrast, the Institute of Race

Relations noted that in the decaying inner city areas of
sub-standard housing, low amenities and high unemployment,
where the white working class and the majority of black people
live, there was ample evidence of the SPGs' operations. Indeed,
because of 'in-built prejudice' and the aggressive tactics used by
these officers in 'high crime' areas such as Lambeth and
Lewisham, there was an unusually high proportion of arrests of
black youths for assault or obstruction. So Lambeth, with a
major concentration of black people, received special attention
from the SPG. 'Swamp 81', for example, was one of many
'attacks' by the Group, characterised by road blocks, early
morning raids and random street checks directed at four
housing estates, all with predominantly black populations.

Thus armed and with the security of full state backing, police
harassment hit a new low. Between November 1975 and June
1976, there were several clashes between the police and black
and Asian youths. It was clear that the black community were
not prepared to be bullied on their 'home ground'. They strongly
resisted the police officers, one of whom reported this fact to the
Parliamentary Select Committee on Race Relations. But this did
nothing to foster much-needed improved relations.

With growing unemployment among school-leavers a mass of
young wageless persons emerged. Financed by Urban Aid, youth
projects were set up in black and Asian communities, where
youths congregated daily. Here confrontation with police officers often led to resistance. The view that as unemployed
workers they were supposed to be demoralised victims ready to
move anywhere, cap-in-hand, imploring employers for jobs, was
based on the traditional view of unemployed workers. Although
their parents might have taken this line, by the mid-1970s, this
attitude was virtually dead among young blacks and Asians,
who were not prepared to be isolated or demoralised. Energetic
and resourceful, and consistently re-inventing themselves, they
hoped that society would respond positively to meet their needs.
Anything less would be contested. Indeed, theirs was a movement of bold resistance and change, of going their own way, and
one which, it seemed, police officers instinctively and persistently attacked as an instance of irresponsible and threatening
behaviour. This was the basis for the tension and conflict

between these young people and the police, which left the authorities to ponder how best to approach what had become an increasingly volatile situation. Their general strategy has been to 'harass, attack and disperse',[23] as was the case in Chapeltown, in Leeds. In the 'war' against the unemployed, individuals became the target.

But perhaps the most disturbing development in recent years has been the alarming deaths of young black men in police detention. In such confrontations, we see the balance of power favouring the agents of law and order, as was evident in a number of recent court judgments that had to be overturned, the victims of injustice eventually freed after wrongful conviction and, in some cases, years of imprisonment. Such travesties of justice had a profound effect on the black and Asian communities from the 1960s to the 1980s.

Black and Asian women not only had to contend with racism, but also with sexism. In particular, many had become more and more concerned with the relationship between education, paid employment and power. It is not surprising that women in the former colonies have dreamed of a good education for their children. Over generations, the black and Asian women's struggle has been one of persistence and resourcefulness, incorporating common themes and a statement of their ongoing 'double-subordination'.

At school, Indian and Pakistani girls faced a double disadvantage: lack of fluency in the English language and in being made to feel unBritish and unworthy. Bearing in mind that the structure of primary education in Britain was implicitly racist (for example, in the books used, the curriculum and teachers' attitudes), it served the purpose of reinforcing racial disadvantage, which exacerbated relations in the classroom. A common feeling among Indian, Pakistani and Bangladeshi children was that they were made to feel ashamed of their backgrounds, some disowning their food, languages and their Indian, Pakistani and Bangladeshi first names, while others desired white skin. The years had, if anything, intensified their feelings of insecurity and inferiority. 'Children between eight and twelve seem too young to fight against cultural racism in school', wrote Amrit Wilson, 'it is as though they are almost stunned into accepting the inferiority with which white society has labelled them.'[24]

Asian girls who were bullied at school tended not to talk about it at home, so that their parents remained ignorant of their ordeal. More tellingly though, many girls from orthodox Muslim and Sikh families felt that even if they did tell their parents, they would not understand.

Religion was important in determining Asian parents' attitudes towards the education of their female children. While some parents regarded their daughters' education as irrelevant, most showed interest, though even they tended to discourage them from entering further education. In the case of Muslim girls, the demands of Islam were at variance with the requirements of the British school system. Moreover, immediately after schooling, most Indian and Pakistani girls faced the prospect of marriage, which ruled out any chance of further education. Indeed, higher education was regarded as 'dangerous', 'destructive' and 'politically immoral'. But the struggle for freedom in school was (and still is) in many instances insignificant compared with the restrictions placed upon these girls in adolescence and eventually in marriage, after which 'they may feel that when oppressed as women they are being oppressed as individuals', Wilson wrote, adding that 'racism is an attack on them as part of their family and community, and these things cannot be separated in the identity of a woman'.[25]

Black feminists, for long ignored by the Women's Liberation Movement, addressed white feminists on the boundaries of sisterhood in the overall struggle. And in response to white feminists' emphasis on patriarchy as being the main source of oppression, according to Hazel Carby, black feminists felt the need to redefine the term, since racism 'ensures that black men do not have the same relations to patriarchal capitalist hierarchies as white men'.

Black and Asian women in Britain constantly challenge the racist mythology of their femininity. The belief that Asian girls will be forced into marriage immediately after leaving school perpetuates the racist attitude that Asian women in career jobs are a waste of time, thus echoing the views of some Asian (Muslim) parents about their daughters' education. There was also the problem of the black woman's efforts to protect and control her own sexuality from racist experimentation such as the contraceptive Depo-Provera. Black women have therefore criticised white feminists for overlooking their struggles both before and after they came to Britain. In so far as black and Asian women's experience is steeped in racism and sexism,[26] it necessarily differs from the experience of white women. So it was that black and Asian women resisted being grafted on to feminism in a tokenistic manner and argued for the transformation of feminism so that their needs could be addressed. They were much concerned that what they said and wrote should not be misused and subsumed in generalities, for individual utterances were not representative of the total experience of all black women.

7 MIGRANT COMMUNITIES: LEADERS AND GROUPINGS (1960–89)

THE TIGER BAY COMMUNITY

For the younger generation in 1960–89, at least, life moved in step with the current popular musical sounds. Calypso, gospel, rhythm and blues and rock'n'roll vibrated the walls of the various clubs and pubs. Here, famous American pop singers like the Platters' lead singer Tony Williams came, sang and fraternised, as musically-minded Tiger Bay boys and girls looked on admiringly and considered their own ambitions and futures. One such youth was Shirley Bassey, born at 182 Bute Street, which leads to the Bay, a youngster of raw, prodigious talent, nurtured near the Bay by her parents who were of West African and Welsh heritage, and their family, neighbours and friends. The legendary Rugby star Billy Boston's father was also a West African, his mother a local white woman. Many other children from such unions have gone on to exemplary achievements. This truly mixed community continued to grow.

In the 1950s, a new wave of Africans 'quite different in character' from the founders of the community, arrived in Tiger Bay. At this time of colonial struggle and the developing movement towards Independence, these Africans were, unlike their predecessors, educated and well dressed, modern men and women who were, in a sense, preparing for power, not only in their own countries, but also in various parts of Britain. The confidence they exuded was not lost on the youthful aspirants in the community. The generational differences had begun to emerge more clearly from mid-century, a trend which was given added impetus by the visits of American GIs, many of whom married Tiger Bay women.

If the 1950s was a decade of change, no one could predict the degree to which the community would be affected by those who felt threatened by Tiger Bay and decided that this area, demonised by various white investigators and other officials, needed to move with the times. When the much-loved trees of Loudoun Square (familiar to generations) were felled to make way for the City of Cardiff development, as Neil Sinclair who grew up there in the 1950s put it, the 'very root of our community garden and the old grey stone wall surrounding it, the seat of our dreams', were pulled down.

Nevertheless, although the Tiger Bay tradition of resilience had fortified and seen them through in earlier decades, many were unprepared for what was to come in the 1960s, the consequences of a 'nuclear explosion', as Sinclair describes it, 'though no one heard a sound'.[1] The City of Cardiff authorities decided that change must come to Tiger Bay as redevelopment projects replaced the much-loved areas of old Cardiff, like the leafy Loudoun Square. The new, 'colourless' council housing estate robbed the Bay and the Docks of its 'magic', which some accept will 'never be regained'. This devastation of the haunts of the old community did not extinguish all that was precious about the past years. As often as possible, after the 1960s, those who had grown up in the old Tiger Bay would get together in social clubs, where they displayed 'passions and spirit' inflamed by up-beat music evocative of childhood and youth, and of an irretrievable past.

In the 1980s, that 'spirit of togetherness' was still alive, and for those people who knew and loved the area, Tiger Bay was particularly legendary. However, for the media, long after the 'war' of 1919, another legend persisted and was maintained until the 1990s by a biased media. In fact, in 1992, Tiger Bay was still associated with prostitutes by none other than a Swansea University professor, who, it seemed, was attracted more to the vice and corruption than anything else there.

Today, the descendants of Tiger Bay are scattered across the world and many of them have been successful. Apart from Shirley Bassey, who has realised her full potential and enjoys international stardom, many of a younger generation have excelled in other fields. Linda Mitchell, for example, who understands the idea and practice of community intimately, is now Head of Community Broadcasting at the British Broadcasting Corporation, while among the many travellers who have answered the call and returned home is Neil Sinclair, who wrote an insider's account of Tiger Bay. Others, like Glenn Jordan, the African-American who first came to Cardiff as a Research Assistant with St Clair Drake, have been smitten by the place.

A few of those who had helped to forge close ties in earlier decades are still involved in community work. Indeed, some of them are founder members of the Butetown History and Arts Centre, launched in the late 1980s, an organisation 'linking a glorious past with a glorious future'. The Centre plays a pivotal role in community relations, providing a range of services, including extensive local history archives, historical research commissions, media products, an exhibitions centre, community arts events and workshops, a newsletter 'Voice of the Tiger', and a number of important publications, apart from Sinclair's book, *A Tiger Bay Childhood: Growing up in the 1930s* by Phyllis Grogan Chappell; *How I Saw It: Old Tiger Bay* and *The Docks* by Harry Cooke; *A Family Affair: Three Generations in Tiger Bay* by Olwen Blackman Watkins; and *Old Cardiff Winds* by Mike Johnson. Under the editorship of Glenn Jordan and with the co-ordination and photographic research of Molly Maher, these publications are in themselves fine achievements; and together they present a more dynamic people's history and culture, a timely corpus of work that would add to a more informed and better judgement.

The founders of the Centre have to keep abreast of funding arrangements. It was their good fortune that they were able to fund a long-awaited extension to the building. Having its own premises, the Centre has generated a greater sense of belonging, but few historians have bothered to visit the area. This is a common complaint among locals. The author has done so and was richly rewarded when he met founder members of the Centre, who related their stories of the old Tiger Bay community from the early 1930s onwards. Now in his early seventies, Gerald Ernest remembered the good and bad times. He had seen dramatic changes; and Vera Johnson talked about life from her perspective as a woman in the community. Others related the stories of Billy Boston, his mother and father, Shirley Bassey and the young football star, Ryan Giggs's antecedents in Tiger Bay. The eyes of these older citizens sparkle, and occasionally sadden, as they relate their stories, a fund of memories of Tiger Bay, which is now undergoing further change in the form of an artificial lake that will reflect the moon, instead of the sound and mood changes of the ebb and flow of the tide as it laps the shoreline of the Bay. Indeed the whole of Tiger Bay is once more being transformed.

Unlike the more ethnically homogeneous St Paul's, Brixton and Toxteth, Tiger Bay is distinctively a 'multiracial and intracultural' community. It never was, as Sinclair noted, a 'black' community. Creating a lake in a new Cardiff Bay, where the natural Bay used to be, does not submerge the meaning or the spirit of the old home town, for the old Tiger Bay has, it is claimed, left an enduring legacy as the 'oldest continuous' multi-ethnic community in Britain, regardless of what happens in the reimaging of the Cardiff Docks in the twenty-first century.

Today, as young descendants and older people of Tiger Bay consider the past, there is much in their collective memory to draw upon, a rich reservoir of images in a much maligned place that is pre-eminent among communities across Britain and indeed Europe, a small but unique site of unrivalled human coexistence. Few places can claim such a rare, almost miraculous achievement of cultural harmony which a native son wistfully attributes to the magic of Merlin, for in his view, only in Tiger Bay 'in the land of the Dragon ... the Tiger can roam in peace'.[2]

LIVERPOOL'S AFRICAN AND WEST INDIAN COMMUNITIES

Liverpool's black African presence over centuries was distinguished by its highly 'segmented structure', with many sub-groups graded according to status and the length of time they had been residents in Liverpool. Nevertheless, this African-West Indian community lacked a common outlook on a range of matters, and was therefore unable[3] to develop the kind of community life and spirit reflective of themselves.

The idea of a 'Negro' (Afro-British) community was, therefore, not an appropriate description, the structure of this grouping being better understood if it was viewed as consisting of many small groups, which became bigger with the unhindered inflow of migrants. Other than their racial similarity, there was little around which other groups could rally. At the beginning of the 1960s, these minority groups could be considered as a community only in a loose sense. Indeed, most members had closer contact as individuals than each group had with the others, and it was clear that the most intimate relationships of a person were contained within his or her own African tribal or national association. In Liverpool, then, the black population had not yet developed institutions representative of the advanced development of community life.

Nevertheless working towards common ends, various African and Afro-West Indian associations were able to achieve some degree of co-operation. Even so, it proved difficult to maintain and crises recurred and disputes resurfaced to disrupt whatever co-operation was established. Whatever their description (tribal or national) these associations were identified either through orientation to the country from which their members came, or towards the city of Liverpool – orientations that can be termed 'traditionalist' and 'modern'.[4]

Given the ethnic composition of Liverpool's complex black population, there was no simple formula on the question of leaders. While traditional leaders were acceptable, they could also have a divisive effect. The shortcomings of this kind of leadership were evident, the main difficulty being that those individuals who became leaders were more concerned with themselves than with the groups they were supposedly representing.

In general, though, Liverpool's black associations were similar to other ethnic groups in Britain. All of them sought solidarity, an understanding and appreciation of their history and all the help they could get to assist in their adaptation to conditions in Liverpool, as the 1960s ushered in social, economic and political changes. Consequently, these groupings evolved into more contemporary forms of organisation with better links nationally. Significantly, it was such co-operation that assisted in the setting up of the Trans-Atlantic Slave Gallery in Merseyside.

THE 'STANDING CONFERENCE' AND THE 'CAMPAIGN AGAINST RACIAL DISCRIMINATION'

In the three defining decades, from the 1960s to the end of the 1980s, the different groups of migrants became more or less settled and continued to learn and gain in confidence as they affected and were, in turn, drawn gradually towards their new social, economic and political environment. Culturally, at least, the migrants and their descendants quickly learned the value of independence, of attaining some sense of themselves, while they participated in and maintained forms of assembly to cope with ever-changing circumstances, which demanded initiative and unusual ability from their chosen or self-appointed leaders.

The West Indian Standing Conference (hereafter referred to as Standing Conference or Conference) came into being in 1958 after the Nottingham and Notting Hill riots. In the West Indies, government officials were alarmed by the sharp turn of events in Britain and sent two community development officers, Edward Burke and Ms Gregory, to London. After discussions with personnel in the Migrant Services Division on social, religious and cultural matters, it was decided to bring into being what became known as the 'Standing Conference', aimed at establishing lines of communication between the various High Commissions in London and the existing West Indian organisations, to explore the possibilities of initiating and strengthening leadership where necessary and to encourage better race relations.[5]

These initiatives were not without some success. A few months before the immigration ban, by the middle of 1961, 18 organisations were working with the Standing Conference. Impressive as this was, tensions that had existed between leaders of the Conference and members of the High Commissions during the early years persisted until 1962, when two events caused a marked change in Conference's position. These were the disbanding of the West Indies Federation and the enactment of the Commonwealth Immigration Act, designed to reduce the number of West Indians, Asians and Africans entering Britain, developments which led to a different approach adopted by Conference to co-ordinate the different West Indian community interests in London, at a time when the perceived goodwill of the indigenous white population had become questionable. At the time, words such as 'prejudice', 'discrimination', 'integration' and 'equal partnership' had much currency. After 1962, Conference leaders had no choice but to steer the Conference away from being a multiracial (black and white) Executive Committee, towards what was seen as the best option – an independent organisation.

The autonomy they sought and effected had other spin-offs: that of arousing their suspicion and distrust of professional researchers engaged in the field of race relations. Conference leaders were particularly critical of Sheila Paterson's work on Brixton,[6] and her views on 'integration' and felt that racial mingling could not suffice for 'real opportunities'. Neville Maxwell, one of the most committed West Indian migrant leaders (and a fervent believer in black /African nationhood, who later wrote *The Power of Negro Action*), voiced his worry over integration which, he said, must be 'a game for two' with the players respecting each other's dignity as human beings and 'recognising merit where it exists – with no reservations'.[7]

It was significant that many leading members of Conference were also active in the churches. Attending church services was a practical as well as a spiritual experience, which encompassed uninhibited singing, expressive of the release of pent-up tensions and daily frustrations that were integral to West Indian community life. Out of such Christian beginnings, concern with the welfare of others was indicative of a sense of responsibility, a prerequisite of leadership which was welcomed, harnessed and honed to make specific representations for members of the community in the forums of industrial relations, housing and local authorities. Interestingly, although political views were aired, not much was said or done, at the time, about voter registration or canvassing. Nevertheless, politics was ever-present, affecting the texture and quality of life of members of the community, as discrimination in the housing market and police harassment took its toll, and tensions and frustrations mounted.

While Conference spokesmen made useful representations in tackling matters relating to housing and the police, they were also well aware of their limitations: essentially that they were not strong organisationally and lacked the funds and facilities that would ensure the strength they desired. The best they could do was to push for improvements, for example, by cementing relations between Conference's constituent groups. Though they did not discuss their difficulties with non-West Indians, among themselves much criticism was vented about apathy and inter-island disagreements, and class and status divisions, concerns that were condemned as self-defeating.[8]

The political zeal of some Conference members propelled them forward and 'individualism' was identified as a problem. Maxwell appealed to members to be less selfish and more civic-minded, to forgo 'a little part' of their freedom and resources for the good of the community.[9] He felt there was too much indifference towards the leadership and called for a less complacent attitude and a broader vision. The 'woeful disorganisation' could not continue. Importantly, the prominence of 'individualism' among West Indians, he argued, had led to them becoming cynical about their leaders and towards groups,[10] which in turn did not help in the development of a national consciousness.

The task before them appeared (and indeed was) huge, for they had to engender a sense of pride in oneself, even among members of such an oppressed group. For those who despaired, the enthusiasm and optimism of Maxwell was refreshing and well-received. Unafraid of being critical of himself and others, he saw 'foresight, enterprise, tact, patience, the art of persuading others and an absolute dedication to Negritude'[11] as necessary leadership qualities, underscored by two even more vital attributes: an independence of mind and an unambivalent identification with rank-and-file West Indians.

So the drift towards disorganisation and 'independence' was central to the preoccupation of Conference leaders, matters which they did not hesitate to publicise. They were conscious that while they adapted as migrants in a new society, they had to be careful to preserve their own identities, but not at the expense of their group cohesion. Moreover, the leadership was preoccupied with reaching more and more West Indians.

They also pondered the question of equality in society. Would they achieve this by co-operation with, or independence from, British organisations? Like other bodies, the membership of Conference contained a broad spectrum of views, from radical to conservative. The majority of the Executive desired recognition by English people, which implied (and indeed was accepted as meaning) less independence. This was a departure from the earlier duality of West Indian attitudes.[12]

Consequently, as the less active members moved closer to British organisations, the cleavage between Conference's members and the leadership widened, a situation which was unhelpful to the group, as the more involved leaders gave their support to other migrant associations opposed to the National Committee for Commonwealth Immigrants. This division had a debilitating effect on Conference, which reflected its powerlessness.

APPROACHES FROM THE TOP: THE CAMPAIGN AGAINST RACIAL DISCRIMINATION

Powerless, black and Asian people in Britain continued to seek, through autonomous organisation, redress for their basic grievances. The arrival of Dr Martin Luther King in London late in 1964 was a symbolic and indeed important event. En route to Stockholm to receive the Nobel Peace Prize for his leadership of the American Civil Rights Movement, King preached in St Paul's Cathedral and, at a meeting organised by Christian Action, he spoke on American race relations. He did not evade the hard questions and directed attention to Britain's racial problems, which he said could become 'tragic and intractable' if they were not openly and honestly addressed. King was no Black Power radical, yet, from his own experience, he sensed the dilemma of blacks and Asians in Britain.

While in London, he also met many Commonwealth migrants who were opposed to racial inequality and a few of their white associates. This group was both impressed and encouraged by King, and after his visit they translated their disgruntlements into action, which took the form of an organisation that was representative of all 'coloured' people in Britain.

The LCP, which had been founded by Dr Moody in 1933, also had this aim, but it did not have a mass rank-and-file following. If this was a weakness, would this new organisation be more effective? Though many key members of the Campaign were from the middle classes, their commitment to the grievances of black working-class people was undoubted. However, as they understood it, the founding of the Campaign was necessarily, at least initially, the task and responsibility of professionals and intellectuals; more specifically, those who had already, in various ways, been engaged in analysing socially and politically the pervasiveness of racism in British society.

There was no doubt about the remarkable impact of King's presence in England,[13] though the impetus for founding the Campaign did not come from King himself. Rather, it was Marion Glean, a well-connected member of the Society of Friends Race Relations Committee, and a keen advocate of multiculturalism in Britain, who was the initiator. She turned to Alan Lovell and Michael Randle (both pacifists), who had indicated their interest in forming an exclusive organisation, and then contacted a few friends: Ranjana Ash (an active member of the Movement for Colonial Freedom), C.L.R. James (the distinguished historian and culture critic) and Barry Reckord (the West Indian playwright and actor). They named the group Multi-Racial Britain.

Soon enough they were to realise how far removed they were in education, employment and social standing from their less fortunate potential supporters. In fact, few (if any) of them had any direct rank-and-file contact in the migrant communities, and only Glean, Ash and James had been in touch with migrant leaders. But although the MRB was a 'forum of debate', it had a role to play. And the opportunity to do so came with King's visit, when Glean took it upon herself to assemble some people not only to greet him, but importantly to have a meeting with him. Thus, the MRB called its first mass meeting, an unprecedented gathering of worthies curious to hear the message and appraise the oratorical skills of the distinguished and honoured African-American.

The following day, in a BBC interview, King said: 'I think it is necessary for the coloured [blacks and Asians were still identified as 'Coloured'] population in Great Britain to organise and work through meaningful non-violent direct action approaches to bring these issues to the forefront of the conscience of the nation wherever they exist. You can never get rid of a problem as long as you hide the problem, as long as you complacently adjust yourself to it.'[14] For Glean's part, she wasted no time; soon a Committee was assembled to launch the necessary organisational moves towards forming an 'umbrella' body to deal with cases of discrimination as they arose, through representatives of the various communities.

A second formal meeting of core members was held later in the year and at a subsequent gathering, which took place on 10 January 1965, the 'Campaign Against Racial Discrimination' was officially suggested and adopted as the name of the new organisation. While there was some regional representation, the London group was overwhelmingly represented. About one-sixth of those who attended were white and included the invaluable experience and expertise of the young English lawyer, Anthony Lester. The central features of the meeting were the formulation and adoption of CARD's aims and objectives and the election of an Executive Committee. Pitt and Glean proved popular, receiving the greatest number of votes. In the proceedings that ensued no one was left in doubt about the 'general distrust' towards the Labour Party. However, while Glean opposed 'working closely' with the Labour Party, Pitt, a staunch supporter of the Party, welcomed the 'enlistment of allies'.

At the time, the early appearance of this difference of views went largely unnoticed. After the debate, the Campaign's guiding principles were agreed.[15] Moreover, it was felt that a National Founding Convention should follow and as an organisation they had much to do to prove their worth, not just to themselves, but to their potential membership and also among 'British sympathisers'. An organisation as ambitious as this had much to learn from the American Civil Rights experience, and while there was clearly a good deal of disagreement, the Campaign's programme was still questionable.

By the mid-1960s, the estimated one million 'black' (non-white ethnic minority) migrant population in Britain comprised three main national groups – Indian, Pakistani and West Indian – peoples whose lives were affected by racial discrimination. The better-educated among them were concerned enough to express their interest in getting some form of political representation. Indeed, it was in fulfilling just such a need that the founders of the Campaign had hoped to bring together West Indians. If such an organisation was to gain credibility, it was recognised that it would have to devote much time and effort to mobilising the very different ethnic minority groups. To that end, important differences were glossed over in preference for more universal values, and fundamental weaknesses remained unaddressed. Nevertheless, the organisers were of the view that any realistic formulation of policy should incorporate two broad sets of relationships: first, co-ordinating activities between the different ethnic groupings, and second, liaising with each group's own organisation. Thus, it was hoped that the Campaign would be a coalition, a union of nationalities, races, classes, languages, cultures, religions and political beliefs.

If in its formative period the organisation lacked clarity, there was no doubt that the Executive Committee's role was crucial. Those elected were regarded as the leading lights on racial matters in Britain, and in the following weeks, the Committee was enlarged to include the Standing Conference of West Indian Organisations', Indian, Pakistani and African representatives. In the months that followed, Glean emphasised CARD's mandate of creating a strong organisation and directed attention to the African-American experience. She argued that their revolts were against the old, coloured, legalistic bourgeoisie of the National Association for the Advancement of Coloured People and the Campaign should, therefore, avoid becoming the NAACP in Britain.[16]

While Glean's argument was admirable, the many authors of the various Campaign-inspired memoranda and other activists, embittered by discrimination in British society, had no experience as rank-and-file organisers and needed no reminders of how far removed they were from migrant workers in the factories, in the services and in community-related work. In applying themselves to the difficulties before them, the Campaign's leaders debated a range of 'images', which they envisaged as models for development, strategies that would eventually and successfully bring them closer to the migrants and closer to having some bargaining power. As it was, the various attempts were abortive. But, the impetus, which was present at the beginning, kept debates lively and gave a certain buoyancy to proceedings.

Throughout the founding phase, members of the legal Committee deliberated on formally presenting the Campaign's views to the British public and government. Pitt's idea, that a petition was the best approach, eventually foundered because of incompetence in co-ordination and what had now become abundantly clear, the inherent weakness of migrant organisations. This realisation helped matters little as tensions increased. Soon enough, the cleavage at the top began to widen. The two factions, the working majority and the 'dissidents', were distinguishable in terms of style, rhetoric and political beliefs, the dissidents concerned with presenting the Campaign as a group, while the pro-government working majority sought anti-discrimination legislation. The outcome was 'fundamental confusion' as the Campaign tried vainly to move forward. With no one leader able to command enough respect to win outright support, the 'verbal war' went on, while the fundamental reality of powerlessness[17] was left untended.

So when the National Founding Convention eventually got under way at Conway Hall, London, in July 1965, there was no serious attempt to amend or change the existing structure. Predictably, tensions persisted and the decision taken by Pitt to join the National Committee for Commonwealth Immigrants had profound effects not only in the Campaign's Executive, but also resulted in withdrawal[18] of the Standing Conference from the Campaign's structure.

Although the Standing Conference (London Region) was among the first groups to affiliate with the Campaign, it did so reluctantly. Nevertheless, after some eight months, Conference was formally associated with the Campaign, but interestingly had little involvement in the activities of the organisation, which was so influenced by Pitt. Central to the Campaign/

Standing Conference split was the personality and career of the Campaign's chairman, David Pitt, whose achievements in British public life were unusual. He was perhaps the most prominent black spokesmen in Britain certainly from about the mid-1950s to this time in the Campaign's history, and was regarded as such by many. But, his view of himself was quite different. In the opinion of one commentator, Pitt saw himself as an Englishman and did not attach too much significance to his birthplace. While he recognised the part that the West Indies had played in his life, the fact that he became so accepting of English norms caused much irritation and opposition from Conference spokesmen, who resented that their own more representative organisation which presented a truer picture of West Indians in Britain was overlooked.

Pitt's high profile had had a long period of gestation. Unlike the less privileged working-class children, he was fortunate in having middle-class parents, which helped enormously in terms of his education, upbringing and expectations. Many West Indian youths with his background set their sights on studying abroad. For Pitt, it was to be medicine. And, as he was to find out, work as a doctor opened other doors for him, which, given his priorities, he unhesitatingly entered. As one of the few West Indian doctors in Britain at the time, he realised the importance and potential of his representation of certain lesser known interests. So he became a Greater London Councillor and a Labour Party parliamentary candidate. His professional status and public-spiritedness brought rewards. It was thought by those who administered the highest offices in the land that Pitt should be elevated to the House of Lords, but many were suspicious and wondered why he was so acceptable. Unlike the Conference leaders, as one observer commented, in British terms, he had 'conventional status' which many members of the Conference lacked.[19] This was further emphasised by the fact that Pitt did not show undue concern for rank-and-file West Indians. Indeed, he distanced himself from Standing Conference, and was, at times, 'contemptuous' of its concerns, while he pressed ahead with canvassing white support for his anti-discrimination work.

He was also well connected and knowledgeable, not only in British party politics, but also in conventional politics in the

West Indies as well, where he had gained his invaluable early experience. Though he was born in Grenada, he became involved in Trinidadian and West Indian politics generally, favouring West Indian Federation. In Britain, he urged West Indians to join the Labour Party even though it had extended the discriminatory immigration policy formulated by the Tories. This action had incensed the leaders of Conference who felt it was futile to engage in Labour Party politics. Moreover, Pitt's actions and, at times, inaction (as when he joined the NCCI and did not protest against the White Paper on Immigration) were reminders of his distance from West Indians in Britain. The differences were clear and perhaps Conference leaders were justified in feeling aggrieved by his political skill in stealing the limelight as the spokesman for West Indians in Britain.

In its relations with the Indian community, specifically the Southall Indian Workers Association, the Campaign was inadequate. Much needed representation was denied to many IWA branches in the Midlands, the North and in Scotland. The Campaign's representations, it seemed, were highly selective, incorporating only a few groups in Bradford, Glasgow, Leamington Spa and Leeds. And even they were contacted infrequently and in an unco-ordinated way.[20]

Few groups were as close to the Campaign as the Southall IWA, a relationship which, it was hoped, would serve as a model for other groups. And even as factional disputes sapped the vital energies of the Campaign, moves to strengthen the organisation were being made, until finally it lost all credibility.

The Campaign's concerns seem to have been considered among government officials as reflected in the announcement of an extension of the Race Relations Act of 1965 (RRA) to the vital areas of migrants' interest: employment, housing, insurance and credit facilities. Paradoxically, on the very day that such measures were announced by the Home Secretary, Roy Jenkins, he also imposed a ban on America's chief advocate of Black Power, Stokely Carmichael, as though the Act would negate any need for further debate on race relations in Britain, where a mere 2 per cent of the population was 'black'.

The ban on the American radical, as many had thought, did not necessarily mean the muzzling of indigenous voices. In fact, after Carmichael's expulsion, Michael Abdul Malik (also known as Michael X), leader of the Racial Action Adjustment Society, became the first prominent victim of the RRA of 1965, which was expected to liberate those who felt entrapped. Such expectations could not be realised though for it seemed that the Act was meant to discipline black activists and spokesmen, rather than white racists. Not surprisingly, Malik's arrest generated a wave of resentment among migrants, many of whom felt that the Conservative politician Duncan Sandys, should be indicted for his inflammatory remarks about the inevitability of race riots in Britain if black and Asian immigration to Britain was not stopped. Soon enough, his real fear, marriage between black and white people was exposed. 'The breeding of half-caste children', he said, 'would merely produce a generation of misfits and create increased tension.'[21] As Black Power spread, and more people became colour conscious, tensions in certain sections of Britain's ethnic minorities in the inner cities arose as a counterpoise to the basic tenets of integration, multiracialism and anti-discrimination legislation, upon which the Campaign was founded. As criticism of the organisation became more widespread, worrying divisions appeared and West Indians became more isolated and unhappy with the 'Anglo/Asian axis' within the Campaign.

So three years after King's meetings in London had excited interest in bringing into existence a viable organisation, the qualities and type of leadership crucial for success had yet to be realistically comprehended and dealt with. In essence, the organisation had not fulfilled the expectations it had aroused. In the ensuing period, disappointment and disenchantment led to more serious divisions and eventually to the collapse of the Campaign. Perhaps the problem that should have been tackled was importantly to recognise the different ethnic groups as specific cases, rather than as one. Thus, the one general organisation obscured much that was specific about the affiliated groups of the Campaign. In effect, what was deemed grand and therefore unusual to all migrants regardless

of geography, industry and culture, was inappropriate to the
particular realities of the many people they supposedly
represented.

Of the nine formal West Indian associations in and around
Moss Side, Manchester, in the 1960s, none could do very much
on its own. About this time, it had become clear to some West
Indians that a new organisation should be formed, not as a
substitute for the associations, but to orchestrate their activities. Accordingly, a Co-ordinating Committee[22] came into being
to monitor the West Indian associations' work.

In time of need, these bodies extended their functions to
those who were not members, especially in instances where
West Indians who attended cellar parties and 'shebeens'
complained of police violence. These complainants were
assisted by the associations though their approach reflected a
certain unsatisfactory casualness. By 1968 race relations in
Britain had deteriorated to such an extent that the majority of
the associations' members socialised, more or less exclusively,
with people from their own backgrounds, thus counteracting
any prospect of integration. Entrenched positions bred
exaggerated fear and as a consequence of scaremongering, the
police were usually severe in monitoring black working-class
social and sports activity in Moss Side. Predictably, such
unwarranted attention deepened hostility between whites and
migrants, whose expectations of progress remained unrealised.

The sense of exclusion among West Indian migrants in
Moss Side was given credence by the Black Power movement
in America and the provocative speeches of Enoch Powell on
the question of immigration. Most West Indians felt that
Powell was expressing a truth which mirrored the feeling and
position of the majority of British people. The optimism
which many migrants had harboured when they first arrived
was now difficult to summon up, especially given the type of
dead-end employment with which they were stuck. And as
members of a settled community, they worried about the
vulnerable position and unpromising prospects for their
children.

Faced with a bleak future, teenage West Indians in the late 1960s and early 1970s, were enmeshed in a learning process, characterised by a heightened sensitivity in their relations with both their parents and older West Indians. The generation gap was the source of much tension and misunderstanding, as older people asserted their authority, while West Indian youth mounted implacable resistance. For some, as scarcity exhausted choice, 'hustling' was all that was left. At this juncture in their evolution, many teenagers seemed to have adopted a 'very West Indian' approach to living in Britain. This should not surprise us when their background is considered. Working-class Jamaican youths, for example, were brought up with a preference for things Jamaican, including speaking patois and responding to the home-grown blue-beat rhythm. But those young people who had either been born or had grown up in Britain had also already imbibed more of some aspects of British culture than others, and were therefore more open than their parents to meet individuals from the other side. The contacts[23] they had outside their own community were perceived as less threatening than their more inward-looking parents and elders. What interested many observers was whether or not this tendency to make inter-racial liaisons would go beyond West Indian youths' teenage years into adulthood.

In other parts of the country such as Easton, West Indian associations had also come into being, largely due to their exclusion from the mainstream of social, economic and political life. From the fringes they attempted to organise themselves, but were frustrated by divisions of class, status and colour, the legacy of colonialism and neo-colonialism. Such distractions presented a number of organisational problems, and for many the safe option was retreat. Politically, the interests advanced by West Indian leaders in both Easton and Moss Side were too narrow in scope, reflecting their island parochiality. Their associations were characterised by ephemerality and fragmentation and did not have the consistency and sense of cohesiveness of other local migrant organisations, namely the Indians and Pakistanis.[24]

BLACK CHURCHES

In 1970, nearly a generation after the first shipload of postwar migrants (the former West Indian volunteers) and African students entered Britain, they experienced a rude shock in, of all places, the Christian churches. The bedrock upon which Eurocentric history was founded was also tainted by racism. West Indian Christians were shocked, especially when they recalled the zealous and seemingly open-minded approach of British missionaries who had gone out to 'save' the uncivilised heathen islanders and previously, their African forebears. The sinfulness of white Christians, it was felt, could not be defended, for they were clearly not practising what they had, for so long, been preaching, and neither, it seemed, did they care, which added to the distress of the more pious and naive West Indians.

Such rejection by the Christian people of Britain, especially in those formative years of the postwar migrant experience, was profound and resulted in West Indians and Africans establishing their own Christian forms and places of worship. The time had come for black Christians to bear their burdens in the way, God willing, they chose. Thus, the substantial departure of white Christians from churches which black people had been attending ushered in a 'quick revolution' among black Christians, who not only transformed these churches, but also established other 'black' churches. Thereafter, the inner cities witnessed an 'evangelical explosion', the opposite of what was happening in white churches, a movement of which Clifford Hill had no doubt: that it arose from working people in the West Indian community, an exhilarating change from the staidness of pious middle-class leadership. No 'ruling intelligentsia' was necessary here for the 'explosion' was organic and therefore instructive, inspired by the heart and therefore all the more powerful in its evocations of things spiritual, of deep beliefs. Charismatic leadership, it seemed, was not apparent.[25]

As was the case with their forebears who used religion to combat the evil of slavery, these people drew upon that spiritual reservoir, which began to bind together elements of the West Indian communities more and more.

All-black churches not only became more visible, but were also respected and respectable, as the community-centred 'house meetings' opened out to accommodate more people, ironically, in abandoned white churches. In turn, this had a ripple effect leading to larger congregations and establishing broader connections with religious bodies in the West Indies, Africa and the United States.

Apart from the growing number of black churches, West Indian 'sects' were also to be found functioning as 'home groups', which held prayer meetings. Even these small gatherings though were beset with the gradual emergence of leadership tensions. Taken together, the growth in total membership of the various West Indian religious sects was dramatic: rising from 10,500 in 1966 to 20,600 in 1970, a development accompanied by the consolidating effect of a similarity of approach in preaching style and how they lived their lives.[26]

Like the African Church of the Cherubim and Seraphim, the West Indian sects were both authoritarian and hierarchical, emphasising strong moral values, sexual faithfulness in marriage and strictures on drugs and profane language. Women, it was felt, should not reveal or accentuate their bodies, thus the wearing of cosmetics, jewellery and certain hair-styles was discouraged and dress had to be unprovocative. Generally members of these sects were expected to make financial contributions. Not all members were from the lower working classes though, as was evident from the membership of the New Testament Church of God, which had a majority of 'new' middle-class members from among the migrants.

Hill was of the opinion that the sects' membership had grown because of their exclusion and sense of alienation as Christians from the white churches. And as the black churches were formed and developed, more and more black Christians attended.

Social deprivation[27] also played a role in bringing about this shift. By the 1970s, the creative aspect of the black churches had begun to rouse even supine followers and there was optimism enough to suggest that it would infect the white population, thus affecting the direction of church history and race relations. Hill, who was in the midst of these developments, expressed his hopes:

If the English churches are to benefit from the vision and spiritual gifts of the Africans and West Indians, then the first step is the recognition of their ministry and the admission of their representation, on a fully equal-status basis, into ecumenical church councils. There are indications that this is beginning to happen, but much more needs to be done, and much more quickly.[28]

Historically, from the eighteenth century onwards, black preachers have been at the forefront of engagements for equal rights. In the 1960s and 1970s, black churches were magnificent and positive in response to racism in the 'house of God'.

ASIAN WORKERS AND COMMUNITY CONCERNS
BEFORE 1970

The migrants who came to Britain from the Indian subcontinent had founded associations, mainly of two kinds: first, those concerned with the various cultural activities of India and Pakistan, and second, those that dealt with matters arising from the communities' relations with British society. Both types of organisations offered leadership roles, accompanied by a degree of social standing and a promise of social and economic inclusion in institutions and organisations of the wider society,[29] from which many Indians and Pakistanis felt excluded.

Wherever Indo-Pakistanis lived in large groupings in the United Kingdom (especially in the Midlands and Yorkshire), there were screenings in local cinemas of Indian and Pakistani films, sponsored by film societies, businessmen and cultural associations. Though film-oriented, these societies also functioned as friendly societies and, at times, private businesses. To all intents and purposes, it seemed that these film-cum-friendly societies functioned as democratically-run organisations, though the film groups had, in the main, adopted a top-down management approach, while the more political associations were organised and structured essentially to monitor difficulties between their members and their new British environment.

For most of the early post-Independence migrants from India and Pakistan, being unable to either speak or write English was

a difficulty which left many disoriented and bewildered. Fortunately there were a few English speakers, who devoted much
time and energy assisting their fellow-villagers and countrymen
in filling in forms and writing letters. Such acts of national
brotherhood bred a sense of social cohesion that would cement
relations and help to build a stronger feeling of communal
security and community.

Manmohan Singh Basra was a prominent figure in the Indo-
British scene at this time. He came to Britain in 1953 and
became involved in helping his fellow migrants. But the size of
the problem warranted a more organised, systematic approach.
So Basra, in association with a few other Indians, formed the
Indian Workers Association in 1956 (a name derived from an
earlier organisation) in South Staffordshire. It was soon 150
strong.[30]

The membership of this organisation was drawn, in the
main, not only from among Punjabi pedlars in the Midlands,
but also factory workers from Coventry. In London a similar
group was founded and together they worked diligently,
co-opting the talents of Indian students and intellectuals for
the cause of Independence. In many instances, these
well-educated Indians were at the forefront of the India
League's deliberations and representations. Now though they
recognised the value of supporting the Indian Workers'
Association, which was organised around work, thus reflecting
a strong trade union orientation as opposed to the League's
more direct political concerns. Against this background, by
the 1960s, the IWA had emerged as the most important
organisation among Punjabis in Britain. Election for the
IWA's offices were hard fought and rank-and-file members
were no less interested as they weighed the pros and cons of
hopeful candidates' potential campaigns.

In these Punjabi communities, not surprisingly, men of
influence came to the fore. Often they were of independent
means, whose power and support came from the loyalties of
those they may have helped in the past. Such leaders' following
also consisted of kinship ties.[31] So secure was the support of
many of these men that it did not matter whether they formed
alliances or took an independent path.

Why were influential Punjabis so interested in IWA politics? At least three reasons have been advanced. The first is a strong desire among Punjabis for unity, the second, their adoption of a common and easily recognisable physical appearance and dress; and third the combined effect of 'brotherhood', inextricably linked to their sense of belonging and community. Historically, the value of rituals endemic in Sikhism was a reminder to the individual of his/her role in relation to the corporate life of the Sikh society.[32] This religious fervour, loyalty and pride bonded them as Sikhs.

Homogeneity is a word that can be used to describe the Punjabis' involvement in IWA politics. In the late 1960s an estimated 90 per cent of this community shared the same social background. They came from small villages, where they had done, more or less, the same type of work and for similar reasons. Their migration to Britain did not end the similarities, for in the field of employment they did similar jobs for the same pay, and beyond the workplace there was a commonality to certain general problems. This mutual experience helped enormously towards group consolidation.

With a high premium placed on unity among Punjabis, and the dedicated efforts aimed at achieving this goal by Indian Communists and social workers, well-organised Punjabi communities were established relatively quickly, which was just as well, for by 1967 IWA politics in Britain had been subjected to significant change, a reflection not only of the political scene in India, but also of the influence[33] of British life on these migrants.

That change was manifested in the formation of new Associations in Southall and Birmingham, reflecting different viewpoints which, in turn, were the result of four main trends: first, migrant settlements were evolving into more permanent communities characterised increasingly by families, instead of single men; second, migrants were gaining more knowledge and confidence in dealing with the British way of life, so that fewer of them were dependent upon their countrymen's help; third, these communities were differentiated in terms of caste, religion and education; and fourth, members of these communities were unhappy with their low status in British society.

So for all their similarities, the political circumstances in the Southall, Coventry and Birmingham communities were different. The Coventry Punjabis were, at one stage, alone as a unified community association, a unity that had, alas, become a memory by the summer of 1967, when there were two associations in the city at loggerheads. Each conducted its essential functions[34] with diligence and single-mindedness as though the other did not exist.

A little further north, in Birmingham, the Punjabi community seemed more concerned with stamping out racial discrimination.

This leadership was not lacking in either ambition or innovation. They called upon all Punjabis in the Midlands to rally to their support and pressed ahead with their uncompromising protest in the form of meetings and marches, thus underlining their imaginative leadership and a marked shift from the old formulas tied and weighted down by tradition.

Southall presented yet another interesting organisational scenario. Before 1968, the alliances that had been struck had regrouped to form at least eight smaller bodies, each vying for overall control of the same IWA,[35] a diversity of feeling which led to the lowest ranks, in terms of caste and religion, forming their own organisations.

In those communities where the IWA was without a place of its own for worship, or a cinema to screen its films, there was the likelihood that it could either follow the Coventry example or take the militant path of the Birmingham IWA, the latter appearing especially attractive in the early 1970s. But while the 1960s was a crucial time in their existence, IWA leaders and their followers had to relate to British institutions, as memberships of different kinds were open to them, including the trade unions, constituency Labour parties and inter-racial committees: namely, the Voluntary Liaison Committee, associated with the NCCI. For their part, the government was keen to see migrants on their bodies, which they funded. The fact that migrant leaders were willing to cooperate reflected the serious concern that migrants felt as victims of racial discrimination.

After due consideration, many spokesmen could see no other way forward, even though they were fully aware that such contributions as they made would be overwhelmed by the concerted oppositional voices of white British organisations. Indeed, this was the dilemma of the IWA leaders, who continued to seek common ground.

It had become clear that the Southall IWA and the Birmingham IWA could not agree on the strategy to be used in trying to persuade the British government to accept migrants as full members of society and therefore to abolish racial discrimination. As late as 1967, the Southall IWA leaders still believed that there was a chance that the NCCI and CARD would be able to deliver some form of anti-discrimination legislation. The Birmingham leaders could not accept this, for they reasoned, realistically, that the Labour Party would not take the risk of introducing such legislation, because it would seem to be taking the side of the migrants just when race and immigration control were at the centre of political debate, a political environment in which the different parties could well see black and Asian migrants (as they had done previously) as the cause of some of Britain's economic and social ills.

Against this background, the pent-up resentment of migrant workers had become a detached and highly charged aspect of British industrial relations, as racial disadvantage in employment became intolerable. Daily work relations thus took precedence over the disputes in the Gurdwaras, as Punjabi workers took part in struggles that challenged an unsuspecting British public and, more particularly, the traditional customs and practices underpinning British industrial relations.

Generally the IWAs continued with their inward-looking social work, though more and more, at the leadership level, personal influences were being overtaken by younger, less patient workers who, in the 1970s, added strands of resistance which focused on the workplace, where Indian, Pakistani and African Asian workers expressed industrial solidarity as never before.

ASIANS IN THE 1970s AND 1980s: THE WORKERS' STRUGGLE

By the end of the 1960s, it had become more or less accepted that Indian and Pakistani migrants were to be found in tedious, low-paid and sometimes hazardous employment, jobs that were quite unsuitable for the ambitious and talented among them.

In Courtauld's Red Scar Mills, Preston, Asians constituted a third of the workforce, a significant presence, to say the least. In Southall, Asian workers were to be found largely in four factories and, by the mid-1960s, 90 per cent of the unskilled employed by Woolf's factory were Sikhs from the Punjab.[36] At both the Courtauld and Woolf factories, migrant workers and employers faced each other in industrial conflict that would occur elsewhere; and in the years to come, an identifiable pattern would emerge.

The influx of African Asians in the early 1970s gave added impetus to the movement for change in the workplace as workers, largely from Kenya and Uganda, came out in open rebellion, organising themselves against insensitive and oppressive employers. Public confrontation with vested British interests was relatively new to IWA leaders, whose parochialism was now tested.

In the previous decade, the IWAs had become involved in their members' work experience and, in so far as they could, they supported both work and community-related issues, as they affected the migrant population. But all their interventionist gestures, important as they were, were increasingly seen as inadequate to the needs of a new and independent element in the community of workers, who sought representation beyond the restrictions of its Punjabi majority. Moreover, cleavages in the associations' political orientation in relation to politics in India made it difficult to accommodate the appropriate struggles of African Asians, Asian youths and the British-born among them. Soon the IWAs were found to be unable to cope with problems of Asian youth. Thus, politically and industrially, the IWAs declined as a provider of strong leadership.

The growing incidence of strikes in and around Birmingham could not be ignored and any retreat towards insularity was unacceptable, especially to those at the sharp end of the daily workplace struggles. Jagmohan Joshi did not hesitate to shoulder his share of responsibility by providing leadership that necessarily involved confrontation. Part of that more 'radical' Asian leadership meant coming to terms with Black Power which had propelled many young West Indians and Africans towards forming militant organisations.[37] While many IWA activists felt uncomfortable with Black Power, some made connections with the Black Panther Movement and other radical black groups. Nevertheless, from the late 1970s to the early 1980s, Afro-Asian solidarity came of age, it was a time of impressive solidarity when bus-loads of IWA members from Birmingham, joined West Indian and Africans from Brixton, Notting Hill and elsewhere in London in their denouncement of the Labour government. Perhaps their most impressive joint demonstration was against the Kenyan Asian Bill.

Elsewhere, in Leicester, for example, 4,000 people marched against the Bill, the IWA being the organising intelligence which helped to bring together the student and left-wing sections of British society, the Black Power groups, West Indians and Asians, the largest contingent, drawn from Birmingham, Southall, Leamington Spa, Derby, Coventry and Leicester, who showed their solidarity and support behind the banners of the IWA. Although these demonstrations did not stop the speedy passage of the Bill, they reinforced the belief that, whenever necessary, blacks and Asians could and would combine for common purposes. For all their good work, though, the IWAs were rarely the sole initiator and militant force in any industrial dispute. More often than not, it was only after Asian workers had acted that the IWAs offered assistance. And perhaps this was as it should be, for the IWAs were not, and indeed could not, act as a trade union.

So a new labour force had appeared to challenge the IWAs, to dare them to go further. Perhaps the IWAs realised their limitations, but, in a few cases, opposed the 'impatience and independence' of this refreshingly new 'battalion on the Asian industrial front'.[38]

Many African Asians had, as we saw earlier, worked in British factories and in a relatively short time, through industrial action, they changed the nature and course of the Asian workers' struggle. Unlike most of the Indians and Pakistanis who could not speak English, the African Asians were English-speaking. Their factory experience of shift work led them to believe they were exploited because of the colour of their skin.

With this awareness of racial injustice, they courageously demonstrated their moral fortitude during the industrial action taken at Manfield Hosiery Mills, Imperial Typewriters and Grunwick. Acting largely outside the constraints of traditional migrant organisations, their causes posed many challenges, not only to the established IWAs, but importantly to wider working-class solidarity, and in the whole system of industrial relations.

ENTERPRISE AND RELIGIOUS PLURALISM

Apart from the role and contribution of the vast majority of Asians as wage-earners, there was also an insistent momentum of enterprise building up, within the Asian communities. As population increased, the Asian corner-shop fast became ubiquitous. If the English are a nation of shopkeepers, one Pakistani businessman in Birmingham declared, so are Asians and 'we're proving it daily in England'.[39]

The sense of cohesiveness which Asians felt was strengthened as cultural differences and a lack of fluency in the English language continued to alienate many from the British. In this context, the advice, concerning the importance of language to Empire,[40] given to Queen Isabella by the Bishop of Avila, before Spain's colonisation of the New World, was instructive. As it was, the Asians' 'unfamiliarity' with English (the language of Empire) was a blessing in disguise, which protected them from rapid assimilation. There was, however, more to be gained by learning the language than by not doing so, as the migrants soon realised. Those who had recently come to England relied on the 'assistance and guidance' of their compatriots who had either preceded, accompanied or had come after them. A sense of community was strong, a bonding which could not, however, transcend the language difficulties, for without some fluency in English, the prospect of jobs for Asians would continue to be elusive and, for some years to come, they were encumbered by a daily routine of monotonous and menial tasks. Asians could not, for example, be employed in the public sector, where they came in contact with the English-speaking public, and so they were confined to factory and foundry work. Such limitations had implications on the patterns of settlement of both West Indians and Asians. For example, by the mid-1960s, there were only half as many Pakistanis in Greater London as there were West Indians.[41] And there were also more West Indians employed by London Transport than Asians. Consequently, there was a greater Asian presence in the provinces where the cost of living was much lower than in London. After all, the reason why Asians migrated to Britain was essentially to make money, and in their zeal and determination to do so, jobs with overtime earnings were eagerly sought. Generally, Asians did not mind a long working week, provided they were financially compensated, so that they could send regular remittances to dependants in India and Pakistan and, increasingly to assist their families, who joined them in Britain.

Culturally, Asians were conscious of their alienation from British society and culture, for unlike the Caribbean region, Asia was not a 'creation' of Europe. Asians' social habits were therefore different. They did not drink alcohol, visit pubs or dance halls. Instead, they went to Asian cafés and to the cinema to see Indian and Pakistani films, to keep in touch with their past, a strange dual existence! In effect, Asians tended to be in an economic straitjacket, which kept them culturally estranged.

Isolated from the wider society, Asians created their own communities, thereby avoiding rejection and conflict with Britons in most areas of British life, except employment. More enterprising Asians were loath to work for others and began enterprises that would meet the distinctive requirements of language, religion, dietary practices and culinary tastes of the Asian communities. With the growth of this community, the demand for grocers' and butchers' shops rose[42] in the Asian communities of Southall and Bradford, and Asian business branched out into wholesale and retail enterprises in a whole range of goods, clothing, restaurants, corner shops, travel agencies, banks, electrical goods, petrol stations, cinemas, taxi cabs, bookshops, off-licences and pubs.[43] This astonishing economic progress proclaimed the fact that they had not only become self-sufficient, but also confident enough to reach beyond their communities and cater to the needs of the wider society. Soon, Indian-made clothing and

Indian and Pakistani restaurants and grocers were serving a growing clientele which, more and more, included a cross-section of the British public. But the more successful Asians were not content. They established mortgage companies, private loan companies and finance brokers, to service a network of Asian businesses of varying sizes.

From this broad-based economic foundation, it was necessary to maintain and improve infrastructural interrelationships, and one way forward was to inform the community of all that was available to them. To this end an Asian press in Britain was launched. Following Mahmood Hashemi's pioneering work in 1961 on the Urdu weekly *Mashriq*, and the publication of nine weeklies in various Indian languages, including Urdu, Punjabi, Gujarati, Bengali and Hindi, there was also the English language *India Weekly*. These publications addressed the concerns and desires of thousands of Indians and Pakistanis, who felt more in touch with the larger world. Overall, the various Asian communities were better informed of each other's activities and at weekends cinemas across the country showed Indian films to large audiences (an estimated 100,000 in the 1950s), which had grown almost a decade later, into an enterprise with a turnover of £1.5 million.[44]

However, growing prosperity seemed to have, in some respects, slowed down the urgency to learn English. Towards the end of the 1960s and thereafter, there was a steady influx of English-speaking East African Asians, which reached a climax with their expulsion in 1972, when an estimated 25,000 arrived in Britain; and by 1973, according to one historian, the number of Asians in Britain from Central and East Africa had reached some 200,000.[45] Many of these people were influential in their former countries' financial, business/trading and industrial sectors. So enterprising were they that by January 1974, instead of searching for employment, a 'substantial minority' of them were actually creating jobs. As a consequence, the Uganda Resettlement Board, originally set up to accommodate them, was abolished. The initiative and resourcefulness of these African Asians enriched the wider Asian community. Many branched out into the retail trade and their fluency in English afforded them certain advantages over those Asians from the

Indian subcontinent. Consequently, the majority of these merchants and corner shopkeepers were categorised as lower or middle class, as the Asian community, as a whole, became more sharply stratified.

Unlike the African Asians and West Indians in the 1970s and 1980s, the problem of a greater command of the English language needed to be tackled so that Indians and especially Pakistanis and Bangladeshis could become more competitive and therefore more effectively integrated in the wider society. In this respect, the BBC designed broadcasts to help both Asian women at home and Asian men at their workplaces. Early indications were that these approaches were promising,[46] though there was still some way to go before most of the targeted Asians would become conversant with English. One is reminded here of how different it might have been for the alien Englishmen and women when they were lording it in India! At most, few members of the British community in India would have bothered to dip into an English-Hindustani dictionary.

So the gradual process of the acculturation of Asian parents was contrasted with the more rapid accommodation of British 'ways' by their children, who were being socialised in British schools. In this process, as it relates to young Asians, Hiro has argued that because most of them were bilingual, the English language was enriched with 'idiom, imagery and original turns of phrase'; and he was confident that regardless of the fate of their mother tongue, like the Jewish people who came to Britain before them, religious identity would continue unchanged, for although Jews in the various parts of the world speak different languages, they remain Jews. In the same way, the majority of Indo-Caribbean people, who rarely speak Urdu and Hindi, have retained their Hindu, Muslim and Sikh beliefs and names.[47]

Sikhs, who form an integral part of the Indian community in Britain, are followers of Guru Nanak (the founder of Sikhism) and Guru Gobind Singh, who created the male Sikh's religious identity, which incorporates long hair, comb, long underpants, steel bangle and dagger. He established the brotherhood of the Khalsa Panth and male Sikhs were named 'singh' (lions).

The distinctive features of the male Sikh have been a contentious issue in Britain because they denied them employment, while other Indians and Pakistanis were accepted. Predictably, this type of discrimination was unacceptable to them, and called into question the relationship between religious identity and economic interest, a matter on which there had to be compromise, though this did not mean any diminution of religious fervour. At the centre of their activities were the Gurdwaras (places of worship) which served as a pivotal point for social, welfare and other communal activities. By the 1960s, no fewer than 40 Gurdwaras had been established throughout Britain as places of refuge and sources of individual and communal renewal. Politics was never far from the thoughts of Sikhs, whose particular concern had been the campaign for a Punjabi-speaking state in India under Sikh control. Closer to their place of work, however, Sikh beards and turbans had excited much interest and have continued to arouse much controversy,[48] thus bringing their religious and political identities into focus.

The high profile of Sikh assertiveness contrasted sharply with that of the 'unobtrusive' Hindus who, in spite of being far more numerous than the Sikhs had, by the end of the 1960s, fewer places of worship. Hindus are quite unlike other religious devotees (Sikhs, Muslims, Christians and Jews) in that their belief system encompasses a body of religious literature and scripture, underpinned by a caste system, which in the past has perpetuated gross inequality. In modern India, however, urban developments have increasingly been making such a system untenable, though in some villages it is still a long way from bringing equality to the millions of Untouchables. It must have been disappointing for those Indians who benefited from the caste system to find that in Britain people thought less of caste than they did of colour and 'race'. Nevertheless, caste among Hindus in Britain persisted.

While some Punjabis were Hindus, the majority of migrants from the Gujarat were Hindus; and although they spoke different languages, the first part of their names[49] was derived from Hinduism. But, the growing need for castelessness and equality is a matter which Hindus, Sikhs and Muslims have had to seriously consider.

Islam in Britain has continued to grow since the first Asian migrants began coming to Britain. Islam, described by one

Asian writer as 'physically less obtrusive' than Sikhism, is more focused in its holy scripture and more strict in its edicts, the Friday prayer being one of the important practices of the faith. Of the 80 mosques that existed in Britain in the 1960s, most were the work of devout Pakistanis, for whom such places served as the hub of social/welfare activities, which not only helped to unify the varying elements, but also to transcend racial and national boundaries.

Growing up in a Christian country, it is important for Muslims to retain their religious identity, for since the Crusades of the Middle Ages tension and suspicion have distinguished Muslim/Christian relations. One of the areas of special concern to Muslims in Britain is the religious instruction for their children in Christian schools. After much protest, more educational authorities have conceded that Islamic instruction should be provided by recruiting Muslim volunteers to give Muslim children such classes as are necessary in school.

Fasting is observed by Muslims, especially in the period of Ramadan, and, like followers of the Jewish faith, Muslims regard Jesus as just another prophet. They believe in the prophet Muhammad, who founded Islam in the seventh century AD.

Pakistanis, like Indians, are largely self-sufficient, which emphasises their exclusion from the mainstream of British society. This, in turn, has encouraged a careful nurturing of their languages, dress and cuisine, and from this cultural basis, they have launched innumerable business undertakings, not only to the benefit of their community, but also that of the wider public.[50]

Outside England and Wales, of particular interest is the Asian community in Scotland, which made steady progress socially, culturally and politically in the 1970s and had gained in confidence enough to field their own candidates during the 1974 parliamentary elections. Nevertheless, the community was not free of racial prejudice and with the coming of age in the 1970s of Asians born in Scotland, the level of awareness of racism rose dramatically. For these young people, this was an experience they could not avoid, a minefield through which they trod warily. Unlike their Indian- and Pakistani-born parents who were in awe of the British rulers, Asian youths and their white counterparts had to play out the problem at a different level and at a different pace. It needs to be said, though, that they were less patient and less tactful than their parents. The hidden pain of their tolerant parents was often impatiently and brutally revealed by this new generation of Asian Scots.

Almost in tandem with their opposition to racism, in the decade of the 1970s, there was a surge of religious fervour and associated activities among Asian youths, an affirmation of their attachment to their place of birth, regardless of its location in Britain. In fact, north of the border, of one thing members of the Asian community, especially the young, were clear: Scotland was their home, and they set about putting into practice what they felt and believed in, building places of worship and schools. Before the end of the decade, Glasgow had a new mosque, the source of much pride.

Members of other groups such as Africans, Afro-Caribbeans and others were steadily entering the country, mostly as students. However, towards the end of the decade, it seemed that the intermittent migration of Asians to Scotland from other parts of the United Kingdom had virtually stopped.[51]

In the 1980s, marked progress in commerce and business was made by Asians, as more of them engaged in trading which was extended and consolidated. Small became large in terms of business premises and, as far as quality of goods was concerned, good became better. Taken together, these Scottish Asians were emerging as a dominant force in job creation, and one or two individuals, such as Sher Mohammed and Yaqub Ali, achieved outstanding successes,[52] thus becoming role models for aspiring Asians. There have also been many failures, but the spirit of enterprise persisted among many who were not successful at first. Soon enough they explored other avenues. Overall, the result was greater diversification and creativity in providing services such as petrol stations, estate agencies, video film leasing and insurance brokers and property development, hitherto unimaginable undertakings that could only succeed in response to public demand and entrepreneurial skill and judgement.

What clearly emerged from the success of the many Asian enterprises was a new approach adopted by a new kind of entrepreneur: one who could reconcile his business goals with his community interests, and crucially beyond that, win the confidence of the wider world of British enterprise. It is not surprising that such men are held in high esteem within their communities, men who must overcome many barriers, without losing their own sense of identity. Significantly, such leaders reflect the pluralistic nature of Indian and Pakistani societies, where different linguistic, religious and racial groups are to be found, acting and reacting in response to ever-changing circumstances. And just as 'Western values' are underscored by common assumptions and norms that hold together diverse cultures (British, American, French, Dutch and German), Indians, Pakistanis and Bangladeshis also shared attitudes commonly called 'Eastern values'.[53]

THE INDO-CARIBBEAN COMMUNITY:
THE 1970s TO THE 1980s

By the 1970s, other smaller groups of Asian descendants were visible, especially those from the Caribbean, who were engaged in a range of activities in Britain. To make known their distinctive identity, they formed the Indo-Caribbean Association, which sponsored sports and cultural events. On a much larger scale, perhaps the most impressive social activity each year, and for a number of years, has been the Indo-Caribbean-led *Caribbean Times*-sponsored Community Awards, hosted by Arif Ali, which honour blacks and Asians across the spectrum of human endeavour, for their outstanding and meritorious community work.

For many years now, the Indo-Caribbean Cultural Association has brought together members of this widely dispersed community, through its annual educational, social and cultural activities. The children of these migrants, born and bred in Britain, proclaim through their actions and life-styles a new vision of Britain's future, an outlook inspired by those who have preceded them and those who are still among us, who represent a range of excellence, among them sportsmen of world renown, especially in the field of cricket – Sonny Ramadhin and Rohan Kanhai; businessmen, lawyers, doctors, academics, politicians and statesmen (Shridath Ramphal, former Secretary-General of the Commonwealth) and, of course, distinguished authors of non-fiction and fiction, including the prize-winning novelists Sam Selvon, the Naipaul brothers, Vidia and Shiva, and the acclaimed playwright Mustapha Mathura.[54]

RUDY NARAYAN

No roll call of Indo-Caribbean achievement in Britain would be complete without the important contribution of Rudy Narayan. For over three decades, he has been 'one of the most charismatic and controversial figures' in the legal profession, acting on behalf of black and Asian people, especially youths.

Narayan was born in Guyana on 11 May 1938 and came to Britain in 1952 with the ambition of studying law. He entered Lincoln's Inn at the age of 19 and after National Service, became a prominent and outspoken critic of racial disadvantage in Britain. In a profession so tradition-bound, Narayan's dissenting voice was conspicuous. If many in the legal profession were reticent about complaints of racism, Narayan was having none of it. It was his fearlessness and determination to get to the truth that underscored his career. Predictably, he was on a collision course with the establishment. But Narayan was unperturbed, representing victims of miscarriages of justice. Soon he became the best-known black lawyer in Britain for his defence of the Thornton Heath 10, the Cricklewood 11 and the Bradford 12, among other high-profile cases which expressed deeply-rooted prejudices in British society and caused many British officials to rethink long-held beliefs.

Narayan's sustained attack on established practices eventually brought about his disbarring from the legal profession, after being subjected to at least five disciplinary tribunals in 25 years of professional life. Upholding the law and advocating fair play for the poor and oppressed were among his passionate concerns so it is not surprising that before his death, he was hoping to be re-admitted to the Bar. He was for many black and white Britons (both rich and poor) an extraordinary legal advocate, whose book *Barrister for the Defence* was published in 1985.

Between the mid-1980s and 1991, his courage and skill brought many triumphs, notably in 1985 when he forced Sir Patrick Mayhew, the Attorney General, to admit that the Race Relations Act of 1976 had failed in its purpose and to concede that new legislation was needed; in 1973 when he founded the much-needed Society of Black Lawyers; and in 1995 (after his removal from the Bar) his leadership of protests following the death of Wayne Douglas, a young black man who had died in police custody; and in the setting up of Civil Rights UK in 1994. Though his tactical approach was often controversial, no one can doubt Narayan's courage, his eloquence, unorthodox style and unique blend of personality derived from his Indo-Caribbean upbringing and his experience in Britain. For the ordinary people who sought his help he was their champion. He was 60 years old when he died on 28 June 1998.

On 10 July, the day of his funeral, 'Brixton stood still to pay its respects', the *South London Press* reported. No one who had attended his funeral service in St Matthew's Church (and the reception held later that evening, with 500 people in attendance at Lambeth Town Hall) could deny the deep respect he commanded among fellow-professionals and his huge popularity among a wide cross-section of British society.

In his tribute, Michael Mansfield QC praised Narayan, his former colleague and friend, for his outstanding gifts and said that although they were both law students and practitioners of the law, the one important and telling difference between them was Narayan's colour. Nevertheless, as a pioneer, his monumental life and work during very trying times in Britain will no doubt continue to benefit and guide us today and the generations to come. In fact, it needs to be said that long before the Stephen Lawrence Inquiry brought about unprecedented publicity to the murder of the teenager, Rudy Narayan had for decades been denouncing racism in the police force and malfunction within the British legal system for which he paid the price of being denied the practice of his chosen profession.

In addition to the Indo-Caribbean community, though less numerous, thousands from the Indian diaspora, form part of the diverse mix of Asian and Indian-descended groups in Britain, comprising Sri Lankans, Mauritians, South Africans and

Fijians, among whom can be counted men and women of the highest calibre in the various professions and, of course, their British-born children who are poised to make contributions to British society, as they aspire towards the fulfilment of expectations that will hopefully be realised instead of being frustrated.

AFRO-ASIAN COMMUNITY INITIATIVES:
THE 1970s AND 1980s

In the evolution of the various groupings, successes in community-building had to be balanced by failures. Indeed, during the 1970s and the 1980s, there was much intense activity within and between the black and Asian groups, a troubled time of racial inequality, racial attacks and racial harassment that revealed hitherto hidden goodwill and support between these two main ethnic groupings. These were crucial years in terms of organisation. The full impact of racial disadvantage, reflected in various ways within vibrant, evolving communities, was exacerbated by police harassment of black youth, the baiting behaviour of fascist groups and the escalating racial violence (both at the individual and institutional levels) and drew positive responses, so that in the 1970s, the most vulnerable and beleaguered sections of the black and Asian communities resisted their oppressors, but did not react unduly; though one felt that rebellion would eventually come, as indeed it did in the 1980s.

In retrospect, the 1970s were years of deceptively slow consolidation, when the groups that formed the Black People's Alliance emerged to address their different problems, while at national level, the focus was on co-ordinating the fight against racism,[55] amidst ever-rising provocation from extremist organisations.

If the previous two Immigration Acts were detrimental to migrant interests, the 1971 Act was no less so, and was seen as yet another step towards the heightening of tension as state racism became even more pervasive. At this time too, an area of concern was the problem of education for West Indian children. In this connection, the North London West Indian Association, led by Jeff Crawford, won considerable support from black parents in various parts of London and evolved to become more politically assertive. Crawford was not shy in coming forward to give voice to what were more widely-based community matters. No one was left in doubt, for example, of the devaluation of black children in Educationally Sub-Normal schools. The prospects were worrying for many black parents and teachers, who decided that no more time should be lost in registering their concerns. Thus a Conference on ESN schools was called and Bernard Coard made more public the problem in his book *How The West Indian Child is Made Educationally Sub-Normal*.[56] Experience of the black child in relation to the British education system had the desired effect, as black leaders and their organisations initiated a number of supplementary schools in London, including the Kwame Nkrumah, Malcolm X Montessori Programme, the George Padmore and Marcus Garvey schools, and significantly a library in Hackney was named after the distinguished historian and thinker, C.L.R. James.

The black communities' provision of education for itself did not stop there though. It was felt that a West Indian child or youth should have as broad-based an education as possible. So it was that various projects were set in motion to teach black pupils typing, photography, Swahili, clothes-making, drawing and sculpture, poetry, drama and play writing. Older students were assisted by Roy Sawh, the Indo-Caribbean activist, who promoted radical views at the 'Free University for Black Studies'. Concern for the education of these deprived children triggered interest in welfare as the unemployed and homeless were welcomed at hostels and youth clubs. To add to their education, there were information centres and bookshops (stalwarts engaged in publishing and education were John La Rose, Sarah White and Eric and Jessica Huntley) and a number of community-inspired weekly and monthly newspapers, such as *Black Voice*, *Grassroots*, *Freedom News*, *Frontline*, *Uhuru*, *BPFM Weekly*, *The BWAC Weekly*, *Black Liberator* and other short-lived publications, reflective of the quickening pace of change and the evolving complexity of the black and Asian communities.

For their part, the British authorities could only see a 'black', mass rather than a range of multi-coloured, multi-cultural people, an attitude which suited their political strategy of containment. This approach was evident when the police raided and disbanded the Racial Action Adjustment Society's Black House and broke up the Universal Coloured Peoples' Association. The nucleus of the Association was undeterred and formed other militant organisations in a concerted attempt to counter-act unrelenting and, for the black and Asian communities, worrying police and fascist harassment and violence, as Black Power's success darkened the mood and intentions of those who owned and governed the country.[57] There was no doubting the force and pervasiveness of this timely black ideology which traced its origins to the radical Pan Africanists in Manchester of 25 years earlier, dedicated men and women who had come, as it were, full circle, though then none of them could have predicted so ready an acceptance and application of what they had audaciously proclaimed here in Britain.

Many leaders and commentators felt that blacks and Asians had to deal with the forces ranged against them, not only as a people, but also as a class. After the strikes and the increasing incidence of Asians being murdered, the old methods of organisation had become inappropriate. In certain sections of the Asian community, greater urgency was expressed, for example, by the Southall Youth Movement which called on its members to de-fend their community against fascist aggression. So with the rise of racially-motivated assaults and murders, young Asians formed defence committees in the areas most endangered – in London (Brick Lane, Hackney and Newham), Manchester, Lewisham and Bradford. Like the earlier strike committees, these young Asians were very concerned with solidarity, not only within their Asian communities, but also with West Indian youths, and at times came together to express common cause through political groups such as the Hackney Black Peoples' Defence Organisation and Bradford's United Black Youth League.

Radical political groupings in these years also emerged, incorporating Afro-Caribbeans, Asians and Africans, who were unhappy with the white Left's preoccupation with themselves, rather than appraising and integrating the black and Asian experiences. While they paid greater attention to the British experience, as black political groups had done before, they also made international connections, as imperialism's second phase was conducted from America. Common to them were their anti-imperialist and anti-racist orientations, arising from lived experiences in their Western European communities.

As before, though perhaps more crucially, in the late twentieth century, a press was necessary in politicising black and Asian people. Among the publications at this time, mirroring more contemporary issues, were the bilingual Urdu and English publications *Samaj in a Babylon*, *Black Struggle* and *Mukti*, supplemented by a number of other newspapers, journals, news sheets and newsletters. Although now, and historically, these publications represented different stages in the black and Asian struggles, the major targets of their concern varied little, if at all, namely the government and the police, and the stain of racism that had infected both.

Faced with ever-changing strategies, Afro-Asian leaders and groupings responded by making qualitative changes. Educated, middle-class, authoritarian and accommodationist leadership could no longer justify itself, and more and more, state racism and racial discrimination forced the black and Asian communities to undertake their own representation to address these issues. It was significant that through the 1970s and 1980s, members from the black and Asian intelligentsia increasingly felt threatened and expressed their concern. Their leadership and other skills were well received by the communities, but unlike a previous generation of migrant leaders, they were, in turn, grounded in the realities of grassroots political struggle,[58] for clearly their concerns were intertwined and becoming more recognised, as was the ongoing assertiveness of black and Asian women.

THE BLACK WOMEN'S MOVEMENT

If, in the early 1960s, the idea of sari-clad Asian women on picket lines was unthinkable, by the end of the 1970s, this phenomenon had become part of the history of British industrial relations, which indicated new lines of development. In their industrial disputes, they found that other women were willing to assist them. Their courageous stand and the support they received aroused among them a sense of sisterly solidarity,

which was more or less coincident with the emergence of a
'black' women's movement.[59] The aggression of the National
Front and other right-wing groups, and the continuing threats of
Paki-bashing, encouraged black and Asian resistance. Both the
struggles and the leaderships in this resistance were of a new
kind, a reflection of the difficulties women faced in the late
1970s and 1980s.

By now, black and Asian women had learned to press ahead
with the issues particular to them, without waiting for the support of the white women's liberation movement, with which
there were clear cleavages in terms of their social, economic and
political positions. This had the effect of increasing Asian and
black women's awareness, and thus their willingness to resist
further encroachments on what they regarded as irreducible
areas of concern. They formed the Organisation of Women of
African and Asian Descent, an umbrella organisation which debated issues and balloted its members nationally, worked closely
with Afro-Caribbean groups and granted its member associations
local autonomy. In scope and depth, OWAAD's representations
were ambitious. Its leaders sought ways of orchestrating their
experiences, of dovetailing strands of struggles into campaigns,
highlighting the general through the particular, without compro-
mising each other's difference. Afro-Asian women were opposed
to discrimination based on class, race and gender, and together
they organised the first 'black' women's centre.[60] From here, they
planned strategies to counteract racism as it existed in the educational, social and welfare services.

Early in the 1980s, Afro-Asian women were again at the
forefront of industrial protest, significantly when trade union
power was being undermined by a right-wing government. They
also collaborated with black socialists against state harassment.
As the campaign of the women's movement ran its course in
the 1980s, it assumed a distinctive identity, which complemented wider groupings of blacks and Asians.

The start of the 1980s had dramatic implications for the manner in which race relations should be looked at thereafter. While
black and Asian leaders and groupings had been warning of the
effects of individual and institutional racism on the two main
communities, little was done, as policing, which demonised

black youths, brought an 'accumulation of blunders' to a climax, as the old slave port of Bristol became the scene of a riot which exploded in 1980. The strategy of 'dispensing justice on the streets', resorting to 'arbitrary' and in some cases mass arrest had much to answer for. The riots had galvanised black and Asian leaders, who found a common cause, and achieved a hard-won maturity, a deeper feeling of belonging, in spite of their exclusion.

In the aftermath of the 'Bristol riot', attention was directed to racist attacks in London and most regrettably on the burning to death of 13 young West Indians in New Cross in January 1981, which brought more distress to the black community. The cumulative effect of these acts of malice and hatred was a heightened wave of deep-seated resentment reflected in feelings that were given expression in the New Cross massacre demonstration in March 1981. Thereafter, police/ethnic minority groups' relations remained troubled. Naturally, the New Cross tragedy struck deep responses within the black communities, where there was enough tinder[61] needing only a spark, which was lit (after a long period of intense police harassment) in Brixton on Friday, 10 April 1981. This area of postwar migrant settlement was set ablaze and in its scale, duration and intensity the violence dwarfed the Bristol riot, though not its enormous symbolism and impetus. The damage to property was extensive – £10 million worth. But the human cost of years of inner city neglect prior to this event was incalculable. Youths (blacks, Asians and whites) responded to their perceived neglect to their lives and, between April and July 1981, they rioted in as many as 29 cities and towns across Britain in an unforgettable summer of crowd violence.[62]

This is an interesting juncture at which to pause for a backward glance at British race relations which have indicated in consecutive official reports the extent of racial discrimination and racial disadvantage suffered by the ethnic minorities. Their location in society has signalled a national black and Asian consciousness, the result of a culture of race and class[63] oppression, though increasingly class was being replaced by culture.

An integral part of the cultural transmission of imperialist ideas was (and still is) racism, and by the 1980s, the anti-working class Thatcher regime had already embarked on its determined move to the right in policy-making, a movement that had, in turn, generated new initiatives and new images of late twentieth-century Britain from among the more assertive movers and shakers, the leaders and their followers within the black and Asian communities. But while they acted together, they were also fully aware of the divergent paths of their development in Britain.

ASIANS IN THE 1980s

After the violent scenes of the early 1980s, in spite of the Scarman Report and subsequent efforts to improve understanding between black people and the police, it was the evolution of the Asian communities that was striking in the strides they made during the preceding decade. Most of the Asian youths who had confronted 'Skinheads' and the National Front were not troublemakers, but residents who felt that their opposition was necessary and as such it had to be forcefully made. The stand they took galvanised many in their communities. Southall was, however, not Brixton and the conflict was not prolonged.

Asians in the Southall Youth Movement were not parochial, and continued to show that they could be flexible, radical and progressive, reaching out to other oppressed groups. At various times, they co-operated and acted in solidarity with Afro-Caribbean organisations, because they felt that their 'political colour' was black, though some would later seek a redefinition, even beyond the unsatisfactory omnibus designation 'Asians'. Such actions augured well for the future as more young Asians became participants as employees who represented their ethnic group at town hall level, a capacity in which they displayed their innate talent and skills in liaising between people in the community and local government officers. Confidence among Asians generally was boosted and their success was undoubted when in 1986 there was a three-fold increase in the number of councillors from ethnic minorities, an indication, according to one writer, that both Asians and Afro-Caribbeans had moved closer to 'being integrated into mainstream' British politics.[64] These continuous shifts and changes in the direction of integration were reflected the following year when an Asian,

Keith Vaz, was elected as the Member of Parliament for Leicester East (the first Asian MP since Saklatvala).

In the mid-1980s, Asian cornershops, clothing stores and chemists continued to proliferate, and an Asian middle class emerged, many of them home-owners. On council housing estates, however, there was an increase in racial tension, as Asians were terrorised by persistent racial harassment, ranging from threatening letters, excrement daubed against doors and walls, to physical and verbal abuse. In some cases, their homes were petrol-bombed while they slept, too often with fatal results. Their fear of harassment in certain areas such as Tower Hamlets in London, grew by the minute.

The majority of Asians (over 70 per cent of them home-owners), however, lived in relative security. Indeed the economic profile of some Asians in Britain by the end of the 1980s was impressive. According to the *Sunday Times* there were an esti-mated 200 Asian millionaires, compared with 1,800 millionaires in Britain as a whole. If this suggests Conservative Party links, that would be more or less correct, for by the early 1980s, the Anglo-Asian Society of the Conservative Party, was ten times bigger than the party's Anglo-West Indian Society.[65] In this decade, while there was a mood of militancy among young Sikhs, many of whom had also adopted a more conservative attitude evident in styles of dress and a return to traditional values, many of the followers of Islam not only reacted strongly to Indian-born author Salman Rushdie's novel *The Satanic Verses*, but also maintained a high profile during the controversy arising from it.

Pakistani Muslims in Britain accounted for the largest single group of adherents to Islam, whose insistence on their child-ren's education generated the leadership among them to inaugu-rate, in 1979, the Union of Muslim Organisations of the United Kingdom and Eire. In the 1980s, they followed closely and anxiously the troubled affairs of their co-religionists in Iran, Iraq and Afghanistan. The rise and undisputed authority of the Ayotallah Khomeini in Iran was welcomed by Muslims in Britain but when Rushdie, who lives in Britain, published his *Satanic Verses* in which he allegedly depicted the Prophet Muhammad and his wives in a demeaning and negative light, Islamic traditionalists or, as some referred to them, 'fundamentalists', were enraged to such an extent that in various parts of Britain demonstrations were held and, in one instance, a copy of the book was burned and the author denounced for his defamation of Islam. Thereafter, events took a gradual, but irrevocable down-turn as Muslim leaders in Britain asked Prime Minister Thatcher to ban the book and bring charges against Rushdie. Having lobbied various politicians, they sought the support of the Islamic world to deal swiftly and firmly with what they perceived to be a blasphemous, and indeed, satanic book. Soon Bradford with its large Asian Muslim population became the focus of a campaign to ban the book and prosecute both the author and his publisher.

The publication of an American edition of the novel further inflamed tempers, and demonstrations in Islamabad, the capital of Pakistan, were successful in that the book was banned, though at the heavy cost of at least one person being shot dead. When news of these events reached Iran, the Ayotollah was asked to deal with the matter. And so Ayotollah Khomeini, as we know, declared his religious decree, the Fatwa, which sentenced Rushdie to death. Rushdie immediately withdrew from public life and, as the heated debate on lifting the Fatwa ('an extreme form of literary criticism', as V.S. Naipaul put it) persisted, there were more demonstrations in Britain and abroad, as diplomatic calls reached Islamic leaders to resolve the death threat. The media took every opportunity to record the latest developments, scores of books about the 'Rushdie Affair' appeared and the novelist became an international celebrity. Leading churchmen condemned this incitement to murder and politicians from Britain and the European Community have been engaged in top-level talks with the Iranian government ever since.

The events so far have highlighted Islamic values in Britain, thus giving greater credence to the traditionalists' viewpoint at the expense of lessening the tendency of British-born Muslim youth towards the adoption of a more flexible, less traditionalist approach, which had been evolving over the years. So in the face of religious attack, many British-born Muslim youths became militant, forming organisations in Bradford and London in defence of the British Muslim community, which accounted for almost half of the Asians in Britain.[66] The focus was on the fundamental aspects of Islam: the arousal of a new awareness of the faith which merited study, both ideologically and socially. In strengthening waning belief, any sense of inferiority Muslims may have felt was dispelled as the debate retained its high national and international profile, which Muslim youth increasingly saw as being underscored by British racism. In effect, the 'Rushdie Affair' shored up many interrelated concerns within the Muslim community, notably in Bradford. Any attack on Islam was perceived as an assault on Muslims and their culture. The death of Khomeini in 1989 did not lift the death sentence. The 'Rushdie Affair' should not, however, obscure the real issues confronting Muslims in Britain, for historically, Muslim minorities have 'sought tolerance-cum-pluralism not formal equality', according to Tariq Modood, who argues that in Britain, Muslims are offered a 'formal equality', but this is not reflected in its 'institutional and legal arrangements'. The relationship 'between equality and pluralism', he believes, is central to race relations in Britain, an issue which Muslims should address.

Modood proceeds past the 'hang 'em and flog 'em' interpretations of the Holy Quran and directs our attention to the heart of the Rushdie Affair, which he says is neither about Rushdie's life, freedom of expression nor indeed about Islamic fundamentalism, book-burning or strained relations between Iran and Britain. He identifies the central issue as being the 'rights of non-European religious and cultural minorities in the context of a secular hegemony'.[67]

Adding his comments to the 'Rushdie Affair', Professor John Rex posed the question: Has anyone the right in a multicultural society to denigrate and blaspheme against the religion of another group? He answers that Rushdie's book does infringe the principle of integration and mutual tolerance, but warns that though there is scope for dialogue, one cannot be optimistic about the Muslims' integration in British society. Acknowledging the popular perception in Britain that all Muslims are fundamentalists,[68] Rex does not hide his dislike of a minority asserting or demanding their rights. He much prefers to let the matter rest with the tyranny of the majority, rather than the principle of mutuality, which he refers to in passing. The fact remains that the Rushdie Affair is still with us and, as one writer has pointed out, less than a year after Rushdie's book was published, Asians who were Muslims became 'British Muslims' their confidence growing, thus redefining their beliefs in relation to those of other groups, including, of course, the majority of people in British society. While it would not be easy for the British public or government to accept the idea of overwhelmingly brown Muslims dictating terms for social integration within white society, Hiro maintains that implicit in this is 'a power relationship tilted in favour of the newcomer, who is attached to a cultural heritage that has been for centuries in struggle with Christian Europe'. More and more as the 1980s gave way to the 1990s, the relationship between the ethnic minorities on the one hand, and the white population, on the other, revealed the long gestating complexities, some new trends and surprisingly different and clearer patterns of development. But let us first consider briefly the political context of these changes.

8 TOWARDS THE MILLENNIUM: ETHNIC MINORITIES IN THE 1990s

Race has become metaphorical – a way of referring to and disguising forces, events, classes and expressions of social decay and economic division far more threatening to the body politic than biological 'race' ever was. Expensively kept, economically unsound, a spurious and useless political asset in election campaigns, racism is as healthy today as it was during the Enlightenment. It seems that it has a utility far beyond economy, beyond the sequestering of classes from one another, and has assumed a metaphorical life so completely embedded in daily discourse that it is perhaps more necessary and more on display than ever before.

Toni Morrison, *Playing in the Dark* (1992)

A BRIEF OUTLINE OF THE POLITICAL BACKGROUND

Politically, as Britain entered the 1990s, the ethnic minorities were faced with a number of changes. The Conservatives still held power, but a beleaguered government led a 'sick', empire-less economy, whose representatives made strong remarks in the forums of Europe regarding the European Union.

Against this background, the Labour Party leader, John Smith, died suddenly. His successor, the much younger Tony Blair, was joined by John Prescott, as deputy leader. Already, after heated intra-Labour Party discussion and debates about the merits of 'Black Sections', the largest black and Asian populations in British history now had some representation with the election of four 'black' Members of Parliament – three from the African-Caribbean community (Diane Abbott, Bernie Grant and Paul Boateng) and one Asian, Keith Vaz. Many articulate people from the ethnic minority communities were enthusiastic, but the black journal *Race Today* suggested that those more militant blacks who had aspired to office (but had ultimately failed the parliamentary selection process) were better-off being out than in Parliament.[1] One who did not get in was Sharon Atkin, who had been replaced in a 'safe' seat in 1987 by another candidate, because Neil Kinnock (then Party leader) did not like her outspoken views on black political representation. Since then while middle-class blacks and Asians felt encouraged and optimistic, many thousands more were deeply unhappy that their plight was ignored. Indeed the links between crowd violence, the economic crisis of the late 1970s and inner city deprivation, disadvantage and decay surrounding young black and Asian people were largely denied by government ministers. At various times, including successive Notting Hill Carnivals, instead of defusing and preventing crowd violence, the state has tried to repress it. Thus with few choices, collective racial violence continued to be an alternative means of expression for the groups concerned, as indeed it was earlier, especially in the 1970s and 1980s, a time of ever-tightening authoritarianism and black and Asian disaffection.[2]

In the run-up to the 1997 general election the leaders of the three main parties (John Major, Tony Blair and Paddy Ashdown) answered questions put to them by young Asians, in a live television programme. To the question: Why should Asians vote for each leader's party? Major's response was that he liked to think of himself as 'colour blind', and he strung together fine words about a plural society and the quality not the colour or the number of such candidates chosen by his party to contest the elections. Blair and Ashdown also chose their words carefully. In the months that followed, these leaders, with more pressing matters on their minds, continued to address the non-white electorate in the same vague manner. Racial tolerance is one thing, but racial discrimination and disadvantage constitute quite another. Since then, they have continued to make speeches assuring blacks and Asians that they are integral to British society.

The theme of unity was yet again in the foreground of British politics in relation to Northern Ireland, where a number of Asians work and live. How was this to be achieved? Unemployment in this region was among the highest in the United Kingdom, a problem that did little to relieve the heightened tensions, especially among extreme elements of the Catholic and Protestant communities.

The people of the Province continued to hope but just when the IRA ceasefire seemed like holding, the murders, violence and exploding bombs were again a deadly presence. As the 1 May 1997 Election Day approached, the questions uppermost in people's minds were: Could Labour's decline be about to end? Or would the Conservative Party claim a fifth consecutive victory? Alas, for the Conservatives, this was not to be. Tony Blair became the youngest British Prime Minister in the twentieth century, after guiding his 'new' Labour Party to power with a landslide victory, a majority of 179 seats. In this wave of New Labour popularity (with more women MPs than ever before) two more 'black' MPs, Muhammad Salwar and Oona King, joined the above-mentioned four, who had retained their seats, in the House of Commons. In the context of these political developments, how did the various ethnic minority groups evolve? And what were (indeed are) their main concerns?

ETHNIC MINORITIES IN THE 1990s

From the beginning of the 1960s to the late 1990s, the ethnic minority population has risen from less than 1 million to an estimated 3 million,[3] and there has been a significant shift from the non-white (ethnic) population being essentially 'black' Afro-Caribbean to a majority 'Asian' population. From the outset, the non-white migrants have not been homogeneous and although the simple black/white division has been used in the past, increasingly and especially in the late 1990s, such a general division is wholly inappropriate. So for the purposes of this recent period and, indeed as a reflection of the evolution of the migrant communities vis-à-vis the wider white population, at least six groups will hereafter be referred to: Caribbeans, Chinese, Indians, African Asians, Pakistanis and Bangladeshis.

Before 1982, there had been three major surveys on ethnic minorities in Britain: *Racial Discrimination in England* (1966),

Racial Disadvantage in Britain (1974) and *Black and White Britain* (1982). More recently, in 1994, a fourth survey revealed important changes and developments, both within the various ethnic minority groups and between them and the white population. While some of the areas of interest had previously been looked at, the themes selected, presented and the conclusions reached here are drawn essentially from the findings of several authors of the latest Policy Studies Institute report, which raises many questions of central and ongoing concern.

Families and Households

One of the striking differences identified in the 1990s is the age difference among the more recent ethnic minority migrants. It is significant that all the minority groups had a larger number of children and fewer elderly people than the white population. Pakistanis and Bangladeshis were among the leaders in this respect.[4]

In terms of age distribution, 40 per cent of all South Asians (Indians, African Asians, Pakistanis, Bangladeshis) were under 16 in 1982. This figure fell to 35 per cent in 1994, when Caribbeans and Asians showed a 'small increase' in the numbers of elderly people. While the vast majority of children in each of the ethnic groups are British-born, only among the Bangladeshis was there a very significant number of children who were not, and very few non-white elderly people had been born in Britain.

There were important differences among those of working age born in Britain: Caribbeans being just over half, between a quarter and a third of Indians and Pakistanis, and only an estimated one-seventh of African Asians, Bangladeshis and Chinese.

In just over a decade since the last survey, the proportion of members of minority groups born in Britain had increased, the largest shift appearing among African Asians, the smallest among Indians. Bearing in mind that a fairly large number of ethnic minority adults (especially from the Caribbean) were also born in Britain, 'new births are increasingly into the second British-born generation'. And among the younger children in the five years before 1994, the greater was the likelihood that their parents were also British-born. As the latest research noted: 'a sixth of Pakistani and Bangladeshi babies, a quarter of Indian and African Asian babies, and three-quarters of Caribbean babies had at least one British-born non-white parent'. Thus, the migrants can be regarded as the first generation, while their grandchildren can be described as the third generation.[5]

Much has changed over the past 30 years and family structures have been influenced by a number of factors, including economic, technical, moral, social and political influences.

The patterns which Caribbean and Asian people have incorporated since they came to Britain reflect both their traditional values and those of the adopted country. Because their migration took place within the life-span of many of them, it characterised their age-structure as a group.

Caribbean and South Asian family structures differ from their white counterparts, but not in the same way. As the most recent survey noted the 'most striking' feature is that of negligible interest in long-standing relationships, especially in formal marriage. For all age groups, men and women from this group were the least likely of all the ethnic minority groups to be married, and most likely to be either separated or divorced. Yet, their unconventional partnering patterns indicated a direction which is being adopted by many whites too. Of those who were married or lived as married, as many as half of the British-born Caribbean men and one-third of women chose a white partner. Caribbean women have children at an early age, and almost a third of Caribbean families with children were unmarried mothers, as much as 'five times the proportion among whites'.

As the researchers pointed out, these patterns of child-rearing raise a number of issues, importantly child-rearing as one-parent families and concern especially with the children of Caribbean heritage, where one parent is white and the other black; and where the child is brought up in the culture of the one parent rather than the other. In the cases where the mother is white, it raises the question of how the Caribbean heritage will be passed on in the years to come.[6]

South Asian families, on the other hand, though different from the whites, were much further removed from the Caribbeans. In fact, if Caribbeans were trendsetters, South Asians (especially Pakistanis and Bangladeshis) were some distance behind. Unlike Caribbeans, South Asians were more concerned with marriage than their white counterparts, divorce and separation being quite rare. Members of this general group were, unlike Caribbeans, more inclined to partner one of their ethnic group, though this does not preclude Asian/white couplings. In fact, as many as one-fifth of British-born Indians and African-Asian men had white wives.

There was also a similarity between white women and Indian and African-Asian women in terms of their child-bearing age. Pakistani and Bangladeshi women, on the other hand, differed from the above groups in that they not only began their families at an earlier age and ended child-rearing later, they also had more children than was common among families in Britain. Taking South Asian mothers as a whole, 'virtually all' of them had married and 'almost all' of them retained this status.[7]

Another distinguishing aspect of the Asian family is that, unlike white people who usually move away from their parents once they form their own families, married South Asians with children often live in the same dwelling as the husband's father. So marriage does not necessarily mean physical separation from the father's household. But such South Asian family patterns have been subjected to change, as in the case of Indian and Pakistani households, which since the early 1980s have had fewer children, especially those who were born in Britain; and, as we saw earlier, attitudes towards marriage continued to be less 'traditional'. The situation for Bangladeshis though is different. Bangladeshi women tend to marry early and have many children.

In terms of their family structures, of all the ethnic minority groups, Pakistanis and Bangladeshis differ most from whites. It has been suggested that while an ever-growing number of British-born Pakistanis and Bangladeshis make adjustments to their attitudes towards marriage and the family, this will be counterpoised by more traditional values based on Islamic teachings concerning intimate relations between men and women, and contraception. Consequently, religion could either hinder or change Pakistani and Bangladeshi families or the family could become a matter of disagreement.

Also at issue, in relation particularly to Pakistanis and Bangladeshis, were families with low incomes, and the effect of this on the community and especially on the welfare of the children. In so far as British social policy is not oriented to large families, the poverty of both these groups is likely to continue.

Then there is the matter of concern for older members of the South Asian family. Because the early migrant population had few elderly people of Asian origin, the need for social care of this kind was not a priority. However, much time has elapsed and today there are many who are over 60 years of age. Fortunately, more often than not, they live in the same household as their adult children, and in this they differ from the white elderly.

This diversity of family structure within and between the various ethnic groups has clear implications for British social policy. Whatever the assumptions on partnering and parenting patterns that will go into the making of policy, one should have no illusions that such a formulation will, as Berthoud and Beishon found, 'operate unequally on different ethnic groups in a multiracial society'.[8]

Educational Qualifications and the English Language

By the early 1980s, two-thirds of South Asian men and an estimated half of the women spoke English well, even fluently; almost ten years later, more than three-quarters of the men in each Asian group had become fluent in English. Though age and length of residence in Britain were important, the former was especially significant for those who were over 25 when they came to Britain in that they were 'least likely to have a facility in English regardless of their age today'.

In terms of educational qualifications, among those of working age, apart from the Chinese, African Asians and Indians were the best qualified groups. These were followed by men from the white population and Caribbeans; and while Pakistanis were less qualified than African Asians and Indians, Bangladeshis were even less so. Among women, it was found that white women were less likely to be as qualified as Caribbean women. But this was not the full story, for there was another demarcation between the ethnic groups and that was the nature of the qualifications of those best qualified. Were they academically or vocationally inclined? While Caribbeans and whites were among the most vocational, African Asians and other South Asians were less so. Thus the situation in contemporary Britain reflects not only the 'different starting points of different groups, of different experiences in the educational system', but also the strong determination of the ethnic minorities to gain the maximum benefits from their educational efforts, as revealed generationally between the migrants and their descendants, who are today's young people.

Although most migrants had no qualifications on arrival, with time, they can be divided as being either poorly qualified or highly qualified: Caribbeans, Pakistanis and Bangladeshis constituting the former category, while Indians, African Asians and Chinese form the latter group. Such a division is, however, further qualified by distinguishing whether or not the qualifications they had were British and if they were, how widely they were distributed. If women were less qualified among South Asians, the opposite was true for Caribbeans, and while 'overseas' qualifications figured prominently among South Asians, British qualifications predominated among Caribbeans. The overall effect was a widening of the gap between those who were highly qualified and those who were less so.

As far as the 'second generation' was concerned, those in the 25–44 age group seemed to have made 'significant progress', Caribbean men in particular leading the other ethnic minority groups in the middle and higher ranges, but not at degree level. On the other hand, although Pakistani women were successful at degree level, the number of those in this group with no qualification was more or less unchanged. Unfortunately, the Bangladeshis' position remains a cause for serious concern. By contrast, at higher levels, Indian and African Asian women have made progress: African Asian women being pre-eminent among those most likely to achieve degree standard than others of their age group. Compared with white males, men from both the Indian and African Asian groups were more likely to achieve degree qualifications.

There is, however, another segment of the ethnic minority population of more recent origin, the 'new generation', those in the 16–24 age group, fewer of whom were lacking a qualification than those of the older generations. Unfortunately, among Pakistanis and Bangladeshis are to be found the largest numbers of those without qualifications; and young Caribbean men have not improved their position vis-à-vis those who were older, an alarming statistic, with twice as many men as women having no qualifications. Much better off were the Indians, African Asians and Chinese, whose positions were almost as good as those of whites generally. Even more impressive is the fact that at degree level, these minorities' positions were 'distinctly better'. And to give added hope and encouragement to those not so well favoured, the progress of ethnic minority women (with the exception of Caribbean women) with degree qualifications was better, when compared with white women. In spite of these relative successes, young Pakistani and Bangladeshi women are 'considerably less' qualified and therefore unable to compete for available jobs; and so too were young Pakistani, Bangladeshi and Caribbean men similarly placed.

There is still much optimism among many in the least qualified ethnic groups who are engaged in a determined effort to obtain relevant qualifications by furthering their education. For many, qualifications are indispensable if they are to enhance the chances of well-paid employment in what has been described as a 'meritocratic' society 'open to the talents of all'9 regardless of their background. The idea that gaining higher, better qualifications will be economically rewarding is perhaps naive, though it is important to bear in mind the pivotal role of employment to the many concerns of the ethnic minorities.

Employment

Employment has remained the central issue in relation to the 'life chances and equality' of the ethnic minorities. Since the late 1980s, a straightforward black/white analysis can no longer be used to appraise a number of hitherto hidden differences (and similarities). As Tariq Modood argued in the Policy Studies

Institute survey, instead of explaining racial inequality, the need now is to explain racial inequality and ethnic disadvantage. Moreover, bearing in mind that the basic division in employment is by ethnicity and not a simple black/white divide, the different ethnic groups have come to occupy different positions on different aspects of employment.

By the early 1990s, there was evidence that the position of Indians and African Asians in terms of the fairly even division of their employment in manual and non-manual employment was 'similar' to that of white men. Other groups fared less well. As many as two-thirds of Caribbeans, Pakistanis and Bangladeshis were manual workers. And in terms of becoming employers and managers of large businesses, all minorities were less likely of such attainments than were white men. Nevertheless, an encouraging number of South Asians and Chinese were to be found at the 'broad professional', and at managerial and employer levels, largely because of their engagement in self-employment.

Although the attainment of employment at certain job levels was closely linked to the employees' academic qualifications, this was not necessarily the case. Even for those who were qualified though, there were differences between the groups, which separated workers with O-level standard education from the skilled manual and intermediate and junior non-professionals. While whites were 'evenly divided', only a quarter of Caribbeans were to be found in the 'other' non-manual employment. South Asian groups (although Pakistanis and Bangladeshis were concentrated at the lower end of the employment pyramid due to their large presence in semi-skilled manual employment) had twice as many employees in 'other' non-manual jobs, compared with skilled manual work.

Not only were highly qualified ethnic minority men more likely than their white equivalents to be in the professions, but there were also among qualified South Asians more men in non-manual work compared with Caribbean men and whites, who were to be found more in non-manual occupations.

Unlike ethnic minority men, fewer women were to be found at the higher professional, managerial and employers levels, though the variation among the different groups was similar, with Chinese women heading the list, followed by South Asian women and Caribbeans. Significantly, however, a majority of women in these groups were in non-manual employment. Unlike the men, Indian and Pakistani women in top non-manual occupations were likely to be self-employed. Nevertheless, it was found that gender divisions in employment were likely to be of greater importance than differences in race and ethnicity. Taken together, regardless of gender, members of all the ethnic minority groups had one thing in common in relation to their white counterparts: their chances of being in the top positions were fewer and so too were their chances of working in large organisations.

Qualifications had become increasingly influential in the pattern of ethnic minority employment by about the mid-1990s. While white and Chinese women were 'broadly similar' in the posts occupied (about a quarter of those with A-level or higher qualification being in the professional, managerial and employers' category), African Asians were not far behind. On the other hand, a higher proportion of whites with A-levels or higher qualifications were in semi-skilled or unskilled work than 'any other group', the Caribbeans being closest. Qualified South Asian women, with little prospect of a job, were more than likely to remain unemployed instead of accepting unskilled employment. And while three-quarters of the ethnic minority women (except Pakistanis) with O-level qualifications were employed at intermediate or junior non-manual positions, Pakistani women remain of particular interest. They not only had the smallest number of women without qualifications in non-manual work, but also the highest proportion of qualified workers at O-level standard in semi-skilled manual work, thus bearing a more striking resemblance to their men than to other women.[10]

On the crucial question of the conditions of service, apart from the highest number of hours worked each week by men and women in the higher reaches of the non-manual positions, for those who worked a 30-hour week, there was little difference in the hours spent at work at different job levels. Except for the fact that men worked about five hours more than women, the differences were marginal among the South Asian groups.[11] Almost a decade earlier, Caribbean men had worked longer by about an hour, while Caribbean women and South Asians (both men and women) spent less time at work. Furthermore, while the hours of white workers remained more or less the same, the differences between white and ethnic minority men had grown in the public sector.[12]

Though minority migrants and shift work have become synonymous, recently there has been a relative decline, especially among South Asians. By 1994, Caribbean men were more likely than whites to be engaged in shift work, though for South Asians this practice had changed, with South Asian women being least likely to do so, essentially because of job losses in the textile industry during the previous decade and also due to the upward occupational mobility in the last few years, notably of Indians and African Asians.

Men from the minority groups were engaged in shift work that was available, while women predominated in the public sector. This pattern of work was most common in the public services – health, emergency and public transport. Interestingly, the younger the worker, the less likely was he or she to do shift work.[13] Nevertheless it was found that, unlike South Asians, Caribbean men in the 16–34 age group were as likely to work shifts as those older; and young Caribbean women were less likely to do so than older women.

The chances of assuming supervisory responsibilities were greater for those in non-manual posts than in manual, and for all groups, at both levels, men had better chances of becoming supervisors than women. Predictably, there were group differences, not only between the ethnic minority groups, but also between them and whites. Men were two-thirds as likely to achieve supervisory grades as their white counterparts. And significantly among male manual employees, Caribbeans approximated those of whites, but in 'varying degrees'. All the Asian groups were unlikely to supervise at this level, though the likelihood of Pakistanis and Bangladeshis doing so were even more remote. Another variation, and an interesting one, is that among those employed in the private sector, at the manual level, Caribbean workers were more likely to be found in supervisory roles than the other ethnic groups. And among women in manual work, Caribbeans were more likely than whites to be supervisors, while South Asians were less likely to be in such posts, a reflection of their 'strong presence' in the public service industries.[14]

Although Caribbeans, Indians and African Asians approximated the same proportion of white men employed in manufacturing, only Pakistanis were more numerous. And while Bangladeshis (and Chinese) were less represented in the manufacturing sector, Caribbean and Indian men were highly concentrated in engineering, notably in the motor industry. But even though most of the minority groups had a larger number of employees in transport and communications than whites, African Asians were far ahead of the others in the retailing business. At the other extreme, while white men were relatively well represented in the financial sector (one in eight) African Asians and Indians were at least equal and were likely to exceed this ratio.

It becomes clear that the different ethnic minority groups contribute to industrial production differently, each contributing more to some sectors than to others. And importantly, all have more restricted access to the various economic sectors than white men, though, in some areas, the presence of Caribbean men approximates that of white men.

For their part, Bangladeshis represent the 'most extreme' case as reflected in their confinement to catering, thus adding to their large numbers as manual workers in just one area of employment – in the kitchens of restaurants. Concentration in such jobs has resulted in 'occupational segregation', which highlights the very high unemployment among Bangladeshis. All minority groups are poorly represented in agriculture, forestry, fishing, energy and water, which are relatively small employers.

Unlike white men, white women are most likely to be in the retail trade, education and medical care. Overall, women were not concentrated in manufacturing, though South Asian women figured more prominently than whites and Caribbeans. In fact, Indian and Pakistani women were to be found across manufacturing, half of them in clothing and footwear. And while retail and finance attracted most groups, apart from African Asians, Caribbean women were (and still are) well represented in hospitals and medical areas at twice the rate of white women, which accounts for their persistently high engagement in shift work. And like Pakistanis and Indians, they outnumber whites in the public sector. This has been reduced in recent years, resulting in the loss of thousands of jobs, as the ownership of various public bodies became part of the private domain of the economy. None the less, it remains the main area of Caribbean employment, accounting for an estimated one-third of its employees, especially Caribbean women, with a large presence in the Health Service and in local government departments.

Further, the relationship between the public sector and ethnicity provides some contrasts. Compared with other ethnic minority men and white men employed in the private sector, it was found that those minority men who worked in the public sector tended to be in non-manual jobs and from these positions their chances of rising higher up the non-manual occupational pyramid were better.[15]

The contentious issue of equal opportunities, debated over the years, was more likely to be implemented by the larger establishments in the public sector. Nevertheless, although equal opportunity policies have been put in place, their lack of effectiveness has aroused much and justifiable concern, especially since they are so dependent on the availability of vacancies at higher levels, which suffered restrictions as the public sector was reshaped, thus making such policies more or less redundant.

On the issue of earnings, the figures reveal that white men earn more than their ethnic minority counterparts, though some African Asians enjoy parity with whites, followed in descending order by Caribbean men, Indians, Pakistanis and Bangladeshis. Earnings also varied among the different religious groups. Taken together, the Pakistani, Bangladeshi, Indian and African Asian Muslim population increased their mean weekly earnings. On the other hand, there was a marked difference in the mean earnings of Hindus and Sikhs, the former earning much more than the latter. The 'comparative position' of African Asians and Hindus, as the survey found, compared with other South Asians, 'is a striking new development'. But while the earnings differential between whites, Indians and Pakistanis has not disappeared, Asian men have improved their position significantly by gaining more places at the top levels of earnings, in positions that were hitherto the domain of whites alone. A similar historical shift has taken place between Hindu and Sikh men who, from having average similar earnings, were nevertheless separated by a gap, with Hindus being better-off than Sikhs in both job levels and pay.[16]

For those ethnic minority women workers in full-time employment, weekly earnings lagged behind those of men. On average, though, these women's earnings were much higher than white women's, a finding which necessitates a reassessment of the concept of 'double discrimination' in relation to non-white women. This argument promoted the view that in addition to being discriminated against as a woman, the ethnic minority woman was further disadvantaged, compared to white women, an argument which, according to the latest research, can no longer be taken for granted.

Moreover, the claim current two decades ago that qualifications were irrelevant to the higher earnings potential of non-white workers cannot be sustained in the 1990s. Not all ethnic minority groups adopted this negative approach to educational qualifications. Optimism was always to be found, especially among South Asians, who impressed upon their children the value of education, if not in the short term, then to their long-term prospects. It is this attitude that has brought about the new profile of ethnic minority groups' earning power, a positive and encouraging approach for those who are less well educated and therefore unqualified to earn more.

And yet, one must be cautious, for even with qualifications, there were (and are) many who are unable to find appropriate work, often because of discrimination, but also because there were fewer jobs. Self-employment is one alternative, but there is no guarantee that the self-employed earn more than those who opt for paid work, a significant factor in the decision-making process among those with the same qualifications who tended to view self-employment as a less attractive alternative.

Although employed white men had higher earnings in the 1990s than self-employed men (except for African Asian men), the opposite was the case among the ethnic minorities. Overall, male members of these groups have achieved parity (and even higher earnings) than whites, thus emphasising the importance of self-employment and qualifications in reducing earnings.

Unlike their men, ethnic minority self-employed women were differently placed. Not only did they earn more than their white counterparts, the evidence shows that for them self-employment was a financially rewarding experience.[17]

By 1994 it was found that the proportion of Chinese, African Asians and Indians in self-employment had increased and was greater than that of whites, that Pakistanis had proportional parity with whites, while Caribbeans and Bangladeshis could only manage half that amount.

Consideration of the rates of self-employment revealed 'significant variations' between the different ethnic minority groups. For example, Bangladeshis had drawn up 'almost level' with whites, while Pakistanis showed the greatest dependency on self-employment, which is not surprising given the serious problem of unemployment among both groups. Gender and ethnicity differentials were also important 'for in most groups' women accounted for only half the rate of self-employed men. And among the ethnic groups, Caribbeans registered the lowest rate of self-employment, with women less likely to be self-employed than men.

Where were these self-employed ethnic groups to be found? And where in the various sectors of the economy were they located? Interestingly, the Fourth PSI Survey informs us that:

> While half of white self-employment is in construction, agriculture and manufacturing, half of minority ethnic self-employment is in retail (South Asians, except Bangladeshis) or catering (Chinese and Bangladeshis) though one-third of all self-employed Caribbeans were in construction, 20 per cent of whites were in the financial sector, as were the Caribbeans and the African Asians, but while only 6 per cent of whites were in the educational and medical sector, Caribbeans, Indians and African Asians were about twice the proportion. One in five of Pakistanis and one in seven of Bangladeshis and Caribbeans were in transportation, primarily as taxi and mini-cab drivers, compared with only 5 per cent of whites.[18]

While the ethnic minorities are highly concentrated in inner city areas, it is here that self-employed whites figured most prominently. Indeed, all the minority groups had their highest rates of self-employment, not in the large urban areas, but in those parts of the country with 'below average' ethnic minority density, especially among African Asians, Indians and Chinese, who had, in many cases, established large, job-creating establishments. Not surprisingly the income generated by such forms of self-employment had risen to the extent that there was 'relatively little' separating whites from the ethnic minorities as a whole, entrepreneurs' earning over £500 a week. Self-employed African Asians were among the highest earners, followed by Indians, Chinese and Caribbeans, whose incomes ranged from £385 to more than £500 per week. Although high unemployment, racism and other factors motivate self-employment, there is no doubt that, compared with whites, the average earnings of ethnic minority men and women were higher in self-employment than in waged employment.[19] Always aiding such ventures were 'cultural factors' (thrift and enterprise, for example), thus consolidating and drawing upon a given community's resources – information, labour, capital and financial institutions. The concerns generated by such networks, in turn, give rise to greater interest in qualifications and self-improvement, which eventually benefits all in these communities.

Over these past two decades, there seems to have been a shift towards more openness among 'economically active' white people, 90 per cent of whom believed that employers denied applicants jobs because of their race and religion, only 5 per cent less than the same belief held by Caribbeans. Consistently high percentages of other minority groups (except for Bangladeshis) also confirmed the existence of discrimination in employment.

In spite of its complexity, it is significant that as many as a quarter of all ethnic minority people believed that the discrimination they experienced was based on a combination of their race and religion. An estimated 40 per cent of South Asians believed this to be true, especially the younger members of this general grouping.

While whites and Caribbeans see 'Asians' as the 'victim' group, for their part, the South Asians regard their 'Asianness' as the main target for prejudice. But an even greater number of Indians, African Asians and Pakistanis think of Muslims rather than 'Asians' as the group most affected by prejudice. The Chinese, on the other hand, regarded 'black' people (essentially those of Afro-Caribbean and African descent) as facing most prejudice. Such differences as exist do not mask the fact that all the ethnic minority groups were in no doubt that Asians face more prejudice than any other group; and for their part, Asians see this as prejudice aimed at their religion. Indeed, Muslims have increasingly become hated targets, arousing Islamophobia to such a degree that it has become a 'growing strand of racism', necessitating an urgent review of anti-discrimination legislation to safeguard the rights of and protect those persons who most need it. Hindus and Sikhs also felt they were denied employment because of their religion.

The question of equal opportunities at work was not a question of either/or, but one that has led to more complex answers. While some felt there were equal opportunities for all employees where they worked, 'regardless of race, colour or religious or cultural background', others, particularly those under 35 years of age, were more likely to experience discrimination.

Employees in both the private and public sectors also highlighted contrasts in relation to equal opportunities. African Asians, Pakistanis and Bangladeshi men employed in the private sector had no doubt about the reality of equal opportunities where they worked, but Caribbeans and Indian men were less convinced.

The public sector, on the other hand, reflected other contrasts, with South Asians and Caribbean women taking opposing views, two-thirds of the former believing there were equal opportunities, while only one-third of the latter thought so. There was, however, unanimity among the ethnic minorities in one part of the public sector, the Health Service, on which they stood opposed to their white co-workers. As many as 25 out of 32 Caribbean women employees felt equal opportunities did not exist at their workplace, an especially serious problem because the health authorities are among the biggest employers of ethnic minority workers.[20]

Concerning racism in the workplace and trade unions by the mid-1990s, most encouraging were the TUC initiatives in conjunction with the CRE's efforts generally and crucially in relation to those employers in the private sector of the economy, where union membership among poorly paid members of ethnic minorities was low. While whites were less likely to join unions than ethnic minority employees (and although shop steward representation had increased among some ethnic groups) low-paid non-white women in 'unregulated' jobs were under-unionised and therefore 'vulnerable'.[21] Not surprisingly, the degree of dissatisfaction was great and, yet again, there was a trend favouring the idea of autonomous black and Asian workers' groups for which the strongest support came from those engaged in manual and non-manual work. Within the Labour Party, there has been strong resistance from the leadership to incorporate some of the pre-1979 government's attitude towards what used to be called collective bargaining. Since then, and as a result of having lost a series of general elections, the Party has had to adopt new labour strategies. Thus, the landslide victory of New Labour heralded a new era and, no doubt, new policies in the future, aimed at curbing disruptive strikes. The more discerning among the poorer sections of society are not fooled into accepting that 'New Labour' will be beneficial to them, for the indications are clear that their concerns would not be given undue priority, while New Labour middle-class liberals enjoy their ascendancy. Even amidst the euphoria, the less fortunate can still hear the words of Prime Minister Blair who warns that trade unions must not expect special treatment from the new 'people's government'. Emphasising this point so early, Blair has quashed the hopes of many thousands of blacks and Asians, who are highly visible within the contemporary system of industrial relations, in so far as such a 'system' exists.

How have the different ethnic groups been affected? A 'pattern of inequality' amongst the ethnic minority groups had been present, though not clearly perceived, from the outset. By the 1970s, differences in economic background and education between African Asians and Indians, as one category, and Pakistanis and Bangladeshis as another, had emerged though they were subsumed by generalisations in the 1980s, with references to the ethnic minority groups as 'blacks' and 'Asians' and even more generally as 'black' in relation to a 'black/white' dichotomy which obscured all distinctions. In the 1990s, however, increasingly the differences between the ethnic minority groups have been emphasised as well as aspects of their commonality.

Crucial to this shift in emphasis is the period 1982–94, when all minority groups were subjected to structural change and therefore had to adapt to new circumstances, the most significant being an 'upward occupational shift'. With the exception of the Pakistanis, all the minority groups were faced with a fall in demand for work at skilled manual and foreman levels

Particularly for Indians, African Asians and Pakistanis, there was a proportional decline in those employed in semi- and unskilled manual jobs. But the rate of progress persisted for some minority groups. For example, in 1982 (apart from the African Asians) an estimated 80 per cent of South Asian and Caribbean men were in manual work. By 1994, however, they accounted for an estimated two-thirds. In just over a decade, it was found that the position of Indian men had changed 'substantially'. Having been essentially in manual employment in the 1980s, approaching the mid-1990s, as a group, they had moved 'much closer' to whites, African Asians and Chinese. So although Caribbeans, Pakistanis and Bangladeshis remained largely in manual jobs, between the 1980s and mid-1990s all the minority groups had improved their positions relatively to whites, with whom only African Asians have attained parity. And because in this period self-employment expanded, many ethnic minority men in non-manual and manual employment achieved upward mobility.

In terms of job levels, women's employment was not unlike men's. Indeed more women moved into non-manual employment than men, especially ethnic minority women. For those in full-time employment by the 1990s, African Asian women had improved their position, though women from the other minority groups were less well represented than they were in the 1980s. And although in intermediate and junior non-manual employment categories, Caribbeans, Indians and African Asians were disproportionately placed, Pakistani and Indian women in full-time work remained largely in manual work. Nevertheless, the trends in the 1990s reveal upward mobility for ethnic minority employees who are vacating manual positions for non-manual ones, reflecting a 'general pattern' of 'declining differentials' between white people and some ethnic minority groups. And while some minorities will further improve their relative economic positions, as the survey warned, the differentials between the different minorities could well become greater as those groups in advantaged positions continue to make progress. So in the 1990s, it has become increasingly difficult to refer to the ethnic minorities simply as being concentrated in low-skill, low-paid work. According to the survey, three bands of employment sum up the position of ethnic groups in relation to whites. First, disadvantage in the top jobs in large businesses; second, relative disadvantage; and third, severe disadvantage. Among those represented in these three categories are the Chinese and African Asians, the Indians and Caribbeans and the Pakistanis and Bangladeshis, respectively.[22]

Thus far, racial disadvantage emerges as very much a part of the ethnic experience, with an estimated one-third of private employers discriminating against Caribbeans and Asians who had applied for jobs. Even Asian applicants' names were enough for some discriminating employers, which begs the question: What can be done to remedy the problem? The Commission for Racial Equality publishes its findings regularly, which show that the number of complaints of racial discrimination have risen steadily, a trend recognised by 90 per cent of white people. No wonder it is argued that all economically active non-white groups are victims of 'an ethnic penalty', a term which relates to the sources of disadvantage likely to lead an ethnic group to do 'less well' in the job market than whites with similar qualifications, even though 'discrimination is likely to be a major component'.[23]

Among the British-born ethnic minority members there is no doubt that the 'second generation' suffer ethnic penalties, as they search for higher level non-manual jobs. The 'advantage' accrued to the first generation Caribbean women was not experienced by the second generation, for whom being born in Britain did not confer special treatment. Therefore, there is little difference in the pattern and extent of ethnic penalties between the two generations. And regardless of the fact that there may have been more non-manual jobs and an increase in openness in competition, it is a fact that the over-achievers were not adequately rewarded and for those who persist in attaining better jobs, many could not avoid the conclusion that they had to be 'not just as good, but better than their white competitor' to get the job.[24]

While 'race', discrimination or ethnic differences are attributable to racial disadvantage, economic restructuring, as Modood in the survey points out, is 'most important'. Consequently, the changing labour requirements for both the ethnic minorities and the white population have brought with it further job losses at low skill levels, as the service sector expanded offering jobs at higher levels and in lower graded part-time employment. This economic shift, combined with demographic shortages (resulting in 'differential disadvantage' of the various minority groups), forms the employment context,[25] that core area of migrants' and their children's preoccupations, which has so profoundly affected other aspects of their lives.

Earnings and Standards of Living

There were clear indications that the 'extent of poverty' was particularly disturbing and worrying for Pakistani and Bangladeshi households. As we saw earlier, Pakistanis and Bangladeshis figure at the lowest levels in employment, but significantly over 'four out of five' Pakistani households' income declined to a level that was just about one-fifth of white pensioners. And to give their plight a further reference, Richard Berthoud informs us that in relation to impoverished groups of national concern (for example, pensioners, disabled people, one-parent families and the unemployed) they were poorer.

Indeed a 'huge difference' emerges between them and the other groups. While the Chinese and African Asians are upwardly mobile, with Indians and Caribbeans in positions of some advantage in employment, Pakistanis and Bangladeshis are seriously disadvantaged. In relative terms, during the early 1990s at least, the Chinese were better off than Indians and African Asians, while the Pakistanis and Bangladeshis were (and still are) worse-off than Caribbeans. Overall, however, much of the improvements that have accrued to Indians and African Asians must be tempered, for all minorities were disadvantaged in relation to the white population, a conclusion confirmed, in part, by the yardsticks measuring living standards.

Indians and African Asians owned more consumer durables than whites, essentially because they had larger households. Nevertheless, with the exception of the Chinese, it was found that all the minority groups possessed fewer durable goods, and again Pakistanis and Bangladeshis were the most deprived groups. Yet, given their incomes, in terms of financial difficulties and debts, the Asian communities generally appeared to be at least 'no worse off', indeed at times, in some respects, better-off than anticipated. On the other hand, with insistent and rising rent debts, Caribbeans were financially the most vulnerable group. So, on the issue of income and standards of living, most worry and concern have been directed to Caribbeans, Pakistanis and Bangladeshis.[26] In turn, this affects where they live and the quality of the homes they inhabit.

Neighbours and Housing

The fact that ethnic minority households were different in their neighbourhoods and the type of housing they occupied from white households was yet another area underscored by disadvantage, though the extent and form of disadvantage varied. Indeed, housing and neighbourhood disadvantage was a complex and composite issue which included low incomes and a history of living in poor areas. Ethnic minorities were most likely to be living in the towns in which they had first settled. While Caribbeans, Bangladeshis, Chinese and Pakistanis were strongly represented in the inner cities, Indians and African Asians had moved to better locations outside the cities. Nevertheless the urban concentration of ethnic minorities reflects a general pattern of segregation from their white counterparts. Furthermore, certain metropolitan 'wards' tend to be populated by more members of a particular ethnic group than others.[27]

This 'residential segregation' was not static, though such changes as have been taking place do not alter the fact that many members of minority groups not only exercise their preference for residing among those of other ethnic groups, but also prefer to remain amidst their own particular group. On the other hand, there were inherent dangers in this for such concentrations were accompanied by a 'concentration of disadvantage'.[28] Too often we find members of the minority groups living in areas characterised by high unemployment and consequent deprivation and frustration in the form of vandalism to property and communal facilities. Often these conditions persuaded them to move on.

Housing has remained a matter of much concern. In the mid-1990s we find that, apart from Pakistanis, while the other ethnic minority groups had only marginally improved their positions, Bangladeshis (perhaps the most disadvantaged of the deprived minority groups) had achieved improved levels of owner-occupation. Differences between the different groups, did not, however, alter the general tendency regarding owner-occupation as Indians, African Asians and Pakistanis maintained their position ahead of whites, Chinese and Caribbeans. If Bangladeshis were a cause for concern, so too was the tenure pattern of Caribbean households, comprising members under 45 years old, who were in the category of low owner-occupation, but with high representation in social renting.

Differences in tenure between the ethnic groups were attributable to variations in the geographical pattern of settlement which, in turn, is the outcome of historical, economic and cultural influences. Jane Lakey has found that the 'relatively low level' of owner-occupation among Chinese, Bangladeshi and Caribbean households reflected their strong presence in inner London, their below-average incomes and, in the case of Caribbeans and Chinese, the 'predominance of small (lone parent and single adult) households'. By comparison, Indian, African Asian and Pakistani households were the leading home-owners among the ethnic minority groups, in spite of their 'relatively low' earnings.

Surprisingly, apart from their preponderance in social housing, Caribbeans, like Indians, African Asians and Pakistanis, tended to prefer ownership, but even though a high proportion of Caribbean owners lived in former council accommodation, as a group, it was suggested that they were unlikely to become owners of council property.

While owner-occupiers lived in houses, tenants were accommodated in flats. Among the flat-dwellers in inner London were Caribbean, Bangladeshi and Chinese tenants, while Bangladeshis and Caribbeans were overwhelmingly housed in medium and high-rise blocks of flats. By comparison, Indian and African Asian households seemed to have benefited from their owner-occupation investment, becoming in 1994 'as likely as white households to occupy detached or semi-detached properties', thereby improving their position of more than a decade earlier, when they were largely confined to terraced houses. Pakistanis and Bangladeshis, on the other hand, were over-represented in terraced housing, the two groups most likely to be without central heating, baths and inside toilets, conditions indicative of the poor standard of their living space. In the main, members of both groups were largely on the lowest incomes and, as a consequence, they struggled to provide better accommodation for their families through owner-occupation. Given their large households, predictably Pakistanis and Bangladeshis were (and still are) the most disadvantaged of the ethnic groups, as far as overcrowding is concerned. So if whites were among the most satisfied in relation to neighbourhoods and housing, Caribbeans and Bangladeshis were the least content.[29]

Health

On matters relating to health and health services, differences are found between minority groups. For instance, compared to whites the health status of Indians, African Asians and Chinese were roughly equivalent, while that of Caribbeans, Pakistanis and Bangladeshis was regarded as being much less so. Before the 1990s, several studies on the various ethnic minority groups were not differentiated from each other, and this was reflected in the literature generally. The various groups were categorised as 'black', 'Asian' and 'South Asian', which tended to hide crucial differences and therefore give an inaccurate and misleading picture.

While an earlier study on the 'possibility of high rates of heart disease among South Asians' did not consider that such rates were applicable to all South Asians, James Nazroo, in his analysis published in 1997, noted that 'only those South Asians with Pakistani and Bangladeshi origins had higher rates of heart disease than whites, [while] Indians and African Asians had rates that were similar to the white rate'. He also pointed out the ethnic variations in health, which suggested that even within each of the ethnic groups there was a 'clear relationship between socio-economic status and health'.

Although all ethnic minority groups (apart from the Chinese) consulted their general practitioners more often than whites, the quality of primary health care offered to them was poorer, especially 'in terms of meeting the language needs and preferences for the gender and ethnicity of doctors consulted'. This was reflected in the plight of those not fluent in English who were 'three times more likely than others to prefer to see a doctor of the same ethnic background as themselves', an indication of communication problems that could well be reflected in the 'under-referral to secondary health care for ethnic minority groups compared with whites'.[30]

Racial Harassment

As we have seen, racial violence and harassment in Britain is not new. The experience of crime in relation to ethnic minority groups varies, showing a similarity in the proportion of physical attacks on whites and South Asians, compared with a much higher figure for Caribbeans and much lower for the Chinese. Property damage also showed differences between Bangladeshis and the other ethnic groups. Importantly, within the context of such experiences of crime, racial harassment was prominent, with 13 per cent of the members of ethnic minorities suffering from 'some form' of racial harassment, while 12 per cent were racially 'abused or insulted' over a twelve-month period.

Given that the total adult ethnic minority population of England and Wales (Scotland excluded) was about two million, according to one estimate of the number of those subjected to racial harassment over one year, an estimated 20,000 persons had been racially attacked, 40,000 persons were victims of property damage and 230,000 persons were either racially abused or insulted. So over a quarter of a million people suffered racial harassment in one form or another during the period.

Who were the victims of such violent behaviour? Among the 'most vulnerable' were men under 45 years of age; and more than half of those who had experienced racial harassment were subjected to 'repeat victimisation' over twelve months. Moreover, a staggering 60,000 people had experienced racial harassment five or more times.

We are taken further into this dark and depressing matter through the findings of Satnam Virdee, who confirms the identities of the perpetrators of such harassment. An estimated three-fifths of those who had been racially attacked or abused identified their assailants as a 'complete stranger'; while the victims of property damage saw the offender as either a neighbour or an acquaintance. As disturbing, if not more so, is the extent of racial harassment at the workplace, where the attackers were both young and older men.

Overall, racial harassment has affected all the ethnic minority groups, though not all those directly involved were forthcoming in reporting their experience. But among those who did, about half were dissatisfied with the manner in which the police responded. These victims were in no doubt that the police officers involved were indifferent to their plight, and thus police responses were seen as racist and as siding with the assailants. Such perceptions give added credence to the difficulties implicit in the relationship between Caribbeans and the police. By the 1990s, two-thirds of South Asians too had no confidence in the police. And to compound the unsatisfactory relationship, the police themselves were accused of 'actually engaging' not only in damaging property, but also in racial attacks and the abuse of members of minority groups.

Predictably, a 'significant proportion' of the ethnic minority population were deeply concerned about racial harassment, though few complained to the police. Nevertheless fear moved them to act, to avoid 'some common everyday scenarios' so that the level of racial harassment to which they were subjected would be reduced. Such actions leave no doubt that racial harassment has impacted significantly on the 'quality of life' of many ethnic minority people. Recent racist murders, notably the case of Stephen Lawrence, have outraged many black and Asian people (and increasingly more white people) throughout Britain, whose support and respect for the parents of the teenager have grown over the past five years of their struggle for justice. But in spite of the Lawrence Inquiry revelations the number of *reported* cases of racial attacks during 1989–99 had increased by 350 per cent, according to John Grieve of the Metropolitan Police.

Groups have formed to defend ethnic minorities – the recurrence of a phenomenon of the late 1970s, when the Shadwell Community Defence was established to give much-needed protection to threatened Asians in East London.[31] Whatever its merits, there was, perhaps surprisingly, no unanimity of support for such defence groups among the ethnic minorities.[32] Thus life-threatening racial attacks were viewed by the different minority groups in relative terms. The poorest and most vulnerable, namely Pakistanis and Bangladeshis, unable to move out of the inner cities, are left to fight their own battles and are seen by more fortunate members of ethnic groups (including other Asians) as having themselves to blame!

Underpinning the themes and developments of the ethnic minority groups in relation to British society, is the fact that the rightward direction of Thatcherism and Conservative governments over many years has, in part, been responsible for some 'surprising' changes among the ethnic minority groups and, between them and the indigenous white British population.

Culture and Identity

Tariq Modood has examined the theme of 'culture and identity' in relation to the ethnic minority groups in British society. What people believed about themselves was important, most of them identifying themselves as members of their particular group, though an associational or community identity did not necessarily mean participation in all of that group's cultural activities. Also of importance in a limited list were religion, language, clothes, marriage, schools and trips to the country of birth.

South Asians were strongly influenced by religion, language and dress, religion in particular being of more value to them than to white people. But although one South Asian language was spoken by the vast majority of members of this general grouping, it was found that such a practice was not being adopted by younger South Asians. Dress too has been subjected to change, not least among South Asian men. More particularly, as Modood points out, there are many contrasts within the general grouping, between African Asians and Indians, as opposed to Pakistanis and Bangladeshis on religion, 'arranged' marriages, preference for single-sex schools for female children, preference for schools of an acceptable religious denomination, the wearing of Asian-style clothing and marriage with cousins, especially among Pakistanis. Many of these differences are due to the longer duration of the settlement of Indians and African Asians, who were followed by Pakistanis and Bangladeshis, the latter groups being less amenable to cultural change.

Among South Asians, a strong associational identity was related to the age of those who had migrated. It was evident though that some British-born Asians' associational ethnic identity was strong, even when they were not involved in 'core cultural practices'.[33]

On the other hand, while a Caribbean associational identity is also related to age, it is a more complex one. For example, those who came to Britain as children tended to display a stronger associational Caribbean/black identity than those who had grown up in the Caribbean. Moreover, the British-born of Caribbean parents have a 'relatively weaker' Caribbean/black identity, though possessing a 'stronger group identity' than Asians.

According to Modood, this strong black/Caribbean associational identity was forged in Britain, through a process that was coloured by a 'considerable degree of racial rejection' which, in turn, has given rise to an 'ethnic distinctiveness', reflected in the growth and development of black churches, the Caribbean patois-Creole language, and hair and dress styles characteristic of the region. Simultaneously, another trend had been set in motion. As if to counteract the separation of Caribbean ethnic distinctiveness, Caribbean men and women were engaged in 'racial mixing', partnering whites. And while some Asians are also engaged in this process of assimilation, theirs is a 'relatively linear' development, compared with the emergence of a 'more complex' Caribbean/black identity, which shows that while almost one-half of the 35–49 year olds sampled do not think that they are British, one in six British-born Caribbeans do not think that they are part of the Afro-Caribbean group. Such generational shifts, especially among Asians in terms of cultural practices, further supports the argument for changing ethnic identities.

For the second generation, cultural practices were not acquired simply from their parents, but also from white British society. As they see it, they were (and are) sharing in British culture, even though they fully appreciate their family-centred community values and hold on to a strong sense of pride in their ethnic group, all the more so as they confront racial exclusion and ethnic stereotyping by whites. Therefore, their identities are not weak, but vibrant and changing. In the life of many members of the second generation, especially in the last two decades, changes to the 'bases of identity-formation' have brought about a greater degree of conscious minority assertiveness, thus adding a political edge to their deliberations and actions.[34] Global change in terms of culture and identity is paralleled by developments in Britain, where minority cultures, as Modood states, 'may be long-term features of British society, but the ways in which minorities conceive of themselves and the cultural syntheses that are taking place are various, changing and generating new mixed forms of ethnicity'.[35] Indeed in the 1990s, diversity and divergence between the ethnic minority groups have become clearer.

Given the 'moral covenant' which underpins the relationship between British society and the ethnic minorities, both have responsibilities they must honour. And while Britain is claimed to be a relatively 'safe' country for black and Asian people, the inequities are stark and no one should be complacent about the sobering fact that racial equality, so urgently desired by those who are denied it is nevertheless the achievable goal.[36]

However, important as the *factual* approximations of the above survey and other samplings of migrants and their descendants are to our understanding, they tell, for the most part, the material aspects of the story of black and Asian people in Britain who, it must be said, have always responded imaginatively.

REIMAGING BRITAIN:
LITERARY AND ARTISTIC IDENTITY

> Excising the political from the life of the mind is a sacrifice that has proven costly ... A criticism that needs to insist that literature is not only 'universal' but also 'race-free' risks lobotomizing that literature, and diminishes both the art and the artist.

> Toni Morrison, *Playing in the Dark* (1992)

In retrospect, the history of Britain's Imperial experience should teach some invaluable lessons. But in spite of the dispersal of British cultures to the United States, Canada, Australia, New Zealand and South Africa, tradition and xenophobia still haunt the British imagination. While class is still an issue in British politics, ethnicity (that other social construction) remains a factor of future political significance.

Just prior to the 1990s no fewer than eight cultures coexisted in the British Isles and the long-standing presence, history and culture of blacks and Asians in Britain, which accrues a profound and incalculable contribution to Britain at every stage of its modern history, must be added. Summing up his *History, Religion and Modern Identity in Britain*, Keith Robbins argued that unity has been 'precarious' because of a lack of uniformity, and arguments in favour of devolution for Scotland and Wales have become even more threatening in modern Britain. Nevertheless, there is little doubt that the Empire played some part in 'British nationality'. 'Britishness', as Robbins noted, 'has always been an elusive concept, but it would be a mistake to suppose that its comprehensive capacity is exhausted.'[37]

While the Conservatives were still holding on to their totalising approach to power, which was (and still is) at variance with the discordant voices of a growing mass of people in a disunited kingdom, the distinctive voice of the poet Seamus Heaney was heard, expressing his sense of Irishness, his identity, in the 'Frontiers of Writing' by suggesting that there is 'nothing extraordinary about the challenge to be in two minds', having been brought up in a minority culture in Northern Ireland, but educated within the dominant British culture. This duality has the effect, he says, of emphasising his identity rather than eroding it. And whether or not the British dimension is resisted by the minority, the fact remains that history and geography have brought them together, to coexist 'willy-nilly'. Even if institutional arrangements could bring about political harmony, he recognises the predicament of being a member of a minority and states that 'within our individual selves we can reconcile two orders of knowledge which we might call the practical and the poetic; to affirm also that each form of knowledge redresses the other and that the frontier between them is there for the crossing'.[38]

As we approach the end of the century, and as ethnic minorities increasingly define themselves as British and identify and see Britain as their home, Heaney has acknowledged the trend towards reimaging Britain. Indeed the 'frontier' is there for the crossing and having already considered the more pragmatic dimensions of the ethnic minorities, let us finally turn to those among them who have sought to redress the balance of diversity and disadvantage, and of image and reality.

Africans and Asians and their descendants from both diasporas are inscribing their discourses. They have been, and are today, striking back, not only as we have seen in the foregoing story of their struggles, but also crucially by using their powerful imagination to reimage Britain, to bring a sense of balance and harmony that was so lacking, through literature and art. In this process, many Afro-Asians schooled in the British education system, have felt the need to leave their peripheral colonial 'home' for the freedom of the metropolis. The sons and daughters, usually of the well-to-do classes in India, Africa, the Caribbean and the United States, they all came to Britain and have had, in various ways, to reinvent themselves, to express themselves creatively, with new distinctive images.

Musically, Bob Marley and Peter Tosh's reggae legends live on, and the rhythms of Africa, the Caribbean, Latin America and the United States are potent sounds in the dance halls and discos of Britain's black communities and increasingly in the wider

society. Such fusions as Bhangra and Jungle are but two of the
latest popular styles, to which black and Asian youths dance and
with which they continue to experiment. Unlike Samuel Coleridge Taylor, whose 'exotic' compositions were still essentially
European, Tunde Jegede, the foremost and one of the few Kora
players in Britain, emerged in the 1980s and since then has
developed his own style, as performed in 1991 at the inaugural
concert and world premiere of African Classical Music in Britain
at the Purcell Room[39] in London's South Bank Centre, a performance during which the author presented an Introduction to
this music. Since then many concerts across Britain and the
Continent have been staged and recordings of Jegede's unique
music have been issued. Though his audience is still relatively
small, he is passionate about what he does in this relatively little
known genre. He is always full of ideas and continues to com-
pose. Still only in his mid-twenties, he has carved a musical
niche for himself and feels charged to deliver not only the 'classical' aspects of this 'African' music, but also those elements of it
which relate to other musical idioms in a fusionist sound. The
BBC recently screened a documentary of his life and work, a
reflection of his stature in this musical genre.

Keith Waithe, the improvisatory flautist, composer and jazz
fusionist, who blends the sounds of the East and the West with
his unique Caribbean nuances, continues to thrill audiences
from different cultural backgrounds. His concert tours to many
parts of the world and the rising demand for his music in Britain
confirm his creative standing at the cutting edge of today's most
innovative music.

In the dramatic arts, too, distinctive productions provide
evidence of new perspectives on Afro-Asian history and on life
and living. In films, radio, television and in theatres, black and
Asian plays are portraying the lives and struggles of those who
came to Britain and survived, and those who did not. Crucial
precedents have been set and it is worth reviewing some of them.

Just prior to and between the 1960s and the 1990s, images of
black people, against strong odds, continued to appear on British
film and television screens. Apart from Nina Baden-Semper's
riveting performance in *The World in a Room*, prior to her
famous Barbie role in *Love Thy Neighbour*, if there were few parts

either written for or offered to black actresses, there were many more opportunities for black women in the music business and variety shows, a time when the home-grown talent of Shirley Bassey flourished. However, the sounds of Jamaica (before Marley's time) were also being heard through the lively Millie with her foot-tapping hit 'My Boy Lollipop'. Significantly, this was a period of transition, from blue-beat to reggae. But the images of black people on television that achieved the largest audiences were those of the African-American characters played by Bill Cosby, Greg Morris and Michelle Nicholls in *Star Trek*,[40] whose on-screen performances, were indicative of future possibilities.

Before moving on, however, it is important to place historically the contributions of Gordon Heath and Lionel Ngakane to British film and television. After playing Othello in Kenneth Tynan's 1950 production, Heath was again cast in the part by Tony Richardson for a BBC television production, in which his powerful performance generated much debate and comparison with Lawrence Olivier's film portrayal of the same role. More television and film roles followed, but Heath, like other black actors such as Earl Cameron, Cy Grant and Errol John, was neither put under contract, nor promoted by the film studios. 'There were few openings' for such actors in British films, Bourne argues, 'and they could not expect to be promoted in the same way that Dirk Bogarde [the English actor] would have been'. Ironically, at this time, the African-American Sidney Poitier was making huge strides in Hollywood, so much so that he became the biggest threat to the few excellent black actors in Britain. Heath died in Paris in 1991, 41 years after the young South African Lionel Ngakane had arrived in England.

Ngakane's interest in journalism led him to do an interview with Zoltan Korda, who was about to do a film based on the book *Cry, the Beloved Country*. After their meeting, Korda offered the part of Absalom to Ngakane. But although his portrayal of this role was praised, Ngakane was more interested in film direction. He continued to act in British-made films during the 1950s, but seized the chance of making his directorial debut with *Sunday in London*, before his better known, prize-winning work *Jemima and Johnny* in the early 1960s.

Ngakane has lived in England for many years and does all he
can to promote African cinema.

Another black actor and personality of the 1950s and 1960s
was Earl Cameron, who appeared memorably in the films *Pool
of London, Emergency Call, Sapphire, Flame in the Streets* and
Guns at Batasi and on television. The film *Sapphire* received the
British Academy Award for Best Film, soon after the 1958 riots.

In the small grouping of black performers in Britain, Cam-
eron came to know and to work with Nadia Cattouse, Amanda
Ira Aldridge (daughter of the great nineteenth-century African-
American actor) Connie Smith and Sidney Poitier, and white
film directors, such as Zoltan Korda, Basil Dearden, Brian
Desmond Hurst, Roy Baker and the English actor, John Mills.[41]

Other outstanding performers of the period were Errol John
and Carmen Munro. Born in British Guiana in 1932, Carmen
came to London in the late 1950s, not to become an actress, but
to further her education. She joined the West Indian Drama
Group in 1957 and her earliest stage appearance was in Eugene
O'Neill's *Anna Christie*, in which she gave a creditable performance. Carmen went on to act in many parts in West End
theatres, in plays by Tennessee Williams, Alun Owen, Jean
Genet and George Bernard Shaw. With time, she became
increasingly proud of her involvement in black theatre in
Britain. Some of her portrayals were of works by young black
British dramatists such as Caryl Phillips, Michael Abbensetts
and the African-American import, Loraine Hansberry's famous
play *A Raisin in the Sun;* and after partnering Yvonne Brewster
as Assistant Director of *The Black Jacobins* by C.L.R. James, she
directed *Alas, Poor Fred* in 1986 and Derek Walcott's *Remem-
brance* a year later. But it is her strong stage presence that lives
on, performances that have been described in superlatives by
critics. Apart from a good deal of radio work, her engagement for
television has been very impressive. Though she will perhaps be
best remembered for her role in *The Desmonds*, which co-
starred the Guyanese-born Norman Beaton.

Munro views herself as a 'drama queen' who is unafraid to
stand up in her own 'light'. She is happy with her career as an
actress and, as she put it, 'always in competition with myself'.
Commenting on struggling actresses, she said: 'You have to work

with the time you live in ... you can't change anything from the outside, you have to be in it and change it from within.'

Joining her in the select group of the acting profession's most respected black actresses is Corinne Skinner-Carter, whose innumerable performances on the stage, radio, in films and television have endeared her to millions.[42]

In the last four decades, huge audiences have been watching British television's 'soaps' and gradually from the 1960s to the 1990s, more and more black and Asian actors and actresses have appeared in *Coronation Street*, *Emergency Ward 10*, *Crossroads*, *Brookside*, *Eastenders*, *Empire Road*, *Brothers and Sisters*, *Black Silk* and, of course, *The Desmonds*. Taken together, they represent a substantial part of British popular culture.

While the Trinidad-born actor Rudolph Walker continues to act, a number of young black actors and actresses are beginning to provide the British public with their dramatic 'shine', not only in theatres, but also in films and on television. Often in Britain, we have tended to overlook budding and manifest black talent, a category within which that other Trinidad-born actor Errol John must be firmly placed.

A Man From the Sun was a landmark film, distinguished for being the sole British television drama about Caribbean migrants in postwar Britain, some 40 years before *The Final Passage* was screened in 1996. John's appearance in *A Man From the Sun* was regarded as a 'most memorable' and 'lasting impression'. Soon after his arrival as a migrant, he expressed his feelings in the words of a letter at once sad, yet hopeful: 'Dear Mama; after this little time things is not too bad. I'd like to send you some money but I not got a job jus' yet. England is a wonderful strange place, but it's my home now, for better or worse.'

Errol John's film and television career, which began in the early 1950s with *The Emperor Jones*, continued with *The Heart of the Matter*, *The Love Lottery*, *Simba* and *Odongo*. As a playwright, he won the prestigious Observer Drama Competition for his play *Moon on a Rainbow Shawl*. Nevertheless, his love of acting prevailed. In the succeeding years, he was seen on British television in *For the Defence*, *Cry the Beloved Country*, *The Member of the Wedding*, *No Hiding Place*, *First Night: (The Dawn)*, *Rumpole of the Bailey*, *Crown Court* and in films, including *The Nun's Story, The Sins of Rachel Cade, PT 109, Guns at Batasi, Assault on a Queen* and *Buck and the Preacher.*

John had a rare presence, and his sensitive performances have left lasting impressions on those who witnessed them. He has worked with some of the biggest names in the theatre and in the film and television world, but frustration remained, which has something to do with concerns expressed by other black actors, actresses and performers in Britain: that African-Americans are given roles which actors like himself could have handled. He was confident that he was as good, perhaps better than the African-American imports. At the time, many believed that instead of casting Sidney Poitier, John would have been perfectly cast in the role of Mark Thackeray in the 1967 film *To Sir, With Love.*

In the last years of his life, he became a solitary figure. When he was found dead in his room in London on 10 July 1988, some reflected on the chances that did not come his way, because of the bias of box office-oriented producers and film officials directly responsible for casting. None the less, Errol John's legacy as a fine actor and a proud human being are lasting images of a man from the sun, which a new generation of black actors and actresses are investigating as part of a continuum in evaluating their own potential and identities in relation to ever-changing British society.[43]

In a medium which, since the inaugural screening of *The Wandering Negro Minstrels* has grown into the fabulously wealthy and powerful film industry, control of the various studios remain paramount. Thus, the images of blacks and Asians have yet to be freed from their residual colonial constraints. However, more and more independent black and Asian film-makers are striking back with their own creations of powerful moving portrayals, not simply to entertain, but also to serve as a timely corrective to the gross prejudices and misrepresentations of the Imperial past.

The Asian presence in British film and television is powerfully evocative of the Empire and includes the film appearances of Sabu and Indian images in *The Jungle Book, Kim, Bhowani Junction, The Man Who Would be King, Nine Hours to Rama, Bhaji on the Beach, My Beautiful Launderette, Jewel in the Crown, A Passage to India* and Richard Attenborough's acclaimed *Gandhi,* films that have attracted huge British audiences. Few, however, could doubt the authenticity, beauty and power of Satayajit Ray's films and indeed the pervasive effect of the song and dance musicals on Asian audiences in Britain. In fact, the Indian and Pakistani film fraternities, formed in the 1950s in Britain,[44] continue to enjoy Asian movies, a demand which is fed by the almost endless film productions from the world's largest film industry in Bombay. Today, many talented black and Asian actors, actresses and comedy players perform nightly (Lennie Henry being by far the most successful), as and when 'black' shows are adequately funded. These actors are becoming more and more familiar on our television screens in both comedy and drama, their images appearing in different guises in a whole range of popular shows.

Black photographers have been relatively successful in recent years. Armet Francis continues to work, and some of his best photographs have been published in two books: *The Black Triangle*[45] and *Children of the Black Triangle*. Black film-makers too have been striving to bring their videos and films to the screen in the hope of reaching a wider public than they have hitherto, but often they are left frustrated, their projects unfinished usually because of a lack of funding.

Evocations from the heart of Afro-Asian visual artists, especially by painters, depict the tragi-comic realities of their peoples' minority status and predicament in Britain. For decades, they have been confined to small budgets which, in turn, restrict their attempts to gain access to the best venues and thus reach wider audiences. In fact, it was not until 1989 that a major exhibition of works of art by Afro-Asian artists, 'The Other Story', was exhibited at the Hayward Gallery in London, signalling a fundamental change in the art world in the postwar period. For the artists this came none too soon. Among them were the modernists Ronald Moody, Ivan Perries, Francis De Souza, Avinash Chandra, Aubrey Williams, Ahmed Parvez, Frank Bowling, Balraj Khanna and Avtarjeet Dhanjal; and those who considered art to be no longer an object but an idea with no set pattern of expression, such as Iqbal Geoffrey, David Medalla and Rasheed Araeen. (More recently, the internationally acclaimed British artist Anish Kapoor has had his first major show at the Hayward Gallery.) And then there were those who, because of the intense and unforgettable experiences of 'loss and displacement', use the language of 'deconstruction of dominant forms, through borrowing and hybridising' like Gavin Jantjes (the South African), Mona Hatoum (the Palestinian) Eddie Chambers (black British-born), Keith Piper (black-British) and Lubaina Himid (an independent black woman artist) who, in 1983, organised an art exhibition in the Africa Centre. Very much a woman who believes 'We will be who we want, where we want, in the way that we want, when we want, and the time is now and the place here and there and now'. One of her favourite themes has been the deconstruction of such European masters as Pablo Picasso and William Hogarth, whose work 'The Countess's Levée', a pastiche, is described as a satire examining the position of black people in British society and especially in the world. She substantiates contemporary characters for Hogarth's and, as in the image of 1743, black people are today still 'marginalized onlookers', but she turns Hogarth's black servant into the black artist and the black child slave into the 'spirit of Resistance', thereby creating a message of unity and resistance for black people in Britain.

Other artists' work at 'The Other Story' exhibition depicts cultural difference. The problem with creating such a synthesis is that it either 'obscures difference by assimilating it, or makes it re-emerge as a sign of Otherness', though the cultural difference in its reassertion, as Rasheed Araeen (one of the artists and curator of the exhibition) claims, have the merits of also being a 'critique to the dominant forms'.

Among those thus engaged were Anwar Jalal Shemza (an Indian who came to Britain in the 1950s), Uzo Egonu (an African who came to Britain in 1945), Donald Locke (a Guyanese who came to England in 1954), Saleem Arif (an Indian) and the East London-born Sonia Boyce, who integrates 'material into the creation of a pictorial space which tells stories', which address the black woman's experience in white society. She is intent on the recreation of self by using her own image not as a mirror, but as a metaphor, the means through which she emphasises core issues relating to the 'regeneration of a cultural identity within a racist society'. She deals with imagery which transcends stereotypes and, in form and subject matter, encourages broad-mindedness by demonstrating that drawing is (or can be) as expressive a medium and carry as much potential as painting. 'The picture plane is seen as a space to be patterned in every sense of the word, in order not to imitate the world, but to create it.'[46]

With the passage of time, the migrants' and migrant writers' experiences were expressed in many works of fiction and non-fiction such as George Lamming's *The Emigrants* (1954) and *The Pleasures of Exile* (1960), Andrew Salkey's *Escape to an Autumn Pavement* (1963) and V.S. Naipaul's *The Mimic Men* (1967). In *The Emigrants*, Lamming addresses the nature of the migratory experience: 'The interpretation me give hist'ry is people the world over always searchin' and feelin', from time immemorial, them keep searchin' and feelin'.' In the 'postmodern' world, an ever-increasing body of literary texts related to migration, *Writing Across Worlds*, are among the major themes being expressed today. As citizens not just of one country, but many, one writer proclaims the 'boundless kingdom of the imagination, the half-lost land of memory'.[47] Migration has become an important subject of study for both social scientists and literary scholars, who together can advance our understanding. Of all the writers who came to London, Sam Selvon, in his trilogy *The Lonely Londoners*, *Moses Ascending* and *Moses Migrating*,[48] perhaps evokes best the black migrants' attempts to recreate 'home' in a 'city of words'. The migrants' entry into Britain confronted Selvon with his own identity. It is just such a confrontation which inspired him to use language in his art to decolonise, both in style and content, the traditional imperialist novel. His black Londoners are rootless characters through whom he uses language to remake the city in their own image. He used the 'oral calypsonian ballad' to good subversive effect, a striking departure from the strictures of 'Queen's English' or 'Standard English'. Indeed his efforts at literary decolonisation both colonises England in reverse and looks forward to the later works of Caribbean poets and writers, such as James Berry, Michael Smith, Earl Lovelace, Grace Nicholls, Louise Bennett, Jean Breeze and Linton Kwesi Johnson, who combine the literary with the oral.

Michel Fabre has said of Selvon that he 'does not assimilate into the mainstream (of writing 'standard' English) he explodes it'.[49] And adding his subversive mix to the oral tradition, John Agard, like other Caribbean writers who use standard English, challenges its privileged status in the continuum of the language in *Listen, Mr. Oxford Don:*

> 'Me not no Oxford don
> me a simple immigrant
> from Clapham Common
> I didn't graduate
> I immigrate.
>
> But listen Mr Oxford don
> I'm a man on de run
> And a man on de run
> is a dangerous one
>
> I ent have no gun
> I ent have no knife
> but mugging de Queen's English
> is the story of my life
>
> I don't need no axe
> to split/ up yu syntax
> I don't need no hammer
> to mash/ up yu grammar...
>
> So mek dem sen one big word after me
> I ent serving no jail sentence
> I slashing suffix in self-defence
> I bashing future wit past tense
> and if necessary
>
> I making de Queen's English accessory/ to my offence'.[50]

Whether or not the novel is dead, these writings, creations by people from the former British Empire, whose British-born children are, in effect, redressing the balance by writing back in a new linguistic mixture, are a vital and inescapable task at the heart of the postcolonial enterprise. Given that postcolonial literature is 'essentially political', its creation and study necessitate serious questioning of the axioms upon which the whole discipline of English has been founded, for they are 'not immutable "truths", but changeable social and political constructions'.[51]

Like Boyce, the generations of writers of postcolonial literature and other Afro-Asian artists before her, who learned to draw and to 'paint', the multitude of black and Asian British youths in the 1990s (who are among the majority of the 'underclass', the long-term unemployed, with precious little space for manoeuvre) are engaged, through momentary configuration of images and attitudes, in reinventing themselves within the 'Britannic melting pot'.

They, like their forebears, have struggled for the right to demonstrate their sense of identity in the heart of the former Empire. Today's youths demonstrate a strong sense of belonging: they want to win for Britain. And when they do, they proudly parade the Union Jack. They do not want to be misrepresented, like a Norman Tebitt pastiche. They are engaged in a massive pop culture that is seemingly everywhere in Britain; and instead of 'Rule Britannia', the popular contemporary trend now is 'Cool Britannia', a phenomenon that can also be found all over Europe. British identity is flagged up time and again in the debate over Europe, as though it is something specific and common to everyone. The absurdity of this is emphasised when one considers that pluralistic Britain is considering whether or not to become more fully involved with pluralistic Europe. In making a decision as to Britain's future in the Community, those in power should not forget the groundswell of feeling, reflective of the 'new' Britain of British youths, and of black and Asian people generally. For their part, the actions they take proclaim that they too are integral to the historical flux, by inscribing as a corrective to the Western versions their own histories, participants in the act of cultural renewal, of making and remaking themselves, of enforcing the crucial connection between anti-racism and culture, thus giving meaning to life as lived and creatively expressed in their own hybridised art forms which defy, redefine and transform 'Englishness' and 'Britishness' through a regenerative and liberating accommodation of multiple British identities. Thus blacks and Asians vis-à-vis other groups have been making positive contributions to the process of reimaging Britain.

At the end of the bloodiest century in recorded human history, diversity and disadvantage have underscored this multifaceted black, Asian and 'British' history of racialised interdependence which, in turn, has been characterised by black and Asian peoples' dignity, courage and self-belief. But although the 'brothers' and 'sisters' are still denied the 'upper hand', they have learned much about the use of colour. Such an imposition subjected and consigned black and Asian people to the wretchedness and frustration of being at the margins of a racial divide along economic, social and political lines. From these unpromising circumstances, in the fast-changing technological world of recent decades, a new and proliferating multicoloured, cross-cultural mosaic of cultural tolerance (reflecting more light and less shadow, subtle nuances giving perspective to a modernist version of an essentially primal story) has appeared to contradict certain prevailing norms and values, the legacy of white mythologies. This post-Empire counterpoise, has been converted into highly-charged creative 'unBritish' lifestyles, new and positive images of their humanity imprinted on a time-worn canvas, portrayals that are evocative of the art of living with difference in a society whose elites, contrary to political realities and incontrovertible evidence of a pervasive racist culture, still perceive themselves and British institutions, not as striving for, but as providing the ever-elusive equal opportunities for all.

Few would argue against the advances made, but the vision of cock-eyed powerbrokers, architects of the economy and patrons of the arts continues to inspire in those they mislead a desire and urgency to add their individual and collective brushstrokes in the making of a truer, though less defined and unfinished picture of British life and living, which insists that the people in this 'sceptred Isle', far from being the 'Lords of humankind', have been and are of many cultures, with a tendency to look outwards and more realistically at themselves and release the imagination from the Empire within.

Clearly, at least from the time of the Viking invasions, among the peoples of the British Isles the legacy of British traditions is integral to what has evolved in today's multicultural Britain. So in speaking about contemporary British cultural identity certain questions arise. For example: Whose

Britain? Whose culture? And whose identity? We should therefore be concerned with Britain as a complex society, in terms of age, gender, sex and the family, ethnicity, language, youth, culture, class, politics, the environment and heritage; a diverse Britain with conflicting group interests. Not surprisingly each of these groupings has its own interpretation of Britain and none can claim to be solely representative because each is influenced by region, religion, education and profession. We should therefore speak in the plural, of identities in terms of British culture, rather than identity. By so doing, in this post-Empire, devolutionary, pro-Europe period of British history, British civilisation and society – in the face of the uncertainties of a fast-changing world, in which the ugliness of racism looms large – should not miss the opportunity at the new millennium not merely to acknowledge but also to celebrate the *creative potential* of human difference.

NOTES

Prologue
1. Kiernan 1969.
2. Hulme 1992.

PART ONE: THE 'BLACKAMOORES" PRESENCE (1500–1900)

Chapter 1 Africans and Asians in the British Isles
1. Swire 1966: 20; Magie 1922: 1, 434–7, Latin text and translation;
   Birley 1971: 10–11, quoted Gundara and Duffield 1992: 9–15.
2. Visram 1986: 2–3.
3. Kearney 1989.
4. Taylor 1934: 42–3; Fryer 1989: 3.
5. Parker 1965.
6. Seeck 1876: Breeze and Dobson 1976.
7. Paul 1902: 106; Laing 1834: Vol. II, 386; Edwards, in Gundara and
   Duffield 1992: 16–24.
8. Johnson 1971; Edwards, in Gundara and Duffield 1992: 4.
9. Maan 1992: 62–3.
10. Jones 1965; Cowhig 1985: 1–25.
11. Graham-Dixon 1996.
12. Williams 1944: 4–7.
13. Rodney 1988: 84–5.
14. Williams 1944: 4–7.
15. Strachey 1959: 68; Fryer 1989: 4.
16. Walvin 1997: ix–xiii.
17. Craton 1974: 140, 152.
18. Ragatz 1928: 53.
19. Thomas 1997.
20. Acts of the Privy Council, Vol. XXV1, 1596–7: 16–21; Hughes and
    Larkin 1969: Vol. 3, 221.
21. Shyllon 1974: 230.
22. Sancho 1782.
23. Cugoano 1787.
24. Long 1774: Vol. 2, 364–5, 383; Edwards 1793: Vol. 2, 75; Carlyle
    1853; Trollope 1860; Walvin 1973.
25. Shyllon 1974; Gretchen 1995: 1–28, 133–64.
26. Norton: 1972; 1974.

27. PRO: T/1/631 and 632.
28. Sharp 1788.
29. PRO T/1/646; Shyllon 1974: 150.
30. Cugoano 1787: 139–42.
31. Colley 1996.
32. PRO: T/1/643; Shyllon 1974: 140–6.
33. Equiano 1969: xlv.
34. George 1925; Shyllon 1974: 146.
35. Parliamentary Papers 1789, Vol. 82; Shyllon 1974: 156.
36. Equiano 1969: 236–9.
37. Smith 1838: 26–7; Egan 1821; Fryer 1984: 23–330.
38. Yorke 1931; Garrick 1782: Vol. III, quoted Gretchen 1995: 29–67; Smith 1949: 14–15; Dabydeen 1985: 37.
39. Shyllon 1974.
40. Visram 1986: 1.
41. Ibid.: 2.
42. Ibid.: 3–4.
43. Hammond and Hammond 1925: 196–9.
44. Hansard Parliamentary Debates, 3rd series, vol. 148 (1858) cols 1338, 1354. Digby 1901: 33; Marshall 1976; Baines 1835: 218; Fryer 1989: 20.
45. Visram 1986: 11–15.
46. Wedderburn 1790.
47. Ackroyd 1996.
48. Wilkinson 1820.
49. Prince 1831.

Chapter 2 Afro-Asians after Emancipation

1. Kearney 1989: 13, 102–3.
2. Robbins 1994: 8.
3. Ibid.: 26–28.
4. Inden 1990: 262–5.
5. Robbins 1994: 57–61.
6. Ibid.: 78.
7. Graham-Dixon 1996: 75–9, 197.
8. Majumdar et al. 1950: 810; Gadgil 1971: 33–6; Fryer 1989: 21–2.
9. Chaudhuri 1955: xxii, 198; Ghosh 1930: 50ff; Majumdar 1962–63: Vol. I, 48–143; Stokes 1970: 110; Chatterji 1857: 224; Chaudhuri 1957: 269; Malleson 1878–80: Vol. III, 205; Fryer 1989:107–10.
10. Ackroyd 1995: 844.
11. Ireland 1861: Vol. II, 159–60, 256; Dilke 1868: Vol. II, 225; Kaye 1864–76, 170, 235–7; Fryer 1989: 109–10.
12. Visram 1986: 7–8.
13. Ramdin 1982: 23–4.
14. Hitchins 1931.

15. Campbell 1923.
16. Basham 1975; Herodotus 1972; Banaji 1933.
17. Frere 1883: 355; Banaji 1933: 36, 202–3.
18. Ramdin 1995.
19. Ramdin 1995.
20. Tinker 1974.
21. Mangru 1987; 'The Sex-Ratio Disparity and its Consequences under Indenture in British Guiana' in *India in the Caribbean*: 211–30; Reddock 1986: 27–49.
22. Ramdin 1995: 40–1.
23. *Punch* 1848: Vol. XV, 265, reprinted in Thackeray 1855–7: Vol. I, 126–31; Kingsley 1850: 167, 174, 194.
24. 'Death of a Celebrity', *Mercury* (Hobart Town) XVII/3007 (11 August 1870); Saville 1982: Vol VI.
25. Seacole 1853; Ramdin 1987: 29–35.
26. Holzman 1926: 70–91; *Memoirs of William Hickey*, ed. Spencer, Vol. II, 228, 262, 275; Hecht 1954: 50–4; Visram 1986: 11–13.
27. *The Times*, 20 July 1852; IOR 1782: 181; Visram 1986: 19–20.
28. IOR: L/P&J/6/435; *London City Mission Magazine*, 2 July 1900: 172–4; *Kelly's Hackney and Homerton Street Directory, 1900–1901*; Sims 1906: Vol. III, 279, 281; Visram 1986: 28–30.
29. Mayhew 186: Vol. IV, 366; IOR: L/MAR/C/902, 33ff; Letter from East India Company Chairman to the Hon. Nicholas Vansittart, 23 February 1815 in *Copy of All Correspondence*, 1816: No. 279, 3; Visram 1986: 38–9.
30. Report from the Committee on Lascars, 1814–15: No. 471, 9–13; Harris et al. 1814: 17; Visram 1986: 40.
31. *Collectanea: Or a Collection of Advertisements and Paragraphs from the Newspapers, Relating to Various Subjects*. D. Lyons (comp.), 223 v; *London City Mission Magazine* 1867; Visram 1986: 57–61.
32. Maan 1992: 84.
33. Salter 1873; *The East in the West; Or Work Among Asiatics and Africans in London* (London: S.W. Partridge & Co., 1896).
34. Malabari 1893: 80–1.
35. Langland 1964: 502.
36. IOR: MSS EUR F.84/126a; Visram 1986: 33.
37. *London City Mission Magazine*, January 1867: 4–16; Salter 1873: 236–9; Visram 1986: 55.
38. Salter 1873: 203; *London City Magazine*, August 1857: 217; Visram 1986: 60–2.
39. Maan 1992: 77.
40. Fisher 1996: 2.
41. Hamilton 1796; Moirer 1824; de Montesquieu 1721; Fisher 1996: xiii; Macpherson 1928; Harvey 1988; Moodie 1788: Pearse, T.D., '*Memoir*' *Bengal Past and Present*, Vols. 2–7 (1908–11); Rennell, J., *Marches* (1792) and *Journals* (1910 edition); Scott 1827–28;

Shipp, J., *Memoirs* (1829); Williams, J., *Historical Account* (1817; 1970 reprint); Williams. T., *East Indian Vade Mecum* (1810).
42. Fisher 1996: 4.
43. Mahomed 1820; 1822, 1826, 1838.
44. Guy's Hospital Reports, Vol. XLIII; *British Medical Journal*, 29 November 1884; Visram 1986: 67–9.
45. Vagdama 1984: 41.
46. Alexander and Anand 1980: 167–203; Visram 1986: 71–3.
47. *Illustrated London News*, 17 July, 1852.
48. Visram 1986: 74–5.
49. Allen 1981: 50–3.
50. Sayers 1915; Coleridge Taylor 1979; Parry 1912: 638.
51. Reynolds 1928.
52. Marshall and Stock 1958.
53. Fryer 1984: 256.
54. Allen 1894: 213; V/119 (10 November 1894): 229; *Fraternity*, 1/15 (15 September 1894): 3; Fryer 1984: 277–9.
55. Hill 1992: 99–123.
56. Froude 1888; Thomas 1969.
57. Mathurin 1976; Hooker 1975: 119, 121.
58. Visram 1986: 82–4.
59. Ibid.: 91–2.
60. *The Times*, 15 November 1933; Visram 1986: 92–7.
61. *The Times*, 4 August 1928; Visram 1986: 97–102.
62. Shyllon 1992: 209.
63. *Llafur* 3, 1 (Spring 1980): 5–29. See Law and Loy 1981.
64. Fyfe 1971: 189–90.
65. Duffield 1971: Vol. 2, 102; Kosmin 1978–79.
66. Shyllon 1992: 211.
67. Ibid.

PART TWO: BRITAIN AND EMPIRE (1900–62)

Britain: An Historical Outline

1. Childs 1995: 1.
2. Robbins 1994: 162, 88–166.
3. Graham-Dixon 1996: 206.
4. Robbins 1994: 205–6.
5. James 1962.
6. Graham-Dixon 1996: 225.
7. Robbins 1994: 172–251.
8. Fryer 1884: 133–90.

Chapter 3 Racism, Empire and Labour

1. Said 1994: xxiv.
2. Lenin 1969: 63.

3. Robbins 1994: 96–7.
4. Eldridge 1996.
5. Curtin 1971: 1.
6. Porter 1975: 46.
7. Hobson 1902.
8. Fryer 1989: 66–81.
9. Tinker 1974: ch. 7.
10. Ibid.: 330, 365–6.
11. Ibid.
12. Ibid.
13. Ramdin 1982: 89–92.
14. Dutt 1949: 23–4.
15. Henderson 1965; Ramdin 1987: 64–7.
16. Little 1947: 34–6, 56–7; Sinclair 1993.
17. Little 1947: 59, 61; Ramdin 1987: 75–82.
18. *Western* Mail *and South Wales Echo*, 8 July 1935; Ramdin 1987: 83–4.
19. *Guardian Review*, 25 March 1998: 6–7.
20. Sinclair 1993: 88–130.
21. Richmond 1954; Ramdin 1987: 86–99; Bousquet and Douglas 1991.
22. Ramdin 1987: 85–99.
23. Richmond 1954; MacPherson 1947.
24. Ellinwood, in Ellinwood et al.1978: 199.
25. Visram 1986: 117–39.
26. Ibid..
27. Fuller 1952: 188–9; Visram 1986: 139–43.
28. Maan 1992: 99–148.
29. Ibid.: 114–21.
30. Ibid.: 124.
31. Ibid.: 125–9.
32. Ibid.: 132.
33. Ibid.: 139–40.
34. Ibid.: 132–3, 139–44, 146.
35. Ibid.: 146–7.
36. Ibid.: 149–50.

Chapter 4 Afro-Asian Challenges

1. Green 1987: 174–89.
2. Little 1947: 172.
3. Shyllon 1977: 212.
4. Tupper 1938: 20, 40, 50–1; Thornton 1939: 215, 219–20; Little 1947: 34–6, 56–7, 59; *Western Mail*, 12 June 1919, p. 5.
5. *The Sunday Pictorial*, 6 September 1942.
6. Smith 1980: 318.
7. Parliamentary Debates, 5th Ser. Vol. 38 (1942), Cols. 670–1.

8. Thorne 1974.
9. Macdonald 1992: 150–68.
10. Ramdin 1987: 90–7; Shirsat 1974.
11. Shirsat 1974: 18–19.
12. Saha 1970.
13. *The Daily Worker*, 20 January 1936.
14. Morris 1976: 380; Saha 1970.
15. See Nield and Saville, in Bellamy and Saville 1982: 237.
16. George 1974: 1–13.
17. Ibid.
18. *The Observer*, 30 November 1974; George 1974.
19. Visram 1986: 161
20. Ibid.: 166–7.
21. George 1974; Lenyel 1962; *Dictionary of National Biography*. 560–1.
22. Vaughan 1950: 54–5.
23. Ibid.: 108–37.
24. Vaughan 1950.
25. Ibid.: 26, 34, 41.
26. Ibid.: 46.
27. Ibid.: 63–4.
28. Ibid.: 111.
29. Ibid.: 130.
30. Drake, J.G. St. Clair, 'Value Systems, Social Structure and Race Relations in the British Isles'. PhD Thesis (University of Chicago, 1954): 106.
31. Morris 1972.
32. Hooker 1967; Geiss 1968.
33. Hooker 1967: 53–4, 93–7.
34. Ibid.: 97.
35. Ibid.: 101.
36. *The Defender*, 16 February 1946.
37. Hooker 1967: 106.
38. Ibid.: 106–8.
39. Ibid.: 116.
40. Padmore 1956: 11.
41. Hooker 1967:139–40.
42. Padmore 1948; Phillips 1960; Geiss 1974.
43. Bennett 1960.
44. Naipaul 1987.
45. Lamming 1960.
46. Parliamentary Debates, House of Commons, 5 December 1958, Cols. 1580–1.
47. Hiro 1992.
48. Ibid.
49. Maan 1992: 162.
50. Selvon 1975.
51. Glass and Pollins 1960: 45–6.

52. Eggerton 1957: 65–6.
53. Glass, and Pollins 1960: 48–9.
54. Gladstone 1924: 202; Glass and Pollins 1960: 50–2.
55. Glass and Pollins 1960: 52.
56. Ibid.: 54.
57. *The Times*, 20 May 1959.
58. *The Times*, 29 May 1959.
59. Ibid.
60. Selvon 1975.
61. Glass and Pollins 1960: 6, 54, 68, 72.
62. Ibid.
63. Cabinet Papers, 1954:1; *The Times*, 2 January 1985.
64. Glass and Pollins 1960: 68–72.
65. Report of the Proceedings of the 90th Annual Trades Union Congress, September 1958: 459.
66. Glass and Pollins 1960: 76–8.
67. *The Times*, 26 August 1958.
68. Ibid.: 131.
69. Glass and Pollins 1960: 146.
70. Ibid.: 146–8.
71. Parliamentary Debates, House of Commons, 5 December 1958, Col. 1588.
72. Glass and Pollins 1960: 148.
73. *The Daily Telegraph*, 25 May 1959.
74. *The New Statesman*, 9 May 1959.
75. *The Times*, 6 October 1959; Ramdin 1987: 219.
76. Glass and Pollins 1960: 194.
77. Ibid.: 209.
78. Scobie 1972.
79. Hiro 1971: 48; Ramdin 1987: 204–26.
80. Foot 1965: 129.
81. Bourne 1998: 2–4.
82. Ibid.: 5–8.
83. Ibid.: 8–10.
84. Ramdin 1987a: 10.
85. Shipman 1970: 463.
86. Bourne 1998: 43–64.
87. Kobal 1971; Shipman 1970; Larkin 1994; Bourne 1998: 69–73.
88. Bourne 1998: 82
89. Ibid.: 125–9.
90. Ibid.: 130–2.
91. Ibid. 132–6.
92. Ibid.: 136–9.

PART THREE: THE EMPIRE WITHIN (1956-98)

An Historical Overview of the United Kingdom

1. Robbins 1994: 268.
2. Ibid.: 277.
3. Ibid.: 278.
4. Kearney 1989: 282.
5. Robbins 1994: 282-5.
6. Address Given by the Home Secretary on 23 May 1966 ... to a Meeting of the Voluntary Liaison Committees (London: NCCL, 1966); Rose et al. 1969: 514.
7. Gourvish and O'Day 1991; Morgan 1990; Dutton 1991; Callaghan 1987; Healey 1989.
8. Young 1989.
9. Askwith 1998: 6-7.
10. Ibid.
11. James 1963.
12. Williams 1958.
13. Hoggart 1957.
14. Snow 1962.
15. Robbins 1994: 336-7.
16. Ibid.: 337-8.
17. Graham-Dixon 1996: 225-341.
18. Guptara 1986.
19. Robbins 1994: 365.
20. Ibid.: 383.
21. Childs 1995: 235-6.
22. Freedman 1988.
23. Wiener 1981; Middlemas 1991; Robbins 1994: 367-71
24. Robbins 1994: 400.
25. Childs 1995: 239.
26. Ibid.: 241-2.

Chapter 5 The Migrant Workers' Story

1. Castles and Kosack 1973.
2. Peach 1968: 23-6; Smith 1976: 64, 73, 75-6; Phizacklea and Miles 1980: 16-19.
3. Trollope 1860.
4. Ramdin 1998.
5. Nanan 1990; Vertovec, quoted in Karran 1994: 185-205.
6. Morokvansic, in Phizacklea 1983.
7. Ramnarine, in Dabydeen and Samaroo 1987: 119-41.
8. Karran 1994: 188-9.
9. Goulbourne 1988: 7.
10. Knowles 1952: xii.
11. Foot 1965; *New Society*, 17 June 1965; Torode 1965.

12. 'Who Are Imperial Typewriters?', *Race Today* (July 1974): 201.
13. Dhondy 1974; *Race Today*, July–August 1974.
14. Dromey. and Taylor 1978: 14.
15. 'The Grunwick Strike: The Bitter Lessons', *Race Today*, November–December 1977.
16. In the 1960s and 1970s the designation Caribbean became increasingly acceptable. Afro-Caribbean, rather than 'West Indian', came into vogue, a definition which, by default, meant that the other main non-white ethnic group from the Caribbean, the 'East Indians', became 'Indo-Caribbeans'.
17. Foner 1977: 224–5.
18. Ibid.: 226; 'Black Women and Nursing: A Job Like Any Other', *Race Today*, August 1974.
19. *Race Today*, August 1974
20. Ibid.: 228.
21. Ibid.: 228–30.
22. 'Caribbean Women and the Black Community', *Race Today*, May 1975.
23. Hassan and Dick 1983.
24. 'The State of Play at Fords', *Race Today*, May–June, 1982.
25. *Third World Impact* 1982: 36.
26. Allen and Bornat 1970: 2–3.
27. Ibid.: 5; Ahmat et al. 1983.
28. Policy Studies Institute 1993; Labour Research Department 1993: 2–3.
29. *Black Workers and Trade Unions* 1993: 15–18.
30. Ibid.: 16.
31. Ibid.: 25–7.
32. *Black Trade Unionists Solidarity Movement*, Issue No.1 and *Declaration* (London: BTUSM, Dcember 1981).
33. Ibid.
34. Select Committee on Race Relations and Immigration 1974: xxii.
35. Ramdin 1987: 337–69.

Chapter 6   Migrants in Transition and Authoritarianism

1. Ramdin 1987: 370–94.
2. Emecheta 1974.
3. Carmichael 1971: 27.
4. Ibid.: 18.
5. Ibid.: 201, 224–5.
6. Hiro 1992: 146–7.
7. Ibid.: 149.
8. Ibid.: 145–52.
9. Ibid.: 152–63.
10. Parekh 1981: 19.
11. *Race and Class*, Vol. XXIII, Nos. 2–3, 1981–2.

12. Hiro 1992: 164–73.
13. Maan 1992: 182–200.
14. *Unemployment and Homelessness* (London: Community Relations Commission, 1974): 10; Coard 1971.
15. Cashmore and Troyna 1982: 101–2.
16. Cashmore and Troyna 1982; Cashmore 1979.
17. Gilroy 1982: 291–4.
18. Roberts, in Cashmore and Troyna 1982: 101–2; Demuth 1978: 22–3.
19. *Daily Mirror*, 19 June 1979; Roberts in Cashmore and Troyna 1982: 105.
20. Bunyan 1981–2: 154.
21. Ibid.: 154–64.
22. Ibid.: 167–8.
23. *Race Today*, Editorial, July–August 1976; Bunyan 1981–2: 149.
24. Wilson 1978: 93.
25. Ibid.: 168–9.
26. Carby 1982: 232; Wilson 1978: 122–3.

Chapter 7 Migrant Communities: Leaders And Groupings

1. Sinclair 1993: 88–100.
2. Ibid.: 130.
3. Law and Loy 1981; Law and Henfrey 1981; Manley 1958–59.
4. Manley 1958–59; Richmond 1954.
5. Manley 1958–59; Little 1957: 589.
6. Heineman 1972: 66, 103.
7. Paterson 1963; Heinemann 1972: 69, 104.
8. Maxwell 1965: 19.
9. Pearson n.d.
10. Heinemann 1972: 77–8.
11. Maxwell 1966: 39–40.
12. Ibid.: 37.
13. Glass and Pollins 1960: 200.
14. Heinemann 1972: 16.
15. *Peace News*, 11 December 1964.
16. Heinemann 1972: 21.
17. Ibid.: 28.
18. Ibid.: 44.
19. *The Guardian*, 28 February 1966; Ramdin 1987: 426–7.
20. Heinemann 1972: 87.
21. Ibid.: 110.
22. Ibid.: 207.
23. Kinder 1966: 161.
24. Ibid.: 215–18.
25. Pearson n.d.
26. Hill 1971: 3.

27. Ibid.: 5.
28. Ibid.; Foot 1965; Deakin 1965.
29. Hill 1971: 20.
30. Desai 1963: 88.
31. Hiro 1971: 156.
32. De Witt 1969: 49.
33. Mansukani 1965: 204.
34. De Witt 1969: 110.
35. Ibid.: 126.
36. Ibid.: 128.
37. *Race Today Collective* (1983): 8.
38. Ibid.: 17, 20; see Ramdin 1987.
39. *Race Today* (1983): 20.
40. Hiro 1971: 116.
41. Hanke 1959: 8.
42. Report of the Race Relations Board 1969–70: 58.
43. Rose et al. 1969: 443; Hiro 1971: 121.
44. Butterworth 1967: 14.
45. Hiro 1971: 123–4.
46. Humphrey and Ward 1974: 151.
47. Rose 1969: 321; Hiro 1971: 125–6.
48. Hiro 1971: 126
49. Ibid.: 127–31.
50. Ibid.: 132.
51. Ibid.: 133–7
52. Maan 1992: 172–5.
53. Ibid.: 176–80.
54. Hiro 1971: 145–52.
55. See *Contemporary Authors; International Authors and Writers Who's Who; Contemporary Dramatists.*
56. Sivanandan 1981–2: 130.
57. Coard 1971.
58. *Race and Class* (1981–2): 135.
59. Ibid.: 143.
60. *Race and Class* (Summer 1985).
61. *Race and Class* (1981–2): 147.
62. *Daily Express*, 13 April 1980.
63. Joshua and Wallace 1983: 11; The Kerner Commission 1968, Part III, 73–7; Rudé 1981; Hobsbawm 1959; Thompson 1971; 'Black and Blue: Race and Violence in Britain', *Third Way*, Vol. 8, No. 5, 1985.
64. Thompson 1968: 10–11; Robinson 1983: 38.
65. Hiro 1971: 176–7.
66. *The Sunday Times*, 30 July 1989; Hiro 1971: 180.
67. Modood, in Donald and Rattansi 1992: 260–74.
68. Rex 1996: 240.

Chapter 8   Towards the Millennium: Ethnic Minorities in the 1990s

1. *Race Today* (1987–88).
2. House of Commons, Hansard, 1997.
3. *Ethnic Minorities in Britain* 1997: 1.
4. Ibid.: 32–3.
5. Ibid.: 23.
6. Ibid.: 56–7.
7. Ibid.: 58.
8. Modood, Beishon and Virdee 1994; *Ethnic Minorities in Britain* 1997: 58–9.
9. Modood 1997: 60–82.
10. Modood 1997: 105.
11. Ibid.: 106.
12. Brown 1984: 211.
13. Jones 1993: 74.
14. *Ethnic Minorities in Britain* 1997: 105–6.
15. Ibid.: Table 4.20, 111.
16. Ibid.: 113–14.
17. Ibid.: 116.
18. Ibid.: 124–5.
19. Ibid.: Table 4.24, 128–9.
20. Beishon, Virdee and Hagell 1995; see also *Ethnic Minorities in Britain* 1997: 134–5.
21. Wrench and Virdee, in Acker et al. 1995; *Ethnic Minorities in Britain* 1997: 135–7.
22. *Ethnic Minorities in Britain* 1997: 143–4.
23. Heath and McMahon 1997: 1.
24. *Ethnic Minorities in Britain* 1997: 145.
25. Ibid.: 145–9.
26. Ibid.: 180–1.
27. Lakey 1997: 220.
28. Ibid.: 221.
29. Ibid.: 223.
30. Ibid.: 256–8.
31. Ibid.: 287–9.
32. Ibid.: 286.
33. Ibid.: Tables 9.36 and 9.37, 334–6.
34. Ibid.: 337.
35. Ibid.: 338.
36. Ibid.: x.
37. Robbins 1993: 292, 328.
38. Heaney 1996: 203.
39. Jegede 1991.
40. Bourne 1998: 140–1.
41. Ibid.: 148–61.

42. Ibid.: 163–75.
43. Ibid.: 191–222.
44. For more on Asians, see Bourne 1988.
45. Francis 1985.
46. Boyce 1989: 100–4.
47. Rushdie, quoted in White 1995: 16.
48. Selvon 1956; 1975; 1983.
49. Fabre, in King 1979: 123.
50. Agard 1985: 44.
51. Ashcroft, Griffiths and Tiffin 1989: 196–7.

BIBLIOGRAPHY

Acker, et al., (eds), *The New Workplace and Trade Unions* (London: Routlege, 1995).

Ackroyd, Peter, *Blake: A Biography* (London: Sinclair Stevenson, 1996).

—— *Dickens: A Biography* (London: Sinclair Stevenson, 1995).

Agard, John, 'Listen, Mr. Oxford Don' in *Mangoes and Bullets* (London: Pluto Press, 1985).

Ahmat, Y, et al., 'The Textile Industry and Asian Workers in Bradford', *Race Today* (London: March–April, 1983).

Alexander, M. and Anand, S., *Queen Victoria's Maharajah Duleep Singh, 1838–1893* (London: Weidenfeld and Nicolson, 1980).

Allen, David Ravern, *A Song for Cricket* (London: Pelham Books, 1981).

Allen, R.V., 'Celestine Edwards: His Life, Work and Death', *Lux*, V/118 (3 November 1894); *Fraternity*, 1/15 (15 September 1894).

Allen, S. and Bornat, J., *Unions and Immigrant Workers: How They See Each Other* (Runnymede Trust Industrial Unit, 1970).

Anstey, Roger, *The Atlantic Slave Trade and British Abolition, 1760–1810* (London: Macmillan, 1975).

Ashcroft, B., Griffiths, G. and Tiffin, H., *The Empire Writes Back* (London: Routledge & Kegan Paul, 1989).

Askwith, Richard, 'The Forgotten Hero', *The Guardian Review*, 25 March 1998.

Atwood, Thomas, *The History of the Island of Dominica* (J. Johnson: 1791).

Baines, Edward, *History of the Cotton Manufacture in Great Britain* (London: H. Fisher & Co.,1835).

Banaji, D.R., *Slavery in British India* (Bombay: Toporavela Sons & Co., 1933).

Barker, Anthony J., *The African Link: British Attitudes to the Negro in the Era of the Slave Trade* (London: Frank Cass, 1978).

Barley, M.W. and Henson, R.P.C. (eds), *Christianity in Britain 300–700* (Leicester: Leicester University Press, 1968).

Bartlett, C.J., *British Foreign Policy in the Twentieth Century* (Basingstoke: Macmillan, 1989).

Basham, A.L. (ed.), *A Cultural History of India* (Oxford: Clarendon Press, 1975).

Beishon, S., Modood, T. and Virdee, S., *Changing Ethnic Identities* (London: Policy Studies Institute, 1994).

Bellamy, J. and Saville, J. (eds), for William Cuffay, see *Dictionary of Labour Biography*, Vol.VI (Basingstoke: Macmillan, 1982).

Beishon, S., Virdee, S. and Hagell, A., *Nursing in a Multi-Ethnic NHS* (London: Policy Studies Institute, 1995).

Bennett, L., 'Colonization in Reverse', *Jamaican Labrish* (Kingston, Jamaica: the author, 1960).

Berthoud, R., 'Income and Standards of Living', in *Ethnic Minorities in Britain* (London: Policy Studies Institute, 1997).

Best, G., *Mid-Victorian Britain 1851–1875* (London: Weidenfeld & Nicolson, 1971).

Birley, A., *Septimus Severus: The African Emperor* (London: Eyre & Spottiswoode, 1971).

—— *The People of Roman Britain* (London: Batsford, 1979).

Black Trade Unionists' Solidarity Movement, Issue No. 1 and Declaration (London: BTUSM, December 1981).

Blackett, R.J.M., 'Fugitive Slaves in Britain. The Odyssey of William and Ellen Craft', *Journal of American Studies*, 12 (April 1978).

Blyden, Edward W., *Christianity, Islam and the Negro Race* (Edinburgh: University of Edinburgh, 1967).

Bolt, Christine, *Victorian Attitudes to Race* (London: Routledge & Kegan Paul, 1971).

Bourke, A., *'The Visitation of God'? The Potato and the Great Irish Famine* (Dublin: Lilliput, 1993).

Bourne, Stephen, *Blacks in the British Frame: Black People in British Film and Television, 1896–1996* (London: Cassell/The Arts Council of England, 1998).

Bousquet, B. and Douglas, C., *West Indian Women at War: British Racism in World War II* (London: Lawrence & Wishart, 1991).

Boyce, Sonia, *The Other Story: Afro-Asian Artists in Post-War Britain* (London: South Bank Centre, 1989) pp. 100–4.

Breeze, D.J. and Dobson, B., *Hadrian's Wall* (London: Allen Lane, 1976).

Briggs, A., *Victorian People* (London: Odham's Press, 1954).

—— *The Age of Improvement 1783–1867* (London: Longman Green & Co., 1959).

—— *Victorian Cities* (London: Odham's Press, 1963).

Britain's Ethnic Minorities: Diversity and Disadvantage. The Fourth Policy Studies Institute Survey (London: Policy Studies Institute, 1976).

Britnell, R.H., *The Commercialisation of English Society, 1000–1500* (Cambridge: Cambridge University Press, 1993).

Brown, C., *Black and White Britain. The Third Policy Studies Institute Survey* (London: Heinemann Educational Books, 1984).

Brown, K.M., *Kingdom or Province? Scotland and the Regal Union, 1603–1715* (Basingstoke: Macmillan, 1992).

Bunyan, T., 'The Police against Black People', *Race and Class*, Vol. XXIII, Nos. 2–3 (Autumn–Winter 1981–2).

Bush, B., *Slave Women in Caribbean Society, 1650–1830* (London: James Currey, 1990).

Butterworth, E., *A Muslim Community in Britain* (London: Church Information Office, 1967).

Callaghan, J., *Time and Chance* (London: Collins, 1987).

Campbell, J. (ed.), *The Anglo-Saxons* (Oxford: Phaidon, 1992).

Campbell, J., *Edward Heath* (London: Jonathan Cape, 1993).

Campbell, P., *Chinese Coolie Emigration to Countries within the British Empire* (London: P.S. King & Son, 1923).

Cannadine, D., *The Decline and Fall of the British Aristocracy* (New Haven, Conn. & London: Yale University Press, 1990).

Carby, H., 'White Women Listen! Black Feminism and the Bounds of Sisterhood' in *The Empire Strikes Back* (London: CCCS, 1982).

Carlyle, T., *Occasional Discourse on the Nigger Question* (London: Thomas Bosworth, 1853).

Carmichael, S., *Black Power Back to Pan Africanism* (New York: Random House, 1971).

Carr, A.D., *Medieval Wales* (Basingstoke: Macmillan, 1995).

Cashmore, E., *Rastaman* (London: Allen & Unwin, 1979).

Cashmore, E. and Troyna, B., *Black Youth in Crisis* (London: Allen & Unwin, 1982).

Castles, S. and Kosack, G., *Immigrant Workers and Class Structure in Western Europe* (London: Oxford University Press, 1973).

Chatterji, N., 'A Century of India's Freedom Struggle', *Journal of Indian History*, XXXV (1857).

Chaudhuri, S.B., *Civil Disturbances during the British Rule in India, 1765–1857* (Calcutta: The World Press Ltd, 1955).

—— *Civil Rebellion in the Indian Mutiny, 1857–1859* (Calcutta: The World Press Ltd, 1957).

Childs, D., *Britain since 1939: Progress and Decline* (London: Macmillan, 1995).

Clanchy, M.T., *England and its Rulers, 1066–1272* (London: Fontana, 1983).

Coard, Bernard, *How The West Indian Child is Made Educationally Sub-Normal in the British School System* (London: New Beacon Books, 1971).

Coleridge Taylor, A., *The Heritage of Samuel Coleridge Taylor* (London: Dennis Dobson, 1979).

Colley, L., *Britons: Forging the Nation, 1707–1837* (London: Vintage, 1996).

Colley, L., 'The Significance of the Frontier in British History' in *More Adventures with Britannia*, William Roger Lewis (ed.), (London: I.B. Taurus, 1998).

Collinson, P., *The Religion of Protestants: The Church in English Society 1559–1625* (Oxford: Clarendon Press, 1982).

Connolly, S.J., *Religion, Law and Power. The Making of Protestant Ireland, 1660–1760* (Oxford: Clarendon Press, 1992).

Cowhig, R., 'Blacks in English Renaissance Drama' in *The Black Presence in English Literature*, D. Dabydeen (ed.), (Manchester: Manchester University Press, 1989).

Craton, M., *Sinews of Empire: A Short History of British Slavery* (London: Temple Smith, 1974).

Cugoano, O., *Thoughts and Sentiments on the Evil of Slavery or, the Nature of Servitude as Admitted by the Law of God, Compared to the Modern Slaves of the Africans in the West Indies* (London, 1791).

Cunliffe, B.W., *Iron Age Communities in Britain* (London: Routledge, 1991).

Curry, A., *The Hundred Years War* (Basingstoke: Macmillan, 1993).

Curtin, Philip D., *The Atlantic Slave Trade: A Census* (Madison: University of Wisconsin Press, 1972).

—— *Imperialism* (New York: Harper & Row, 1971; London: Macmillan, 1972).

Dabydeen, D., *Hogarth's Blacks* (London: Dangaroo, 1985).

—— (ed.), *The Black Presence in English Literature* (Manchester: Manchester University Press, 1985).

Dasent, J. R. (ed.), *Acts of the Privy Council of England, New Series, XXVI, 1596–7* (London: Stationery Office, 1902).

Daunton, M., *Progress and Poverty. An Economic and Social History of Britain 1700–1850* (Oxford: Oxford University Press, 1995).

Davies, C.S.L., *Peace, Print and Protestantism: 1450–1558* (London: Hart-Davis MacGibbon, 1976).

Davis, D.B., *The Problem of Slavery in the Age of Revolution, 1770–1823* (Ithaca, NY & London: 1975).

—— *Slavery and Human Progress* (Oxford: Oxford University Press, 1984).

—— *The Problem of Slavery in Western Culture* (New York: Oxford University Press, 1988).

Deakin, N., *Colour and the British Electorate* (London: Oxford University Press, 1965).

De Muth, C., *Sus: A Report on the Vagrancy Act 1824* (London: Runnymede Trust, 1978).

Derry, J., *Politics in the Age of Fox, Pitt and Liverpool* (Basingstoke: Macmillan, 1990).

Desai, R., *Indian Immigrants in Britain* (London: Oxford University Press, 1963).

Devine, T.M. (ed.), *Scottish Emigration and Scottish Society* (Edinburgh: John Donald, 1992).

De Witt, J., *Indian Workers' Associations in Britain* (London: Oxford University Press, 1969).

Dhondy, M., 'The Strike at Imperial Typewriters', *Race Today*, July–August, 1974.

Dickson, W., *Letters on Slavery* (London: J. Phillips, 1789).

Digby, W., *'Prosperous' British India: A Revelation From Official Records* (London: T. Fisher Unwin, 1901).

Dilke, C.W., *Greater Britain* (London: Macmillan & Co., 1872).

Donald, J. and Rattansi, J. (eds), *'Race', Culture and Difference* (London: Sage, 1992).

Douglas, D.C., *William the Conqueror* (London: Eyre & Spottiswoode, 1964).

Drake, J.G. St Clair, 'Value Systems, Social Structure and Race Relations in the British Isles' (PhD thesis, University of Chicago, 1954).

Dromey, J. and Taylor, G., *The Workers' Story* (London: Lawrence & Wishart, 1978).

Duffield, I., 'From Slave Colonies to Penal Colonies: The West Indian Convict Transportees to Australia', *Slavery and Abolition*, 7, 1 (May 1986).

—— *Duse Mohamed Ali and the Development of Pan Africanism, 1866–1945*, 2 vols. (PhD thesis, University of Edinburgh, 1971).

—— (ed.), *Essays on the History of Blacks in Britain* (Aldershot: Avebury, 1992).

Dutt, Palme R., *Britain's Crisis of Empire* (London: Lawrence & Wishart, 1949).

Dutton, D., *British Politics since 1945: The Rise and Fall of Consensus* (Oxford: Oxford University Press, 1991).

Edwards, B., *The History, Civil and Commercial of the British Colonies in the West Indies*, Vol. 2 (John Stockdale, 1793).

Edwards, P., 'The Early African Presence in Britain' in J. Gundara and I. Duffield (eds), *Essays on the History of Blacks in Britain* (Aldershot: Avebury, 1992).

Edwards, P. and Walvin, J., 'Africans in Britain, 1500–1800' in Martin L. Kilson and Robert I. Rotberg (eds), *The African Diaspora: Interpretive Essays* (Cambridge, Mass.: Harvard University Press, 1976).

Egan, P., *Life in London* (Sherwood, Neely & James, 1821).

Eggerton, J., *They Seek a Living* (London: Hutchinson, 1957).

Eldridge, C.C., *The Imperial Experience: From Carlyle to Forster* (London: Macmillan, 1996).

Ellinwood, DeWitt C. and Pradhan, S.D. (eds), *India and World War I* (New Delhi: Manohar Publications, 1978).

Emecheta, B., *Second Class Citizen* (London: Allison & Busby, 1974).

Equiano, O., *The Interesting Narrative of the Life of Olaudah Equiano or Gustavus Vassa, The African Written By Himself*, 2 vols. (London: 1789).

Evans, E.J., *The Forging of the Modern State, 1783–1870* (London: Longman, 1983).

Fabre, M., 'Sam Selvon' in Bruce King (ed.), *West Indian Literature* (London: Macmillan, 1979) p. 123.

Falkus, M. and Gillingham, J. (eds), *Historical Atlas of Britain* (London: Granada, 1981).

File, N. and Power, C., *Black Settlers in Britain, 1555–1958* (London: Heinemann Educational Books, 1981).

Fisher, M.H., *The First Indian Author in English: Dean Mahomed (1751–1851) in India, Ireland and England* (Delhi: Oxford University Press, 1996).

Floud, R. and McCloskey, D. (eds), *The Economic History of Britain since 1700* (London: Cambridge University Press, 1981).

Foner, N., *Jamaica Farewell* (London: Routledge & Kegan Paul, 1977).

Foot, P., *Immigration and Race* (London: Penguin Books, 1965).

—— *The Rise of Enoch Powell: An Examination of Enoch Powell's Attitude to Immigrants and Race* (Harmondsworth: Penguin Books, 1969).

Foster, R.F., *Paddy and Mr. Punch: Connections in Irish and English History* (London: Allen Lane, 1993).

Francis, A., *The Black Triangle*. Introductory Text by Ron Ramdin (London: Seed Publications, 1985).

Freedman, L., *Britain and the Falklands War* (Oxford: Basil Blackwell, 1988).

Frere, H.B., *The Fortnightly Review* (1883).

Froude, J.A., *The English in the West Indies* (London: Longman & Co.,1888).

Fryer, P., *The History of Black People in Britain* (London: Pluto Press, 1984).

—— *Black People in the British Empire* (London: Pluto Press, 1989).

Fuller, J.O., *Madeleine, The Story of Noor Inayat Khan* (London: Victor Gollancz, 1952).

Fyfe, C., *History of Sierra Leone* (Oxford: Oxford University Press, 1962).

Gadgil, D.R., *The Industrial Evolution of India in Recent Times, 1860–1939* (Bombay: Oxford University Press, 1971).

Geiss, I., *The Pan African Movement* (London: Methuen, 1974).

George, M.D., *London Life in the Eighteenth Century* (London: Kegan Paul, 1925).

George, T.J.S., *Krishna Menon: A Biography* (London: Jonathan Cape, 1974).

Gilroy, P., *'There Ain't No Black in the Union Jack': The Cultural Politics of Race and Nation* (London: Hutchinson, 1987).

—— 'Steppin' Out of Babylon: Race and Class and Autonomy' in *The Empire Strikes Back* (London: Centre for Contemporary Cultural Studies, Hutchinson, 1982).

Ghosh, Rai Sahib Jaimini Mohan, *Sannyasi and Fakir Raiders in Bengal* (Calcutta: Bengal Secretariat Book Depot, 1930).

Gladstone, F.M., *Notting Hill in Bygone Days* (London: Fisher Unwin, 1924).

Glass, R. and Pollins, H., *Newcomers* (London: Centre for Urban Studies and George Allen and Unwin 1960).

Glean, Marion, 'Whatever Happened to CARD?', *Race Today*, 5, 1, January 1973.

Golding, B., *Conquest and Colonization: The Normans in Britain, 1066–1100* (Basingstoke: Macmillan,1994).

Goulbourne, H., *West Indian Cultural Leadership* (CRER: University of Warwick, 1988).

Gourvish, T.R. and O'Day, A. (eds). *Britain since 1945* (London: Macmillan Education, 1991).

Graham, B.J. and Proudfoot, L.J., *Historical Geography of Ireland* (London: Academic Press, 1993).

Graham-Dixon, A.. *A History of British Art* (London: BBC Books, 1996).

Green, J., 'John Alcindor (1873–1924): A Migrant's Biography', *Immigrants and Minorities*, 6, 2, (July 1987).

Gretchen, G., *Black England: Life before Emancipation* (London: John Murray, 1995).

Griffiths, R.A., *Conquerors and Conquered in Medieval Wales* (Gloucester: Alan Sutton, 1994).

Grigg, J., *Lloyd George* (London: Methuen, 1985).

Gronniosaw, U., *A Narrative of the Most Remarkable Particulars in the Life of James Albert Ukasaw Gronniosaw, an African Prince, As Related by himself* (Bath: S. Hazard, 1770).

Gundara, J. (ed.), *Essays on the History of Blacks in Britain* (Aldershot: Avebury, 1992).

Gunn, S., *Early Tudor Government 1485–1558* (Basingstoke: Macmillan, 1995).

Guptara, P., *Black British Literature: An Annotated Bibliography* (London: Dangaroo Press, 1986).

Guy, J., *Tudor England* (Oxford: Oxford University Press, 1988).

Haig, C. (ed.), *The Cambridge Historical Encyclopaedia of Great Britain and Ireland* (Cambridge: Cambridge University Press, 1985).

Hakluyt, R., 'The Voyage of M. John Lok to Guinea, Anno 1554' in *The Principal Navigations, Voyages, Traffiques and Discoveries of the English Nation* (Glasgow: J. MacLehose and Sons, 1904).

Hamilton, E., *Translation of the Letters of a Hindoo Rajah* (1796).

Hammond, B. and J.L., *The Rise of Modern Industry* (London: Methuen, 1925).

Hanke, L., *Aristotle and the American Indians* (Bloomington & London: Indiana University Press, 1959, 1970).

Hansard Parliamentary Debates, 3rd series, Vol. 148 (1858) cols 1338, 1354.

Harding, R., *The Evolution of the Sailing Navy 1509–1815* (Basingstoke: Macmillan, 1995).

Hargreaves, J.A., *Sport, Power and Culture: A Social and Historical Analysis of Popular Sports in Britain* (Cambridge: Polity Press, 1987).

Harkness, D., *Ireland in the Twentieth Century* (Basingstoke: Macmillan, 1996).

Harris, W. et al., *Lascars and Chinese: A Short Address to Young Men of the Several Orthodox Denominations of Christians* (1814).

Harvey, A., Soldier (n.p.: 1988).

Harvie, C., *Scotland and Nationalism: Scottish Society and Politics 1707–1994* (London: Routledge, 1994).

Hassan, L. and Dick, P., 'Health Workers after the Strike', *Race Today* (March–April 1983).

Hay, D. et al.: *Albion's Fatal Tree: Crime and Society in Eighteenth Century England* (London and Harmondsworth: Allen Lane 1975).

Healey, D., *Time of My Life* (Harmondsworth: Penguin Books, 1989).

Heaney, S., *The Redress of Poetry: The Oxford Lectures* (London: Faber and Faber, 1996).

Heath, A. and McMahon, D., *Education and Occupational Attainments: The Impact of Ethnic Origins*, Paper 34. Centre for Research in Elections and Social Trends, 1997).

Hecht, Jean J., *Contractual and Colonial Servants in Eighteenth Century England* (Northampton, Mass: South College, 1954).

Heinemann, B., *The Politics of the Powerless: A Study of the Campaign against Racial Discrimination* (London: Oxford University Press, 1972).

Henderson, I., 'The Attitude and Policy of the Main Sections of the British Labour Movement to Imperial Issues, 1899–1924' (B.Litt thesis, Oxford University, 1965).

Herodotus, *Histories* (Harmondsworth: Penguin Books, 1972).

Hill, C., *Black Churches: West Indian and African Sects in Britain* (Community and Race Relations Unit of the British Council of Churches, 1971).

Hill, R. A.: 'Zion on the Zambesi: Dr. J. Albert Thorne, A Descendant of Africa, of Barbados and the African Colonial Enterprise: The Preliminary Stage 1894–97' in *Essays on the History of Blacks in Britain* (Aldershot: Avebury, 1992).

Hiro, D., *Black British White British* (London: Eyre & Spottiswoode, 1971; revised and expanded edition, London: Paladin, 1992).

Hitchins, F.H., *The Colonial Land and Emigration Commission* (Philadelphia: University of Philadelphia, 1931).

Hobsbawm, E. J., *Primitive Rebels: Studies in Archaic Forms of Social Movement in the Nineteenth and Twentieth Centuries* (Manchester: Manchester University Press, 1959).

Hobson, J.A., *Imperialism* (London: James Nisbeth & Co., 1902).

Hoggart, R., *The Uses of Literacy: Aspects of Working-Class Life* (London: Chatto & Windus, 1957).

—— *Townscape with Figures* (London: Chatto & Windus,1994).

Holderness, B.A., *Pre-Industrial England* (London: Dent, 1976).

Holt, R., *Sport and the British* (Oxford: Oxford University Press, 1990).

Holzman, J.M., *The Nabobs of England: A Study of the Returned Anglo-Indians, 1760–1785* (New York, 1926).

Hooker, J.R., *Henry Sylvester Williams: Imperial Pan Africanist* (London: Rex Collings, 1975).

—— *Black Revolutionary: George Padmore's Path from Communism to Pan Africanism* (London: Pall Mall Press, 1967).

Houston, R.A., *Social Change in the Age of Enlightenment. Edinburgh 1660–1760* (Oxford: Clarendon Press, 1994).

—— and Whyte, I.D. (eds), *Scottish Society 1500–1800* (Cambridge: Cambridge University Press, 1989).

Hughes, A., *The Causes of the English Civil War* (London: Macmillan, 1991).

Hughes, L. and Larkin, J.F. (eds), *Royal Tudor Proclamations 1588–1603 'Licensing Caspar Van Senden to Deport Negroes' 1601* (Yale University Press, 1969) Vol. 3.

Hulme, P., *Colonial Encounters, Europe and the Native Caribbean, 1492–1797* (London: Methuen, 1986).

Humphrey, D. and Ward, M., *Passport and Politics* (Harmondsworth: Penguin Books, 1974).

Hussey, G., *Ireland Today* (London: Viking, 1994).

Hutton, R., *Charles the Second, King of England, Scotland and Ireland* (Oxford: Clarendon, 1989).

—— *The British Republic 1649–1660* (Basingstoke: Macmillan, 1990).

—— *The Rise and Fall of Merry England. The Ritual Year 1400–1700* (Oxford: Oxford University Press, 1994).

Inden, R., *Imagining India* (Oxford: Basil Blackwell, 1990).

Ireland, W.W., *History of the Siege of Delhi by an Officer Who Served There: With a Sketch of the Leading Events in the Punjab Connected with the Great Rebellion of 1857* (Edinburgh: Adam and Charles Black, 1861).

James, C. L.R., *The Black Jacobins: Toussaint L'Ouverture and the San Domingo Revolution* (London: Secker & Warburg, 1938).

—— *Beyond a Boundary* (London: Stanley Paul/Hutchinson, 1963).

Jeffreys, K., *The Labour Party since 1945* (Basingstoke: Macmillan, 1993).

Jegede, T., *African Classical Music: Inaugural Concert Programme* (London: London Arts Board, 1991).

Jenkins, J.A., *The Liberal Ascendancy, 1830–1886* (Basingstoke: Macmillan, 1994).

Johnson, L.A., *The Devil, the Gargoyle and the Buffoon: The Negro as Metaphor in Western Culture* (London: Kennikat Press, 1971).

Jones, B.A. and Mattingly, B., *An Atlas of Roman Britain* (Oxford: Basil Blackwell, 1990).

Jones, E., *Othello's Countrymen: The African in English Renaissance Drama* (London: Oxford University Press, 1965).

Jones, J.G., *Early Modern Wales, c. 1525–1640* (New York: St. Martin's Press, 1994).

Jones, J.R., *Country and Court, 1660–1714* (London: Edward Arnold, 1978).

Jones, T., *Britain's Ethnic Minorities* (London: Policy Studies Institute, 1993).

Joshua, H. and Wallace, T., *To Ride the Storm* (London: Heinemann Educational Books, 1983).

Karran, K., 'Indo-Caribbean Women in Britain: Why Did They Migrate? A Preliminary Investigation', *Indo-Caribbean Review* (Ontario: University of Windsor, 1994).

Kavanagh, D. and Seldon, A. (eds), *The Thatcher Effect* (Oxford: Clarendon,1989).

—— *The Major Effect* (London: Macmillan, 1994).

Kaye, J.W., *A History of the Sepoy War in India, 1857–8* (W.H. Allen & Co., 1864–76).

Kearney, H., *The British Isles: A History of Four Nations* (Cambridge: Cambridge University Press, 1989).

Keen, M., *England and the Later Middle Ages* (London: Methuen, 1973).

Kerner Commission, 1968, Part III.

Kiernan, V., *European Attitudes Towards the Outside World in the Imperial Age* (London: Weidenfeld and Nicolson, 1965).

Kilson, M. and Rotberg, R.F. (eds), *The African Diaspora: Interpretive Essays* (Cambridge, Mass.: Harvard University Press, 1976).

Kinder, C., 'West Indians in Moss Side: The Effectiveness of Voluntary Organisations in Integrating West Indians' (B.Litt. thesis: Oxford University, 1966).

King, B. (ed.), *West Indian Literature* (London: Macmillan, 1979).

Kingsley, C., *Alton Locke, Tailor and Poet* (London: Chapman & Hall, 1850).

Kirby, D.P., *The Earliest English Kings* (London: Unwin Hyman, 1991).

Knowles, K.G., *Strikes – A Study in Industrial Conflict* (Oxford: Basil Blackwell, 1952).

Kobal, J., *Gotta Sing, Gotta Dance: A Pictorial History of Film Musicals* (London: Hamlyn, 1971).

Kosmin, Barry A., 'J.R. Archer (1863–1932) A Pan Africanist in the Battersea Labour Movement', London: *New Community*, V11 (1978–9).

Labour Research Department, *Black Workers and Trade Unions* (London: Labour Research Department, 1993).

Laing, L. and J., *The Picts and the Scots* (Stroud: Alan Sutton, 1994).

Lakey, J., 'Neighbourhoods and Housing', *Ethnic Minorities in Britain* (London: Policy Studies Institute, 1997).

Lamming, G., *The Pleasures of Exile* (London: Michael Joseph, 1960).

Langford, P., *A Polite and Commercial People: England, 1720–1783* (Oxford: Oxford University Press, 1989).

Langland, E., *Victoria* (London: 1964).

Langley, J.A. *Pan Africanism and African Nationalism in West Africa, 1900–1945: A Study in Ideology and Social Classes* (Oxford: The Clarendon Press, 1973).

Larkin, C., *The Guinness Who's Who of Film Musicals and Musical Films* (Enfield: Guinness Publishing, 1994).

Laslett, P., *The World We Have Lost* (London: Methuen, 1971).

Law, I. and Loy, L., For Continuity of Liverpool's Black Community in the Nineteenth Century. See Paper presented at International Conference of Blacks in Britain, Institute of Education, University of London, September 1981.

Lenin, V.I., *British Labour and British Imperialism* (London: Lawrence & Wishart 1969).

Le Patorel, J., *The Norman Empire* (Oxford: Clarendon Press, 1976).

Lenyel, E., *Krishna Menon* (New York: Walker & Co., 1962).

Lewis, R., *Marcus Garvey: Anti-Colonial Champion* (London: Karia Press, 1987).

Little, K., *Negroes in Britain* (London: Kegan Paul, 1948).

—— 'The Role of Voluntary Associations in West African Urbanization', *American Anthropologist,* Vol. 59, No. 4 (1957).

Loades, D., *The Mid-Tudor Crisis, 1545–1565* (London: Macmillan, 1992).

Locke, J., *An Essay Concerning Human Understanding,* Peter H. Nidditch (ed.), (Oxford: Clarendon Press, 1975).

Long, E., *The History of Jamaica* (London: T. Lowndnes, 1974).

Lorimer, D.A., 'Black Slaves and English Liberty: A Re-Examination of Racial Slavery in England', *Immigrants and Minorities,* 3/2 (July 1984).

—— *Colour, Class and the Victorians: English Attitudes to the Negro in the Mid-Nineteenth Century* (Leicester: Leicester University Press, 1978).

Loyn, H.R., *The Norman Conquest* (London: Hutchinson, 1982).

Maan, B., *The New Scots: The Story of Asians in Scotland* (Edinburgh: John Donald Publishers, 1992).

MacCulloch, D., *The Later Reformation in England, 1547–1603* (Basingstoke: Macmillan, 1990).

MacDonald, R.J., 'The Wisers are Far Away. The Role of London's Black Press in the 1930s and 1940s' in *Essays on the History of Blacks in Britain* (Aldershot: Avebury, 1992).

MacKenzie, J.M., *Propaganda and Empire: The Manipulation of British Public Opinion 1880–1960* (Manchester: Manchester University Press, 1984).

MacPherson, Sir J., *Development and Welfare in the West Indies, 1945–6* (London: HMSO, 1947).

MacPherson, W.C. (ed.), 'The Journals of Alexander Champion, Allan MacPherson and John MacPherson' in *Soldiering in India, 1764–1787* (Edinburgh: Blackwood & Sons, 1928).

McCalman, I., 'Anti-Slavery and Ultra-Radicalism in Early Nineteenth Century England: The Case of Robert Wedderburn', *Slavery and Abolition,* 7, 2 (September 1986).

—— *Radical Underworld: Prophets, Revolutionaries and Pornographers in London, 1795–1840* (Cambridge: Cambridge University Press, 1988).

Magie, D., *Scriptores Historiae Augustae* (London: Loeb Library, 1922).

Mahomed, S.D. (Dean), *Cases Cured by Sake Dean Mahomed, Shampooing Surgeon and Inventor of the Indian Medicated Vapour and Sea Water Baths* (Brighton: 1820).

—— *Shampooing, Or Benefits Resulting From the Use of the Indian Medicated Vapour Bath* (Brighton: 1822, 1826, 1838).

—— *Travels of Dean Mahomet, A Native of Patna in Bengal* ... (n.d.).

Majumdar, R.C. et al., *An Advanced History of India* (London: Macmillan & Co., 1950).

—— *History of the Freedom Movement in India* (Calcutta: Firma, K.L. Mukhopadhayay, 1962–3).

Malabari, B.M., *The Indian Eye on English Life or Rambles of a Pilgrim Reformer* (Westminster: A.Constable & Co., 1893).

Malleson, G.B., *History of the Indian Mutiny, 1857–1858, Commencing from the Close of the Second Volume of Sir John Kaye's History of the Sepoy War* (London: W.H. Allen & Co., 1878–80).

Mangan, J.A., *The Games Ethic and Imperialism* (London: Viking Press, 1986).

Mangan, J.A. (ed.), *Pleasure, Profit and Proselytism: British Culture and Sport at Home and Abroad, 1700–1914* (London: Frank Cass, 1988).

Mangru, B., *Benevolent Neutrality: Indian Government Policy and Labour Migration to British Guiana, 1854–1884* (London: Hansib, 1987).

—— 'The Sex-Ratio Disparity and its Consequences under Indenture in British Guiana', in *India in the Caribbean* (London: Hansib, 1987).

Manley, D.R., 'The Social Structure of the Liverpool Negro Community With Special Reference to the Formation of Formal Associations' (PhD thesis, University of Liverpool, 1958–59).

Mansukani, G.S., *The Quintessence of Sikhism* (Amritsar: Shiromani Gurdwara Parbandhak Committee, 1965).

Marshall, H. and Stock, M., *Ira Aldridge: The Negro Tragedian* (London: Rockliff, 1958).

Marshall, J., *East Indian Fortunes: The British in Bengal in the Eighteenth Century* (Oxford: Clarendon Press, 1976).

Marshall, P., *An Agenda for the History of Imperial Britain*, cited by Linda Colley, in *More Adventures with Britannia* (London: I.B. Tauris, 1998).

Marwick, A., *British Society since 1945* (London: Allen Lane, 1982).

Mason, M., *The Making of Victorian Sexuality* (Oxford: Oxford University Press, 1994).

Mathurin, O.C., *Henry Sylvester Williams and the Origins of the Pan African Movement, 1869–1911* (Westport, Conn., London: Greenwood Press, 1976).

Matthias, P., *The First Industrial Nation: An Economic History of Britain 1700–1914* (London: Methuen, 1969).

Maxwell, N., *The Power of Negro Action* (London: the author, 1966).

Mayhew, H., *London Labour and London Poor* (London: 1861).

Middlemas, K., *Power, Competition and the State*, Vol. 3 (Basingstoke: Macmillan, 1991).

Miles, R., *Racism and Migrant Labour* (London: Routledge & Kegan Paul, 1982).

Mitchison, R. (ed.), *Why Scottish History Matters* (Edinburgh: Saltire Society, 1991).

Modood, T., 'British Muslims and the Rushdie Affair' in J. Donald and A. Rattansi (eds), *'Race', Culture and Difference* (London: Sage Publications, 1992).
—— 'Qualifications and the English Language' in *Ethnic Minorities in Britain* (London: Policy Studies Institute, 1997).
—— 'Employment' in *Ethnic Minorities in Britain* (London: Policy Studies Institute, 1997).
—— 'Culture and Identity' in *Ethnic Minorities in Britain* (London: Policy Studies Institute, 1997).
Moirer, J., *Adventures of Haji Baba* (1824).
Montesquieu, C. de Secondat, *Lettres Perses* (1721).
Moody, J., *History* (1788).
—— *Remarks* (1788).
Morgan, K. (ed.), *The Oxford Illustrated History of Britain* (Oxford: Oxford University Press, 1984).
—— *The People's Peace: British History 1945–1989* (Oxford: Oxford University Press, 1990).
Morokvansic, M., 'Women in Migration: Beyond the Reductionist Outlook' in A. Phizacklea *One Way Ticket: Migration and Female Labour* (London: Routledge & Kegan Paul, 1983).
Morris, M., *The General Strike* (Harmondsworth: Penguin Books, 1976).
Morris, S., 'Moody – The Forgotten Visionary', *New Society*, Vol. 3 (Spring 1972).
Morrison, T., *Playing in the Dark* (Cambridge, Mass.: 1992).
Naipaul, V.S., *The Enigma of Arrival* (London: Penguin, 1987).
Nanan, S., 'Voices From the Boundary: The Indo-Caribbean Experience in Britain' (MA thesis, University of Warwick, 1990).
Nazroo, J.Y., 'Health and Health Services' in *Ethnic Minorities in Britain* (Policy Studies Institute, 1997).
Nield, B. and Saville, J., 'Saklatvala', in J. Bellamy and J. Saville (eds), *Dictionary of Labour Biography*, Vol. VI (London: Macmillan, 1982).
Norton, M.B., *The British American: The Loyalist Exiles in England, 1774–1789* (Boston: 1972; London: 1974).
Ormrod, W.M., *Political Life in Medieval England, 1300–1450* (New York: St. Martin's Press; Basingstoke: Macmillan, 1995).
Ottaway, P., *Archaeology in British Towns: From the British Emperor Claudius to the Black Death* (London: Routledge, 1992).
Padmore, G. (ed.), *Colonial and Coloured Unity* (Manchester: Pan African Federation, 1948).
—— *Pan Africanism or Communism? The Coming Struggle for Africa* (London: Dennis Dobson, 1956).
Palliser, D., *The Age of Elizabeth* (London: Longman, 1983).
Parekh, B., *The Experience of Black Minorities in Britain* (Milton Keynes: The Open University, 1981).
—— 'Foreword', *Ethnic Minorities in Britain* (London: Policy Studies Institute, 1997).

Parker, J., *Books To Build An Empire: A Bibliographical History of English Overseas Interest to 1620* (Amsterdam: N. Israel, 1965).

Parry, Sir H., ' A Tribute from Sir Hubert Parry', *Musical Times*, LIII (1912).

Paterson, S., *Dark Strangers* (London: Tavistock Publications, 1963).

Paul, Sir James B., *The Poems of William Dunbar* (Edinburgh: 1902).

Peach, C., *West Indian Migration to Britain: A Social Geography* (London: Oxford University Press, 1968).

Pearse, T.D., 'Memoir', *Bengal Past and Present*, Vols 2–7 (1909–11).

Pearson, D.G., 'West Indian Communal Associations in Britain: Some Observations', *New Community*, Vol. 5.

Perkin, H., *The Rise of Professional Society: England since 1880* (London: Routledge, 1989).

Perry, K., *British Politics and the American Revolution* (Basingstoke: Macmillan, 1990).

Phillips, J., *Kwame Nkrumah and the Future of Africa* (London: Faber and Faber, 1960).

Phizacklea, A. amd Miles, R., *Labour and Racism* (London: Routledge & Kegan Paul, 1980).

Phizacklea, A., *One Way Ticket: Migration and Female Labour* (London: Routledge and Kegan Paul, 1983).

Policy Studies Institute, *Britain's Ethnic Minorities* (London: Policies Studies Institute, 1993).

Pollard, A.J., *The Wars of the Roses* (Basingstoke; Macmillan Education, 1988).

Porter, R., *English Society in the Eighteenth Century* (London: Allen Lane, 1982).

Pounds, N.J.G., *The Culture of the English People* (Cambridge: Cambridge University Press, 1994).

Powell, D., *British Politics and the Labour Question, 1868–1990* (Basingstoke: Macmillan, 1992).

Prestwich, M., *The Three Edwards* (London: Weidenfeld & Nicolson, 1980).

—— *English Politics in the Thirteenth Century* (Basingstoke: Macmillan Education, 1990).

Prince, M., *The History of Mary Prince: A West Indian Slave, Related by Herself*, 1st edition (London, 1831).

Pugh, M., *The Making of Modern British Politics, 1867–1939* (Oxford: Basil Blackwell, 1982).

—— *State and Society: British Political and Social History 1870–1992* (London: Edward Arnold, 1994).

Race and Class, Vol.XXIII, Nos. 2–3, 1981–2.

Race and Unemployment (London: Labour Research Department, 1989).

Ragatz, L., *The Fall of the Planter Class in the British Caribbean, 1763–1833* (New York: 1928).

Ramdin, R., *From Chattel Slave to Wage Earner: A History of Trade*

Unionism in Trinidad and Tobago (London: Martin, Brian & O'Keeffe Ltd, 1982).

—— *Paul Robeson: The Man and His Mission* (London: Peter Owen, 1987).

—— *The Making of the Black Working Class in Britain* (Aldershot: Gower & Wildwood House, 1987).

—— *The Other Middle Passage* (London: Hansib Publishing Company, 1995).

—— *Arising from Bondage: A History of East Indians in the Caribbean, 1838–1997* (London: I.B. Tauris, 1999).

Ramnarine, T., 'Over One Hundred Years of East Indian Disturbances on the Sugar Estates in Guyana' in D. Dabydeen and B.Samaroo (eds), *India in the Caribbean* (London: Hansib/University of Warwick, 1987).

Reddock, R., 'Indian Women and Indentureship in Trinidad 1845–1917: Freedom Denied?', *Caribbean Quarterly*, Vol. 32 (September–December 1986).

Rennell, J., *Marches* (1792).

—— *Journals* (1910).

Report of the Race Relations Board, 1969–1970, Appendix X, p. 58.

Rex, J., *Ethnic Minorities in the Modern State* (London: Macmillan, 1996).

Rex, R., *Henry VIII and the English Reformation* (Basingstoke: Macmillan, 1993).

Reynolds, D., *Britannia Overruled* (London: Longman, 1991).

Reynolds, H., *Minstrel Memories: The Story of Burnt Cork Minstrelsy in Great Britain from 1936 to 1927* (London: Alston Rivers, 1928).

Rich, P.B., *Race and Empire in British Politics* (Cambridge: Cambridge University Press, 1986).

Richmond, A.H., *Colour Prejudice in Britain* (London: Routledge & Kegan Paul, 1954).

Robbins, K., *The Eclipse of a Great Empire: Modern Britain 1870–1992*, second edition (Harlow: Longman, 1994).

—— *History, Religion and Identity in Modern Britain* (London: Hambledon, 1993).

—— *Nineteenth Century Britain: Integration and Diversity* (Oxford: Clarendon Press, 1988).

Roberts, B., 'The Debate on Sus' in Cashmore, E. and Troyna, B. (eds), *Black Youth in Crisis* (London: Allen & Unwin, 1982).

Robeson, S., *The Whole World in His Hands* (Seacacus, NJ: Citadel Press 1981).

Robinson, C.J., *Black Marxism* (London: Zed Books, 1983).

Rodney, W., *How Europe Under-developed Africa* (London: Bogle L'Ouverture Ltd, 1988).

—— *A History of the Upper Guinea Coast* (Oxford: Clarendon Press, 1970).

Roger, N.A.M., *The Wooden World: An Anatomy of the Georgian Navy* (London: William Collins, 1986).

Rose, E.J.B. et al., *Colour and Citizenship* (Oxford: Oxford University Press, 1969).

Rudé G., *Protest and Punishment: The Story of the Social and Political Protesters Transported to Australia, 1788–1868* (Oxford: Clarendon Press, 1978).

—— *The Crowd in History: A Study of Popular Disturbances in France and England, 1730–1848* (London: Lawrence & Wishart, 1981).

Rule, J., *Albion's People: English Society 1714–1815* (London: Longman,1992).

—— *The Vital Century: England's Developing Economy 1714–1815* (London: Longman, 1992).

Rushdie, S., *Satanic Verses* (London: Viking, 1988).

Rushdie, S., Text delivered to the International Parliament of Writers, Strasbourg, November 1993; reported in *Times Literary Supplement* (25 February 1994).

Russell, C., *The Crisis of Parliaments, 1509–1660* (London: Oxford University Press, 1974).

Saha, P., *Shapurji Saklatvala: A Short Biography* (Delhi: Asia Publishing House, 1970).

Said, E., *Culture and Imperialism* (London: Vintage, 1994).

Salter, J., *The Asiatic in England: Sketches of Sixteen Years' Work among Orientals* (London: Seely, Jackson and Halliday, 1873).

—— *The East in the West; Or Work among Asiatics and Africans in London* (London: S.W. Partridge & Co., 1896).

Sancho, I., *Letters of the Late Ignatius Sancho, An African* (London: 1782).

Saville, J., 'William Cuffay', in *Dictionary of Labour Biography*, Vol. VI (London: Macmillan, 1982).

Sayers, W.C. Berwick., *Samuel Coleridge Taylor, Musician: His Life and Letters* (Cassell and Co. Ltd, 1915).

Scarisbrick, J.J., *Henry VIII* (London: Eyre & Methuen, 1976).

Scobie, Edward: *Black Britannia* (Chicago: Johnson Publishing Co., 1972).

Scott, R., 'Journal', *Naval Military Magazine*, Vols 1–4 (1827–28).

Seacole, M., *The Wonderful Adventures of Mrs. Mary Seacole in Many Lands* (James Blackwood, 1858).

Searle, G.R., *The Liberal Party: Triumph and Disintegration 1886–1929* (Basingstoke: Macmillan,1992).

Seaward, P., *The Restoration, 1660–1688* (Basingstoke: Macmillan, 1991).

Seeck, O. (ed.), *Notitia Dignitatum* (Berlin: Weidmann, 1876).

Select Committee on Race Relations and Immigration, *Employment*, Vol. 1, Report (London: HMSO, 1974).

Selvon, S., *The Lonely Londoners* (London: Longman, 1956).

—— *Moses Ascending* (London: Davis Poynter, 1975).

—— *Moses Migrating* (London: Longman, 1983).

Sharp, G., *A Short Sketch of Temporary Regulations Until Better Shall*

Be Proposed For the Intended Settlement of the Gold Coast of Africa, Near Sierra Leone (London: 1788).

Shipman, D., *The Great Movie Stars: The Golden Years* (London: Hamlyn, 1970).

Shipp. J., *Memoirs* (1829).

Shirsat, K.R., *Kaka Joseph Baptista* (Bombay: Popular Prakashan, 1974).

Short, B. (ed.), *The English Rural Community* (Cambridge: Cambridge University Press, 1992).

Shyllon, F.O., *Black Slaves in Britain* (London: Oxford University Press, Institute of Race Relations, 1974).

—— *Black People in Britain, 1555–1838* (London: Oxford University Press, 1977).

—— 'The Black Presence and Experience in Britain: An Analytical Overview', in *Essays on the History of Blacks in Britain* (Aldershot: Avebury, 1992).

Sims, G., *Living London* (London: Cassell, 1906).

Sinclair, N., *The Tiger Bay Story* (Cardiff: Butetown History and Arts Project, 1993).

Sivanandan, A., *Race and Resistance: The Institute of Race Relations Story* (London: Institute of Race Relations, 1974).

—— From Resistance To Rebellion: Asian and Afro-Caribbean Struggles in Britain', *Race and Class*, XXIII, 2–3 (1981–2).

Smith, D.J., *The Facts of Racial Disadvantage* (London: Political and Economic Planning, 1976).

Smith, G.A., 'Jim Crow on the Home Front, 1942–1945', *New Community*, VIII/3 (Winter 1980).

Smith, J.T., *Vagabondia, Anecdotes of Mendicant Wanderers through the Streets of London* (London: S. Orr, 1838).

—— *Nollekens and His Times*, ed. G.W. Stonier (London: Turnstile Press, 1949).

Solow, B L. and Engerman, S.L. (eds), *British Capitalism and Caribbean Slavery* (Cambridge: Cambridge University Press, 1987).

Snow, C.P., *Two Cultures* (London: Chatto & Windus, 1962).

Spencer, A., *Memoirs of William Hickey*, 4 vols, Vol. II (London: Hurst & Blackett, 1913, 1948).

Spufford, M., *Contrasting Communities: English Villagers in the Sixteenth and Seventeenth Centuries* (London: Cambridge University Press, 1974).

Stevenson, J., *British Society 1914–1945* (London: Allen Lane, 1984).

Steward, R., *Party and Politics 1830–1852* (Basingstoke: Macmillan, 1989).

Stock, M. and Marshall, H. *Ira Aldridge: The Negro Tragedian* (London: Rockliff, 1958).

Stokes, E., 'Traditional Resistance Movements and Afro-Asian Nationalism: The Context of the 1857 Mutiny Rebellion in India', *Past and Present* (August 1970).

Strachey, J., *The End of Empire* (London: Victor Gollancz, 1959).

Swire, O.F., *The Outer Hebrides and Their Legends* (London: Oliver Boyd, 1966).

Taylor, E.G.R., *Late Tudor and Early Stuart Geography 1583–1650* (London: Methuen & Co., 1934).

Thackeray, W., *Miscellaneous Prose and Verse*, Vol. 1 (Bradbury & Evans, 1855–7).

Thatcher, M., *The Downing Street Years* (London: HarperCollins, 1993).

Third World Impact, fifth edition (London: Hansib, 1982).

Thomas, H., *The Slave Trade: The History of the African Slave Trade, 1440–1870* (London: Picador, 1997).

Thomas, J.J., *Froudacity: West Indian Fables by James Anthony Froude Explained* (London: T. Fisher Unwin, 1889).

Thompson, E.P., *The Making of the English Working Class* (Harmondsworth: Penguin Books, 1968).

—— 'The Moral Economy of the Crowd in the Eighteenth Century', *Past and Present*, Vol. 50 (February 1971).

Thompson, F.M.L., *The Rise of Respectable Society. A Social History of Victorian Britain, 1830–1900* (London: Fontana, 1988).

Thorne, C., 'Britain and the Black GIs: Racial Issues and Anglo-American Relations in 1942', in *New Community*, III/3 (Summer 1974).

Thornton, R.H., *British Shipping* (Cambridge: Cambridge University Press, 1939).

Tinker, H., *A New System of Slavery* (London: Institute of Race Relations (Oxford: Oxford University Press, 1974).

Todd, M., *Roman Britain* (Brighton: Harvester, 1981).

Trollope, A., *The West Indies and the Spanish Main* (London: Chapman & Hall, 1860).

Troyna, B. and Cashmore, E., 'Growing up in Babylon' in *Black Youth in Crisis* (London: Allen & Unwin, 1982).

Tupper, E., *The Life Story of Captain Edward Tupper* (London: Hutchinson, 1938).

Unemployment and Homelessness (London: Community Relations Commission, 1974).

Vagdama, K., *Indians in Britain: The Indian Contribution to the British Way of Life* (London: Robert Royce, 1984).

Vaughan, D.A., *Negro Victory: The Life Story of Dr. Harold Moody* (London: Independent Press, 1950).

Vincent, D., *Bread, Knowledge and Freedom: A Study of Nineteenth Century Working Class Autobiography* (London: Europa, 1981).

Visram, R., *Ayahs, Lascars and Princes* (London: Pluto Press, 1986).

Virdee, S., 'Racial Harassment' in *Ethnic Minorities in Britain* (London: Policy Studies Institute, 1997).

Wallace, T. and Joshua, H., *To Ride the Storm* (London: Heinemann Educational Books, 1983).

Walvin, J., *Black and White: The Negro and English Society, 1555–1945* (London: Allen Lane, Penguin Books, 1973).

—— (ed.), *Slavery and British Society* (London: Macmillan, 1982).
—— *The Fruits of Empire* (London: Macmillan, 1997).
Warren, W.L., *Henry III* (London: Eyre & Spottiswoode, 1973).
Wedderburn, R., *Truth Self-Supported; or, a Refutation of Certain Doctrinal Errors Generally Adopted in the Christian Church etc.* ... (London: 1790[?]).
—— *The Horrors of Slavery; Exemplified in the Life ... of ... Robert Wedderburn ... in which is included the Correspondence of ... his brother A. Colville, alias Wedderburn, etc.* (London: 1824).
—— *A Few Hints Relative to the Texture of Mind and the Manufacture of Conscience Published for the Benefit of the Rev. R. Wedderburn, etc.* (London: T. Davison, 1820).
—— *The Trial of Rev. Robt Wedderburn ... for Blasphemy ... edited by Erasmus Perkins* (London: 1820)
—— *A Critical Historical and Admonitory Letter to ... the Archbishop of Canterbury, upon the following Important Questions ...* (London: 1820).
White, P., 'Geography, Literature and Migration', in *Writing across Worlds* (London: Routledge, 1995).
Wiener, M., *English Culture and the Decline of the Industrial Spirit, 1850–1981* (Cambridge: Cambridge University Press, 1981).
Wilkinson, G.T., *An Authentic History of the Cato Street Conspiracy with the Trials at Large of the Conspirators for High Treason and Murder* (London: Kelly, 1820).
Williams, E., *Capitalism and Slavery* (Chapel Hill: University of North Carolina, 1944).
Williams, J., *Historical Account* (1817; 1970).
Williams, P., *The Tudor Regime* (Oxford: Clarendon Press, 1979).
Williams, R., *Culture and Society, 1780–1950* (London: Chatto & Windus, 1958).
Williams, T., *East Indian Vade Mecum* (1810).
Wilson, A., *Finding a Voice: Asian Women in Britain* (London: Virago, 1978).
Wrench, J. and Virdee, S., 'Organising the Unorganised: "Race", Poor Work and Trade Unions' in P. Acker, C. Smith and P. Smith (eds), *The New Workplace and Trade Unions* (London: Routledge, 1995).
Wrigley, E.A. and Schofield, R.S., *The Population History of England, 1541–1871* (London: Edward Arnold, 1981).
Wrightson, K., *English Society 1580–1680* (London: Hutchinson, 1982).
Yorke, Philip C. (ed.), *The Diary of John Baker* (London: Hutchinson, 1931).
Young, H., *One of Us: A Biography of Margaret Thatcher* (London: Macmillan, 1989).
Young, J., *Britain and European Unity, 1945–1992* (Basingstoke: Macmillan, 1993).

Index

Compiled by Sue Carlton